THE
FARMHOUSE
COOKBOOK

THE
FARMHOUSE
COOKBOOK

YVONNE YOUNG TARR

Quadrangle / The New York Times Book Company

NEW YORK

NOTE: For advice on the pickling, preserving, and canning of fruits and vegetables we consulted an expert—the United States Department of Agriculture. Many of the recipes and most of the information in these sections of the book are from:

"Home Canning of Fruits and Vegetables," Home and Garden Bulletin No. 8
"How to Make Jellies, Jams, and Preserves at Home," Home and Garden Bulletin No. 56
"Making Pickles and Relishes at Home," Home and Garden Bulletin No. 92

Library of Congress Catalog Card Number: 73–79937

International Standard Book Number: 0–8129–0398–6

Design by Betty Binns

Production by Planned Production

I dedicate this book

to JOAN

With a special thanks to
Ruth Grossman, my editorial assistant,
whose help and dedication
have been of inestimable value
in putting together this book.
Thanks also to
Sylvie Mutchler of Trout Run, Pennsylvania,
for parting with so many of
her treasured recipes.

Contents

Introduction

THIS IS A TIME when many of the ends seem to have become undone, when many of the familiar ties have been loosened, when things once considered wholesome are thought to contain poisons, when the perfect order of things seems perfectly out of order.

This is a time when many know it is desperately necessary to retie the loose ties, to retrace the lost steps, to find a way back to the good beginnings; when to go backward is to go forward. There is a need to replant our roots, to grow our own unpoisoned foods, to bake our own bread, to have some control over our own subsistence, to re-establish that perfect order of things. America is a country with a longing for the country life. There has been an exodus of residents from the cities and suburbs. They rush to the country for a weekend, a summer, a fall, a spring. Some have even opted for year-round country living. They feel the need to free themselves from their concrete environments and split-level lives to dig their toes in the soil, to watch plants growing and bearing fruit, to see clearly the changing of the seasons. City residents and many country ones, too, are buying farms and building homes where they can plant, grow, and harvest their own food; where they can store root crops in their own root cellars, make pies from their home-canned cherries, unearth frozen parsnips from their own outdoor storage bins, and in general, recreate the warm and hearty life-style of the early American farm family.

City breakfasts of toast and coffee are giving way to hearty repasts of farm-fresh eggs, slab bacon, hashed brown potatoes, pan-cakes, and still-warm home-baked breads spread with strawberry preserves from the berry patch. These wholesome foods—garden-fresh vegetables and herb salads, tree-ripened fruit salads, thick soups, roast birds, stuffings, dumplings, country puddings, pies, cakes, and cookies—all are part of the farm-family way of life.

This is a book concerned with growing, cooking, and feasting in the Farmhouse manner. Instructions are given for planting, caring for, and harvesting your own foods; for storing and canning, freezing and preserving them, for mulching and composting and caring for the soil in which they grow, but most important, for planning, cooking, and preparing feasts of Farmhouse Favorites. The recipes in this book have been tested and retested to prepare them for your kitchen. The special section on the cooking of garden vegetables alone contains 150 recipes. The section on Meats, Poultry, Game, and Fish is intended to fill your table with healthy and satisfying main courses. The section on Desserts and Sweetmeats should provide a variety of treats rich and tempting enough to satisfy your sweet tooth for years to come. Recipes marked with three stars *** throughout this book are those I would particularly like to bring to your attention. These have been resounding successes and are frequently requested by my family and friends.

These recipes have been gleaned from hundreds of books on hearty and scrumptious eating, Early American and country cookbooks, and from my own files. If you would like to find your way back to a healthier, more wholesome way of life—whether you grow your own foods or merely wish you could—this book is meant for you.

FOOD
OF
YOUR
OWN

Gardening organically

A GARDEN IS more than a plot of soil dotted with edible vegetation. A garden can be a harbor for the soul—a living barrier against the frenzies and frustrations of the outside world. Kneeling, trowel in hand, in the midst of the damp cool furrows, your green beans rising to the left of you, your sweet corn to the right, peace settles slowly like a blanket over your frazzled nerves. There seems to be an integral calm in the very odors and sounds of a garden—earth smells, bird songs. The business person direct from the tensions of the city may find peace glowing pleasantly within, minutes after returning "home" to the soil.

Even the most gregarious and extroverted rarely chatter while working in a garden. Humans who enter the land of plants and soil seem to revert to the language of its inhabitants—one of surface silence, of touch, of experienced but unspoken feeling.

If you are to profit most from your garden you must do your gardening yourself. Plant and rake and care for your garden with your own time and fingers. The garden that is plowed, planted, and completely cared for by the gardener is the gardener's garden no matter who may harvest and consume the fruits.

We care for the things we take care of and those things we

care for lovingly grow beneath our fingers. I feel that vegetables and fruits are merely the by-product of a successful garden: the real harvest is a soothed and mended psyche, a body tanned and healthy, a chance to retrace our origins—to rechart the life cycle and put ourselves back in touch with reality.

In these chaotic times it is healthy not only to eat fruits, vegetables, and herbs that we are certain contain no poisonous insecticides but also to know that if necessary we can discard the plastic containers, the middlemen, the sprays, the subsidized farming, and feed ourselves as we were meant to do.

Think of soil as a complex dough composed of a flour of inorganic rocks, sand, and silt, mixed through with dead organic matter, and set vitally alive by earthworms, fungi, and bacteria that live in it. This dough has been resting, growing, living, and breathing in its own fashion for some time.

Dust settled on the barren earth, seedlings sprang up and grew and spread their seeds, and died. Plant children grew up from the hearts of their plant parents, algae formed, amoebas amoebaed and trilobites trilled (or whatever it was the trilobites did) in the steaming mists of past ages, and life survived.

Generation upon generation of primeval plant families, insects, and gargantuan beasts grew up, munched, crunched, and in general did their natural things, and then quite conveniently bit the volcanic dust and generously provided us with the wherewithal in which to plant our present-day gardens—our soil.

Now, if nature has provided thus far, if bees have been buzzing about pollinating flowers, if birds have been doing their bit, eating insects and the like, if worms have been busily aerating the soil, and all manner of creeping and crawling and fluttering and buzzing things have managed to keep the earth prolifically vegetated for some time, why, you may ask yourself, does present-day man insist upon the need for chemical gardening? Why does he feel that not one apple or pea or bean or strawberry or squash can possibly survive without the assistance of dangerous chemical sprays and powders?

That is an intelligent and sensible question and, as one might suspect, there is an intelligent and sensible answer.

Unfortunately we have been propagandized into looking for manufactured miracles when natural miracles are all around us. What could be more miraculous than the way spring happens every year without help from any of us? No presidental pronouncements need be made, no congressional committees need be formed. The flower bed nearly makes itself, the blanket of snow disappears without being washed and folded and stored in mothballs. Buds pop up from the ground on schedule without one word of motherly coaxing. How presumptuous of us to think that without our chemical interference nature cannot survive, our gardens cannot grow. They can, and will, if given half a chance.

There *is* method behind the seeming madness of organic gardening and that method is: (1) return *to* the soil as much natural life-giving matter as your vegetables have taken *out* (or perhaps a bit more) and there will be no need for chemical additives of any kind; (2) if your plants are growing in organically enriched soil they will be strong enough (with a little help from *friendly* insects and birds) to withstand the onslaught of blights of nature. This method is so simple, effective, and natural that more and more farmers and gardeners across the country are beginning to see it as logic, not fad.

Organic gardening is not and never has been a mystic or spiritual involvement with psychic processes. You need neither belong to a grain-eating Eastern cult nor a fanatic Western counterculture to become a proponent. Organic gardening is, simply, a return to the growing practices of the early American farmer, to a time prior to the manufacture and use of many lethal plant sprays and farming practices.

The following material is intended as a guide to help you choose what you want to grow and what would grow best given the particular variables in your garden. You will find suggestions on what to plant, when to sow seed, what produce grows best in your climate and/or type of soil, plus practical harvesting information. Consult seed catalogs, garden encyclopedias, local farmers, and knowledgeable neighbors for more specific or precise directions.

The Home and Garden Bulletins Nos. 7 and 9, published by the U.S. Department of Agriculture,* are invaluable sources of information. In addition, many state universities publish bulletins on growing vegetables and fruits which are available free of charge to state residents.

Novice gardeners are understandably puzzled by the multitudinous bits and pieces of information needed to plan and plant a gar-

* Available from the Superintendent of Documents, U.S. Government Printing Office, Washington, D.C. 20402; 25 cents each.

den. The following general information may help to answer some of your basic questions.

Compost

While it is true that soil is the heart of the garden, compost is the blood line that feeds, replenishes, and delivers life-giving essentials to that soil. To build a compost heap is to repeat and accelerate the processes nature has carried out so many millions of times—that of turning leftover leaves, weeds, grasses, twigs, nuts, seeds, animal hair, feathers, manure, dust, etc., into new and revitalized growing materials.

Three basic materials must be included in any successful compost heap: *manure* or commercially prepared compost starters which provide bacteria; *healthy green plants* which provide minerals; and *nitrogen* (provided by hair, bone meal, feathers, soybean meal, etc.) to accelerate the proliferation of the bacteria needed to break down the other materials into compost.

It is perfectly satisfying to finally find a use for raked leaves, cut grass, egg shells, coffee grounds, vegetable peelings, fruit skins, etc. The compost heap accepts them all. You need only shred the leaves, weeds, hay, and other large ingredients with a power mower or shredder before adding them to the heap.

Pile the collected debris 5 or 6 feet high, sprinkle liberally with water (but do not soak), cover the top (not the sides) with a tarpaulin to keep off heavy rains, and your compost heap is underway. If the heap is thriving it should register temperatures of around 150 degrees by the second day. Lower temperatures indicate too few nitrogen-producing elements and too little manure in the pile. Readjust these elements and begin again.

Build your compost heap in an out-of-the-way corner of the garden. Wet it down occasionally when rainfall is light, dust with limestone from time to time, and fork the pile once in a while to speed decomposition. Good compost takes time to build but the wait is worth it.

Manure is usually sold in dehydrated form, shredded, dried, or pulverized. If fresh manure is available, be sure it is well rotted before working it into the soil. Fresh manure, unless it is applied to the soil in the fall and left to rot over the winter, can badly burn plants.

Cover crops, also called green manure, are another good source of organic matter. Ryegrass, rye, buckwheat, or clover are often alternated with vegetables during the ordinary course of crop rotation, and then are plowed under to condition the soil. The strong root systems of cover crops help to make heavy soils friable and reduce the erosion of sandy soil. Ryegrass is particularly good because as a cool-weather crop it can be planted after many vegetables are harvested, has most of its growth in the fall, and may be turned under the ground come spring.

Liming and pH

The pH scale indicates the degree to which soil is acid or alkaline. A pH of 7.0 is neutral. Any pH count below 7.0 shows that soil has some degree of acidity. Any pH above 7.0 indicates an alkaline or sweet soil. Most vegetables will grow satisfactorily in a slightly acid soil where the pH is from 6.0 to 7.0.

New gardens should be tested to determine the degree to which they are acid or alkaline. Soil-testing kits are available through seed catalogs or at most garden stores. If you prefer not to do it yourself, most state university or agricultural stations will test your soil, and many garden supply stores provide these tests as a service. Finely ground limestone or dolomite (which contains magnesium) should be applied to garden soil only when a test proves the soil too acid. The pH count of moderately alkaline soils may be brought nearer to neutral by adding compost.

Mulches

Weeding your garden and cultivating it to keep the soil friable are two of the more laborious aspects of gardening. You can save yourself work by applying a mulch after seedlings have been thinned. In addition to smothering weeds, mulches eliminate the danger of damaging shallow-rooted plants by too zealous cultivation. They conserve moisture, too, and help to keep the ground cool.

There are various materials used for mulching. Some have certain shortcomings, but any will serve the purpose. Following is a list of the more common mulches.

Grass clippings are always available, but should be applied thinly because they tend to mat.

Leaves are always on hand, are economical, and help enrich the soil, although some tend to pack flat.

Straw and hay are not too attractive and may contain weed seeds, but in decomposing both enrich the soil. Apply them in a thick layer.

Salt hay is weed free but does not decompose. Save it every year for next year's use.

Peat moss is neat and fairly inexpensive, but often mats and keeps moisture from penetrating soil. Mixing it with sawdust or wood shavings helps.

Sawdust is excellent but consumes a lot of the nitrogen in soil. Use a fertilizer with a high nitrogen content before applying.

Buckwheat hulls are lightweight and clean but wind may scatter them easily.

Black plastic absorbs the sun's rays during the day and radiates it back at night, thus protecting early-planted crops from frost injury. Plastic is also useful in speeding the early growth of such warm-weather crops as melons, peppers, and tomatoes. Soil must be well soaked before the plastic is laid. Lay it out in strips or in large pieces punctured with holes through which the plants can grow. Anchor plastic securely to the soil so it won't loosen on windy days.

Fertilizers

The finest and most basic fertilizer comes from your compost heap. Sift the compost and spread the fine particles several inches thick over the entire garden. Plow, spade, or rake this into the top 3 to 4 inches of soil. Let the garden rest for 1 week.

If it is possible, prepare your garden in the fall rather than the spring. This will give the compost a chance to break down and give the earthworms an opportunity to find a home in the rich soil of the garden. Plow the compost under and mulch heavily. Work the ground well in the spring.

In addition to nourishing the garden with compost, you may need a bit of extra help from commercial fertilizers. Any material which helps supply the elements essential to plant growth may be properly called fertilizer. Many of these materials are organic, that is, derived from animals and plants: dried animal manure, sewage, sludge, bone meal, cottonseed meal, soybean meal, dried blood, etc., or they may be composed of inorganic products derived from minerals or mineral by-products. Only natural ground rock sources of phosphorus, potash, and limestone, not quicklime, should be used in the organic garden.

If the garden soil has been properly prepared vegetables will probably grow without the supplemental feeding fertilizer provides.

Commercial fertilizers are designed to restore or increase the nitrogen, phosphorus, and potassium (potash) content of soil. Nitrogen stimulates leaf growth and strong green color in vegetables; phosphorus promotes early and strong root growth; and potash improves plant vigor and helps to build strong root systems.

Most commercially mixed inorganic fertilizers are packaged and sold as complete or balanced fertilizers. The proportion of nitrogen, phosphorus, and potash is indicated by 3 hyphenated numbers displayed on the bag. The numbers refer to these 3 elements, in the above order, that are contained in the package. When you buy 10 pounds, or even 100 pounds of, say, 5-10-5 fertilizer, you are buying a package containing 5 percent nitrogen, 10 percent phosphorus, and 5 percent potash. The rest is filler which makes these nutrients safe and easy to work with. Inorganic, dehydrated fertilizers generally carry a higher percentage of plant nutrients than the organic fertilizers, but both basically do the same job.

Vegetables need fertilizers at regular intervals. Side-dress, or scratch fertilizer around your vegetables when transplanting or thinning, then water the soil thoroughly to help the plants absorb the feed. Continue to side-dress regularly as the vegetables begin to grow more vigorously.

Both organic and inorganic products are sometimes sold as limited-purpose fertilizers, that is, the numbers on the package will indicate that one fertilizer will have more nitrogen, or perhaps more potash, than is usual in a balanced fertilizer. There are also special fertilizers, designed to sweeten acid soils. There are fast-acting fertilizers, which give spectacular results within a short time. There are also slow-acting fertilizers, which are not so dramatic but which have fewer drawbacks. With slow-acting fertilizers there is little chance of burning your plants by overfertilizing, and you will not have to apply fertilizer as often, but they do take time to release the essential nutrients needed by the soil. A knowledgeable nurseryman can help you find the proper fertilizer for your soil and plant requirements.

Soil

Ideally soil should be a deep, fine, sandy or silt loam. These soils promote good drainage, where water will soak deeply and uniformly into the ground instead of standing in puddles or running off too quickly. Most plants don't like wet feet so avoid low, wet, mushy ground. Take sample shovelfuls of earth from various parts of the area available for your garden. If one section seems to be richer, more loosely packed or full of worms than the others, by all means plant in that spot unless there is a drainage problem. If you are not partial to gnarled and twisted produce, remove rocks and stones from garden locations, especially where root vegetables are to be planted.

Where to Plant

You may be the wildly enthusiastic gardener who prefers a large flamboyant garden bursting with stately cornstalks, rambling squash plants, and multicolored peppers, or you may prefer a small salad garden with room for only lettuce, scallions, herbs, and tomatoes. You may begin by growing tomatoes, herbs, or even beans in a large patio planter, or you may merely tuck some vegetables in among your flowers. No matter what your preference, it is probably best to start your garden on a small scale. As you grow in confidence and know-how, so will your garden grow.

Vegetables should be grown where they will receive full sun for at least 5 or 6 hours during the middle of the day. The plot should be fairly level and should be located as close as possible to a source of water for easy irrigation. If your land is hilly, plant in rows across the hill to keep both soil and water from running off.

Plowing

First, dig a 10- to 12-inch trench where you plan to plant your garden. Determine the depth of the topsoil by noting the texture and color of the earth. The line where the color changes is where the topsoil ends and the subsoil begins. Be sure to plow 2 inches above this line so the subsoil will not be turned up.

Unless it is quite small, your garden will probably be plowed by a farmer. Take note of the direction the furrows run. The plowed rows should run the opposite way the following year.

Watering

Vegetables vary in their water requirements but most will be satisfied with 1 to 2 inches of water per week uniformly soaked around the roots. If normal rainfall is scant be sure to water plants regularly, especially during the hottest part of the season. The water should penetrate to a depth of at least 3 inches. Water loss through evaporation is high at midday so try to keep water off the foliage by using a perforated hose, which soaks only the soil. If you use a sprinkler, water in the morning to give the leaves a chance to dry out by nightfall, thus minimizing the danger of fungus disease in your garden.

When to Plant

Many crops do well when planted as early as the soil can be worked. More delicate varieties should not be planted until all danger from frost is past. Some vegetables must be planted during early summer for fall or winter harvest, others thrive if they are planted in the fall and harvested in the spring. Approximate times for planting in different areas of the country are given in the individual sections.

In general, ground should be turned over for planting when it is dry enough to work. Pick up a handful of topsoil from your garden and squeeze it into a ball. If the ball crumbles when you tap it with your finger, the soil is ready to prepare for planting.

Pest Control

Your garden soil has been turned over and enriched with compost; seeds and seedlings have been planted; a mulch has been laid; and a regular fertilizing schedule has begun: your garden is no longer a dream but a reality. Suddenly, a terrible feeling arises that out among those straight green rows the soil and air are teeming with plant pests, all scheming to undo your labor of love.

Simply defined, plant pests are insects, fungus organisms, rodents, mites, snails, slugs, or weeds; in other words, anything that causes damage or disease in the garden. Before resorting to wholesale chemical spraying at the first sign of trouble, consider alternative methods to protect the vegetables.

Begin by buying only disease-resistant seeds and seedlings. Turn over the soil every fall after garden cleanup. This will expose many insect larvae in the soil to freezing temperatures during the winter.

Enrich the soil with organic fertilizers before planting and keep the seedlings adequately fertilized. Healthy, vigorous plants have a good head start in combating disease and pests.

Housekeep the garden: pull out weeds, pick up trash, and get rid of diseased plants. Don't handle healthy plants after pulling out diseased ones without washing your hands. Rotate your crops: some disease organisms are carried over in the soil from year to year. Slip paper collars around the vulnerable seedlings of tomatoes or members of the cabbage family to protect them from cutworms.

Fight force with force. Many valuable insects such as lady bugs, lacewings and praying mantises are natural enemies of the harmful bug population. Encourage insect eating birds such as robins, bluebirds, chickadees, and wrens, by hanging out suet and building a birdbath, but be sure to throw netting over the berry bushes whose fruits the birds love so well.

Saucers of stale beer set in the garden lure slugs to their doom by drowning. Rabbits love soybeans. Plant these at the outside of your garden to preserve tender young lettuce, carrots, etc. Mice hate the smell of mint so plant this around the edge of your garden.

If the infestation is not overwhelming, some bugs may be stripped from leaves and stalks by hand. Japanese beetles, for instance, can be picked off and dropped into a jar of kerosene. Some insects can be washed off by a heavy stream of water from your garden hose.

Transplanting

Many vegetables need an early start for a long growing season. In areas where frost lingers late into spring, start seeds indoors in flats or peat pots. Peat pots make especially good containers for seedlings, because they may be transplanted, pot and all, without disturbing the root ball.

Use disease and weed-free soils or other suitable lightweight planting mediums, available at garden supply stores. You may also sterilize ordinary soil by sifting it first and then setting it in an oven preheated to 160 to 170 degrees for 30 minutes on 2 successive days.

Your seedlings will require a warm and sunny spot to grow indoors, preferably near a window or under adequate artificial light. Keep the flats or peat pots uniformly watered, but take care not to saturate the soil. Thin the seedlings, or transplant to peat pots if started in flats, when the first true leaves appear above the rounded seedling leaves. Seedlings will be spindly and weak if they are crowded too closely together.

Harden-off is the term used to describe acclimatizing or toughening to outdoor conditions seedlings which have been raised indoors. When they have developed one set of true leaves move the seedlings to a cold frame, or gradually expose them to lower temperatures and stronger sunlight.

Hot caps are used to protect some vegetables from cold weather. They can also be used to harden-off seedlings if sufficient ventilation is provided. Widen the slits in the caps as the days warm up.

Disturb the seedlings as little as possible when transplanting them to the garden. Water them about 2 hours before setting them out. Try to keep the soil ball around the roots intact—this is where peat pots come in handy. Transplant on a cloudy day, or give a little light shade to the seedlings to protect them from full sun for a few days after transplanting. This will help them recover more quickly. You may give the young plants an added boost with a transplanting fertilizer prepared by mixing 1 part of commercial liquid fertilizer with 12 parts of water.

A *cold frame* is a sloping, large, bottomless box, constructed of wood with standard glass sash or wood-framed plastic sheeting set on top. The box is placed outdoors directly over the soil, and seedlings, plants, or cuttings are raised inside it. Climate control is provided by raising or shutting the glass or plastic top.

A *hotbed* is a cold frame equipped with an electrical heating source, and is usually a more elaborate and permanent structure than a cold frame.

Damping-off is the diseased condition of seedlings, caused by fungi that rot the stems at soil level and produce wilting. Seeds may be treated with disinfectant before planting. Use only sterile soil and keep the moisture supply uniform. Don't saturate the growing medium in your flats or pots.

Blanching is the term given to the process of shielding the leaves, stalks, or florets of certain vegetables from the sun to whiten or lighten them. The blanching process for celery, cauliflower, leeks, escarole, and curly endive is described in their individual sections.

Growing your own vegetables

A SUCCESSFUL VEGETABLE garden takes planning. Thought must be given to the size of the vegetables, their compatibility, when each matures, and crop rotation. Here are a few points to consider:

Provide continuous sun for your growing plants by arranging the rows according to height, so that one won't shade the other.

Make successive sowings 2 or 3 weeks apart, or make simultaneous plantings of early, midsummer, or late varieties of a crop. These take different lengths of time to mature and ensure a full picking basket all summer and fall.

Take advantage of the germination speed of quick-growing crops like radishes. They help to mark the rows of slow-germinating vegetables like lettuce, and harvesting them helps keep the soil friable.

Plant perennial vegetables such as asparagus and rhubarb to one side of the garden, where if undisturbed, they will continue to flourish for many years.

Select named varieties of seed or transplants for planting, and buy them from a reputable seedsman to be assured of high-quality, disease-resistant plants.

Seed should be planted shallowly in early spring. Warmer

weather and lighter loams call for deeper seeding. The soil should be freshly sifted, or dug and finely raked, before planting. Space seeds uniformly, and avoid crowding the seedlings by planting too thickly. Take care that the soil covering is pressed firmly down over the seed. Keep the soil moist to speed germination, especially in warm weather.

Seeds may be planted in rows of single plants, sometimes called drills, or they may be planted in hills which means that a cluster or group of seeds is planted in a small circle instead of in rows on level ground. Vegetables such as corn, or those with running vines like cucumbers or pumpkins, do best when planted in hills.

Rotate your crops if possible. The same vegetables planted in the same spot year after year can drain the soil of one or more essential nutrients. Rotate by families: no member of the extensive cabbage family, for instance, should be planted where another cabbage relative has been grown within the previous 3 years; and rotate by single crop: beans, for instance, should be planted in a new soil location each year. Crop rotation also reduces the incidence of disease and insect infestation.

Artichokes

The artichoke, a handsome and exotic-looking vegetable, is grown chiefly in California, where frost-free winters provide the long, uninterrupted period they need to grow to maturity. The edible part of the artichoke is the purple green flower bud. The large outer leaves or scales on the bud have spiny tips, but their fleshy base is tender and edible, as is the base of the bract which forms the artichoke bottom just above the stalk. The choke or spiny center is not edible. Green Globe is a good artichoke variety.

Treating the Soil
The vegetable is a vigorous feeder and needs rich soil that should be further enriched with generous applications of fertilizer.

Planting
Artichokes may be started from seed, either in peat pots and then hardened-off before setting outdoors, or planted directly in the garden. Seedling production is variable, however, so using suckers is the preferred way to start new plants.

Plant the suckers, which are obtained from dividing the parent plant, 6 inches deep and 6 feet apart, in rows 6 feet apart. Cultivate the soil cleanly and provide plenty of water.

Harvesting

Before they bloom cut the flower heads, which are the edible part of the plant. To encourage sucker production, cut back the stalks to the ground. Make new plantings from suckers every 3 years, since plants are usually not productive after that length of time.

Asparagus

Asparagus is one of the very few perennial vegetables, and one of the first to be ready for spring picking. It grows well everywhere except in states bordering the Gulf of Mexico, since a dormant period is necessary during the winter months. Waltham Washington, Mary Washington, or Viking (Mary Washington Improved), are among the best varieties.

Treating the Soil

Asparagus needs well-drained soil with a pH of 6.0 to 8.0. Dig a trench about 15 inches deep (deeper in a heavy clay soil with poor drainage) in the fall or early spring. Spread well-rotted manure to a depth of 4 inches over the trench, and cover it with 4 to 6 inches of rich garden loam. Gradually fill in the rest of the trench by weekly hoeing during the growing season. Fertilize the soil each spring and mulch each fall with manure or any coarse litter.

Planting

Although asparagus may be started from seed, many gardeners prefer to buy established year-old roots and save a year's growing time. If started from seed, the first crop will not be ready for harvest for 3 years, while year-old roots will begin to produce after 2 years.

Seed may be started indoors during the winter months or outdoors in a hotbed in early spring. Soak the seed overnight in lukewarm water before planting 1 inch deep and ½ inch apart. When all danger from frost is past, transplant the seedlings to rows 4 inches apart in your garden or nursery bed. Next spring transplant the yearlings to one side of the garden, spacing them 1½ feet apart in rows 2 to 3 feet apart, where if undisturbed they will continue to grow for many years. Use this spacing for year-old roots as well.

Set the plants 6 inches deep, with their roots spread wide and their budded crowns pointing upward. Carefully mound 1 to 2 inches of soil over the roots, tamping it down well. As the soil is worked during the growing season with weekly or semiweekly hoeing, additional earth will gradually fill the trench and increase the root covering.

Harvesting

Asparagus should not be harvested sooner than the third spring if started from seed, or the second spring when year-old roots are planted. The first crop year, harvest for only 2 weeks; thereafter the vegetable may be harvested for up to 6 weeks. Cutting too late in the season reduces the next year's yield.

Asparagus is ready to be picked when the stems are 6 to 8 inches tall and the buds are compact. Snap the stalks by bending them between the thumb and index finger; cutting may injure other young sprouts. At the end of the season cut the yellowed tops close to the ground, then fertilize and mulch.

Beets

The hardy, easy-to-grow beet, with its beautifully textured red roots and nutritious young green leaves, provides home growers with an economical and important food source for table, canning, or winter storage. Early Wonder and Crosby's Egyptian are excellent early varieties. Detroit Dark Red is tops for all-around purposes, and when planted in midsummer is ideal for winter storage.

Treating the Soil

Beets do well in most well-drained garden soils, although a deep, light sandy soil is best.

Planting

Beets may be planted early for summer harvest and during midsummer for winter storage, since neither light spring nor fall frosts will harm them. Hot weather toughens the roots, so plant early and late in southern climates.

If seeds are started in a hotbed or cold frame, transplant the seedlings with the roots straight down at the same time the first outdoor sowing is made. The beet seed is really a seed clump, with each clump containing 3 or 4 or even more seeds. Sow 2 seed clumps to an inch and cover with ½ inch of soil. The rows should be set 15 to 18 inches apart. When seedlings sprout from a clump, select the strongest and pull up all the others. Feed and water adequately for quick growth. When your plants are 5 to 8 inches tall, thin to 4 or 5 for each foot of row, and use the nutritious beet greens for cooking. Successive plantings should be made at 4-week intervals to ensure a steady supply of tops and roots. Plant until early July, when winter storage varieties may be sown. To raise beets for their greens only, sow the seed thickly in rows 1 inch apart.

Harvesting
The roots of most beet varieties are ideally picked when they are 2 inches across, or about 60 days after planting, although those most suitable for winter storage take a bit longer. If your crop has been planted for greens, harvest when the tops are 5 to 8 inches tall. Remove fall-harvested beets to the storage cellar when heavy frosts are predicted.

Broccoli

Broccoli, a member of the cabbage family, can be planted indoors in late winter and then transplanted for midsummer harvest, and outdoors in late June for a full crop. Good early varieties are Green Comet, Spartan Early, and DeCicco. Fall-harvested types include Cleopatra, Green Mountain, and Waltham 29.

Treating the Soil
Full sun and plenty of plant food and moisture will promote good growth and large, firm, compact heads. Broccoli will grow fairly well in most garden soils but in order for the plants to flourish the soil should be enriched and have sufficient drainage. Do not plant broccoli where any other broccoli plants or cabbage relatives have been grown within the previous 3 years, or the plants may become diseased.

Planting
For midsummer harvest, sow broccoli seed ½ inch deep in peat pots

at least 6 weeks before setting them out in late April or May. Plant the seedlings 2½ feet apart in their peat pots. Plant seeds of late varieties ½ inch deep, in rows 2 feet apart, directly in the garden from the middle to the end of June for fall harvesting. Thin the seedlings to stand 2 feet apart and water freely to help the plants tolerate the summer heat and keep them from wilting. The weather will have cooled before the heat-sensitive varieties mature. Seed should be sown in fall or winter in warm areas for spring harvest.

Be sure to keep the ground well cultivated while the plants are growing. Paper collars set around the seedlings will help to protect them from cutworms.

Harvesting

Broccoli is ready for harvest when the heads are compact and the buds are still tight. Some varieties extend their harvest by producing numerous side shoots and sprouts for several weeks after the main heads are cut.

Brussels Sprouts

Hardy brussels sprouts resemble miniature cabbages and have a subtle cabbagelike flavor, but are not as easy to grow as cabbage. Since light frosts enhance their development, they are not satisfactorily grown in the warmer and more humid areas of the South. Good varieties are Jade Cross Hybrid and Long Island Improved.

Treating the Soil

Brussels sprouts grow well in any kind of enriched soil having a pH of 6.0 to 7.5. Be sure that the soil has proper drainage and that adequate moisture and food are supplied. To discourage plant disease do not plant brussels sprouts where any previous plantings have been made or where any other cabbage-related crops have been planted within the previous 3 years.

Planting

Brussels sprouts need a long growing season. Start your plants as soon as the ground has warmed in early to mid-May. Set the seeds ¼ inch deep in rows 2½ to 3 feet apart, and thin to stand 2½ feet apart. As the sprouts start to develop, pick off the lower leaves and stems. This will make harvesting easier. Don't remove the top leaves, however—sprout formation starts near the bottom and progresses up the stem. Paper collars set around the seedling stems keep the soil cool and moist and protect against cutworms.

Harvesting

The sprouts are edible when they are 1 to 2 inches in diameter. The plants when mature may stand as high as 2½ feet tall, and up to 100 sprouts may cluster around the stem. Picking usually begins after the first frost. Pinch out the growing points on the top of the plant at this time to stimulate quicker growth in the upper sprouts.

To pick the sprouts, break off the leaf below each sprout before breaking the sprout off the stalk. Continue to harvest until below freezing temperatures set in, when you may safely dig up the plants and store in a cool cellar or garage. Leave sufficient soil around the roots and keep the soil moist so the sprouts will continue to flourish.

Cabbage

Varieties of cabbage include those with smooth, green, tightly compressed heads; red cabbage with its tight purple red leaves; and savoy cabbage with looser curled or savoyed foliage.

Choose green cabbage for early, midsummer, or late planting. Golden Acre, Early Jersey Wakefield, Jersey Queen, and Marion Market all prefer cool, moist conditions and will reach their harvest size of 3 pounds by the time hot weather sets in.

Midsummer varieties stand hot weather better. Danish Ballhead or King Cole Hybrid, both weighing 4 to 6 pounds, are good choices.

Danish Ballhead may also be planted for late fall harvest, as may Improved Wisconsin.

Among the red cabbages try Red Acre and Red Danish, and good savoy types are Savoy King or Chieftain Savoy. Plant the early varieties of cabbage in midwestern areas where hot summers prevail. In those regions where winter temperatures rarely dip below freezing, sow outdoors in late summer for late fall harvest.

Treating the Soil

Cabbage needs full sun and well-drained soil with a pH of 6.0 to 7.5. Keep well supplied with water in dry weather.

Cabbage needs uniform, not soaking moisture. The root system is large but runs shallow. Cultivation should be light. To lessen the risk of plant disease, do not plant cabbage in soil where previous crops of cabbage or cabbage-related vegetables (broccoli, brussels sprouts, cauliflower, kohlrabi) have been planted.

Planting

Get seeds for early varieties off to an early start by planting them ¼ inch deep in pots or flats indoors or in a hotbed. Keep the soil moist and the temperature uniform to help the seedlings develop strong roots.

Harden-off the seedlings at 50 to 55 degrees before setting outdoors 2 weeks before the last frost is due. Transplant these early varieties 1 foot apart in rows 2 feet apart.

Set the seeds for midsummer varieties directly in the garden early enough to give them a good start before hot weather sets in. Plant them ¼ inch deep and 2 inches apart, and thin them to stand 1½ feet apart when the second set of true leaves appear. Midsummer types, including savoy cabbage, are excellent for fall harvesting. Late varieties of cabbage may be planted in late May or June because they are less susceptible to summer heat. Paper collars set around all varieties of seedling cabbages help to reduce cutworm destruction and also keep the soil moist and cool.

Harvesting

Pick the cabbage heads as needed when early varieties mature. Their keeping quality is not as good as that of later cabbages, which may be stored in a variety of ways for late fall and winter harvest. Harvest midsummer cabbages in the fall, and late cabbages just before the first freezing temperatures. Consult Outdoor Storage (page 483).

Chinese Cabbage

Chinese, or celery cabbage, resembles lettuce or celery more than it does cabbage, but it boasts a sweeter and more subtle flavor than either. The leaves are eaten raw in salads, or may be cooked like spinach. This vegetable is fast-growing and prefers cool weather. Michihli is a good variety.

Preparing the Soil

Chinese cabbage needs a good soil with a pH of 6.0 to 7.5, enriched before planting with well-rotted manure.

Planting

Because chinese cabbage will run to seed in hot weather, spring planting is not advised. Plant directly in the garden during mid-summer in rows 2 feet apart. Set the seeds ½ inch deep and 3 to 4 inches apart, then thin to 10 or 12 inches when 4 to 6 inches high. Use the thinnings for salads. Continue to pull and use if the plants crowd each other. Fertilize every 3 or 4 weeks.

Harvesting

Plants are mature when 15 to 18 inches tall, about 8 to 10 weeks after sowing the seeds. Harvest by pulling the heads up and cutting off the roots.

Carrots

Carrots come in short, medium, or long types. Choose varieties suited to the soil in your garden.

Gold Pak and Imperator, which have long tapering roots, require a light, sandy soil. For gardens with shallow, rocky, or heavy clay soil try Nantes Coreless, Chantenay, Danvers Improved, Danvers Half-Long, or Oxheart, which is short and broad and has good keeping qualities.

Carrots are a cool-season vegetable best grown where relatively mild temperatures prevail. Excessive hot weather retards their growth and spoils their flavor.

Treating the Soil

The soil must be worked as deeply as possible and enriched with organic matter or fertilizers. Carrots prefer a loose soil with a pH of 6.0 to 7.0. Plant in raised ridges or sprinkle grass cuttings over the soil surface to keep the earth friable.

Planting

Sow carrot seeds as early as the ground can be worked and make successive plantings 3 weeks apart until late June. Seeds should be sown ½ inch deep in rows 1 foot apart. Thin to 2 inches apart for early varieties, and 3 to 4 inches apart for the larger, later varieties. If small young carrots are desired, sow the seeds thinly in midsummer and don't bother to thin them. Quick-growing radishes may be planted between the slow-germinating carrot seeds to mark the rows. Cultivate deeply to keep the soil loose and the weeds out, and water uniformly in dry weather. Pile soil on any exposed roots to keep the tops of the roots from turning green.

Harvesting

Carrots can be pulled when the plants are thinned (these young tender roots are delicious), or they may be allowed to mature and then harvested. Dig before frost sets in and cut off the tops ½ inch from the root crown. Store your fall harvest in a root cellar.

Cauliflower

This temperamental member of the cabbage family requires cool, moist temperatures to produce its familiar thick white clusters of compact florets. Cauliflower grows best in northern regions when planted as an early spring or fall crop, or as a winter crop in milder climates. Select Snowdrift or Early Snowball for early spring planting, and Super Snowball or Snow King Hybrid for fall. All of these must be blanched to produce white heads.

Treating the Soil

Cauliflower needs a deep, rich, loamy soil with a pH of 6.0 to 7.5. Uniform moisture and adequate feeding should be supplied. As with other members of the cabbage family, you can lessen the risk of plant disease if you do not plant cauliflower in any part of the garden where its cabbage or cabbage-type relatives have been planted for the previous 3 years.

Planting

Seeds for early varieties should be sown in March, indoors in flats or pots, or outdoors in a hotbed. Plant the seeds ½ inch deep. When transplanting set individual plants 1½ to 2 feet apart in rows 3 feet apart. In areas where summer temperatures are not excessively hot, plant the seeds in a partially shaded spot in the garden in early June for a fall crop. Transplant to full sun in July. Seeds of fast-growing crops like radishes may be planted between the seedlings and between the rows.

Cultivate weekly until the leaves grow large enough to shade the ground around the stems of the plants, but be careful: cultivate shallowly—the roots are close to the surface. Protect the seedlings from cutworms by slipping paper collars around the stems.

Blanch cauliflower when flower clusters begin to show. Protect the heads from sunlight and weather by gathering up the leaves around the flowers and securing them at the top with string. Be sure that both flower clusters and leaves are dry before blanching begins. Blanching will take 3 or 4 days in warm weather, 7 to 8 days in cool.

Harvesting

To harvest, cut the cauliflower just below the head when the florets are still compact. Cutting after the buds open results in poor quality. If frosts threaten late crops, store immature heads in a cool place with moist soil around the roots and they will continue to mature.

Celeriac

Celeriac is an edible, turnip-shaped root with a flavor similar to celery. It is delicious grated or sliced and eaten raw in salads, boiled and served with cream sauce, or used for soups and stews. Celeriac requires less work than celery, because it need not be blanched and the roots are easier to store.

Preparing the Soil

Like celery, celeriac should be planted in a rich, loamy, moist soil with a pH of 6.0 to 7.0. The ground should be well prepared beforehand and enriched further with a good supply of organic matter. Besides lots of moisture, celeriac should have routine applications of plant food about 3 weeks apart during its very long growing period.

Planting

Plant celeriac seed indoors in regions where frosts persist into early spring, or outdoors as soon as the ground can be worked. Start directly in the garden in the fall in areas where winter temperatures are mild. Cover the seed lightly with soil in rows 2 feet apart. Thin the seedlings 6 to 8 inches apart and keep the soil around them moist and cool.

Harvesting

Celeriac roots grow to 4 inches across when mature, but are at their most tender and have the best flavor when 2 to 3 inches in diameter.

[25]

To harvest, simply pull the roots from the ground, cut off the tops, and use. To store, cover the roots with sand and keep in a cool place until needed.

Celery

This basic and popular vegetable is not usually grown in home gardens. It needs cool temperatures and a rich, friable, uniformly moist soil for the duration of its very long growing season. However, if you are a really avid gardener, it might be interesting to try this one.

Blanching, or protecting the stalks from light to whiten them, is no longer considered essential because green celery has more vitamins, but blanching advocates claim it makes the celery more crisp and tender. Choose varieties such as Summer Pascal or Giant Pascal and also yellow, or self-blanching types like Golden Plume.

Treating the Soil

To prepare the soil for celery before sowing seeds or transplanting, enrich it to a depth of 1 foot with large quantities of organic matter and fertilizer, and rake the top 6 inches very finely. Uniform watering is essential during the long growing months.

Planting

Seed for early varieties may be started indoors in early spring. Scatter the seed in finely sifted soil, then firm and keep the soil moist and cool. Place near a sunny window, or set a pane of glass over the flat. When seedlings are 1 inch tall, transplant to individual pots or to a cold frame or hotbed. Set directly in the garden when the seedlings reach a height of 3 or 4 inches. For easier gardening, start celery from nursery-bought seedlings of this size.

Seeds for fall harvest may be placed outdoors in late April or early May in a cool, damp, well-prepared spot set apart from the garden, and then transplanted as seedlings in July.

Set the celery seedlings 6 to 8 inches apart in rows 2 feet distant from each other if they are not to be blanched, or 3 feet distant if they are. Fertilize every 3 weeks, and keep the soil moist, especially during the summer months and just before harvesting. Surface-cultivate because celery has a small, easily disturbed root system.

To blanch your celery, pile earth around the stalks, except during the summer months when this method may cause rotting. Blanching may also be accomplished by setting boards along the rows of stalks to reduce the amount of light reaching them, or by slipping paper or metal cylinders around each individual stalk. Be sure to leave the tips of the stalks exposed when blanching.

Harvesting

Celery is tender and edible at any point in its growth, but take care to dig your crop before fall frosts. Celery will continue to grow and blanch if packed closely together in a cool cellar with lots of soil surrounding the stalks.

Swiss Chard

Swiss chard is a vegetable unfamiliar to most gardeners. Often referred to as a foliage beet, Swiss chard is grown for its large fleshy leafstalk rather than its root. Its large leaves may be used like other greens, while the green stalks may be sliced and served in any recipe that calls for cut asparagus. Gardeners should try chard at least once, since it is extremely tasty and hardy enough to flourish in hot or cold weather. Try Fordhook, Large Ribbed, Dark Green, or Lucullus. Rhubarb Chard has bright red stalks.

Treating the Soil

Swiss chard grows well under soil conditions similar to those required by beets: that is, any garden soil with good drainage and a pH of 6.0 to 7.5.

Planting

Swiss chard is extremely hardy. Plant it in northern regions in early spring, as soon as the soil can be worked. In the South, sow in the fall for harvesting through most of the following year.

Sow the seeds 1 inch deep in rows 1½ to 2 feet apart. Thin to 4 inches apart when the seedlings are 6 inches tall, and thin again to stand 8 inches apart when the plants are 10 to 12 inches tall. Use the plants removed in thinning as greens.

Harvesting

When the plants reach a height of 10 inches, use a sharp knife to cut off the outer leaves and stalks as needed. Trim off mature leaves to stimulate new foliage growth. Take care not to injure the remaining leaves or the bud and the plant will produce until well after frost.

Collards

Collards, a tall-growing form of kale with coarse green leaves which sprout in treelike fashion, are easy to grow and full of vitamins. Young leaves may be eaten raw in salads, more mature leaves should be cooked. Collards are hardy vegetables, so plant them in midsummer for fall harvest in northern regions, or as a winter or early spring crop in the South. Vates and Georgia are good varieties.

Treating the Soil
Collards are members of the cabbage family, resembling small cabbages when immature, and require the same type of well-drained loamy soil. The pH should be between 6.0 and 7.5. To reduce the risk of disease do not plant collards where any other cabbage or cabbage-related vegetable (broccoli, brussels sprouts, cauliflower, or kohlrabi) has been grown within the previous 3 years.

Planting
Plant collards in midsummer for fall harvest in northern areas of the country, and during the fall for winter or early spring crops in southern regions. Sow the seeds 1 inch deep and 3 inches apart in rows 3 feet apart. Thin to 12 to 15 inches apart when the seedlings are 3 or 4 inches tall. Cultivate carefully since the roots spread wide and lie close to the surface. Fertilize every 4 weeks and keep uniformly supplied with water.

Harvesting
Collard leaves may be harvested when the young leaves are tender, or at any time up to maturity. Collards usually reach their full growth in 80 to 90 days. The plants will continue to produce if the green leaves of the central rosette are allowed to remain intact, so pick only the side shoots.

Corn

There is nothing more delectable than sweet corn fresh from the garden, picked from its stalk just as the cooking water reaches a boil, husked and freed from its silks, cooked quickly, and brought to the table minutes later dripping with melted butter and sprinkled with salt.

Corn comes in many varieties: early, second early, midseason, and late; yellow, white, yellow and white, or black. For early yellow varieties, choose Golden Beauty, Seneca Beauty, Earlivee, or Seneca Golden. Golden Midget, Xtra Early Sweet Hybrid, and Carmel Cross are good second early types. For midseason yellow corn, select Golden Bantam, supreme among standard yellow corn; Golden Cross Bantam, or Golden Chief. An excellent late yellow is Iochief.

Types of white corn include Silver Sweet, an early variety, and Country Gentleman and Stilwell's Evergreen, both late. For the bi-colored, or yellow and white varieties, try Sugar and Gold or Butter and Cream. A hardy black type is Black Mexican. Choose wisely from among early, midsummer, and late varieties and be assured of summer-long harvest.

Treating the Soil

Corn will grow well in almost any type of soil with a pH of 6.0 to 7.0, but rich soil gives a better guarantee of tender kernels and taste. Work well-rotted manure and fertilizer into the ground just prior to planting to enrich the soil where corn is to grow.

Planting

Wait until the ground warms in spring and all danger from frost is past before sowing the seed. Planting too early in cold, damp weather may cause poor germination or rotting seeds. Plant 2 or 3 rows side by side rather than a single row to make it easier for pollination to occur. Drop the seeds 1 inch deep into the soil, about 4 to 6 inches apart in rows 2½ feet apart for early varieties, 3 feet apart for all other types. Thin to 8 to 10 inches apart for early varieties, and 10 to 12 inches apart for later ones. Cultivate shallowly to control weeds or use a mulch.

Make successive plantings of early corn 2 weeks apart until midsummer, or plant early, second early, midsummer, and late varieties at the same time in the spring to guarantee a full summer supply.

Harvesting

Corn is ready for harvesting when the husks are dark green and the silks begin to brown. Feel the corn kernels through their husk wrappers—they should be well-rounded and firm. If they spurt a milky substance when tested with a fingernail they are ready for immediate eating. Twist the corn free from the stalks by pulling them down slightly. Cook corn immediately if possible. If there must be a delay between picking and cooking, keep the ears refrigerated to prevent flavor loss.

Cucumbers

Two main varieties of cucumbers are grown in home gardens: those used primarily for slicing, which are long and tapering; and the short, blunt-ended cucumber which is best adapted for pickling. Good selections among the long cucumbers are Spartan Valor, Burpless Hybrid, Burpee Hybrid, or Victory. For the smaller pickling cucumbers, try Early Hycrop, Gherkin, Bravo, or Wisconsin SMR 18.

Treating the Soil

Cucumbers require an enriched soil with a pH of 5.5 to 7.0. The plants are usually grown in hills (groups of seeds planted together), with 3 or 4 plants to a hill. Prepare the ground in advance of setting out the seeds or seedlings by working organic matter (compost or well-decayed manure) thoroughly into the soil.

Planting

Begin seeds indoors in peat pots, ½ inch deep and 3 or 4 seeds to a pot, about 4 weeks prior to setting out in areas where late frosts linger. Seeds will rot if planted outdoors before night temperatures remain above 50 degrees. When the seedlings are 1½ inches tall, pull out all but the strongest in each pot. Transplant 3 or 4 seedlings to 1 hill. Plant seed directly in the garden in late spring when all danger from frost is past. Sow outdoors in the fall in warmer regions for winter or spring harvest. Seeds should be planted ½ inch deep, 6 to 8 seeds to a hill, spacing the hills about 4 feet apart. Thin the seedlings to the strongest 3 or 4.

Fertilize the plants every 3 weeks, and provide sufficient water during dry weather. Allow the plants to grow freely along the ground or train them to climb on strong trellises. Do not disturb the vines too much, even when picking, and cultivate shallowly if at all. Both vines and blossoms are easily injured, and injury results in misshapen cucumbers.

Harvesting

Pick the fruit as it matures, as continuous harvesting increases the yield. Slicing cucumbers are mature when they are about 8 inches long, while pickling cucumbers may be picked at 1½ to 3 inches. If fruit is allowed to yellow or grow too large the vines will not produce. Roll the vines over carefully, cut the cucumbers from them, and just as carefully roll them back. The vines may tangle or break if handled too roughly.

Eggplant

Tender, glossy eggplant, native to India and the Far East, needs warm temperatures for its very long growing season. Varieties best suited to northern climates, where frosts may linger into spring, are Black Beauty and Black Magic. Try Florida Market for planting in warmer climates. Eggplant matures about 2½ months after the plants are set outside as seedlings.

Treating the Soil

Deep, sandy soil, well enriched with rotted manure or compost is best, although any enriched soil with a slightly acid pH of 5.5 to 6.5 will do. Minimize the risk of plant disease by planting successive eggplant crops in different garden areas each year. Do not plant eggplant where tomatoes or potatoes have been grown within the previous 3 years.

Planting

In areas with a shorter growing season, start eggplant indoors in flats about 8 or 9 weeks before transplanting to the garden. Transfer to individual peat pots or place in a hotbed outdoors when the seedlings are 2 inches tall. The seed should be planted ½ inch deep, and the soil should be kept warm and uniformly moist.

Transplant the seedlings as soon as daytime temperatures reach a constant 70 degrees. Set the plants about 2½ to 3 feet apart in rows 2½ to 3 feet apart, since mature plants will be 2½ to 3 feet tall. Fertilize every 4 weeks during the growing season and water uniformly. Slip paper collars around the seedlings to protect them from cutworm invasion.

Harvesting

Eggplants may be harvested before they reach their mature size of 6 to 8 inches. The fruit has the most delicate flavor when it is ⅔ grown and the purple black skin is glossy. A dull skin means the eggplant is too ripe. To harvest, cut the thick woody stem close to the fruit with a sharp knife.

Escarole and Curly Endive

These crisp greens lend variety and nutlike flavor to salads. Endive has curled or fringed leaves, while the leaves of escarole are broad. Try Salad King or Green Curled Endive. A good escarole variety is Broad Leaved Batavian. Both endive and escarole prefer cool growing temperatures, so midsummer planting and fall harvest are advised in northern areas. When mild winters prevail, both may be planted in the fall for winter or spring harvest.

Both endive and escarole should be blanched, a process of shielding them from the sun which makes the leaves light, more attractive, and somewhat less bitter.

Treating the Soil

Soil for endive and escarole should be well drained, sandy, and enriched with well-rotted manure or compost. A pH of 5.8 to 6.5 is best.

Planting

Sow outdoors beginning in June for a fall crop, and make successive plantings every 2 weeks through the beginning of August to insure a succession of harvests. The seed should be planted ¼ inch deep in rows spaced 1½ to 2 feet apart. Thin to 10 to 12 inches when the seedlings are 2 to 3 inches tall. Use a well-balanced fertilizer every 3 or 4 weeks and cultivate carefully as the roots of these greens are relatively shallow.

Blanch the leaves when the plants are about 15 inches tall. To blanch, tie the side leaves up over the center leaves with string or rubber bands, or shield the plants from the light with boards raised to the proper height with stones or cinder blocks. The blanching process will require 4 or 5 days when the weather is warm and 10 to 14 days when the temperature is cooler. Be sure the greens are dry before covering them or the plants will rot.

Harvesting

Curly endive and escarole take about 85 days to reach maturity, but they can be used prior to maturity providing they have been blanched. Protect growing crops from late autumn frosts by mulching the ground around them.

Herbs

Herbs are simply cultivated aromatic weeds, and since they are descended from hearty weed ancestors, they grow, quite predictably, like weeds. These delightful plants can make even the novice gardener feel like a pro. Just dig up the earth a little, pop in the seeds, dust them over with a bit of sifted soil, and sprinkle them lightly once in a while. After the plants mature they need virtually no attention. If you forget to water them, if you never get around to enriching the soil, so much the better—herbs seem to prefer infertile ground and dry earth. Try them at the edge of your garden, in a flower pot, or even on your window sill. As a matter of fact, some herbs are almost impossible to get rid of once they have a good start. Three years ago I spent an entire summer pulling up mint plants that were taking over my lawn. I turned over the soil to expose the roots to the sun and finally built a tool shed over the roots to make sure that none survived. And guess what is growing out from under that tool shed this year—mint.

I've tried every type of herb garden, from the formal to the herb border to the flowerpot variety, and I've finally settled upon a patch of earth, 8 feet by 8 feet and well-fenced off. I plant annuals such as lemon basil, marjoram, mint, oregano, sage, dill, and anise and let the bulk of the plants go to seed. The following year I merely harvest by pinching off the tops of the plants as soon as they seem hearty enough—because nearly everything comes up, every spring.

Place your herb garden up-wind of your patio or terrace, and when you pick herbs for cooking make a practice of crushing a few leaves of each plant (herbs can survive this rough treatment). Then sit yourself down under a shade tree to snap beans from your garden or to peel potatoes. The breezes will do the rest to soothe you with the fragrance of mingled herbs.

Drying Herbs

Always harvest herbs before their flowers burst into bloom. Snip off the stems at the base, leaving several sets of leaves still growing for next year's supply. Rinse the leaves, dry them well with paper towels, and hang them, several stalks tied together, upside down in a dark, dry, airy place for 3 to 4 days. Place a large paper bag around each group of plants, making sure that the bag does not touch the leaves. Tie the bag at the top, hang it up, and let the herbs continue to dry for 2 weeks. Cut down the bags but do not untie the tops. Rub the bag between your hands until the leaves have dropped to the bottom, then remove the stems from the bag and pick off any clinging leaves. Discard the stems.

Sprinkle the leaves onto cookie sheets, discarding any large pieces of stem, and dry the herbs in an oven preheated to 200 degrees. Dry the leaves in the oven until they crumble when rubbed between the fingers. Store in clean, dry, airtight jars and arrange the jars in a dark, cool place until needed.

Freezing Herbs

Harvest herbs before they bloom and snip off the stems at the base, leaving several sets of leaves still growing for next year's supply. Wash the leaves and dry them well with paper towels. Pack into plastic containers or bags and freeze.

Amounts

In general, frozen herbs have the same strength as fresh and may be used in the same way. Dried herbs have the flavorful oils concentrated in their leaves and are twice as strong. You may substitute half the amount of dried herbs when fresh are called for.

Kale

Kale is a hardy member of the cabbage family, high in nutritive value, rich in vitamins, and absolutely delicious when properly prepared. This one is a gardener's dream—it thrives in cool weather and its flavor even improves after frost, or even freezing. Kale does not form a head like cabbage, but rather has a profusion of curly or ruffled loose green leaves which sprout from a stout central stem. Try Dwarf Green Curled or Dwarf Curled Scotch.

Treating the Soil

Kale will grow readily in most gardens if the soil is properly prepared and fertilized beforehand with well-rotted manure or compost. Ample moisture and good drainage are also required. To lessen the risk of plant diseases, do not plant kale where cabbage or any cabbage-related vegetables have grown within the previous 3 years.

Planting

Kale thrives in cool weather, so plant in midsummer for fall harvest in the North, and as a fall, winter, or early spring crop in warmer areas. Sow the seeds ½ inch deep directly in the garden soil in rows 20 to 24 inches apart. Thin the seedlings to stand 15 inches apart. Keep the soil uniformly moist and cultivate carefully.

Harvesting

Young, tender kale greens are delicious raw in salads or used as a garnish. Pick greens as needed.

Leeks

The leek is a milder and hardier version of the onion, grown for its thick green leaves and layers of white stem which are ideal for seasoning soups or for serving braised. Leeks will need blanching to whiten their stems when half-grown. A popular variety is American Flag.

Treating the Soil

A light, rich, friable soil, with a pH of 6.0 to 8.0, is best for leeks. Mix the soil with well-rotted compost and prepare a well-pulverized trench, 6 inches wide and fairly deep, for each row you plan to plant. Uniformly moist soil and good drainage are very important.

Planting

For midsummer harvest, plant the seeds in flats indoors in February or March. Cover thinly with soil. When the seedlings are 3 to 4 inches tall, set them 1 foot apart in the prepared trenches. Sow the seed in nursery beds outdoors as soon as the weather warms for fall harvest in northern areas, then transplant to trenches as described. In warmer regions, plant in late summer or fall for winter or spring crops.

Gradually fill in and mound up the trenches with soil as the growing season progresses. By the time the leeks reach maturity the stems will be blanched by the mounded soil.

Harvesting

The blanched stems of leeks will often measure 2 inches across at maturity, with leaves that may reach a height of 2 to 3 feet during the 4-month growing season. Young leeks may be pulled up and used at any time after they are blanched. Store your extra crop in a protected cold frame or in a cool, moist place with soil loosely packed around them.

Lettuce

Lettuce, the most popular salad vegetable, is easy to grow and thrives in many different garden locations, even in partial shade.

There are 4 main types:

Head lettuce is distinguished by a solid, firm center ball surrounded by large, crisp, green leaves. Ithaca (early), Great Lakes, and Imperial are good varieties;

Butterhead or Bibb lettuce is a smaller, less compact head with soft, loosely folded leaves which grow paler toward the center. Try Buttercrunch, Summer Bibb, or Matchless (Deer Tongue);

Leaf lettuce has clusters or bunches of loose, wavy leaves, which branch out instead of forming heads. Salad Bowl, Prizehead, Grand Rapids (early), Black Seeded Simpson (early), and Ruby, a colorful red-tinged type, are good varieties;

Cos or *romaine* lettuce has long, narrow, rather coarse upright leaves which are tender and sweet. Try Parris Island Cos or Paris White.

Treating the Soil

Lettuce needs well-drained, friable soil with a pH of 6.0 to 7.0. Good quality in crops is dependent on quick, uniform growth, so be sure to boost the soil with well-rotted manure or compost.

Planting

A cool weather crop, lettuce does best where it can be harvested before hot weather sets in. For early harvest, sow indoors or in a hotbed in late February, covering the seed thinly. As soon as the ground can be worked, harden-off the seedlings and transplant to the garden. Make successive plantings about 10 to 12 days apart directly in the garden thereafter until June. Seeds may also be planted in late August for fall crops.

Distance between plants varies with the type of lettuce planted. Head lettuce needs plenty of room: space it 12 to 15 inches apart. Butterhead and cos lettuce should each be 8 to 10 inches apart, and leaf varieties should stand 6 to 8 inches apart. Plant all seeds ¼ inch deep in rows 1½ feet apart. Thin as indicated. The pulled seedlings may be used for salads.

Lettuce may also be tucked in between slower-growing crops if garden space is at a premium, or quick-maturing vegetables like radishes may be set in between the lettuce plants. Lettuce needs full sun during the spring and fall, but it will do better in partial shade in midsummer, and seedlings may be tucked into out-of-the-way garden corners.

Give lettuce uniform moisture, especially at transplanting time and during hot weather, and stimulate quick growth with adequate plant food every 3 weeks. Mulch around the plants to keep the soil moist and the weeds down.

Harvesting

Different varieties of lettuce mature at different times, but all may be used before maturity is reached. Leaf varieties are fastest, with a growing period of about 45 days. Butterhead types mature after 65 days. Head lettuce takes about 75 to 85 days, and romaine or cos takes a little longer.

Melons

The vine-ripened sweetness of home-grown melons is vastly superior to those commercially grown, but melons must be protected from cold if they are to be successful in the home garden. The many different varieties: cantaloupe (or muskmelon), honeydew, casaba, crenshaw, persian, and watermelon, need a long growing season, a hot, dry climate, and plenty of growing space.

Among the cantaloupe varieties, try Far North, Hybrid Classic, Delicious 51, or Iroquois. Honeydew, casaba, persian, and crenshaw are winter melons and ripen later than cantaloupe. Choose Honey Dew, Sungold Casaba, Persian, or Early Hybrid Cranshaw.

Watermelons are available in sizes as small as your hand or as long as your arm. Sugar Baby and You Sweet Thing Hybrid are both good small to medium varieties. Crimson Sweet average 25 pounds, while Charleston Gray weighs up to 35 pounds when mature.

Treating the Soil

Melons prefer full sun, and a sandy, well-drained, moderately acid soil with a pH of 6.2 to 6.8. Prepare the soil thoroughly beforehand by setting well-rotted compost or manure under the ground where each hill (group of seeds) is to grow.

Planting

In northern areas of the country where spring frosts linger, sow seeds indoors in flats or peat pots, using a light, sterilized, enriched soil. Start the seeds about 4 weeks before setting them outdoors.

Transplant the seedlings to the garden when days are warm and temperatures no longer dip below 55 degrees at night. Set 2 to 4 seedlings in each previously prepared hill, spacing the hills 5 feet apart for the smaller melons, and 10 feet apart for watermelon. Seed may also be sown directly in the garden in the warmer regions of the South and Southwest. Sow them ½ inch deep, 10 or 12 seeds to a hill, and pull up all but the 2 hardiest.

Protect seedlings from exposure to cold and wet weather by covering them with paper hot caps, but be sure to remove these in scorching weather to keep the plants from suffocating. Fertilize your crop every 2 weeks and carefully shallow-cultivate or mulch the plants with coarse litter when the vines begin to run. Remove blossoms and fruit which appear after midsummer so that the vines will direct their energies to the fruit already growing.

Harvesting

Melons mature at different rates, usually taking from 3 to 4 months to reach a peak of vine-ripened perfection. Testing for "full slip" will tell you when cantaloupe is ready to be picked and eaten. With your thumbs, lightly press the disc where the stem joins the melon. If the fruit slips off the vine easily, it is ripe. Pick honeydew and casaba when they are yellow or white and smell sweet. Crenshaw and persian also smell sweet when ripe.

On the average, watermelons need about 3 months of growing time before harvesting, and are ripe when the underside turns yellow and a dull thump is heard when the fruit is tapped lightly on the top.

Okra

The crisp, emerald green young pods of the okra, or gumbo, plant are most familiar to Southern cooks, but the vegetable can be grown successfully anywhere in the North where the summer months are warm. Okra is generally used as a thickener for soups and stews, but it is also delicious when dipped in batter and deep fried. Try Clemson Spineless, Emerald, or Louisiana Green Velvet.

Treating the Soil
Okra must have good drainage or the plants may rot. The vegetable will thrive in any good garden soil with a pH of 6.0 to 8.0. Full sun and continuous cultivation are also important.

Planting
In areas where winter frosts linger, start okra indoors in pots about 4 weeks before setting outdoors. Sow 1 inch deep directly in the garden in warmer regions. Thinned plants should stand 15 to 18 inches apart in rows 3 feet distant.

Harvesting
Okra, a form of hibiscus, produces yellow, red-centered blossoms, with pod formation beginning shortly after the blossoms fall. Pick all pods while they are still green and tender, not more than 1½ to 2 inches long. Keep the pods picked off so that the plants will continue to bear. Pods that you cannot use at once may be frozen for a winter-long supply.

Onions

All varieties of this multipurpose vegetable can be started from seed, sets (bulblets), or small seedling plants. Two types of dry-bulb onion are grown: the pungent American varieties and the milder Spanish, Bermuda, or Portugal onions.

Each type has varieties with white, yellow, and red skins. Good white varieties are White Sweet Spanish and Crystal White Wax, a Bermuda-type. Choose Early Yellow Globe, Ebenezer, Downing Yellow Globe, or Yellow Sweet Spanish among the yellow types, and Burgundy and Southport Red Globe among the red.

Scallions or green onions are the so-called bunching onions, easily distinguished by their small white bulbs and tender green shoots. Good varieties are Evergreen Bunching, Beltsville Bunching, or Hardy White Bunching.

Treating the Soil

A loose and well-drained soil is best for growing onions. It should be enriched with well-rotted compost, and have a pH of 5.8 to 6.5. Soil prepared for seed should be raked fine before sowing is begun, and kept uniformly moist while the plants are growing. Full sun is required.

Planting

When starting onions from seed, sow as early as the ground can be worked and a finely raked seedbed prepared. Plant seeds in shallow (2 to 3 inch) rows 1½ feet apart and keep the soil uniformly moist and weed free. Thin the seedlings to 6 inches apart when 6 to 8 inches tall and use the thinnings as green onions.

To shorten the growing season for onions, many gardeners prefer to purchase sets or small seedling plants from a reliable nursery.

Plant these sets, which are immature bulblets, 3 to 4 inches apart and 2 inches deep in rows 1 to 1½ feet apart, as early as the ground can be worked. Plant 2-inch seedlings 2 inches deep and 3 to 4 inches apart in rows 1 to 1½ feet apart as soon as the danger from frost is past. Keep the soil uniformly moist and well cultivated.

Bunching onions or scallions are planted in the same way as bulb onions but they mature much more rapidly. Make successive plantings for continuous harvest. Bunching onions winter well and may be planted in fall for early spring harvest.

Harvesting

When the bulbs mature and the tops turn yellow, bend the tops down to speed up the ripening process and shift some of the soil away from the top of the bulb. Wait until the leaves turn brown before pulling up the onions, then cut off all but an inch or two of top, spread the onions out, and allow them to dry. Most bulb onions winter well if kept in a root cellar, although the milder varieties do not keep as long. Bunching onions will keep for only a week or two, so use them soon after pulling.

Shallots

A shallot is a small, mild-flavored member of the onion family, similar in appearance to garlic, with leaves which resemble the thin green shoots of scallions.

Shallots are grown from bulbs which divide into cloves or small bulblets as they mature. Plant them in the early spring as soon as all danger from frost is past. Set them in rich, moist soil, 2 inches deep and 2 to 3 inches apart in rows 1 foot apart. Harvest by digging them in the fall when their leaves turn yellow, then hang or spread them in the sun for a week to dry. Store them as onions.

Parsnips

Parsnips have thick, tapering roots and a delicate sweet flavor that is improved by fall frosts. Choose from such varieties as All American, Model, or Guernsey.

Treating the Soil

Soil for parsnips should be rich, loamy, and rock free, with a pH of 5.5 to 7.0. Clay or rocky soils produce crooked or branched roots. Spade the ground to a depth of at least 1½ feet before planting any seed.

Planting

Parsnips need 4 to 5 months of growing to reach maturity, so sow the seed early in the spring as soon as the ground can be worked. Plant seeds ¼ inch deep in rows 2 to 2½ feet apart. Scatter the seed thickly, since it germinates slowly and sometimes does not germinate at all. Cover with a very light layer of sand or vermiculite; if the covering is too heavy, germination may not take place.

When the seedlings are 1 inch tall, thin them to stand 3 to 6 inches apart. Keep the ground uniformly moist and weed free, and fertilize every 4 weeks during the long growing season.

Harvesting

Since frosts do no harm to parsnips and even add to their sweet flavor, the vegetable may be left in the ground and harvested all winter or in the spring. Mulch the plants if you plan to dig them during the winter so that the ground will be soft enough to be worked.

Peas

Sweet, delicious peas are among the earliest home garden delicacies to be harvested. A cool-season crop with smooth-seeded, wrinkle-seeded, and edible-pod varieties, peas are sensitive to hot weather and should be planted in spring in northern areas, and during the fall and winter in the South. Sow early, medium, and late-maturing varieties all at one time, to assure continuous production and an abundant yield.

Good tall or medium-tall varieties are Alderman, Freezonian, Lincoln, Laxton's Progress, and Wando, the latter having been especially bred to stand up to hot weather. Choose from Alaska (early), Little Marvel, or Frosty among the dwarf types. Dwarf Gray Sugar and Mammoth Melting Sugar are good edible-pod varieties. It's a good idea to support all pea vines, including the bush types, on plastic or string netting held in place by stakes to keep the plants from sprawling too much. This will also help to make cultivation and harvesting easier.

Treating the Soil

Peas can be grown in a variety of soil types, but well-drained sandy or clay loams with a pH of 6.0 to 7.0 are best.

Planting

Peas sown in warm weather are usually unsuccessful, so plant seeds outdoors as soon as the soil can be worked. Fortunately, the light spring frosts will not do this vegetable any harm. Dig shallow trenches 2 to 3 inches deep in double rows 8 inches apart. Use the space between the double rows to set up your netting trellises when the seed is sown. If you plant more than one double row of seeds, the space between each set of double rows should measure 2 to 4 feet, depending on the height of the variety. To plant in single rows of trenches, space the rows 2 to 4 feet apart.

Sow the seeds in the bottom of the single or the double trenches, 3 inches apart for the dwarf varieties, 4 inches apart for the taller types. Cover the seed with about 1½ inches of soil and gradually fill in the trenches as the seedlings emerge.

Inoculating the pea seed with a commercial bacterial preparation before planting is a good idea. This preparation helps peas and other legumes take nitrogen from the air and convert it into plant food. It may be purchased from garden supply stores and dusted on.

Harvesting

Peas should be picked while they are still young and tender. If allowed to mature on the vine, they soon pass their peak of sweetness. Edible-pod types, which need not be shelled, should be harvested as soon as tiny peas begin to form inside the shells. Clip all varieties of peas at their prime, and eat or prepare them for the freezer as soon as possible.

Peppers

Two varieties of pepper are available for planting in the home garden: the mild-flavored sweet or bell pepper, and the hot pepper, whose pungent flavor forms the basis for many cooking sauces.

Sweet peppers may be picked green or allowed to ripen to red or yellow. Try Bell Boy Hybrid, Ace Wonder, Peter Piper Hybrid, Yolo Wonder, or Early Calwonder. Hot peppers range from small cherry types to long, slim, tapering kinds. Choose Tabasco, small and very pungent; Long Red Cayenne, slim and tapering; or smooth and elongated Hungarian Yellow Wax, which may be used fresh or dried for spicy soups or stews.

Treating the Soil

Peppers prefer a warm, moist, light soil, with a pH of 5.5 to 7.0. The soil need not be overrich, but it should have a good supply of humus.

Planting

Peppers thrive in warm weather, so start your plants by sowing them indoors in flats in February or March, and keep them in a warm, sunny place. Use a loose-growing medium such as vermiculite or mixed sand and peat for fill for the flats. Sow the seed thinly and keep the flats uniformly moist by watering from underneath. Transplant to individual peat pots when the plants are 1 inch tall. In frostfree areas, seed may be started outdoors in seedbeds and then transplanted to the garden.

Transplant the seedlings to the garden when daytime temperatures turn sufficiently warm and humid but are not too hot and dry. Hot, drying winds and low humidity will cause the blossoms to abort and drop off, producing plants with lots of leaves and no fruit. Space the seedlings 1½ feet apart in rows 2 to 3 feet apart. Paper collars slipped around the stems will protect the plants from cutworm injury.

Harvesting

Peppers may be harvested at any stage, whether green or a fully ripe red or yellow. Use a sharp knife to cut part of the stem along with the pepper. Keeping the stem intact this way helps to preserve them. Store in a cool place where the air is not too dry.

Potatoes

Although potatoes are among the most serviceable vegetables, they are not often grown in the home garden because they require so much space. They are, however, a good crop to plant if your garden is large and you plan to harvest when the potatoes are small and flavorful. The vegetable should in this case be used immediately rather than stored.

Potatoes are a cool-season crop. The most favorable conditions for a good harvest are a temperate climate and ample rainfall. Best suited are the northern areas of the country in spring or summer, and the South and Southwest, where they can be planted in winter for spring harvest.

Potato varieties vary in color, quality, and resistance to disease. Most varieties have brown skins, although there are also potatoes with reddish or blue skins. Irish Cobbler, Early Gem, and Norland (red skinned) are early varieties. Use Red Pontiac (good for boiling) or Kennebec for midseason planting. Kennebec may also be planted as a late crop, as may Katahdin and Russet Burbank, more familiarly known as Idaho or Idaho Baker. Blue Victor has purple blue netted skin enclosing a tasty white flesh.

Plant potato varieties which correspond to your table needs, according to whether you want them for immediate use or for winter storage. Always buy and plant certified, disease-free tubers from reliable seedsmen. Do not plant the potatoes you purchase at a grocery store.

Treating the Soil

The ideal soil for potato growing is a light, sandy loam, with good drainage and a pH of 5.0 to 6.0. Well-rotted manure should be spaded deep into the soil before planting.

Planting

Potatoes are grown from seed sets or from seed potatoes. Use potato sets, which are ready to plant; seed potatoes, which are small 1- to 2-ounce potatoes planted whole; or larger seed potatoes, which may be cut into small blocks weighing 1 or 2 ounces each. Take care to include 2 or even 3 eyes or buds on each block, and to give the cuts time to cure by allowing the pieces to dry for 2 or 3 days in a cool, well-ventilated place. If desired, you may dust your seed with a fungicide such as Captan to minimize loss from rotting.

Planting dates are important. Early varieties should go into the ground as soon as the soil can be worked in early spring, even if frost is still lingering. Plant late varieties a few weeks later. In warmer climates, plant in winter so that the potato crop can be harvested before prolonged hot weather sets in.

To plant, dig trenches about 4 inches deep and space the trenches 2 to 3 feet apart. Place the pieces of seed potatoes, with their eyes up, 12 to 15 inches apart. Cultivate only if necessary, and only deep and often enough to control weeds. After the plants begin to blossom and to set tubers, carefully mound up the soil 3 or 4 inches high around the stems to control weeds and protect the tubers from greening caused by too much exposure to light.

Harvesting

For summer use, dig those tubers of eating size as needed, leaving the vines intact so that other smaller tubers may mature. Mature early varieties may be safely left in the ground for several weeks if the weather is not too hot or wet.

Later varieties are ready to harvest when the vines wither and die back. Leave them underground for 3 to 4 weeks, then dig them up on a clear day when the soil is not too wet, taking care not to bruise the skins. Spread them out for 2 or 3 hours to dry any moisture or loose soil, before storing them in a root cellar or other cool, dark place. Cover the potatoes with bags or paper to prevent greening or a somewhat bitter flavor. Always cut off the greened portions of potatoes and cut out the eyes of old potatoes before cooking.

Pumpkins

Home gardeners often shy away from planting pumpkins because they take up quite a bit of room. Pumpkins are a satisfying crop, easy to grow, and may be tucked in among a row of corn or trained on supports if you need to save space in your garden. Big Max, with fruit up to 100 pounds, and Connecticut Field, averaging 25 pounds, are the old-fashioned, corn-field kinds of pumpkin, great for Halloween carving. Jack O'Lantern is smaller, about 10 to 15 pounds. Small Sugar is excellent for pies and keeps well when stored in a cool dry place.

Treating the Soil
Pumpkins, like squash, need rich, light soil with good drainage. Well-rotted manure, mixed thoroughly and deeply under the ground before planting, will further enrich the soil and increase its water-holding capacity. Pumpkins thrive on full sunlight, although they will tolerate a little shade.

Planting
Pumpkins are sensitive to frost, so start them from seeds planted directly in the garden after the ground has warmed in midspring. Sow 5 or 6 seeds 1 inch deep in hills (groups of seeds), and space the hills 6 to 8 feet apart. Thin the seedlings to the 2 hardiest, and keep the soil uniformly watered in dry weather. Pick off any blossoms or new fruit that develop after midsummer so that each vine's energy will be directed toward those pumpkins already growing.

Harvesting
Pumpkins take about 4 months to mature and should be harvested

[46]

before frost. After the leaves die and the pumpkins turn bright orange, cut them from the vines with a sharp knife, leaving 2 or 3 inches of stem on each fruit. Harden the shells by drying the pumpkins in the sun, protected from wet or cold weather. Store them in a cool, not cold, dry place.

Radishes

Radishes are easy to raise and fast to mature. Plant them along with slower growing crops like corn or lettuce, or with the seeds of other root crops like beets, carrots, and parsnips. The radishes will help to mark rows, and when they are pulled will help to keep soil friable around these other vegetables.

Radishes come in all colors and sizes. Try Cherry Belle, or Champion, a king-size version of Cherry Belle, for round red radishes. French Breakfast is a red radish with an oval shape. Sparkler, round and scarlet with a white tip, is a good early radish. White Icicle is a long, tapered white radish, while Black Spanish, round and black, and pink-skinned China Rose, which has a long, blunted shape and a white interior, are both good winter varieties for planting in fall.

Treating the Soil

Since rapid growth is necessary for radishes to develop crisp, juicy roots, prepare the soil well with well-rotted compost or manure worked several inches deep under the surface. If at all possible prepare the soil during the previous fall.

Planting

Sow radish seeds as soon as the ground can be worked in the spring. Plant them ½ inch deep in rows 10 to 12 inches apart, and thin the seedlings to stand 1 inch apart. Make successive plantings 10 days apart until early June. Radishes grown during hot, dry weather tend to be woody or hot tasting, although this condition can be somewhat alleviated by keeping the soil well watered.

Successive plantings of small, quick-maturing radishes may begin again in late summer, when you may also plant the winter radishes. The latter, being larger, will need more space. Plant them ½ inch deep in rows 1½ feet apart, and then thin them to stand 6 inches apart.

Harvesting

Radishes are ready to eat as soon as they reach the size indicated on the seed packet. Just pull, wash, and serve. Winter radishes may be used fresh or stored in moist sand for use over the winter.

Rhubarb

Rhubarb is a hardy perennial which, like asparagus, should be placed to one side of the garden where its handsome 2-foot stalks will provide rich background color year after year. Northern regions with cool, moist summers and winters cold enough to freeze the ground are best suited to this vegetable, which needs a dormant period during the winter. Try Chipman's Canada Red, Crimson Cherry, or Valentine. Six to 10 roots will yield an ample yearly supply of rhubarb for fresh eating or freezing.

Treating the Soil

Rhubarb can be planted in any well-drained, fertile soil with a pH of 5.5 to 7.0. Its fleshy roots run deep, so work lots of well-rotted manure or compost thoroughly into the soil before planting.

Planting

The best way to start rhubarb plants is from roots obtained from a reliable seedsman. Plant the roots in spring in a well-prepared bed.

Dig a trench 8 to 10 inches deep, and line it with a 4- to 6-inch-deep mixture of soil and well-rotted manure. Place each rhubarb root so that its top lies 3 or 4 inches below the surface of the ground, and 3 feet from its nearest neighbor. Fill in the trench by cultivating when the young stalks begin to shoot up.

Rhubarb is a hearty feeder so fertilize the plants heavily each spring and again in the fall. Mulch the plants over the winter with compost, and give plenty of water in spring.

Harvesting

Rhubarb will take until its third spring of growing before the first crop can be harvested. After that time your plants should yield for a 2-month period every spring. Pull, don't cut, the stalks when they are at least 1 inch thick. Remove the seedstalks as soon as they appear.

Warning: The dark green leaves at the end of the rhubarb stalk are poisonous and should never be eaten.

Rutabagas

Rutabagas, also known as Swede turnips, are a cool-weather vegetable very similar to turnips, except that rutabagas are larger and their smooth cabbagelike leaves are not edible. Try American Purple Top or Long Island Improved, whose pale yellow flesh turns orange and delicious after cooking, or Macomber, a white-fleshed variety.

Treating the Soil
Work well-rotted manure deeply into the ground and rake the soil until it is fine and smooth before setting out the seed.

Planting
Plant rutabaga seed in early summer in northern areas, and in late summer or early fall in frost-free regions. Sow the seed ½ inch deep directly in the garden. Thin the seedlings to stand 6 to 8 inches apart. Cultivate frequently to control weeds.

Harvesting
Rutabagas are ready to harvest about 3 months after planting. Their roots are larger than those of turnips and they therefore take about a month to 6 weeks longer to mature. Although rutabagas are able to withstand light frosts, they must be pulled before extreme winter cold sets in. Trim the taproots and crown, then store in a cool, well-ventilated root cellar.

Soybeans

Soybeans are perhaps best known for the food products derived from them, whether soy sauce, soy flour, soybean oil, soy paste, soybean curd, or dried soybeans. They are also of value commercially as a cover crop in the Midwest and as a forage crop in the South.

Since fresh soybeans provide an excellent source of protein and are rich in other food values and relatively low in carbohydrates, there has been increasing interest in growing the plant in home gardens. The tall, bushlike plants, which often reach a height of 6 feet, produce a multitude of white or purple blossoms which mature into hanging clusters of coarse dark-colored pods.

Soybeans grow well in most areas where corn grows but they require a full growing season. They are short-day plants and pod ripening is usually determined by the length of sunlight they get toward harvest time. Be sure to check with the local agricultural station, however, to determine the soybean variety best suited for your particular area.

Treating the Soil
Soybeans will do well in any type of heavier soil. Inoculating the seed with a commercial bacterial preparation before planting will help soybeans to take nitrogen from the air and convert it into plant food. If you inoculate your seed, be sure to use a fertilizer low in nitrogen.

Planting
Plant soybeans when the ground has warmed, in May or early June, in well-drained, fertile soil. Sow the seeds in rows 2½ to 3 feet apart. Cultivate frequently to control weeds and to keep the soil crust friable. Mulching with 3 or 4 inches of straw is also a good idea.

Harvesting
Harvest the pods, which grow to only 2 or 3 inches, by stripping them from the plants in September or October. Blanching is the best way to remove the beans (of which there will be 2 to 4 in each pod) from their tough pod covers. Place the pods in a bowl, pour in boiling water to cover, steep for a few minutes, then drain and plunge immediately into ice water. The beans should then be easy to remove.

Soybeans may be cooked and served with butter and seasonings, or they can be added to soups or stews. To dry soybeans, allow them to ripen fully on the bush, then shell and dry them thoroughly in a warm place.

Spinach

Spinach is a vegetable with a definite preference for cool weather, since it will bolt, or go to seed, if grown during the hot summer months. Rich in vitamins, calcium, and iron, the dark green leaves of spinach can be used raw in green salads, or steamed using only the water clinging to the leaves.

For early spring planting, choose America or Long Standing Bloomsdale, both savoy crinkly-leaved types. Good varieties for fall are Hybrid No. 7 or Virginia Blight Resistant Savoy. During the summer months try New Zealand, not a true spinach but a good substitute.

Treating the Soil

Spinach needs a light, well-drained soil, not too acid, with a pH of 6.0 to 7.0. Prepare the soil beforehand by thoroughly mixing in humus.

Planting

Plant spinach seed early in the spring, as soon as the ground can be worked. Sow the seed ½ inch deep in rows 12 to 15 inches apart. Make successive plantings at weekly intervals until the middle of May, when New Zealand variety may be planted. Spinach which matures during hot weather is likely to go to seed. New Zealand variety germinates slowly and may be planted in late spring, but soak the seed overnight before setting it out in the garden. Thin the seedlings 3 to 6 inches apart in rows 1½ to 2 feet apart.

In northern areas, plant fall crops in late August or early September. Seed may also be planted in the fall for winter and spring harvest in frost-free regions. Cultivate the soil shallowly and mulch the plants to prevent excessive grittiness in the leaves.

Harvesting

Spinach matures in 6 to 8 weeks and the vegetable may be harvested as soon as 5 or 6 leaves have fully grown. Harvest by cutting the leaves just above the top of the root.

New Zealand spinach develops rich green leaves on the tips of its branches. These may be used in the same recipes as true spinach.

Squash

Squash, one of the least demanding vegetables to grow in the home garden, comes in all shapes, sizes, and colors. Superb summer varieties include Goldneck and Golden Crookneck, both yellow; St. Pat

Scallop or Patty Pan, green tinted scallop types; and Hybrid Aristocrat Zucchini, smooth and deep green.

Choose from such winter squash varieties as Waltham Butternut; Buttercup, a green Hubbard type; Ebony Acorn, green black with pale orange flesh; or Gold Nugget, an orange bush type.

Treating the Soil

All varieties of squash need light, rich, fertile soil and full sun. Because the plants have extensive root systems, thorough soil preparation beforehand, with applications of well-rotted manure or compost worked deep below the surface, is important.

Planting

Plant squash directly in the garden when the ground has warmed up well in the spring. Sow the seeds 1 inch deep in hills (clusters or groups of seeds), about 6 to 8 evenly spaced seeds to each hill. These hills, or groups of seeds, should be spaced 3 to 4 feet apart for bush varieties, and 10 feet apart for the running varieties. When the seedlings appear, fight that parental need to protect and pull out all but the 3 hardiest.

Cultivate the soil shallowly to prevent injury to the roots or use a mulch to keep weeds down and moisture in.

Harvesting

Summer squash is at its best if gathered when the fruits are young and tender, about 6 to 8 inches long, or in the case of the scalloped types, when the fruit is 2 to 3 inches across. Be sure to pick the squash before they mature or the vines will stop producing.

Winter squash, on the other hand, should be left on the vines to mature fully. Their rinds should be hard and tough and their leaves should be brown before they are cut from the vine with 2 to 3 inches of their stems still attached. Allow winter squash to dry in the sun for a week, taking care to protect them from rain or cold weather. Store as directed in Root Cellar Storage (page 486).

Sunflowers

Sunflowers are fun to grow. Plant them in any kind of soil in early spring, give them lots of moisture during dry spells, and they will reward you with mammoth blooms by late summer, plus tasty, nutritious snacks.

Many sunflowers are native to America and are perennials. Mammoth Russian, which bears enormous flowers on stalks that often reach 15 feet, is a good annual variety.

Cut sunflower heads when the seeds fully ripen and start to turn brown. Plastic bags placed over the flower heads will keep birds away until that time, so that most of the harvest will be yours. Dry out the seeds in a 225-degree oven, then raise the heat to 350 degrees and roast for 10 minutes. A country neighbor of mine maintains that the best way to shell sunflower seeds is to turn them through the coarse blade of a meat grinder. This cracks a good portion of the hulls and the meats can be picked out.

Sweet Potato

Sweet potatoes need a growing season of about 5 months and are therefore best adapted to warm climates with long, hot summers. They can, however, be successfully grown in some of the slightly more northern states if the plants are set out in early June and not subjected to any frost.

Sweet potatoes, not to be confused with yams, are grown from sprouts purchased from a reliable seedsman or grown in your own kitchen. During the winter set a sweet potato on toothpicks in a glass of water. Let it sprout, twist off the shoots, root them in water, and let them develop into vines. Plant the vines outdoors in the garden in early June.

Suggested varieties for planting are Orange Jersey, Nema-gold, Puerto Rico, Centennial, or Goldrush.

Treating the Soil
Soil for sweet potatoes should be light and sandy. Tubers tend to be long and stringy if clay soils are used for planting. Spade deeply, fertilize, then prepare ridges of soil 8 inches high and 12 inches across at the base.

Planting
Plant the sweet potato sprouts 15 to 18 inches apart in the previously prepared ridges. Push the sprouts deeply enough into the ridge so that only one or two leaves are left above ground. Shallow cultivation is required until the vines cover the ground thickly, but do not fertilize again or the result will be an overabundance of foliage and few tubers.

Harvesting

Sweet potatoes should be given as long a time in the soil as possible before frost sets in. In frost-free regions, dig them in late fall; in cooler areas, dig them just before frost is forecast.

Dig the tubers on a clear day when the soil is dry. Set them in the sun to dry for 2 or 3 hours, then arrange them in single layers and cure and store them as directed for Root Cellar Storage (page 486).

Tomatoes

Tomatoes are easily the most popular vegetable grown in the home garden. Even those people who don't go in for serious vegetable raising often take time and space to plant this favorite. Home-grown, vine-ripened tomatoes are high in food value, rich in vitamins and minerals, and more juicy and delicious than the ones available in your grocery store.

Tomatoes come in many different varieties, ranging in size from the small cherry type to the whopper hamburger size. There are also pear-shaped tomatoes, golden orange varieties, and tomatoes bred especially for growing in pots. Experiment with a few different varieties; try planting early, midseason, and late types for a steady harvest; but always make sure, whether you buy seeds or seedlings, that you choose disease-resistant varieties.

Some recommended varieties are Springset, Fireball, New Yorker, Better Boy, Beefeater, Campbell 1327, Big Boy, or Heinz 1350. Small Fry is an improved cherry tomato which bears enormous clusters of 1-inch red fruit. A good golden orange type is Sunray. Among the pear-shaped tomatoes, choose bright-red Roma, or Yellow Pear.

Treating the Soil

Tomatoes will grow in almost any type of soil provided the soil is warm, holds moisture well, and plenty of well-rotted fertilizer has been worked in well beforehand. The plants like a slightly acid soil with a pH of 5.5 to 6.5.

Planting

Many gardeners prefer to buy the plant seedlings, but tomatoes may also be started from seed indoors, 6 to 8 weeks before setting outside. Sow the seeds thinly in fine, rich soil, about ¼ inch deep and spaced about 2 inches apart. Transplant to individual peat pots when the seedlings are 1 inch tall.

As tomatoes are very susceptible to frost injury, wait until all danger from frost disappears before setting any seedlings out. Set the peat pots a little deeper than the soil surface and space 2 to 3 feet apart. If you stake your plants or grow them on trellises, as is sometimes done with the larger varieties, they may be set a bit closer. Pinch off the lateral or side shoots of staked plants, so that the plant may direct its energy to one or two main stems. Tie the growing stem securely to the stake or trellis with plastic-covered wire twists, twine, strips of cloth, or any ties that will not cut into the stems.

Cultivate the soil shallowly, or apply a mulch of grass clippings or straw to conserve moisture and prevent blossom-end rot, which is caused by variations in the water supply. It's also a good idea to place paper collars around the stems to reduce cutworm invasion. If fertilizers are used, wait until the fruits grow to 1 inch size and continue at 3- to 4-week intervals.

Harvesting

For maximum juiciness and top quality, leave your tomatoes on the vine until they ripen to full color but are still firm. Any good-size green tomatoes remaining in the fall should be picked before frost sets in and stored in a dark, cool place. Ripen green fruit on a sunny window sill.

Turnips

Turnips are hardy, cool-weather vegetables that are excellent boiled and buttered, or simmered in soups or stews. Try Purple Top White Globe or Tokyo Market Express.

Treating the Soil

Turnips will grow in all types of soil, but well-rotted organic fertilizer should first be worked deep beneath the surface. Rake the soil until it is fine before sowing.

Planting

Plant turnips in early spring, as soon as the ground can be worked, for a summer crop, or in July or August for fall harvest. Sow the seeds ½ inch deep in rows 12 to 15 inches apart, and thin the seedlings to stand 3 to 4 inches apart.

Harvesting

Pull the turnips when the roots are about 2 to 3 inches across. More mature vegetables tend to get woody. Use the tender green tops and thinnest seedlings in salads or cooked as greens. Store as directed in Root Cellar Storage (page 486).

Growing
your own
fruits
and berries

FRUIT TREES provide beauty and shade as well as fruit. They should be carefully worked into your general landscaping scheme. The smaller fruits make attractive trellis or hedge plantings, or serve as ornamental shrubs.

Size of trees is often a factor in growing fruits because many varieties are not self-fertilizing and must be planted with 2 or even 3 additional trees. Small yards or gardens may not be able to accommodate this quantity. If you are planning to plant peach, plum, or cherry trees, remember that their standard-size is smaller than that of apple trees, so buying dwarf trees may not be necessary.

Both standard-size and dwarf fruit trees have advantages and disadvantages. Standard-size trees will produce more fruit and provide a dazzling display of color in spring and welcome shade in summer, but they also take longer to grow to bearing size, require more space, and ultimately demand skilled pruning and spraying services. Dwarf trees bear at an earlier age than standard trees, take much less room, are easier to prune, spray, and harvest, and may even be netted against birds if necessary. However, they are more expensive and their total production of fruit is smaller.

Berries and smaller fruits vary in their climate and soil demands, but all should have full sun and well-drained soil. Spring planting is best for these bushes, vines, and plants except in the South, where fall planting is recommended. Methods of pruning at planting time and yearly pruning thereafter are discussed in the individual sections.

Get expert advice before buying your trees, vines, bushes, or plants. And always buy from a reputable nursery or seed house.

Where to Plant

Fruit trees should be planted where they will receive full sun. The planting site should be on fairly high ground, facing north, if possible, where injury to blossoms by late frost is not as likely. A fertile, sandy loam is best and good drainage is essential.

When to Plant

Plant 1- or 2-year-old trees in the early spring or in fall, when the tree is dormant (not in leaf). Dig the hole big enough to accommodate all the roots in a natural position, and trim off any scraggly, broken, or injured roots. Separate the subsoil from the topsoil; mix the latter with compost. Scatter some of the mixed topsoil over the bottom of the hole before setting in the tree, then fill in the hole with the rest of the topsoil, carefully moving the tree up and down a bit to eliminate any air spaces. Finish by firming the soil down compactly with your feet.

Plant standard-size fruit trees at the depth they grew in the nursery. Dwarf trees must be installed in their sites with the graft union (spot where stem sections from dwarfing stock are joined to standard-size rootstock) about 2 inches above ground level. Otherwise, the tree will grow larger than dwarf-size.

Water the tree when planted, and continue to keep it deeply

watered, especially during the dry season. Mulches of hay or straw help to conserve moisture, but also attract mice and rabbits. To prevent rodent injury, encircle the slender trunk with a wire-mesh cylinder sunk 4 inches below ground level and extending several inches up around the trunk.

Fertilizing

Fruit trees will not usually need fertilizing during their first year. Don't, in any case, fertilize when planting. The sensitive roots might be burned. Fertilize if necessary once the roots are established, and thereafter apply fertilizer yearly in early spring, using a balanced fertilizer rich in nitrogen (Fertilizers, page 8).

Pruning

General directions for pruning are given in the individual fruit sections. Pruning at planting time is necessary because much of the root system is lost when the tree is dug at the nursery. In order to recover and begin new growth the tree must be cut back to leave only 3 to 5 well-placed branches. Pruning in subsequent years should be directed toward shaping the tree and maintaining vigorous growth.

It will usually be necessary to thin the fruit once bearing is well established. Excessive fruit bearing one year prevents flower-bud formation the next. Some thinning is taken care of naturally when the tree itself drops some of its immature fruit about 2 to 3 weeks after blooming (this is called June drop in some areas, for obvious reasons). But selective thinning when the fruits are one-third grown results in larger size and better color in the fruits left on the tree.

Spraying

It is generally agreed that in order to grow high-quality, unblemished fruit your trees must be sprayed to protect them against insects and disease. If you are willing to settle for smaller, less-perfect fruit (such as you often see in natural food stores), by all means do not spray.

Pest problems vary from fruit to fruit as well as from one part of the country to the other. Professional growers follow rigorous spraying schedules. Your best bet is to get expert advice on when to spray and what sprays to use. Always buy disease-resistant stock, and cut off and dispose of all diseased or dead branches and canes.

Planting

Apples

DELICIOUS, VERSATILE, and just plain good for you, apples are nearly everybody's favorite fruit. Home gardeners will find that there are now many varieties of dwarf or semidwarf apple trees, several of which will fit nicely into the same area that one standard-size fruit tree usually takes. These smaller trees may be set out in the lawn, or espaliered against a fence or wall. Dwarf trees will bear 2 to 3 years after planting, semidwarf varieties take 3 to 4 years to bear fruit. With the dwarf trees, thinning, spraying, and harvesting of apples are that much easier.

Apple trees come in many varieties. For summer production, try Red June, Lodi, or Gravenstein. Wealthy, McIntosh, Anoka, Red Duchess, and Cortland are all good varieties which ripen during August and September. Jonathan, Northern Spy, Haralson, Rome Beauty, Golden Delicious, Red Delicious, and Northwestern Greening are among the fall-ripening varieties.

Climate is one of the main factors in deciding whether to plant apple trees. Winter temperatures must average below 48 degrees if the tree is to get the dormant period it requires. Location is another important factor; certain apple trees are best suited for certain areas. Your best guide to selecting the trees adapted to your needs and locality is an experienced nurseryman. Nursery catalogs will also provide selection information. Whatever you choose to grow, whether standard-size, dwarf, or semidwarf be sure to buy only vigorous 1- or 2-year-old trees from 3 to 5 feet tall.

Treating the Soil
Apple trees grow best in a soil with a pH of 5.5 to 6.5. Sandy or loam soils are good, but soils which are either too dry or without proper drainage are unsuitable. Full sun is important.

Take care that the hole you dig is as deep as the one the plant grew in at the nursery. The main idea is not to crowd the roots. In digging, keep the topsoil separate from the subsoil.

Planting
Apple trees should be planted when they are dormant, so spring planting is preferred. Standard-size trees should be placed 40 feet apart, semidwarf need only 20 feet between trees, and dwarf require even less space: 10 to 12 feet apart is adequate.

After digging the hole and separating the topsoil from the subsoil, sprinkle some of the topsoil on the bottom of the hole. Arrange the roots carefully on the bottom of the hole, sprinkle with more topsoil, then combine some well-rotted manure or compost with the remaining topsoil and fill the hole in. Pack the soil firmly around the base of the tree, leaving a slight depression to catch water run-off. Keep the soil around the tree moist during the first spring and summer, and hill the soil slightly in the fall to reduce the injurious effects of winter.

Pruning develops a good network of branches. Cut back 1-year-old trees, which are usually unbranched and straight, to a height of about 4 feet to stimulate side-branch development. Two-year-old trees have many side branches. Cut off all but 3 or 4 strong, wide-angled branches, and prune these to 6-inch stubs. When espaliering a tree, pruning should be rather severe the first few years, less severe after the tree begins to bear fruit.

Some varieties of apple tree are self-pollinating, but it is wiser to plant several different varieties in order to ensure cross-pollination. Varieties best suited for cross-pollination are Golden Delicious, Jonathan, Cortland, and Rome Beauty.

If your trees don't bear, look to overproduction the previous year. Fruit should be thinned after normal June drop, which is the natural drop of some of the young fruit in early summer. Overfertilization is another cause of poor yield, since an excessive amount of fertilizer is not conducive to blossoming and fruit set. Sometimes the cause is a late frost which kills the flower buds.

Harvesting

Always pick apples with the stems attached. Harvesting them by tearing off the stems will cause the fruit to rot much sooner. Apples are ripe enough to pick when the stem releases easily from the fruit spur or twig. Raise the apple up by the stem and give it a slight twist. Yanking apples from the tree may result in breaking off the spur, and thus your next year's crop may be reduced.

Apples continue to ripen off the tree, and storing at high temperatures accelerates this ripening. Always store your crop in a cool (30 to 32 degrees) storage spot. Take care that none are over-ripe when storing: one overripe apple hastens the ripening of all the others.

Apricots

Apricots will grow almost everywhere peaches will grow, but since their attractive pink flowers are in bloom about a week earlier than peach blossoms, the young fruit may be exposed in colder areas to late spring frosts. Most apricots are grown in California, although hardier varieties are being adapted to many other areas.

Favorite varieties on the West Coast are Royal, Blenheim, and Moorpark, the latter being particularly good fresh. Moorpark and Early Golden are good varieties for other areas. Most apricot varieties are self-pollinating and may be planted singly.

Treating the Soil

Choose a site for your apricot tree that is protected from lingering frost—a northern or western location, preferably sloping, or one that is protected by other trees. Any soil is good if supplemented with organic matter and there is adequate drainage.

Planting

Both dwarf and standard-size trees are available. Dwarf trees will need spacing of about 10 to 15 feet; standard trees should be planted 20 to 30 feet apart. Buy 1- or 2-year-old trees, and cut off all but 3 or 4 well-placed limbs. The remaining branches should form

angles greater than 45 degrees to the trunk, and should be cut back
the first year to 2 or 3 inches in height. Pruning thereafter should
be limited to removing branches that crowd the more desirable ones.
Thin the fruit each year to stimulate blossom formation the next.
Fertilize after growth begins, and once again about 6 weeks later.
As long as the leaf color remains a healthy green, only small
amounts of fertilizer will be necessary.

Harvesting

Apricots should be allowed to ripen on the tree to a uniform, golden
color. Pick them only when they are well colored and soft but still
firm.

Blackberries

The name "blackberry" actually refers to all black-fruited, vine-
type berries, including boysenberry, loganberry, and youngberry, as
well as blackberry. All of these are biennials; that is, the canes
grow one season and bear fruit the next, then die and are removed
to make way for new growth.

Blackberry bushes will generally grow in warm or temperate
climates, while blackberry vines are less hardy and need frost-free
climates. Darrow, Bailey, and Eldorado are good bush varieties.
Lawton and Evergreen are bush varieties suitable for the West
Coast. Boysen, Logan, Lucretia, and Marion are all excellent vine
types. Consult a knowledgeable nurseryman for the variety best
suited to your area.

Treating the Soil

Blackberries will grow in any fertile, well-drained soil with a pH
of 5.5 to 7.5. The soil may be further enriched by working compost
deep under the ground where the fruit is to grow. If possible, choose
a southern location where the berries will have continuous summer
sun.

Planting

Blackberries may be planted in fall, winter, or spring in frostfree
parts of the country. In other areas plant as soon as the ground can
be worked in the spring. Spacing of plants depends on whether they
are bushes or vine types. Set bush types 5 feet apart in rows 6

feet apart, berry-bearing vines about 6 to 8 feet apart in rows 8 to 9 feet apart.

After planting, cut the canes back to about 8 to 10 inches high. New canes will quickly start to grow: these should be pinched back on the bush-type plants when the canes are about 2½ to 3 feet tall to keep the plants sturdy and compact. Vine-type canes may ramble to about 8 feet long during their first year. They should then be pinched back to stimulate lateral development of canes. Canes of vine types can be trained on wire trellises by wrapping or tying.

Prune established blackberry canes in early spring to eliminate those that have borne fruit the previous year, plus any broken or weak ones. Those canes remaining on bush types should be thinned 8 to 10 inches apart, and the lateral branches should be reduced to 8 to 12 buds each. Mulch with wood chips or old hay, but be sure to eliminate suckers coming up between the plants or the result will be a tangle of thorny canes.

Harvesting

Wait until the berries are fully ripe before picking; the riper the berry, the sweeter the fruit. Berries ripen over a 2-month period in midsummer and during this time plastic netting will keep birds from eating the berries before you get a chance to.

Blueberries

Buy only named varieties at least 1 to 2 feet tall: transplanting wild bushes is usually unsuccessful. Cross-pollination is necessary to ensure fruit-bearing plants, so purchase at least 2 varieties of cultivated bushes.

The most popular varieties are Bluecrop, Blueray, Earliblue, Berkeley, Jersey, and Herbert, all high-bush types.

Blueberries grow well from Maine to Florida, and west Minnesota and Louisiana. The northern section of the Pacific coast also yields hearty crops.

Treating the Soil

Blueberry bushes require rich, well-drained, acid soil with a pH of 4.50. They often fail in the alkaline soil found in ordinary gardens. Here is where proper composting can work wonders. A mixture of acid peat and sand, or rotted oak or beech leaves and sand should be mixed thoroughly into the soil. Even in acid soils the bushes will profit from mulching with acid peat moss, oak leaves, or sawdust. Full sun and good drainage are required.

Planting

Set the bushes 6 to 8 feet apart in rows 8 feet apart. Cut back the bushes about half-way after planting. Young plants begin to bear by the third year, are established by the fifth, and reach maturity by the tenth. Prune every year during the dormant season, in winter or early spring, removing any old canes or weak growth to give strong young side shoots a chance. Prune back the tips of fruit-bearing canes to ensure good nourishment for the 4 or 5 flower buds that remain. Blossoms should be removed from canes during the first 2 years after planting. Fertilize judiciously and only if the leaves yellow. Use only fertilizers with an acid reaction—no manure or alkaline fertilizers. The bushes may need to be netted when bearing—birds love blueberries too.

Harvesting

The sweetest berries are those that are allowed to ripen at least 1 week after turning blue. July and August are the usual months for harvesting, but berries may ripen as early as May in southern regions.

Cherries

Few fruits can beat the sweet cherry for fresh, juicy, delicious eating, or the tangy flavor of a cherry pie filled with tart sour cherries. Sweet cherry trees are as hardy as peach trees, and sour cherries are even hardier. Both will grow in the same type of climate, usually where the weather is neither too hot nor too dry. There is one problem, however: birds are as fond of cherries as people are, so be prepared to share your crop with feathered friends.

Cherry varieties fall into 3 general classes, sweet, sour, and Duke. Sweet cherries range in color from black to golden pink, and are best for eating right from the tree. Lambert, Windsor, Black Tartarian, Bing, or Napoleon, which is sometimes called Royal Ann, are all scrumptious.

Sweet cherry trees grow quite large and require cross-pollination. If your grounds are not too spacious, hope that your neighbor will plant a compatible variety.

The most widely grown sour cherry is Montmorency. Duke cherries are a cross between the sweet and sour. Both sour and Duke cherries are used mainly for cooking and canning, and are rarely available in grocery stores or at fruit stands. Grow your own, and you'll have an ample supply.

Sour cherries are mostly self-pollinating, however these are small and 2 can usually be fitted in the average home garden. Duke cherries need cross-pollination; either sweet or sour cherry trees will serve the purpose. Seek advice from a local nurseryman or agricultural agent about the best variety to grow in your area, and also the variety best suited for cross-pollinization if needed.

Treating the Soil

Cherries will grow in most soils except heavy clay, but proper drainage is essential, especially for sweet cherry trees.

Planting

Since cherries bloom early in spring, it is best to plant them as soon as the ground can be worked, or even in the fall. Space sweet cherry trees about 35 to 40 feet apart. Plant sour cherry trees closer, about 20 to 25 feet apart, and Dukes about 30 feet apart. Sour cherry trees, because of their deep roots, make ideal lawn trees.

Proper pruning at planting time is most important for cherry trees. If pruned and trained correctly during their early years they will need only light thinning when they begin to bear. When you plant, cut out all but 3 or 4 of the best-placed and widest branches, then prune these remaining branches back lightly. Remember that narrow-angled branches may split under a heavy load of fruit or the weight of ice or snow.

Harvesting

To prevent spoilage, always pick cherries with the stems attached, but take care that you don't break off the fruit spurs as well, since next year's harvest will develop from these. If you feel ambitious, net your trees to frustrate marauding birds before the cherries ripen; otherwise try to share cheerfully.

Citrus Fruits

The term "citrus" covers a wide variety of rounded fruits of varied sizes. The most familiar are oranges, including sweet, navel, and blood oranges; mandarin and Satsuma oranges and tangerines; tangelos, an orange colored cross between the mandarin orange and grapefruit; tangors, midway between sweet oranges and tangerines and best known as Temple oranges; grapefruits; lemons; and limes. All are available in both dwarf and standard sizes.

Citrus trees are grown almost exclusively in the frost-free regions of the South and Southwest. They will not usually tolerate temperatures more than a few degrees below freezing. Occasionally they are successfully raised in colder areas by planting in tubs which can be placed indoors by a sunny window during the winter months and transferred to your garden, tub and all, for the summer.

Different varieties of citrus fruits are particularly suited to different areas. Some, for instance, grow better in the more humid Southeast than in the drier Southwest. Consult a catalogue from a reliable concern, or get advice from a local nurseryman to learn the varieties best suited to your climate and soil.

Treating the Soil

Citrus trees prefer a soil that is light, loose, and well drained. A good supply of water is essential at all times of the year, especially just before and during the ripening period. Frequency of watering will depend on the type of soil and the climate. A good rule is to water deeply but carefully: a constantly soggy soil will rot the tree's roots. Planting your tree on a mound of soil with a catch-basin around the trunk and below the ground level often helps.

Planting

Citrus trees may be planted in spring as soon as the ground can be worked, although winter planting is preferred in the Southwest. In general, 2-year-old trees should be pruned by cutting away all but 3 to 5 of the best-placed branches at planting time. Aside from selective pruning of crowded branches and dead wood as the trees mature, little pruning will be necessary in later years. However, vigorous trees often send forth water sprouts or shoots from their trunks and these should be removed as they appear.

Harvesting

All citrus fruits are mature when they reach true color; ripening should be done on the tree. Most fruit can be left on the tree, even when ripe, to be clipped as needed, although they gradually lose flavor if left too long. To harvest, clip with a knife or shears where the stem meets the fruit.

Currants

Currants are easy to grow, hardy, and do best in colder areas. The fruit is not usually eaten fresh, but is used frequently in jellies and jams. Currant bushes, however, are host to white-pine blister rust disease, and many states and counties prohibit their cultivation. Check with local authorities before you plant. Red Lake and Wilder are good red varieties. For a white currant, try White Imperial.

Treating the Soil

Currants will grow in any well-drained garden soil. They prefer some shade and moist growing conditions, and will not usually tolerate hot, dry climates.

Planting

Set 1- or 2-year-old plants out in early spring, spacing them 5 feet apart. Pruning is necessary once the plants are 4 years old, since after 3 years a cane ceases production of fruit. Prune in the fall or winter and keep the bushes under control by cutting all 3-year-old canes off at ground level. Limit new growth to 3 canes each year. Mulching with grass clippings each spring is the only cultivation currants require.

Harvesting

Pick the fruit when it is ripe but still firm and make into jams and jellies.

Figs

Figs are usually thought of as warm-weather fruit which grow only in the South or in California, but with proper sheltering and protection from cold, figs can be grown as far north as New York. They can even be grown in colder areas if placed in large tubs which can be moved indoors in winter. Brown Turkey and Brunswick (also called Magnolia) will grow in the eastern part of the country as well as in the Gulf Coast states and Southern California. Another variety recommended for planting in the South is Celeste, sometimes called Blue Celeste. Try Kadota or Mission in Southern California.

Treating the Soil
Fig trees like full sun and moist, well-drained, clay-type soil enriched with organic matter.

Planting
Fig trees are self-pollinating, so 1 tree is sufficient for the home garden. To ensure fruit the year after planting, buy a 3- to 4-foot tree. In farm areas plant in winter; in colder regions plant in early spring, as soon as the ground can be worked. Prune the tree to 3 or 4 well-placed branches, and cut these back to 6 or 8 inches. As the tree grows it will seldom need pruning.

Unless your tree is planted in a tub and moved indoors, it's a good idea in colder areas to winter-over the tree by burying its branches under a mound of soil. Bend the tree to the ground or into a prepared trench, then cover with leaves or straw and heaped dirt.

Harvesting
Fruit should be picked when it hangs straight down from the branches. If the figs are to be dried allow them to ripen enough to fall, then spread them in the sun to continue the drying process.

Gooseberries

Gooseberries belong to the same family as currants and are subject to the same growing restrictions. Some states and counties forbid planting these bushes because the gooseberry as well as the currant serves as a host to white-pine blister rust disease. Although their spiny skins make them hard to pick, gooseberries are delicious in pies, jellies, and jams. Pixwell and Poorman are good varieties.

Treating the Soil
Soil requirements are similar to those of currants. Cool, moist soil, enriched with organic matter, is best. Hot, dry soils cause bushes to lose their leaves and fruits, so water freely in hot weather.

Planting

Set plants out in spring, spacing them 5 feet apart. Prune the canes after they have borne fruit for 3 years, cutting them off at ground level during fall or winter. Limit new growth to 3 canes each year; in this way the bush will have 3 canes each of 1-, 2-, and 3-year growth. One-year-old canes may be pruned to encourage branching, but don't let the branching get out of hand. Mulch the bushes each year with a thick layer of fresh grass clippings, which is about all the cultivation they will need.

Harvesting

Ripe fruit is usually stripped from the canes, but take care to protect your hands from thorns.

Grapes

Although grapevines are not a standard feature of home gardens, to my mind nothing symbolizes peaceful country living like a Sunday lunch under a grape arbor.

There are 3 general classes of grapes. American or fox grape varieties will grow in most of the country: try Concord, Catawba, Niagara, or Delaware. Brighton is the only vine among American varieties that needs a different variety planted close by for cross-pollination.

European grapes are those most often used for commercial processing, and are successfully grown for the most part only in the warm valleys of the Southwest. Excellent varieties are Cardinal, Emperor, Thompson Seedless, Ribier, and Muscat of Alexandria.

Muscadine grapes are grown exclusively in the South, where other types of grapes will not produce. Scuppernong, Thomas, Tarheel, and James are good selections. Unlike the American and European grapes, many muscadines are not self-pollinating and it's necessary to plant a self-pollinating variety nearby.

In addition to those mentioned above, many other good American, European, and muscadine varieties are available for home planting. Consult government publications or a local agricultural agent for those best suited to your area.

Treating the Soil

Although grapes are fairly easy to grow, they do need lots of room, require yearly pruning, and should have some sort of trellis or support for the vines. They are versatile and will grow in many different types of soil, but a deep, fertile loam is best. Good drainage is one of the primary requirements; if your soil is heavy clay, add organic matter to improve its quality.

Planting

In colder climates, plant most 1-year-old vines in the spring as soon as the ground can be worked, but in warmer areas plant in the fall, when the vines are dormant.

American and European varieties should be planted 8 feet apart, muscadine grapes about 15 to 20 feet apart. Plant all vines to the depth they grew in the nursery. Right after planting, prune each vine back to 1 stem with 2 or 3 buds. Cultivate your vines shallowly and only enough to keep weeds under control.

Train and prune yearly while vines are dormant to maintain growth and ensure good-quality grapes. Vines may be trained on trellises and arbors or supported by wires secured to posts. The tall, old-fashioned style grape arbors are excellent for muscadine grapes.

The Kniffin system of training vines is the method used most often for American grapes. Two wires, one set 2½ feet above the ground and the other 2 to 2½ feet higher, are attached to sturdy posts set about 10 feet apart. The vines, planted between the posts, are pruned to a single trunk with 4 canes, each tied to a wire.

European grape varieties may be trained to the Kniffin system, or they may be trained to a single wire strung on sturdy posts.

There are also many other specialized methods particularly suited to certain locations. Consult experts for the proper method of training your variety of vine and the fertilizer and spraying your grapes will require.

Harvesting

Grapes grown in the home garden for table use have the best quality and flavor when left on the vine to ripen fully. Grapes which will be made into jellies or jams, however, should be picked just a bit underripe. Protect your ripening crop against birds by throwing netting over the vines.

Peaches and Nectarines

Peaches and nectarines are usually classed together, the nectarine being a natural mutation of the peach. Varieties of both will grow in most parts of the country, and both have the same soil and cultivation requirements. While they are not cold-hardy trees and are damaged by sudden and severe temperature changes, they do require a period of dormancy. For home gardeners the most satisfactory tree, if properly managed by careful pruning and thinning, is the standard size.

Peach and nectarine varieties are divided into freestones, semi-clingstones, or clingstones. All have a wide range in their hardiness to cold. Some varieties will grow only in warmer climates; others will withstand cold very well. Your local nurseryman can advise you about the best variety to plant in your area. Be sure that you plant 2 trees for cross-pollination.

Treating the Soil

A well-drained location with full sun and a soil pH of 6.0 to 7.0 is necessary for peaches and nectarines. Select a site on higher ground, or plant on sloping ground, because the trees will not tolerate a saturated soil.

Planting

Select 2-year-old trees at least 3 to 5 feet tall. Make sure that the hole you prepare to receive each tree is large enough to keep the roots from being crowded. Mix well-rotted manure or compost with some of the topsoil, and arrange the mixture in the bottom of the hole. Cover the roots with more topsoil after setting in the tree. Pack the soil firmly after planting. Keep watered during hot, dry weather. Fertilize after growth begins, and once again about 6 weeks later. If the leaf color remains good, fertilize thereafter once a year, in early spring.

Prune your trees at planting time by cutting them back to a height of 2½ to 3 feet, then remove all but the 3 strongest branches. These should be branches which form a wide angle with the trunk.

Most peach and nectarine trees will bear the third year after planting, and fruit is borne from side buds on 1-year-old shoots. Regular pruning and heavy thinning of fruit will be necessary every year from then on, since these trees usually produce more fruit than their branches can normally support.

Harvesting

Peaches may be allowed to ripen fully on the tree and picked when they come loose easily, or they may be harvested when ripe but still firm and allowed to ripen at room temperature. Green peaches ripened off the tree are inferior in taste to the tree-ripened ones. Nectarines tend to soften rapidly and are best picked when ripe but still firm. Take care that you handle the fruit gently, as both peaches and nectarines bruise easily.

Pears

Pear trees are a favorite with the home gardener and are one of the easiest fruit trees to grow. They can be planted anywhere apple trees are grown, and they are almost as hardy. Both standard-size and dwarf varieties are available. Good varieties are Bartlett, Max-Red Bartlett (with red skin), Bosc, Seckel, Anjou, Clapp's Favorite, and Magness.

Be sure to buy blight-resistant stock, since fire blight may cause both crop and tree damage. Pear trees need to be cross-pollinated, so planting at least 2 varieties will be necessary. Consult a local nurseryman or county agricultural agent for advice both on the variety best suited to your area and what varieties are best planted together.

Treating the Soil

Pear trees prefer a sunny location, with fertile soil that is moist but well drained. Most soils can be made suitable by improving them with peat moss, manure, or compost.

Planting

Pear trees should be planted in lawn areas because, in competing with grass for food and moisture, their growth is not as vigorous as it may be elsewhere. Too vigorous growth is undesirable since trees that grow too rapidly are more susceptible to fire blight. Another method of checking the incidence of fire blight is to under-fertilize, or, if your trees show good twig growth and healthy dark green foliage, don't fertilize at all.

Plant 1- to 2-year-old trees, removing any broken or injured roots before setting the trees in the ground. Prune standard trees back to about 3 feet, and cut branches on both standard and dwarf varieties to half their original size. Remove any limbs that do not angle out more than 45 degrees from the main trunk and keep only 4 to 8 of the strongest branches.

Pear trees need to be thinned every year because they tend to overproduce. Some of this thinning is taken care of by the usual June drop, but sometimes it must be done by hand. Thinning prevents limb breakage and ensures high quality in the fruit that remains.

Harvesting

Standard pear trees will usually bear fruit within 4 to 5 years of planting, while dwarf varieties will set fruit during the second or third year.

All pears should be harvested when slightly underripe, with color just beginning to turn from green to yellow or red. Check for a slight swelling where the stem attaches to the tree spur. If the pear is ready for harvesting, the stem will detach easily without breaking the spur. Ripen your fruit at room temperature, or better still, keep in storage at 32 degrees for a week before eating or cooking. This keeps the fruit from browning too soon at the core.

Plums

The plum is a fine fruit tree which may be grown in standard and dwarf sizes all over the country, although not all varieties can be grown in all areas. Three general groups of plum trees are: European, which include the prune plums; Japanese and Japanese-American hybrids; and native American plum.

Prune plums are plums with a high sugar content, sweet enough to dry on the pit. European plums are hardy and may be grown wherever apples are grown. Some popular varieties are Stanley prune, Yellow Egg, Burbank Grand Prize prune, Blufre prune, and Reine Claude, sometimes called greengage. Two damson plums, also European and excellent for preserves, are French and Shropshire.

Some Japanese and Japanese-American hybrid plums are Kaga, South Dakota 27, Burbank, Santa Rosa, Underwood, Superior, and Shiro.

American plums are very hardy and grow where other fruits will not, although in general they are not as tasty as other types. The best selections are De Soto, Hawkeye, and Cheney.

Since some plum varieties are self-pollinating and others not, care must be taken to plant with the correct second or even third variety for cross-pollination. Consult a local nurseryman or county agricultural station to learn which varieties are best for your area, and which should be planted together.

Treating the Soil
Like all fruit trees, plums require a well-drained, fertile soil which should be further enriched with organic matter.

Planting
Plant 1- or 2-year-old trees, spacing them about 20 feet apart. Spring is the best time for planting in northern areas, while fall or winter planting is recommended for frostfree regions.

Cut off all but 3 or 4 of the strongest branches after planting to provide for good light and air circulation as the tree matures. The remaining branches should form a wide angle from the main trunk. After the initial pruning, the only thinning necessary will be to prevent overcrowding or to eliminate deadwood. This should be done while the trees are dormant. If any signs of black-knot disease appear (look for ugly black growths), immediately cut out, burn, and dispose of the diseased limbs.

Both European and Japanese varieties will respond with bigger and better plums if the fruit is thinned after the normal June drop. Damsons, however, need not be thinned.

Harvesting
Harvest plums for cooking purposes while the flesh is a bit springy to the touch but still firm. Plums eaten fresh or used for drying purposes can be twisted off easily when they are soft and fully ripened.

Raspberries

What could be more luxurious than growing raspberries on your own bushes? Since these delicious berries are fragile beyond belief, supermarkets and fruit stands seldom stock them and when they do the price is high. The only way to be assured of an adequate summer's supply without putting a permanent dent in your bankbook is to grow your own. Choose from red raspberry varieties, which include some types that are amber in color; black raspberries; and purple rasperries, which are hybrids of the red and black varieties.

Raspberries grow best in a mild to cool climate. Different varieties have different growing habits. Consult a local nurseryman to learn which variety is best adapted to your area and purposes. Take care in addition to buy only 1-year-old plants that are certified disease- and virus-free.

Treating the Soil

A deep, rich, sandy loam is best suited for raspberries, but heavier or light soils will do, provided they are first supplemented with organic matter to ensure good drainage. Raspberries are deep-rooted, and the soil must have proper drainage to a depth of 3 to 4 feet.

Choose a fairly protected site where other crops or a cover crop has been grown in previous years. However, to eliminate the risk of disease, don't plant your bushes near wild raspberries or where other raspberry bushes, or tomatoes, peppers, potatoes, or eggplants, have once been planted.

Planting

Spring is the recommended time of year to plant raspberries to give the bushes a chance to mature and harden before cold weather sets in. Space red raspberries 2½ feet apart and black and purple varieties 3 feet apart, both in rows 7 feet apart.

Raspberry canes are biennial; that is, they grow 1 year and produce fruit the next. Once a cane has produced fruit it should be cut off at ground level and burned.

Pruning of all varieties is necessary to remove dead or damaged canes and especially to keep the brambles in check. Suckers should also be removed from between the rows. To prune your bushes, cut 1-year-old canes back slightly; remove 2-year-old canes, weak canes, and unwanted suckers; and cut side branches or long canes back to 6 to 8 inches. Summer pruning, or topping, should be undertaken when red raspberry bushes are 2 to 3 feet high and black and purple varieties 2 feet high. This helps to increase the following year's production of fruit by forcing the bushes to send out side branches.

Cultivate to keep weeds down until the plants blossom, then

mulch with straw to conserve moisture and keep the soil cool. Protect the berries from marauding birds by netting the bushes.

Red raspberries may be propagated by dividing the plants, or by digging up suckers and replanting them elsewhere. Black and purple raspberries are propagated by tip layering. To accomplish this, in late summer place the tip of one long trailing cane deep enough into the soil so that only the end shows. By fall the tip will have rooted, and you may cut it from its parent in the spring, dig it up, and replant it elsewhere.

Harvesting

Wait until the berries have ripened fully before picking them. They will separate easily from the canes when ripe, but handle them gently—the fruit is very easily bruised.

Strawberries

Strawberries are among the most popular and easiest fruits to grow in home gardens throughout the country, but certain varieties are especially adapted to certain climates. Your local nurseryman or a reliable seed catalog can guide you to the variety best suited to your area. Be sure to buy only certified and disease-free plants.

Strawberry plants are available in 2 types. Most varieties are June bearers which produce 1 crop a year, usually in late spring or early summer. Everbearing varieties produce a June crop, plus additional fruit from July to late fall.

Treating the Soil

Strawberries do best in well-drained soils which have been thoroughly prepared beforehand with organic matter and fertilizer. Use a planting site that receives full sun and slopes slightly to promote good drainage. Do not turn over a section of lawn for your strawberry bed, and don't plant strawberries where tomatoes, peppers, potatoes, eggplant, melons, or other related plants have been grown within the previous 3 years. Cultivate the soil deeply, and pulverize it well before setting your plants out.

Planting

Strawberry plants may be set out at any time the ground can be prepared. Early spring is best in most of the country, except the

Gulf states, the Southwest, and the cooler Pacific coast areas, where fall is the time for planting.

Plant as soon as you buy or receive your strawberries—they may be seriously damaged if the interval is too long, especially if kept in plastic bags. Remove blossom buds, old runners, and all but two or three of the youngest leaves just before planting. Set the plant crown level with the ground surface, taking extreme care that only the bottom half of the crown is covered with soil. This is important—plants with crowns set too shallowly or too deep will not produce well.

Two methods are used to lay out strawberry beds. The more common matted-row system is to set plants 2 feet apart in rows spaced 3 to 4 feet apart. Allow only 6 of the runner plants which develop from the parent plant to form a mat around their parent. Snip off all other runners and keep about 4 to 6 inches between each family grouping.

The hill system of planting calls for plants to be spaced 1 foot apart in rows 2 feet apart. Cut off runners as soon as they form.

Pick the flower buds from June-bearing varieties planted in spring before they open the first season; this will increase the yield the following year. Spring-planted everbearing varieties should be shorn of their blossoms the first year also, but only until late summer, when they may be allowed to set fruit. Everbearing strawberries planted in fall need not have blossoms removed.

Shallow-cultivate for weed control, and mulch the strawberry beds with straw or hay to protect the plants from winter injury. Mulching also conserves moisture and makes for cleaner berries. Netting will protect against birds at harvest time.

Harvesting

Leave the fruit on the plants until they ripen to full red, then pick by snapping the stems ½ inch above the berries. Pick all rows clean, and store the berries in a cool place.

FARMHOUSE RECIPES

Hearty
breakfasts
and
lunches

OLD-TIME FARM breakfasts are traditionally larger and more nourishing than the cup-of-coffee-and-off-to-work breakfasts of city
dwellers. Farmers rise hours before the sun and their morning meal
is designed to provide energy enough to last them through the
7-hour working span before they leave their distant fields and come
back home for refueling at lunchtime. The farm breakfast is high
in protein for lasting power. Several meats, potatoes, eggs, biscuits,
whole grain cereals, and fresh or stewed fruits with cream make up
the menu of a typical breakfast.

The recent city dweller, new to country life, may not feel the
need for such a heavy breakfast, but if the first meal of the day is
rather late in starting you will find that a big breakfast effortlessly
slides into an early lunch and you need plan only two meals for the
day—this and an early supper. The extended breakfast is also a
perfect way to entertain house guests and/or neighboring city
farmers. It is more relaxing than a dinner party and the food can
be as varied or simple as you like.

There are no recipes for fried eggs and bacon, ham, or sausage
in this section, although these often form the mainstay of the
country breakfast. There is probably no one who cannot fry, poach,

or scramble an egg, heat ham slices, or fry bacon or sausages. Rather, in this section I have given recipes for more unusual breakfast and lunch dishes such as omelets, corned beef hash, and apple pancakes with which you may not be as familiar.

"Flannel" Cakes

2 cups milk

2 tablespoons lemon juice

2 eggs, separated

1 teaspoon molasses

1½ teaspoons vegetable oil or melted butter

1½–2 cups all-purpose flour

1¼ teaspoons baking soda

¼ teaspoon salt

SERVES EIGHT

Mix the milk and lemon juice together and set aside for about 10 minutes in a warm place to clabber. Combine this soured milk, egg yolks, molasses, and oil. Sift in the dry ingredients and beat well. Beat the egg whites until they form stiff peaks and fold them into the batter.

Pour 3-inch circles of batter onto a hot, well-greased griddle. Cook until brown on both sides, turning only once. Serve immediately with maple syrup or Brown Sugar Syrup (page 473).

Mrs. Metsker's Applesauce Cornmeal

8 McIntosh apples

1 quart water

1 teaspoon salt

2 cups yellow cornmeal

SERVES EIGHT

Core the apples without peeling them. Cut them into ¼-inch slices. Bring the water to a boil, add the salt, and stir in the cornmeal. Mix the apple slices into the hot cornmeal and cook, stirring occasionally, until the cornmeal is thick. Serve accompanied by molasses or brown sugar.

Ponhaws***

No really satisfying farmhouse breakfast is complete
without crisp, golden slices of scrapple or ponhaws
covered with brown sugar, corn or maple syrup.

3 pounds cooked ham, ground or
minced

1 large onion, minced

½ teaspoon salt

¼ teaspoon black pepper

¾ teaspoon powdered sage

2 quarts Clarified Beef Stock
(page 110) or Chicken Stock
(page 111) or canned beef
bouillon or chicken broth

1¼ cups cornmeal

Vegetable oil for frying

SERVES TEN TO TWELVE

Place the minced ham and onion in a large kettle, add the
seasonings, and cover with the stock. Bring to a boil. Moisten the
cornmeal with a bit of hot water, then stir it into the boiling broth.
Use the back of a spoon to press out any lumps. Bring back to a
boil and cook, stirring constantly, for 10 minutes, or until thick.
Cook the scrapple over medium heat for about 1 hour, stirring frequently to prevent scorching. The scrapple should be very thick
and fairly dry.

Spoon the hot scrapple into 2 loaf pans, cool, then refrigerate
until cold. To serve, cut the scrapple into thin slices and fry in
ample oil or fat. When the slices are brown and crisp on both sides,
serve accompanied by syrup.

Old-Fashioned Cornmeal Mush

It is true that Cornmeal Mush takes a bit of getting
used to, but there is actually no breakfast food that is
more nutritious or tasty than this one,
once your tastebuds become attuned.

1 cup cornmeal

1 teaspoon salt

1 cup cold water

1 quart boiling water

SERVES EIGHT

Mix the cornmeal and salt with the cold water to make a paste. Stir this vigorously into 1 quart boiling water in the top of a double boiler. Continue to stir for several minutes, pressing out any lumps with the back of a spoon. Set the mixture over boiling water. Cook for 1 hour or until very thick, stirring frequently. Serve hot with milk, butter, and molasses as a porridge, or chill for 3 or 4 hours in an oiled loaf pan and use for Fried Cornmeal Mush (below).

Fried Cornmeal Mush

Fried mush may sound like a punishment
rather than a treat, but it is delicious
served with maple syrup.

Old-Fashioned Cornmeal Mush
(page 85)
Flour

2 tablespoons butter
2 tablespoons vegetable oil
Maple syrup

SERVES EIGHT

Cut the chilled mush into ¼-inch slices and dredge lightly in flour. Heat the butter and oil together in a large skillet, and fry the slices over medium-high heat until lightly browned on both sides, turning once. Serve immediately with maple syrup.

Egg-Dipped Fried Mush***

Use this easy method to fry mush
to a golden brown in half the time.

Old-Fashioned Cornmeal Mush
(page 85)
2 tablespoons butter

2 tablespoons vegetable oil
Flour
1 egg

SERVES EIGHT

Cut the chilled mush into ¼-inch slices. Heat the butter and oil together in a large skillet. Dip the mush slices first in flour, then in the lightly beaten egg, and fry over medium-high heat until lightly browned on both sides, turning once. Serve immediately with maple syrup.

Dutch Pancake***

Sprinkle this large puffy pancake with
confectioners' sugar and lemon juice for a
delectably simple dessert, breakfast, or brunch dish.

2 cups sifted all-purpose flour	*4 eggs*
½ teaspoon salt	*8 tablespoons (1 stick) butter*
1 cup milk	*Confectioners' sugar*
1 cup light cream or half and half	*Juice of 1 lemon*

SERVES EIGHT

Combine the flour with the salt and sift again. Use an egg beater to blend in the milk and cream, adding a bit at a time and beating well after each addition until the mixture is smooth. Add the eggs one at a time, beating at least 1 minute for each. Set the liquid batter in the refrigerator, covered with a cloth or aluminum foil, for at least 2 hours.

Preheat the oven to 450 degrees.

Melt the butter in a 10-inch glass pie plate by setting it briefly in the oven. Beat the batter a bit more and pour over the butter to a depth of ½ inch. Bake for 15 minutes, or until the pancake rises. Lower the oven temperature to 375 degrees and bake for an additional 10 to 15 minutes. When the pancake puffs and turns crisp and brown, remove from the oven, sprinkle generously with confectioners' sugar and lemon juice, cut into wedges, and serve immediately.

Apple Eggbread

For a simple but tasty breakfast or lunch,
try this oldtime farmhouse recipe.

8 McIntosh apples	3 eggs
4–6 tablespoons butter	3 tablespoons milk
⅓ cup granulated sugar	8 slices bread
5 tablespoons water	Bacon

SERVES EIGHT

Core the apples and cut them into ½-inch slices without peeling them. Heat 2 tablespoons butter in a large skillet and fry the apple rings to a golden brown on one side. Sprinkle with sugar, turn, and fry. Sprinkle with water and simmer 3 minutes.

Heat the remaining butter in a griddle or another skillet. Combine the eggs and milk and dip the bread slices in it. Fry the bread to a crispy brown on both sides, turning once. To serve, place a slice of fried toast on each plate, top with equal portions of fried apples, and surround with hot, crisp bacon.

Bread Crumb Omelet

When the cupboard is bare and everyone is hungry,
serve this economical omelet, spread with applesauce,
strawberry jam, or apple butter.

⅔ *cup fine dry bread crumbs*   5 *eggs*
⅔ *cup hot milk*   2 *tablespoons butter*
1 *teaspoon salt*   *Applesauce, strawberry jam, or*
                                       apple butter

SERVES FOUR

Mix together the bread crumbs and the milk. Cool to room temperature and beat in the salt and eggs. Melt 1 tablespoon butter in each of 2 8-inch skillets, spread half the egg mixture in each, and fry over low heat until the omelets are golden brown on both sides. Spread with applesauce, jam, or apple butter, and serve immediately.

Baked Sandwich Omelet***

2 *tablespoons butter*   4 *ounces mild cheddar cheese,*
8 *slices well-buttered bread,*   *thinly sliced*
  crusts removed   6 *eggs*
  Filling (next page)   2¼ *cups milk*

SERVES SIX

Preheat the oven to 350 degrees.

Dot the bottom of a well-buttered 8-inch-square baking dish with an additional tablespoon butter. Arrange 4 slices of bread over the bits of butter. Cover with one of the fillings below. Top with 4 additional slices bread and the cheddar cheese.

Beat the eggs lightly with milk and pour over all. Bake in the preheated oven for 45 minutes, or until a knife inserted in the middle comes out clean.

[89]

Ham and Cheese Filling

Spread the bread slices with ¼ teaspoon mustard and cover with 1 cup thinly sliced cooked ham and ¼ pound thinly sliced cheddar cheese. Top with bread, additional cheese, eggs, and milk. Season and bake.

Chicken and Mushroom Filling

Arrange 1 cup thinly sliced cooked chicken and 1 cup sliced sautéed mushrooms over the bread slices. Top with bread, cheese, eggs, and milk. Season and bake.

Bacon and Tomato Filling

Arrange 10 strips crisp bacon over the bread slices and cover with 2 sliced tomatoes. Top with bread, cheese, eggs, and milk. Season and bake.

Hard-Boiled Egg and Scallion Filling

Arrange 5 sliced hard-boiled eggs and 9 chopped scallions over the bread slices. Top with bread, cheese, eggs, and milk. Season and bake.

Onion and Canadian Bacon Filling

Arrange 2 thinly sliced onions which have been sautéed in butter over the bread slices. Cover with 10 slices lightly browned Canadian bacon. Top with bread, cheese, eggs, and milk. Season and bake.

Cheddar Cheese and Jam Filling

Spread ¼ cup strawberry or peach jam over the bread slices. Cover with ¼ pound thinly sliced cheddar cheese. Top with bread, additional cheese, eggs, and milk. Season and bake.

Apple and Apricot Jam Filling

Spread ⅓ cup apricot jam over the bread slices and cover with 3 peeled, cored, and sliced McIntosh apples. Top with bread, cheese, eggs, and milk. Season and bake.

Mustard and Cheese Filling

Spread ¼ teaspoon mustard over the bread slices and cover with ¼ pound thinly sliced cheddar cheese. Top with bread, additional cheese, eggs, and milk. Season and bake.

Bacon and Egg Croquettes***

¾ cup minced lean bacon	Salt and black pepper
9 hard-boiled eggs, finely chopped	2 eggs
2¼ cups fine dry bread crumbs	3 tablespoons grated mild cheddar cheese
1 cup thick Easy White Sauce (page 238)	Vegetable oil for frying

SERVES EIGHT

Sauté the bacon until crisp and drain well on paper towels. Crumble the bacon and combine with the chopped eggs and ¾ cup bread crumbs. Moisten the mixture with the white sauce and season with salt and pepper. Chill, covered, for at least 2 hours.

Beat the eggs lightly. Combine the cheese with the remaining bread crumbs. With floured hands, shape the bacon and egg mixture into croquettes. Dip each first in the beaten egg and then in the cheese-flavored bread crumbs. Fry in 2 inches of hot oil until golden brown, turning once. Drain on paper towels before serving hot.

Mushroom and Egg Croquettes

Substitute 1½ cups minced mushrooms sautéed in 1 tablespoon butter and drained for the bacon.

Stuffed Eggs with Curry Sauce

SERVES EIGHT

Cut 8 hard-boiled eggs in half lengthwise. Scoop out the yolks and reserve the whites. Mash the yolks with one of the fillings suggested below. Heap the filling into the egg whites, season with salt and pepper, and arrange in an ovenproof serving dish. Spoon 2 cups Curry Sauce (page 236) over the eggs and bake in a preheated 350-degree oven for 15 to 20 minutes, or until heated through.

Note: Any of the following stuffed egg preparations can also be chilled and served without baking in Curry Sauce.

Mushroom Stuffing

Mash the yolks with 1½ tablespoons sour cream, 1½ tablespoons minced dill, and ½ pound minced mushrooms which have been sautéed in 1 tablespoon butter.

Fish Stuffing

Mash the yolks with 6 tablespoons cooked flaked fish, 1½ tablespoons minced dill, and 1½ tablespoons sour cream.

Celery Stuffing

Mash the yolks with ¼ cup minced celery and 1½ tablespoons sour cream.

Chicken Stuffing

Mash the yolks with 6 tablespoons cooked, minced chicken, 1½ tablespoons minced dill, and 1½ tablespoons sour cream.

Ham Stuffing

Mash the yolks with 6 tablespoons cooked minced ham, 2 tablespoons minced celery, and 1½ tablespoons sour cream.

Walnut Stuffing

Mash the yolks with 1 minced scallion, 4 tablespoons chopped walnuts, and 1½ tablespoons sour cream.

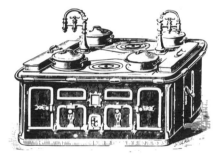

Eggs Simmered in Cream

1 cup light cream   *Salt and black pepper*
8 eggs   *8 slices toast*

SERVES EIGHT

Heat the cream in a large skillet, and drop in the eggs, one at a time. Cover and cook the eggs slowly until the whites are firm. Season with salt and pepper. Serve immediately on toast.

Scalloped Eggs and Onion Lunch Dish***

4 strips bacon, chopped
2 medium onions, sliced
2 cups Easy White Sauce (page 238)

4 eggs
½ cup fine dry bread crumbs
2 tablespoons butter

SERVES FOUR

Preheat the oven to 350 degrees.

Sauté the bacon for 3 minutes, add the onion slices, and continue to cook until the onions are tender. Place 1 cup white sauce in a baking dish and cover with the bacon and onions. Break 4 eggs carefully onto the onion slices and cover with the remaining white sauce. Sprinkle with bread crumbs and dot with butter. Bake for 20 to 30 minutes or until the eggs are as you like them.

Egg Salad with Anchovies

10 hard-boiled eggs, chopped
3 stalks celery, chopped
6 scallions, including 3 inches of green top, chopped
15 flat anchovy fillets, chopped
Salt

Pinch or two dry mustard
Mayonnaise (page 334)
½ cup heavy cream, whipped
Capers

SERVES EIGHT

Combine the eggs, celery, scallions, and anchovies in a large bowl. Season with salt and mustard. Bind the salad with as much mayonnaise as necessary to produce a salad slightly dryer than you prefer. Fold in the whipped cream. Refrigerate for several hours before serving cold, garnished with capers.

[94]

Eggs Baked in Zucchini***

6 medium zucchini
½ teaspoon salt
3 scallions, trimmed leaving 3 inches of green top, and chopped
4 tablespoons butter

6 eggs
2 cups Easy White Sauce (page 238)
2 tablespoons grated cheese (optional)

SERVES SIX

Grate the zucchini into a large bowl and sprinkle with salt. Allow to stand for 5 minutes, then press out all the liquid, reserving it for your stock jar. Dry the zucchini on paper towels.

Preheat the oven to 350 degrees.

Sauté the zucchini and scallions in 3 tablespoons butter for 5 minutes, stirring frequently. Remove the pan from the heat and spread the vegetable mixture in a flat 10-inch baking dish. Use a spoon to make 6 depressions in the mixture, and carefully break 1 egg into each. Dot each of the eggs with ½ teaspoon of butter. Bake for 20 to 30 minutes, or until the egg whites are firm and the yolks are still a bit soft.

Serve the eggs with the sauce on the side. Alternatively, top the eggs with the white sauce after baking, sprinkle with grated cheese, and slide under the broiler for a few minutes, until the top is lightly browned. Serve hot.

Grandmother's Pickled Eggs

5 medium beets, cooked, peeled, and quartered
1½ cups cider vinegar
5 tablespoons granulated sugar
2 cloves garlic, crushed

1½ teaspoons whole pickling spice
¾ teaspoon salt
8 hard-boiled eggs, shelled

SERVES EIGHT

Mix together the beets, vinegar, sugar, garlic, pickling spice, and salt. Let stand for 45 minutes. Place the shelled eggs in a large jar. Add the beets with their marinade. Cover and refrigerate for two or three days, or even a week.

Chicken Livers with Apples and Onions

2½ *pounds chicken livers*

12 *tablespoons (1½ sticks)*
   butter

2 *medium Spanish onions, sliced*
   Salt

Pinch grated nutmeg

4 *medium apples, unpeeled,*
   cored, and cut into ½-inch
   slices

¼ *cup dark brown sugar*

SERVES EIGHT

Cut the chicken livers in half, rinse, and pat dry. Sauté the livers in 8 tablespoons butter until nicely browned on the outside and slightly pink within. Season with salt and pepper and transfer to an ovenproof serving dish.

In a separate skillet, sauté the onion rings in 2 tablespoons butter until the edges are lightly browned. Add to the livers and place in a warm oven.

Add the remaining 2 tablespoons butter to the skillet in which the onions were cooked and sauté the apple slices to a light brown on one side. Sprinkle the tops of the rings with sugar, then turn to brown and glaze the other side. Arrange the glazed apple rings over the liver and onions and serve immediately.

Skewered Chicken Livers and Apple with Honey

2½ *pounds chicken livers*

½ *cup honey*

½ *cup soy sauce*

½ *teaspoon grated nutmeg*

⅛ *teaspoon ground aniseed*

8 *McIntosh apples, unpeeled,*
   cored, and cut into 1-inch
   chunks

SERVES EIGHT

Wash the livers, dry on paper towels, and place in a bowl. Mix together the honey, soy sauce, nutmeg, and aniseed; pour over the livers. Marinate for 15 minutes; remove the livers.

Dip the apple chunks in the marinade. Thread the fruit and livers alternately on skewers, beginning and ending with apple. Broil, turning the skewers several times, until the livers are cooked but still slightly pink in the centers.

Chicken Hash***

4 large chicken breasts, minced

6 tablespoons butter

4 cups coarsely chopped cooked potatoes

1 small onion, minced

Pinch grated nutmeg

Pinch powdered sage

Salt and black pepper

3 tablespoons heavy cream

SERVES SIX

Sauté the minced chicken in 3 tablespoons butter only until the meat is an opaque white. Transfer the chicken to a large bowl and add the potatoes, onion, spices, and cream. Mix well. Heat the remaining butter in a large skillet and cook the hash over medium heat for 15 minutes on each side, or until very crusty and brown, turning once.

Remove the skillet from the heat, set a serving plate on top, and turn over quickly so that the hash is turned out in one piece. Cut into 6 wedges and serve immediately.

Chicken Hash in Parchment Pancakes

Prepare the hash as above, stirring occasionally rather than making a pancake. Make Parchment Pancake Batter (page 104) as directed, using only 1 teaspoon sugar and increasing the salt to ⅓ teaspoon. To serve, fold ½ cup whipped cream into the hash, if desired. Spread a few tablespoons of hash down the center of each pancake, roll up carefully, and place on serving plates. Serve immediately.

Old Country Whipped Cream Chicken Salad***

1 pound mushrooms, thinly
   sliced

1 tablespoon butter

4 cups cubed cooked chicken

1½ cups mayonnaise

1 cup finely chopped celery

2 scallions, with three inches of
   green tops, very finely minced

1 cup heavy cream

4 medium tomatoes, cut into
   eighths

2 tablespoons capers

SERVES EIGHT

Sauté the mushrooms in the butter until golden, adding a bit more butter if necessary. Drain the liquid from the mushrooms, allow them to cool, and add to the chicken. Mix enough of the mayonnaise with the chicken and mushrooms to coat them. Chill the mixture, covered, in the refrigerator for at least 1 hour.

Add the celery and scallions to the chicken mixture and mix well. Whip the cream until stiff and fold gently into the chicken salad. Turn the salad out onto an attractive serving platter or bowl, surround with tomato wedges, garnish with capers, and serve.

Note: Duck, turkey, veal, or fish may be substituted for the chicken.

Rinktum Ditty

*This piquant cheese favorite of the Pennsylvania Dutch
is a nice change-of-pace lunch.*

1 tablespoon butter

2 small onions, minced

1½ tablespoons flour

1 cup milk

1¼ pounds sharp cheddar cheese,
   cubed

1 tablespoon Worcestershire
   sauce

1 teaspoon dry mustard

½ teaspoon salt

¼ teaspoon paprika

½ cup ketchup

1 egg

16 slices toast

SERVES EIGHT

[98]

Melt the butter in the top of a double boiler over boiling water. Add the minced onions and cook until the onions are wilted. Blend in the flour. Stir in the milk a little at a time, blending well after each addition. The sauce should be smooth and fairly thick. Add the cheese to the sauce, continuing to stir until the cheese is melted.

Combine the Worcestershire sauce, mustard, salt, and paprika with the ketchup. Blend into the sauce and cook for 5 minutes. Beat the egg lightly with a fork, stir into the sauce, and cook for 1 minute more. Arrange 2 pieces of toast, cut into strips, on each plate, pour the cheese sauce over, and serve at once.

Farm Fried Pies***

SERVES SIX TO EIGHT

These delicious fried pies may be filled with any of the following fillings. Prepare double the recipe for Pastry for 2-Crust Pie (page 418). Roll out the pastry to medium thickness, cut into 6-inch squares, place 2 to 3 tablespoons of filling on one side of each square, then moisten the edges of the crust and fold the other side over to form a triangle. Use a fork to press the edges together. Fry in 1½ inches of hot oil until brown on one side, turn, brown the other side and serve immediately.

Lamb and Beef Filling

1½ cups ground lamb	4 tablespoons ketchup
2 cups ground lean beef	1 tablespoon prepared mustard
1 small onion, chopped	Salt and black pepper

Sauté the meats and onion until the meat is browned. Mix in the ketchup and mustard and season with salt and pepper.

Lamb, Beef, and Ham Filling

1½ cups ground lamb
1½ cups ground lean beef
½ cup finely chopped cooked ham
3 hard-boiled eggs, finely chopped

½–¾ cup Easy White Sauce (page 238)
Salt and black pepper

Sauté the lamb, beef, and ham until lightly browned. Mix in the chopped eggs. Add as much of the white sauce as necessary to bind the mixture. The filling should not be runny. Season with salt and pepper.

Lamb and Veal Filling

2 cups ground lamb
1½ cups ground veal
¼ cup raisins
2 tablespoons pine nuts

3 tablespoons ketchup
1 tablespoon maple syrup
Salt and black pepper

Sauté the meats until lightly browned. Remove from the heat and mix in the raisins and pine nuts. Combine the ketchup and maple syrup, blend into the meat mixture, and season with salt and pepper.

Mushroom Filling

3½ cups minced mushrooms
4 shallots or 1 small onion, finely chopped
2 tablespoons butter

1 egg yolk
2–4 tablespoons Easy White Sauce (page 238)
Salt and black pepper

Sauté the mushrooms and shallots in the butter until golden brown. Beat the egg yolk and combine with the vegetables. Add as much of the white sauce as necessary to bind the mixture. Season with salt and pepper.

Eggplant Filling

1 medium eggplant, peeled and sliced

Salt

4 tablespoons butter or vegetable oil

1 medium onion, chopped

2 tablespoons pine nuts

¼ cup ketchup

Arrange the eggplant slices on a flat surface, sprinkle with salt, and let stand for 30 to 40 minutes. Dry the slices with paper towels and chop. Heat the butter or oil in a skillet, and sauté the eggplant and chopped onion until soft. Remove from the heat and stir in the pine nuts and ketchup.

Egg and Anchovy Filling

1 tablespoon butter

3 scallions, including 3 inches green top, chopped

5 hard-boiled eggs, chopped

5 flat anchovy fillets, chopped

Melt the butter in a small frying pan and sauté the scallions until golden brown. Mix with the chopped eggs and anchovies.

Cheese Filling

3½ cups grated cheddar cheese

¾ teaspoon dry mustard

Mix the cheese and mustard together.

[101]

Country Pâté

2 *pound piece pork*
2 *pound piece veal*
3 *tablespoons minced shallots*
1 *tablespoon minced fresh dill or*
   1½ teaspoons dried
1 *bay leaf*
⅛ *teaspoon dried thyme*
2 *cloves garlic, halved*

Pinch *grated nutmeg*
   Dry red wine
⅓ *cup dry sherry*
¼ *teaspoon salt*
⅛ *teaspoon black pepper*
8 *strips lean bacon*
20 *stuffed green olives, sliced*

SERVES EIGHT

Slice the pork and veal very thinly into strips and arrange in layers in a large glass dish. Make a marinade by combining the shallots, dill, bay leaf, thyme, garlic, nutmeg, and enough red wine to cover the meat slices in the dish. Refrigerate and marinate the meat for 24 hours.

After draining well, finely mince about ¼ of both the pork and veal slices, or put this same amount through the meat grinder. Season the meats with the sherry, salt, and pepper.

Preheat the oven to 350 degrees.

Line a terrine or loaf pan with bacon, placed side by side extending over the rim of the dish. Remove the meat slices from the marinade and arrange a layer of slices over the bacon. Top this layer neatly with a layer of minced meats and half the sliced olives. Continue the layering, finishing with olive slices. Fold the ends of the bacon strips over the top of the pâté, allowing the center row of olive slices to show.

Set the loaf pan in a pan of water and bake for 1½ hours. Place a small plate or thin piece of wood wrapped in aluminum foil over the pâté after taking it from the oven. Set a 4-pound weight on top of the plate or wood so the pâté cools under pressure. Chill before slicing. Serve with small, thinly sliced sour pickles.

Noodles with Mushroom Sauce***

2 *pounds mushrooms, thinly sliced*

6 *tablespoons butter*

2 *tablespoons vegetable oil*

2 *pounds thin egg noodles*

½ *pound Country Pâté, cut into ¼-inch cubes*

SERVES EIGHT

Cook the noodles according to package directions. Sauté the mushrooms in 3 tablespoons butter and the oil. Drain noodles well. Toss with the mushrooms, the remaining butter, and the cubes of pâté. Serve immediately.

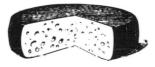

Baked Macaroni and Cheese

If you can't stand macaroni and cheese in a sticky sauce,
you're certain to like this
slightly dry but very cheese-y dish.

1 *pound elbow macaroni*

9 *strips lean bacon, minced*

3½ *cups grated sharp cheddar cheese*

1½ *cups heavy cream, whipped*

1 *cup dry bread crumbs*

SERVES EIGHT

Preheat the oven to 350 degrees.

Cook the macaroni according to package directions. Sauté the minced bacon until crisp and brown, remove with a slotted spoon, and drain, reserving the bacon fat. Set ½ cup of the cheese aside, mix the rest with the drained macaroni, and fold in the bacon bits and whipped cream.

Pour the mixture into a well-buttered casserole. Mix the bread crumbs with the reserved cheese and bacon fat, sprinkle over the top of the macaroni and cheese, and bake for 20 to 25 minutes.

Parchment Pancakes***

A hearty breakfast of potatoes, eggs, and ham
can be extended into an early lunch if you linger
at the table over coffee and sugar-sprinkled
Parchment Pancakes.
These large, paper-thin pancakes are most impressive
when prepared at the table. Use a 15-inch crêpe pan,
or other very large skillet.

3–4 tablespoons butter

6 eggs

1½ cups sifted all-purpose flour

1 tablespoon granulated sugar

¼ teaspoon salt

2 cups milk

Apricot, strawberry, or other jam or apple butter

Confectioners' sugar

2 lemons, quartered

SERVES EIGHT

Season the pan before you start so the pancakes won't stick. Rub the skillet with a little butter. Place the pan over low heat for a few minutes, remove, and wipe the pan. Repeat this process, adding 1 teaspoon butter, and your pan is ready to produce stick-free pancakes.

Prepare the batter just before you are ready to serve the pancakes. Beat the eggs until they are light; continue to beat as you add the flour, sugar, and salt. When the dry ingredients have been absorbed, beat in the milk and continue beating for 3 or 4 minutes.

Have the batter, butter, jam, confectioners' sugar, and lemon wedges near at hand as you begin to cook the pancakes.

Heat 1 teaspoon of butter in the crêpe pan for the first pancake, tip the pan back and forth over the heat to coat the bottom and sides. When the butter is hot, pour 4 or 5 tablespoons batter into the pan. Tilt the pan from side to side to spread the batter very thinly. As bubbles rise to the top, loosen the pancake with a spatula, turn it quickly, and lightly brown the other side.

Use about ½ teaspoon of butter for each additional pancake, and prepare them all in the same manner. Depending upon the size of your pan, there will be enough batter for 4 to 6 very large pancakes.

As each pancake is cooked, slip it onto a plate and spread it quickly with jam. Roll up the pancake, sprinkle with confectioners' sugar, and cut it in half. Serve with lemon wedges.

Peach Parchment Pancakes***

4 cups peeled, pitted, and sliced
   peaches
3–4 tablespoons butter
  Light brown sugar

Parchment Pancake Batter
(page 104)
Confectioners' sugar
1 cup heavy cream, whipped

SERVES EIGHT

Sauté the peach slices in the butter, stirring occasionally, until lightly browned. Sprinkle with brown sugar and turn to brown the other side. Take care not to overcook. Remove the fruit from the heat and set aside while preparing the pancakes.

Have the sautéed fruit and confectioners' sugar close at hand while you make the pancakes. Slip each pancake from the pan as it is finished. Spoon sautéed fruit down the center of each pancake, roll it carefully, and sprinkle with confectioners' sugar. Cut the pancakes in half, set each half on a serving plate, and serve immediately with a bowl of whipped cream.

Apple Parchment Pancakes

Substitute 4 cups peeled, cored, and sliced apples for the peaches. The apples should be tender, but still retain their crunchy texture.

Black Cherry Omelet

8 eggs, separated
⅓ cup granulated sugar
1 tablespoon water
⅛ teaspoon salt
4 tablespoons butter
   Kirsch

Confectioners' sugar
4 cups black cherries, halved and pitted
1 pint heavy cream, whipped and sweetened

SERVES EIGHT

Beat the egg yolks and sugar until thick and lemon colored. Add the water and a pinch of salt to the egg whites and beat until they stand in peaks. Fold the egg whites carefully into the beaten egg yolks.

Melt the butter in 2 medium-size skillets. Divide the eggs between the skillets and cook until the omelets are brown on the bottom and set on top. Fold the omelets in half and carefully slide them onto 2 serving dishes. Sprinkle generously with kirsch and confectioners' sugar and surround with the cherries. Serve with a bowl of whipped cream flavored with sugar and vanilla.

Cold Platters

Cold platters make lovely country lunches when served with crusty fresh-baked bread. Here are a few suggestions for creating impressive and inviting platters of cold salads, vegetables, eggs, and meats.

Heap chicken, turkey, duck, veal, or fish salad (page 249), in the center of a large platter. Surround with rolled and sliced meats, or thin slices of Country Pâté (page 102), tomato halves stuffed with vegetable salads and/or cottage cheese, cold stuffed eggs (page 92), cold artichoke bottoms (page 247), stuffed celery (page 92), and potato salad (page 327). Decorate the platters with sprigs of parsley or other fresh herbs from your garden. Serve well chilled.

SOUPS

Soup Stock

THE MOST delicious soups are those that begin with a stock. Not only is flavor enhanced but the broth takes on added nutritional value. From the basic broth, diverse soups can be created with the addition of other meats and vegetables. Flavor is imparted automatically through the simmering process, but to extract the maximum nutrition there are a few rules that must be carefully followed.

Save bits of raw vegetables, tops of scallions and celery, tender leaves of beets, tough spinach, stems of watercress and dill, limp outer leaves of lettuce—in other words, all of the otherwise good foodstuffs you normally throw away because they are not esthetically pleasing or simply because you are accustomed to treating them as scraps. These should be well washed and refrigerated in a large jar with a lid. They can be kept up to ten days.

Freeze scraps of leftover meat in plastic containers. Meat bones and the carcasses of game birds, chickens, turkeys, or ducks may also be frozen for use in soup stocks. If poultry has been stuffed, carefully remove any remaining bits from the carcass before freezing.

The only vegetables you will not save are potatoes and cabbage.

The former will cloud the stock and the latter will impart too strong a flavor.

Bones contain no vitamins but are high in minerals, which may be extracted from the connective tissue by simmering at about 200° F. preferably for at least 1 hour.

Simmering means cooking without letting the liquid boil. Turn your burner as low as possible and only partially cover the soup kettle to keep the soup from boiling. If stocks are simmered with a tight-fitting lid, they may cloud. To overcome this and still retain the nutritional value, cover with a loose-fitting lid or leave the lid slightly ajar. (The lid *is* important, however, to keep the vitamins from being lost.)

After you have simmered your soup stock, don't feel guilty about straining out and discarding the bones and vegetables used to flavor it. The nutrition has passed from these ingredients into the soup liquid where they await your pleasure.

Beef Stock

2½–3 pound piece lean beef

2 pounds marrow bones, cut into pieces

2 pounds veal knuckle

8 chicken feet, cleaned and skinned

3½ quarts water, or a combination vegetable liquids and water

3 medium onions, studded with 3 whole cloves each

3 large leeks, chopped

3 medium carrots, chopped

5 stalks celery with leaves, chopped

6 sprigs parsley

8 black peppercorns

1 teaspoon salt

YIELDS TWO–THREE QUARTS

Place the beef, beef bones, veal knuckle, and chicken feet in a large soup kettle. Cover with the liquid, and bring slowly to a boil, skimming the scum as it rises to the surface.

When the scum no longer rises, add the vegetables, peppercorns, and salt. Simmer the stock over low heat, partially covered, for 2½ hours. Cool slightly, then strain it through several layers of cheese-cloth and pour into jars. Do not seal the jars until the stock has cooled completely. Discard the bones and vegetables—their taste and nutrition has passed into the stock. When they cool, refrigerate the jars of stock until needed, removing any fat that rises to the surface, or freeze. Refrigerated stock should be brought to the boil every 3 or 4 days to keep it from spoiling; frozen stock will retain peak taste and nutrition 2 to 3 weeks.

Penny-Pincher's Meat Stock

3 pounds beef or veal bones, or both

Any scraps of meat on hand

2 pounds lean beef, cut into pieces

1 roast chicken carcass

8 onions, sliced

12 stalks celery with leaves, chopped

4 quarts vegetable liquids, or a combination vegetable liquids and water

Salt and black pepper

YIELDS TWO—THREE QUARTS

Spread the bones and meat in a roasting pan and arrange the vegetables on top. Bake in a moderate oven for 50 minutes. Remove any fat, then place the bones, meat, and vegetables in a large soup kettle. Cover with the liquid and simmer over low heat, partially covered, for 4 hours, skimming and discarding any scum that rises to the surface.

Cool the stock before straining it into storage jars, then refrigerate. Remove any fat that rises to the top after the stock is chilled. Use as needed, or freeze. Refrigerated stock is at its peak up to 5 days; frozen stock 2 to 3 weeks.

Clarified Beef Stock

*Clarification clears the stock of its tiny
cloudy particles. Use it for clear soups and sauces.*

10 cups Beef Stock (page 108)   3 egg shells
3 egg whites

YIELDS TWO QUARTS

Bring the stock to a boil in a kettle. Beat the egg whites until they are frothy, and add them, along with the egg shells, to the boiling stock, stirring constantly. Lower the heat slightly, and continue to stir while the soup boils for 10 minutes. Remove from the heat, and set the stock aside for 10 minutes while the egg particles settle to the bottom of the kettle. Strain the stock through a fine cloth into another saucepan, and reheat before serving, or pour into containers and freeze.

Beef Consommé

*If space is a factor in your freezer,
make this delicious consommé right after preparing
Beef Stock. Consommé takes less room to store and
is delightful hot or cold dressed with bits of fresh or
cooked vegetable or minced cooked meats.*

12 cups Beef Stock   ½ cup each coarsely chopped
2 pounds chopped lean beef   onion, leek, carrot, and celery
                                  2 egg whites

YIELDS ABOUT EIGHT–TEN CUPS

Bring stock, beef, vegetables, and egg whites to a point *just under a boil.* Simmer for 2 hours then strain through a fine cloth.

Chicken Stock

1 small chicken plus leftover chicken carcass with bits of chicken meat

1 veal knuckle

4 chicken feet, skinned and cleaned

8 chicken necks

3½ quarts vegetable liquids, or a combination vegetable liquids and water

3 stalks celery with leaves, chopped

2 leeks (white part only) sliced

1 turnip, peeled and sliced

1 large onion

1 bay leaf

⅛ teaspoon dried thyme

¼ teaspoon black peppercorns

Salt

YIELDS TWO—THREE QUARTS

Place the chicken, chicken carcass, veal knuckle, chicken feet, and chicken necks in a large soup kettle, cover with the liquid, and bring to a low rolling boil. Simmer very slowly for 1 hour, skimming the scum as it rises to the surface. Add the vegetables, bay leaf, thyme, peppercorns, and salt. Simmer, partially covered, for 2 hours. Remove and reserve the cooked chicken for another use. Strain and cool the stock. Skim off and discard the fat, and refrigerate or freeze the stock. Use refrigerated stock within 5 days and frozen within 2 to 3 weeks.

Chicken Consommé

If space is limited in your freezer, reduce and clarify Chicken Stock. It can be used as is or diluted for use in recipes calling for Chicken Stock.

2½ quarts Chicken Stock (above)

2 egg whites

2 egg shells

YIELDS ONE AND ONE HALF QUARTS

[111]

Place the Chicken Stock in a large kettle, bring to a boil, and continue to boil over medium heat until the stock is reduced by ⅓. This will concentrate the flavor.

To clarify the stock, add the egg whites and shells, and cook the stock over medium heat for 10 minutes. Remove from the heat and set the stock aside for 10 minutes while the particles settle to the bottom of the kettle. Strain the stock through a fine cloth into another saucepan and reheat before serving.

Fish Stock

6 pounds fresh fish, including bones, head, and flesh

2 medium onions

2 leeks

3 quarts water

1 cup dry white wine

1 small bay leaf

2 teaspoons fennel seed

1 whole clove

1 teaspoon salt

YIELDS TWO–THREE QUARTS

Place all ingredients in a deep kettle and bring to a boil. Lower the heat and simmer for 45 minutes. Strain the stock, cool, and store, tightly covered, in the refrigerator where it will keep for several days.

Oxtail Consommé

1 oxtail, cut into 1-inch pieces

2 tablespoons butter

3 quarts Clarified Beef Stock (page 110) or water

2 large onions, sliced

3 medium carrots, diced

3 leeks, coarsely chopped

4 stalks celery, coarsely chopped

2 cloves garlic

1 bay leaf

1 teaspoon salt

10 black peppercorns

1 tablespoon lemon juice

1 tablespoon Worcestershire sauce

SERVES EIGHT

[112]

Wash and dry the oxtail pieces. Heat the butter in a large soup kettle and brown the oxtail pieces on all sides. Add the stock or water, onions, carrots, leeks, celery, garlic, bay leaf, salt, and peppercorns, and bring the mixture to a boil. Boil for 5 minutes, skimming any froth that rises to the surface. Cover the kettle and allow the soup to simmer over low heat for 3 hours.

Remove the kettle from the heat and stir in the lemon juice and Worcestershire sauce. Remove the oxtail pieces, chop the meat into fine dice, and set aside. Strain the consommé and discard the vegetables. Refrigerate the consommé until serving time, remove the fat, and reheat to the simmering point. Serve hot, garnished with the diced oxtail. If desired, dumplings may be added to the consommé at serving time.

Celery Consommé

2½ quarts Beef Consommé (page 110) or Chicken Consommé (page 111)

6 stalks celery with leaves, coarsely chopped

Salt and black pepper

SERVES EIGHT

Bring consommé to a boil over medium heat. Add the celery and simmer together over low heat, covered, for 30 minutes, allowing the celery to thoroughly flavor the soup. Strain the consommé, season with salt and pepper to taste, and serve immediately.

Mushroom Consommé

2½ quarts Beef Consommé (page 110) or Chicken Consommé (page 111)

1½ pounds mushrooms, coarsely chopped

2 leeks, coarsely chopped

2 stalks celery with leaves, coarsely chopped

2 medium carrots, coarsely chopped

½ cup dry sherry

SERVES EIGHT

Place 2 cups consommé in a kettle, add the chopped vegetables, and bring to a boil. Lower the heat and simmer the vegetables, covered, for 40 minutes, or until thoroughly cooked. Strain the consommé into the remaining 8 cups of stock, discarding the vegetables. Reheat and pour into soup bowls. Lace each portion with sherry before serving.

Herb Consommé

2½ quarts Beef Consommé (page 110) or Chicken Consommé (page 111)

¼ cup finely chopped chervil

¼ cup finely chopped chives

¼ cup finely chopped parsley

2 tablespoons minced tarragon

SERVES EIGHT

Bring consommé to a boil, add herbs, and simmer over low heat only long enough to allow the herb flavors to penetrate the soup. Serve immediately.

Additional Consommé Variations

The rich flavor of stock may be enhanced and enriched by the judicious addition of many different garnishes. They can be plain or fancy, created from leftovers, or whatever fresh vegetables are at hand. Raw vegetables can be cooked in stock, adding subtlety and flavor to the broth. Leftover vegetables, noodles, or dumplings, used for texture and garnish, can be added after the stock is heated. Use your imagination to concoct original combinations of vegetables, herbs, and pasta.

Tomato Bouillon

4 tablespoons butter
1 large onion, diced
6 medium tomatoes, peeled, seeded, and chopped
½ clove garlic
Salt

4½ cups Beef Consommé (page 110) or canned beef bouillon
2½ cups tomato juice
Small bay leaf
Sour cream (optional)
Grated orange zest (optional)

SERVES EIGHT

Melt the butter in a large saucepan and add the onion, tomatoes, and garlic clove which has been speared with a toothpick for easy retrieval after cooking. Sprinkle with salt, stir once or twice, cover, and simmer over low heat for 30 minutes.

Remove the vegetables from the heat, discard the garlic, and force the vegetables through a fine sieve. Return the pureed vegetables to the saucepan, add the stock, tomato juice, and bay leaf; cover and simmer over low heat for 30 minutes. Adjust the seasoning. Discard the bay leaf before serving the bouillon, hot or cold. Garnish with sour cream sprinkled with grated orange zest, if desired.

Clam Bouillon with Whipped Cream

6 dozen clams in shells
3½ cups water
Salt and white pepper

Dash Tabasco
½ cup heavy cream, whipped

SERVES EIGHT

Scrub the clams well and rinse in several changes of water. A handful of cornmeal tossed in the water with the clams will force them to void the sand inside the shells. Arrange the clams in a large kettle, add 3½ cups of water, and bring slowly to a boil.

Steam the clams over low heat until the shells open. Strain the broth through a layer of cheesecloth into a large saucepan. Season with salt, pepper, and Tabasco. Discard the shells and save the clams for another use. Reheat the broth if necessary. Serve hot in bouillon cups, and garnish each serving with a spoonful or two of whipped cream.

Miss Faith Fessler's Cream of Carrot Soup***

 8 tablespoons (1 stick) butter
10 medium carrots, thinly sliced
 2 teaspoons granulated sugar
⅓ teaspoon salt
½ cup water
 4 tablespoons flour

½ teaspoon salt
Pinch black pepper
Pinch grated nutmeg
5 cups milk
⅔ cup heavy cream

SERVES EIGHT

Melt 4 tablespoons butter in a skillet, add the carrots, sugar, ⅓ teaspoon salt, and the water. Cover the skillet and cook over low heat for 25 minutes, stirring occasionally.

Meanwhile, melt the remaining butter in a heavy saucepan, stir in the flour, salt, pepper, nutmeg, and milk. Stir constantly until the mixture thickens. Simmer, covered, for 5 minutes.

Remove the carrots from the heat. Set ¼ cup of sliced carrots aside. Combine the remaining carrots with ½ cup of the white sauce and puree in an electric blender until smooth. Place the pureed carrot mixture back in the saucepan with the remaining white sauce, stir well to blend, and simmer over very low heat for 30 minutes. Just before serving, stir in as much heavy cream as necessary to bring the soup to the consistency you prefer. This soup, however, should not be too thin. Garnish with the reserved carrot slices and serve hot.

Cream of Artichoke Soup

3 large boiled artichokes (page 244)

4 cups Easy White Sauce (page 238)

⅛ teaspoon grated nutmeg

Salt and black pepper

1 cup heavy cream

½ cup chopped pecans

SERVES EIGHT

Thoroughly drain the cooked artichokes. Pull off all the leaves and gently scrape the inside of each leaf with a spoon, taking care to remove all the pulp but none of the fibers. Remove and discard the chokes and coarsely chop the artichoke bottoms. Press all the pulp through a fine sieve or puree in a blender.

Mix the artichoke puree with the white sauce, season with nutmeg, salt, and pepper, and stir in the cream. Simmer over low heat until the soup reaches the consistency you like. Serve hot, garnished with pecans.

Lettuce Soup

10 cups Chicken Stock (page 111) or canned chicken broth

4 cups shredded iceberg lettuce

8 egg yolks

½ cup sunflower kernels

3 tablespoons minced parsley

½ teaspoon salt

SERVES EIGHT

Bring the stock to a boil, stir in the shredded lettuce, and boil 3 minutes. Beat the egg yolks in a bowl, and gradually beat in the lettuce and stock. Stir in the remaining ingredients and serve immediately.

Acorn Squash Soup

5 cups water
¾ teaspoon salt
1¾–2 pounds acorn squash,
  peeled, seeded, and sliced
1 cup peeled and thinly sliced
  potatoes
5 cups heavy cream

4 tablespoons butter
⅔ cup chopped spinach
⅔ cup chopped leeks
⅔ cup chopped lettuce
1½ cups cooked rice
2 tablespoons minced parsley

SERVES EIGHT

Bring the water to a boil and add the salt. Add the squash and potatoes and simmer until tender. Press the squash and potatoes, along with the water in which they were cooked, through a fine sieve, or puree in an electric blender. Stir in the cream.

Heat the butter in a skillet. Sauté the chopped vegetables slowly over low heat until they are wilted and all the butter has been absorbed. Add the cooked rice and minced parsley, and stir into the puree. Heat, stirring occasionally.

Country-Style Collard Soup

3 pounds collard greens
1 pound spinach
2 1-pound ham hocks
3 quarts water

1 large onion, chopped
2 tablespoons granulated sugar
Salt

SERVES TWELVE

Cut the stalks from all the collards and wash thoroughly. (The grit is removed by adding ¼ cup of salt to the first washing.)

Rinse 3 or 4 times in cold water with the spinach until the water is clear. Shake the greens to remove the excess water and chop them coarsely.

Place the ham hocks and onion in a deep kettle with the water. Boil for 30 minutes. Add the greens, sugar, and salt, and simmer for 2 hours.

Dutch-Country Dandelion Soup

*Be sure to pick only young, tender dandelion greens
for cooking or for use in salads.*

8 cups dandelion greens	8 egg yolks
3 quarts Chicken Consommé (page 111) or canned chicken broth	1 cup grated mild cheddar cheese Salt and black pepper

SERVES EIGHT

Parboil the dandelion greens for 5 minutes. Drain, chop, and set aside. Place consommé in a soup kettle and bring to a rolling boil. Add the chopped dandelion greens and boil for 10 minutes.

Beat the egg yolks, add the grated cheese, and mix well. Remove the soup from the stove and immediately add the cheese mixture a bit at a time, stirring until the soup thickens slightly. Adjust the seasonings. Serve immediately.

Parsnip Soup

3 strips bacon, chopped	4 tablespoons butter, softened
2 medium onions, minced	5 tablespoons flour
1 stalk celery, minced	¾ teaspoon salt
2 cups cooked parsnips	Pinch black pepper
1½ cups heavy cream	Pinch paprika
6½ cups milk	

SERVES EIGHT

Sauté the bacon for 1 minute in a large heavy skillet. Add the onions and celery and continue to cook over medium heat, stirring occasionally, until the onion is transparent.

Press the cooked parsnips through a sieve into the skillet and add the cream and milk. Blend the butter, flour, and salt with 6 tablespoons of skillet liquid. Blend this paste into the soup, smoothing out any lumps with the back of a spoon. Stir the soup constantly over medium heat until it comes to a boil. Serve hot, sprinkled with pepper and paprika.

Lancaster County Corn-on-the-Cob Soup

1 5-pound chicken, cut into 8 pieces
4 stalks celery, chopped
1 large onion
2 carrots, chopped
10 black peppercorns
3–4 quarts water or Chicken Stock (page 111)

1 teaspoon salt
6 ears corn
2 hard-boiled eggs, chopped
2½ cups diced cooked ham
3 tablespoons minced parsley

SERVES EIGHT

Place the chicken pieces, celery, whole peeled onion, carrots, and peppercorns in a large, deep kettle. Add water or broth to cover, sprinkle with salt, and simmer, partially covered, until the chicken is tender, about 1 hour. Skim as necessary. Remove the chicken pieces, skin them, and set aside. Boil the broth until it is reduced to 10 cups, strain, and return to low heat.

Shuck the corn and drop the ears into the simmering broth. Turn up the heat and boil for 10 minutes. Remove the corn and, holding each one over the kettle, carefully cut the kernels and scrape juice into the soup. Add the chopped eggs, diced ham, and skinned chicken pieces. Heat. Serve with a chicken piece in each bowl and garnish with parsley.

Brussels Sprouts Chowder

1 *pound cooked brussels sprouts*
   (page 259)
5 *cups Easy White Sauce (page*
   238)
2½ *cups heavy cream*

⅛ *teaspoon grated nutmeg*
   Salt and black pepper
4 *hard-boiled eggs, sliced*

SERVES EIGHT

Chop the sprouts coarsely after draining and mix with the white sauce. Add the heavy cream and seasonings, and simmer over low heat, stirring occasionally, until the soup is heated through. Garnish each portion with sliced eggs. Top with Brown Bread Croutons (page 361), if desired.

Pennsylvania Dutch Dried-Corn Chowder***

8 *cups water*
1½ *cups Pennsylvania Dutch*
   dried corn
2 *teaspoons granulated sugar*
   Salt to taste
¼ *pound salt pork, sliced*

1 *onion, chopped*
1 *green pepper, seeded and*
   chopped
1 *potato, peeled and cubed*
2 *cups light cream*

SERVES TEN

Measure 4 cups water into a large saucepan. Add the corn, sugar, and salt, and soak for 3 hours. Add the remaining water and simmer the corn for 1 hour, or as directed on the package.

Fry the salt pork. Discard the pork and reserve the fat. Sauté the onion, green pepper, and potato in the pork fat for 15 to 20 minutes, or until the potato is soft. Add to the corn mixture, stir in the light cream, and simmer for 10 minutes. Correct the seasoning and serve.

Sue Ellen's Black-Eyed Pea Soup

3 cups dried black-eyed peas
4 cured ham hocks
3 stalks celery with leaves, chopped
1 large onion, chopped

3 medium tomatoes, peeled, seeded, and chopped
3 large cloves garlic, crushed
⅛ teaspoon ground cloves
Salt and black pepper

SERVES EIGHT

Rinse the peas in water to cover and pick them over. Pour off the liquid, re-cover with water, and bring to a full boil. Remove from the heat and soak the peas for 1 hour.

Rinse the ham hocks and place them in a large kettle with water to cover. Bring to a boil, lower the heat, and simmer until the meat is nearly tender. Discard the skin and the bones, chop the meat, and return it to the broth in which it was cooked.

Drain the peas and add them with the celery, onion, tomatoes, garlic, and cloves to the kettle containing the ham. Bring to a full boil, lower the heat, and simmer for 1 hour, or until the peas are tender, adding more liquid if necessary. Adjust seasoning. Serve hot with Farm Country Spoon Bread (page 350).

Note: One pound slab bacon can be substituted for the 4 ham hocks.

Pennsylvania Dutch Milk Soup with Pretzels

Hot milk and butter come to the table as a delicious soup garnished only with pretzels. Tasting is believing.

8 cups milk
4 cups light cream or milk
8 teaspoons butter

Black pepper
Pretzels

SERVES EIGHT

Mix the milk and cream together in a saucepan, add the butter, and cook gently, stirring frequently, until the butter melts and the milk and cream are heated through. Divide the soup into 8 soup bowls, season with pepper, and serve, accompanied by a bowl of pretzels for guests to break into the warm milk mixture.

Old New England Revival Soup

⅓ *pound slab bacon or salt pork, diced*

4 *large onions, sliced*

4 *large potatoes, peeled and sliced*

½ *medium head cabbage, cut into 1-inch shreds*

5 *cups Chicken Stock (page 111) or canned chicken broth*

2 *tablespoons flour*

⅓ *cup water*

 Salt

⅛ *teaspoon black pepper*

½ *teaspoon granulated sugar*

 Butter

¼ *teaspoon powdered sage*

SERVES EIGHT

Brown the bacon in a large, heavy soup pot or skillet. Add the onions, potatoes, and shredded cabbage. Cover with the stock and bring to a boil. Lower the heat, cover, and cook gently until the potato slices are tender, about 30 minutes.

Blend together the flour, water, salt, pepper, and sugar. Add ½ cup of the soup to the flour mixture, stir until smooth, and mix into the soup. Bring the soup to a boil, stirring constantly. Serve hot, dotted with butter and sprinkled with sage.

Whole Wheat Bread Soup***

6 strips bacon, diced

2 medium onions, chopped

½ teaspoon dark brown sugar

1 tablespoon flour

6 cups Clarified Beef Stock (page 110) or canned beef bouillon

2 cups tomato juice

2 cloves garlic, minced

3 tablespoons vegetable oil

8 slices whole wheat bread, crusts removed

4 hard-boiled eggs, chopped

5 scallions, chopped

Grated cheddar cheese

SERVES EIGHT

Sauté the bacon for 3 minutes, add onions, and cook until the onion is golden and transparent. Sprinkle with sugar and flour and stir well. Add 2 cups stock and bring to a boil, stirring constantly. Press this mixture through a sieve, add the remaining stock and tomato juice, and simmer for 15 minutes.

Sauté the garlic in the oil in a separate skillet. Brown the bread slices in the garlic oil. Place 1 slice of bread in each of 8 bowls. Ladle the soup over the bread and top with portions of chopped egg, scallions, and cheese.

Grandmother's Oatmeal Soup***

1½ cups rolled oats

12 cherry tomatoes, sliced

6 scallions, chopped

4 cloves garlic, crushed

6 tablespoons butter

8 cups Clarified Beef Stock (page 110) or canned beef bouillon

1 teaspoon salt

⅛ teaspoon grated nutmeg

SERVES EIGHT

Lightly brown the oats in a large heavy skillet. Do not burn. Set the toasted oats aside. Sauté the tomatoes, scallions, and garlic for 1 minute in the butter. Add the stock, salt, nutmeg, and oats. Boil for 5 minutes over medium heat. Serve hot.

Ham and Kale Soup***

*This hearty kale soup is flavored with ham
and thickened with oatmeal.*

1 ham bone with a bit of meat
8 cups water
1½ pounds kale

10 tablespoons quick-cooking
rolled oats
Salt and black pepper

SERVES EIGHT

Place the ham bone and water in a soup kettle and bring to a boil. Skim off the froth, lower the heat, cover, and simmer for 2 hours. Remove the ham bone and chop the meat. Mince the kale and add to the stock. Cover and boil gently for 20 minutes. Add the oats and chopped ham and boil for 10 minutes more. Adjust the seasoning and serve piping hot.

Spring Soup

2 cups shredded lettuce
4 stalks celery, chopped
2 medium onions, chopped
4 sprigs parsley, minced
3 tablespoons butter
4 small potatoes, peeled and sliced
2 carrots, sliced

3 quarts Chicken Stock (page 111) or canned chicken broth
1 teaspoon salt
6 scallions, including green tops, chopped
1 tablespoon minced fresh dill, or 1½ teaspoons dried
⅛ teaspoon black pepper

SERVES EIGHT

Sauté the lettuce, celery, onions, and parsley in the butter. Add the potatoes, carrots, salt, and stock. Boil gently for 20 minutes. Stir the scallions, dill, and pepper into the soup and continue to cook for 5 minutes. Adjust the seasoning and serve.

Herb Soup

6 tablespoons butter

6 tablespoons minced fresh herbs
  (chives, tarragon, dill, thyme)

4 tablespoons flour

¼ cup rice

9 cups Beef Stock (page 108) or
  canned beef bouillon

Salt and black pepper

2 egg yolks

4 tablespoons sour cream

SERVES EIGHT

Heat the butter in a soup kettle and sauté 4 tablespoons of the minced herbs. Mix in the flour and rice, stirring for several minutes until all the rice kernels are coated with butter. Gradually stir in the Beef Stock. Bring to a boil, then immediately lower the heat, and simmer until the rice is tender. Adjust the seasoning.

Beat the egg yolks, add the sour cream, and beat again. Gradually add 1 cup of soup to the egg yolk mixture. Blend thoroughly and slowly stir into the hot soup in the kettle. Serve immediately, sprinkled with the remaining 2 tablespoons of herbs.

Farm-Style Vegetable Soup

8 tablespoons (1 stick) butter

1 large onion, coarsely chopped

4 medium carrots, chopped

2 leeks, coarsely chopped

2 stalks celery, chopped

1 clove garlic, minced

4 medium tomatoes, peeled,
  seeded, and chopped

2 tablespoons minced parsley

¼ pound salt pork, finely chopped

2 large potatoes, peeled and
  diced

1 cup dried lentils

½ pound green beans, broken
  into 1-inch pieces

2 quarts Beef Stock (page 108)
  or canned beef bouillon

Salt and black pepper

2 summer squash, coarsely
  chopped

2 zucchini, coarsely chopped

1 cup shelled green peas

½ cup pastina

Croutons

SERVES EIGHT TO TEN

Heat the butter in a deep soup kettle. Sauté the onion, carrots, leeks, celery, and garlic until the onions turn golden. Add the tomatoes, parsley, and salt pork and cook for 5 minutes, stirring occasionally. Stir in the potatoes, lentils, and green beans.

Cover the kettle and simmer the vegetables over very low heat for 20 minutes, stirring from time to time. Add the stock, season with salt and pepper, and bring the soup to a boil. Lower the heat, re-cover the kettle, and simmer the soup for 1½ hours, stirring once in a while, and adding hot water from time to time if the soup becomes too thick.

Add the squash, zucchini, peas, and pastina and cook 30 minutes more. Serve the soup piping hot, garnished with croutons.

Vegetarian Bouillabaisse***

2 tablespoons vegetable oil
1 large onion, chopped
3 large potatoes, peeled and thickly sliced
3 cups boiling water
1½ cups shelled peas

¼ teaspoon dried thyme
Generous pinch saffron
Salt
2 1-inch strips orange zest
4 eggs
Fried Bread (page 359)

SERVES FOUR

Heat the oil in a large, deep skillet, and sauté the onion until soft and transparent. Add the potato slices; cook briefly on each side without letting them brown. Pour the boiling water over the vegetables, stir in the peas, thyme, saffron, salt, and orange zest. Cover the skillet and cook over medium heat until the potatoes are barely tender.

Push a few of the potato slices to the side of the skillet, and crack 1 egg into the broth. Repeat with the remaining eggs, making room for each by pushing the potatoes aside. Cook only long enough for the eggs to poach. To serve, place a slice of Fried Bread in each soup bowl, top with a poached egg, and ladle the soup and vegetables over all.

Sauerkraut-Gingersnap Soup***

2 pounds sauerkraut

10 cups Beef Stock (page 108) or canned beef bouillon

3 large onions, chopped

6 thick slices from a slab of bacon, diced

2 medium potatoes

1 tablespoon tomato paste

½ teaspoon fennel seeds

½ teaspoon caraway seeds

1 teaspoon paprika

½ teaspoon salt

1 cup diced baked or boiled ham

8 gingersnaps, crumbled

SERVES EIGHT

Drain the sauerkraut and simmer it in the stock for 30 minutes. Sauté the onions and bacon until the onions are transparent. Peel and grate the potatoes and soak them for 5 minutes in cold water.

Add the onions, bacon, drained potatoes, tomato paste, fennel seeds, caraway seeds, paprika, and salt to the sauerkraut mixture. Cover and boil gently for 30 minutes more. The soup may be refrigerated overnight and reheated the following day, if desired.

Ten minutes before serving, add the ham and gingersnaps to the soup.

Red Wine Borscht***

1¼ pounds beets, peeled and grated

10 cups Clarified Beef Stock (page 110) or canned beef bouillon

1 cup dry red wine

⅓ cup lemon juice

⅓ cup granulated sugar

Salt and black pepper

1 cup sour cream

8 scallions, chopped

8 small potatoes, boiled and peeled (optional)

SERVES EIGHT

Place the grated beets in a large saucepan, add the stock and red wine, and bring to a boil. Cover the saucepan, lower the heat, and simmer until the beets are tender, adding more liquid if necessary.

Stir in the lemon juice and sugar, adjusting the amounts of these ingredients to make a sweet and sour borscht to your taste. Season with salt and pepper and serve hot, topping each portion with a dab of sour cream and chopped scallion. If desired, serve with a boiled potato in each soup bowl.

Cold Beery Borscht***

1 pound beets, peeled and grated

1 pound beet greens, chopped

6 cups Clarified Beef Stock (page 110) or canned beef bouillon

3 cups beer

1 pound cooked and then shelled shrimp

1 large cucumber, peeled and chopped

7 scallions, including 3 inches green top, chopped

5 tablespoons minced dill

2 lemons, thinly sliced

5 cups sour cream

Salt and black pepper

5 hard-boiled eggs, coarsely chopped

SERVES EIGHT TO TEN

Place the grated beets and chopped beet greens in a saucepan with the stock. Simmer, covered, over low heat until the beets are tender. Remove from the heat and cool. Stir in the beer, shrimp, cucumber, scallions, dill, lemon slices, and sour cream. Season with salt and pepper to taste, and chill the soup for several hours. Serve cold, garnished with the chopped hard-boiled eggs.

Lamb and Buttermilk Soup

2 pounds lamb bones
1 pound piece lean lamb
2 stalks celery with leaves,
  chopped
2 leeks, chopped
1 white turnip, peeled and diced
2 small carrots, thinly sliced
2 onions, coarsely chopped

2½ quarts water
2½ cups buttermilk
4 tablespoons butter
4 tablespoons flour
  Salt and black pepper
2 tablespoons minced parsley

SERVES EIGHT

Rinse the lamb bones and meat, and place them in a soup kettle. Add the celery, leeks, turnip, carrots, onions, and water. Bring to a boil slowly, skimming frequently. Lower the heat and simmer, uncovered, for 2 hours.

Remove the bones and set them aside. Remove the piece of lamb, chop it, and set it aside. Strain the soup and discard the vegetables. Return the bones to the kettle with the strained broth and simmer until the broth is reduced to 5½ cups.

Bring the buttermilk to room temperature. Melt the butter in a large skillet. Stir in the flour, add the buttermilk, and stir constantly until thick and smooth. Discard the lamb bones and add the broth, 1 cup at a time, to the buttermilk mixture, stirring well after each addition. Adjust the seasoning, stir in the reserved lamb, and simmer for 8 to 10 minutes. Serve hot, sprinkled with minced parsley.

Lamb and Yoghurt Soup

1 cup raw long-grain rice
5 tablespoons butter
1 large onion, chopped
7 scallions, including 3 inches
  green top, chopped
¼ cup chopped mint
1¼ pounds ground lamb

¾ teaspoon ground cuminseed
  Minced garlic to taste
  Salt and black pepper
5 cups Chicken Stock (page 111)
  or canned chicken broth
5 cups yoghurt
1 cup sour cream

SERVES EIGHT

[130]

Cook rice according to package directions. Heat the butter in a large skillet and sauté the onion, scallions, and mint until the vegetables are soft. Add the ground lamb, season with cuminseed, and minced garlic, salt, and pepper to taste. Continue to cook the mixture, stirring occasionally, until the meat is nicely browned, then remove from the heat.

Place the stock and yoghurt in large soup kettle, stir until well blended, and add the cooked rice and lamb mixture. Cook over low heat, stirring constantly, until the soup is steaming hot, but not boiling. Serve hot, with a dollop of sour cream in each serving. Garnish with additional chopped fresh mint leaves if desired.

Calf's Head Soup

Typical of the more complex recipes of Early American farmhouse kitchens is this Calf's Head Soup.

1 calf's head (with brain and tongue), split

½ pound salt pork

2 tablespoons plus 1 teaspoon salt

3 tablespoons white vinegar

1 cup pearl barley

6 black peppercorns

10 whole cloves

¼ teaspoon mace

3 sprigs parsley

8 stalks celery

4 leeks

2 medium carrots

3 small turnips

3 medium onions

2 tablespoons minced parsley

SERVES TEN TO TWELVE

Wash the calf's head and place it, along with the salt pork, in a large kettle. Cover with cold water to which 2 tablespoons of salt have been added, and soak for 3 hours. Remove the brains, place them in a bowl, sprinkle with the vinegar, and let stand for 3 hours, turning once. Drain the head and salt pork and place in a large soup kettle. Rinse the barley and add to the kettle along with the remaining salt, peppercorns, cloves, mace, and parsley. Pour in water to cover and bring to the boil, skimming the foam. When the foam no longer rises, lower the heat, partially cover the kettle, and simmer for 2 hours.

Coarsely chop the celery, leeks, carrots, turnips, and onions. Add the vegetables to the kettle along with more water, if necessary, to cover the calf's head once again. Continue to simmer, covered, for 1½ hours.

Cover the brains with cold water and bring to a slow boil, lower the heat, and simmer for 10 minutes. Drain, clean, chop, and add to the soup. Remove the calf's head and salt pork from the soup and slice the meat. Skin and slice the tongue. Slice the salt pork. Return the meat to the kettle and serve the soup sprinkled with minced parsley.

Cheddar Cheese and Walnut Soup

3 tablespoons butter
4 cups heavy cream
4 cloves garlic, crushed

4 cups grated cheddar cheese
4 egg yolks
¼ cup chopped walnuts

SERVES EIGHT

Bring water to the boil in the bottom of a double boiler. Place the butter, 2 cups cream, and the garlic in the top of the double boiler. Add the cheese and stir over hot water until melted. Beat the remaining 2 cups cream with the egg yolks, add to the cheese mixture, and stir until hot. Do not allow the soup to boil. Serve immediately, topped with the chopped nuts.

Broccoli and Egg Soup

1 pound broccoli
1 cup shredded lettuce
1 tablespoon butter
1 teaspoon white vinegar
2 cups Easy White Sauce (page 238)

4 hard-boiled eggs, chopped
Salt and black pepper
White Bread Croutons (page 361)
Grated parmesan cheese

SERVES EIGHT

Rinse the broccoli, discard the outer leaves, and peel the thick stalks. Place the vegetable, stem down, in a large saucepan, add water to cover the stems but not the florets, and cook until the florets are tender when pinched between thumb and forefinger. Remove the broccoli from the pan, reserving the water. Slice the stalks, set aside the tender florets, and add the sliced stalks to the water in the pan. Boil until the water is reduced to 2 cups, then discard the sliced stalks because their flavor is already concentrated in the water.

Sauté the shredded lettuce briefly in the butter and vinegar until wilted. Chop the broccoli florets, reserving several whole ones for use as garnish. Stir the white sauce, lettuce, chopped broccoli, and chopped eggs into the reduced broccoli water. Cook, stirring occasionally, over low heat until the chowder heats through. Season with salt and pepper to taste. Serve hot, garnished with the reserved florets. Pass bowls of croutons and cheese separately.

Poor Man's Chowder

6 *strips lean bacon*
3 *medium onions, sliced*
8 *frankfurters, sliced*
4 *large potatoes, peeled and cut*
  into eighths
2 *cups corn kernels*
2½ *teaspoons salt*
¾ *teaspoon black pepper*

1 *teaspoon caraway seeds*
1½ *teaspoons dried thyme*
2 *beef bouillon cubes*
2 *cans beef bouillon*
2 *cups water*
1 *cup dry white wine*
4 *cups milk*

SERVES EIGHT

Place the bacon in a deep, heavy kettle and sauté until brown and crisp. Drain on paper towels and reserve. Brown the onions and frankfurters in the bacon fat until the onions are golden. Add the potatoes, corn kernels, salt, pepper, caraway seeds, thyme, bouillon cubes, beef bouillon, and water. Bring to a boil, cover, and simmer gently for 30 minutes, or until the potatoes are tender. Stir in the wine and the milk, but do not allow the soup to boil. Serve immediately, sprinkled with the reserved chopped bacon.

Catfish Chowder

4 *pounds catfish*
2 *large onions, finely chopped*
2 *large cloves garlic, finely*
  chopped
3 *medium tomatoes, peeled,*
  seeded, and chopped
8 *medium potatoes, peeled and*
  cubed

½ *cup finely chopped celery*
½ *cup finely chopped fennel*
½ *cup minced parsley*
⅓ *teaspoon grated orange zest*
  Salt and black pepper
⅓ *cup olive oil*
8 *slices buttered toast*

SERVES EIGHT

Skin the catfish, clean, and cut into 1½ inch pieces. Place in a deep kettle. Arrange the vegetables and herbs over the fish and sprinkle with orange zest, salt, and pepper. Pour in the olive oil before adding water to cover. Bring to the boil, lower the heat to medium, cover, and cook until the potatoes are tender. To serve, put a slice of buttered toast in each soup bowl and pour in the chowder.

Trout Chowder

9 cups Fish Stock (page 112)

6 medium potatoes, peeled and diced

2½ pounds trout

1½ teaspoons salt

⅛ teaspoon black pepper

⅓ teaspoon chili powder

1½ tablespoons chopped chives

2 tablespoons butter

SERVES EIGHT

Put the Fish Stock in a large soup kettle, add the potatoes, and simmer for 20 minutes. Skin and bone the trout and cut into 1½ inch chunks. Add the fish to the kettle, together with the salt, pepper, and chili powder. Simmer for 10 minutes. Adjust the seasoning and serve hot, garnished with chopped chives and bits of butter.

Cold Pumpkin Soup

3 cups canned pumpkin puree (or pumpkin prepared as instructed on page 308)

3 cups milk

¼ cup honey

¼ cup maple syrup

¼ cup orange juice

¼ teaspoon grated nutmeg

2 cups heavy cream

SERVES EIGHT

Stir the pumpkin puree, milk, honey, and maple syrup together in a heavy saucepan. Cook for 2 minutes over low heat, then add the orange juice, 1 tablespoon at a time. Continue to simmer for 3 minutes more, stirring constantly. Chill the soup.

To serve, whip the cream and fold half of it into the cold soup. Dollop spoonsful of the remaining cream into each serving.

Elsie Dunlop's Honey-Buttermilk Soup

5½ cups buttermilk	*1 cinnamon stick*
3½ cups milk	*½ cup honey*
3 tablespoons tapioca	*¼ cup granulated sugar*
1 tablespoon lemon juice	*Salt*

SERVES EIGHT

Place the buttermilk, milk, tapioca, lemon juice, and cinnamon in a soup kettle. Simmer over low heat for 1 hour, stirring frequently to prevent burning. Stir in the honey, sugar, and salt, stirring until well mixed. Remove the cinnamon stick and serve immediately.

Blackberry Soup

The perfect dessert for a sizzling summer's night is this chilled berry soup.

1 quart blackberries	*1⅓ cups granulated sugar*
2½ cups light sweet wine	*½ cup blackberry brandy*
1 2-inch cinnamon stick	*3 cups sour cream*

SERVES EIGHT

Wash the berries, pick them over, and discard any bad ones. Reserve ½ cup of the largest to use as garnish. Place the remaining berries in a soup kettle and add the wine, cinnamon, and sugar; bring slowly to a boil. Lower the heat and simmer 8 to 10 minutes. Strain the soup into a bowl, pressing the berries through a strainer. Chill at least 4 hours.

To serve, stir in the brandy and fold in the sour cream. Garnish with the reserved berries.

Meat, poultry, game, and fish

Meat

Farm-Cured Bacon

This recipe for curing bacon
dates back to the early 1800s.

Pack the meat in salt and allow it to remain five weeks. Then take the hams up, wash off, and wipe dry. Have some sacks made of about seven-eighths shirting, large enough to hold the hams and tie above the hock. Make a pot of sizing of equal portions of flour and corn meal, boil until thick, and dip each sack until the outside is well coated with sizing. Put the hams in bags, and tie tight with a strong twine and hang by the same in the smokehouse.

Farm-Pickled Bacon

*The smell of this old-style bacon frying makes
the good old days now!*

100 pounds side of bacon from
  fresh-killed country hogs

7½–8 pounds salt

3½ pounds dark brown sugar

3 ounces saltpeter (potassium
  nitrate)

4 gallons spring water

Place the sides of bacon on a board and rub all over with fine salt. Allow to stand for 48 hours.

Combine 7½ pounds salt, sugar, and saltpeter and stir into the water. Boil for 15 minutes. Remove from the heat, skim off any foam, and cool the brine to room temperature.

Set the sides of bacon in a clean oak barrel. Pour the brine over the bacon, setting a heavy weight on top to keep the meat underneath the brine. Bacon prepared this way will keep 1 year. When needed, have the bacon smoked in sections in a smokehouse.

Farm-Made Sausage Meat

*This tried-and-true dish from the past gets
everyone into the kitchen on time!*

20 pounds home-dressed lean pork

10 pounds clarified pork fat

1 cup salt

2 tablespoons black pepper

2 teaspoons granulated sugar

2 teaspoons ground ginger

2 tablespoons powdered sage

Cut the meat and fat into small pieces. Combine the salt, pepper, sugar, ginger, and sage and mix with the meat. Put the seasoned meat through a sausage cutter twice, then pack into sterilized jars. Cover tightly and store in a cool place until needed.

Farm-Dried Beef

*This tasty snack will sustain
you on your outings as it did our forefathers.*

2 cups salt
¼ pound dark brown sugar

1 teaspoon saltpeter (potassium nitrate)
20 pounds beef round

Place the salt, sugar, and saltpeter in a bowl and rub out any lumps with the back of a spoon. Place the meat in a large bowl, rub ⅓ of the dry ingredients into all surfaces, and allow to stand for 24 hours, turning several times.

Use another ⅓ of the salt, sugar, and saltpeter mixture to rub into the meat on the second day. Set the meat aside again for 24 hours, turning occasionally. Repeat the process, using the remaining dry mixture and letting the meat stand, turning occasionally, for 24 hours. Keep the meat in the bowl for another week. At the end of this time, hang the meat up until it no longer drips, then wrap in clean muslin. Store in a cool place. If the beef becomes hard after long storage, soak it in cold water, wipe it dry, and wrap in clean muslin before storing again.

Farm-Cured Ham

*Like the country folk of the past, you
can enjoy this time-ripened delight.*

3 pounds salt
½ pound brown sugar
100 pounds ham
3 ounces saltpeter (potassium nitrate)

½ cup black pepper
Additional salt
Cayenne

Combine 1 pound salt with the brown sugar and saltpeter. Rub this mixture over the hams and allow to stand for 24 hours.

Mix the remaining 2 pounds salt with the black pepper and rub into the hams. Let the meat stand for 5 days. Use as much salt as necessary to rub over the hams again, then set the meat aside for 30 days.

Brush the salt from the meat and have the hams smoked in a smokehouse, or smoke them yourself for 10 days, using hickory wood. Each ham should be rubbed all over with cayenne after it has been smoked, then carefully wrapped in brown paper. To finish the process, wrap the hams in muslin bags and hang with the hocks down. Hams prepared this way will keep indefinitely, and time will improve their quality and flavor.

Baked Hams

Hams have always been associated with the best of country cooking. Time was that every farm family bred, fed, slaughtered, cured, and smoked its own hogs and took pride in the unique and subtle flavors of their hams. Nowadays, relatively few farmers have the time, skill, or equipment to carry out all of these procedures themselves. There are still many kinds of country-cured hams available however, each with its own distinctive and tantalizing flavor.

Country hams differ in taste because of the type of feed given to the hogs or the method of smoking. Virginia hams, of which the most famous is probably Smithfield, differ from the country hams in neighboring Maryland, Tennessee, or North Carolina, as well as from the country hams of Missouri or Pennsylvania.

If country hams are available, by all means use them. Any of the commercial hams, however, will do in the following recipes. Take care with any ham, except for the precooked variety, to cook it through thoroughly. To test for doneness, pull the small bone lying alongside the large bone at the shank end. If it comes out easily, the ham is done.

Baked Country Ham

Follow the directions that come with the country ham, or prepare the ham according to the following directions before glazing and baking.

Soak the ham for 24 to 48 hours, using several changes of water, then scrub it well with a stiff brush, rinsing thoroughly. Preheat the oven to 325 degrees. Remove the skin and set the ham, fat side down, in a roasting pan. Add enough liquid: beer, champagne, ginger ale, cider, or water, so the pan is ¾ full. Cover and bake the ham, figuring 20 minutes to the pound, in the preheated oven, turning once.

Cool the ham after taking from the oven and discard the liquid. Raise the oven temperature to 350 degrees. Combine 6 tablespoons flour, 2 teaspoons dry mustard, and 4 tablespoons dark brown sugar with enough water to make a paste. Spread the mixture evenly over the top and sides of the ham and bake for 1 hour longer. Or top with any of the following sweet or savory glazes:

Orange Glaze

1 cup light brown sugar   ¾ cup orange juice

Spread the brown sugar evenly over the surface. Raise the oven temperature to 400 degrees for 15 minutes, then reduce the heat to 350 degrees and baste frequently with the orange juice during the remaining 45 minutes of baking.

Cider Glaze

½ cup cider   ½ cup cider vinegar
½ cup molasses

Combine these ingredients and baste the ham frequently with the mixture during the last hour of baking.

Beer Glaze

1 cup brown or maple sugar   2 tablespoons cider vinegar
1 teaspoon dry mustard   Beer

Mix the sugar and mustard with the vinegar. Add enough beer to make a smooth paste. Score the ham fat in a diamond pattern with a sharp knife. Spread the glaze over the ham, stud with cloves, and continue to bake for 1 hour longer.

Red Cherry Glaze

1 pint jar home-canned or
   commercial cherries

1 cup currant jelly

½ teaspoon dry mustard

1 cup fruit juice (orange,
   pineapple, apple, etc.)

2 teaspoons cornstarch

⅓ cup water

Drain the juice from the cherries into a saucepan, reserving the cherries. Add the currant jelly and mustard to the juice and boil the mixture for 2 minutes. Brush the ham with the currant jelly–cherry juice glaze, then add the reserved cherries to the remaining glaze and pour into the bottom of the pan. Return the ham to the oven and bake for 1 hour longer, basting frequently with the sauce.

To serve, place the ham on a serving platter. Place the roasting pan with the remaining glaze over low heat, adding 1 cup of fruit juice. Mix the cornstarch with the water and add to the pan, stirring constantly until the sauce is clear and thick. Serve in a sauceboat along with the ham.

Baked Ham in Crust

1 ham

Pastry for 2-Crust Pie (page 418)

1 teaspoon dry mustard

4 tablespoons dark brown sugar

1 egg yolk

1 tablespoon cream or milk

Country hams require soaking before baking. Follow the package directions or soak and bake according to directions given in Baked Country Hams (page 142).

Prepare pastry and chill the dough while the ham is baking. Take the ham from the oven and cool. Make a paste with the mustard and brown sugar moistened with water, and spread this over the top and sides of the ham.

Preheat the oven to 425 degrees.

Roll out the pie dough. To transfer it easily, loosen the dough from the board with a table knife, fold the dough in half, and then fold it over again. Drape the dough carefully over the top and sides of the ham, unfolding as you go. Trim the crust evenly around the bottom.

Brush the crust with the cream or milk mixed with an egg yolk. Make a hole in the top crust to create a vent for steam. You may make decorative petals or other shapes out of any trimmed leftover crust and attach them in a pattern around the steam vent and over the crust by dipping them first in the cream-egg yolk mixture.

Bake the ham in its crust in the preheated oven for 15 to 20 minutes, then lower the heat to 350 degrees and bake for an additional 30 to 45 minutes, or until the crust is brown and the ham is heated through.

Ham Baked with Pineapple Rings

1 ham   *Maraschino cherries*
1 cup brown sugar   *Molasses*
 Pineapple rings

Press 1 cup brown sugar into the scored fat of the ham. Arrange pineapple rings, centered with maraschino cherries, over the top and sides of the ham and secure them with toothpicks. Brush the rings with molasses, and bake according to directions that come with the ham. The leftover pineapple liquid may be used in making gravy (page 240).

Dutch Fried Ham with Apple Rings

2 slices ham, 1 inch thick

2 tablespoons butter or bacon
   drippings

8 medium McIntosh apples

2 eggs

½ cup milk

1 cup all-purpose flour

½ teaspoon salt

   Vegetable oil for frying

   Brown sugar

   Ground cinnamon

SERVES EIGHT

Brown the ham slices on both sides in the butter or bacon drippings. Lower the flame and cook the meat, covered, for 30 minutes or until well done, turning the slices several times.

While the ham slices are cooking, core the apples and cut them into ½-inch slices without peeling them.

Beat the eggs lightly, then mix with the milk, flour, and salt to form a light batter.

Transfer the ham slices to a serving dish and *keep them warm*. Pour the drippings left in the skillet into another skillet and add enough oil to bring the depth to 1 inch. Do not use the pan in which the ham slices were cooked or the apple slices will stick. Dip the apple slices in the batter and fry to a golden brown. Drain briefly on paper towels before sprinkling with a mixture of brown sugar and cinnamon, and arrange around the ham. Serve immediately.

Farmhouse Ham Hock, Beans and Potatoes

String beans and potatoes rise above their
humble beginnings when they are cooked with
ham hock and served sprinkled with vinegar
in the old-fashioned manner.

1 ham hock	6 medium potatoes
2 quarts water	Salt and black pepper
1 pound green beans	Cider vinegar

SERVES EIGHT

Place the ham hock in a large kettle, cover with water, and bring to a boil. Reduce the heat, cover the kettle, and simmer the ham for 1½ hours.

Rinse the beans, snap off the ends, and place in the kettle with the ham. Cook over medium heat for 15 minutes. Peel and quarter the potatoes, and add them to the kettle. Continue to cook for 20 to 25 minutes, or until the potatoes are tender.

Remove the ham hock, cut off any bits of meat, and chop finely. Place the vegetables in a serving bowl, cover with 1 cup cooking liquid, and the minced ham. Season to taste and serve immediately with a cruet of vinegar on the side to sprinkle over the vegetables, if desired.

Frau Moyer's Ham and Apple Pie

Pastry for 2-Crust Pie (page 418)	⅛ teaspoon ground cloves
4 cups thinly sliced baked ham	⅛ teaspoon black pepper
4 cups thickly sliced, peeled, and cored apples	2 tablespoons butter
4 tablespoons dark brown sugar	4 tablespoons cream
1 teaspoon flour	1 egg yolk

SERVES EIGHT

Preheat the oven to 425 degrees.

Line a 10-inch glass pie plate with crust. Arrange half the ham slices in a layer on the crust and top with a layer of apple slices. Sprinkle 2 tablespoons brown sugar, ½ teaspoon flour, and a pinch each of cloves and pepper over the apples. Dot with 1 tablespoon butter. Repeat the process, using the remaining ham and apple slices. Sprinkle with the remaining sugar, flour, and spices, and top with the remaining butter and 3 tablespoons cream. Cover with top crust which has been slashed in several places to allow steam to escape. Brush the crust with 1 tablespoon cream mixed with the egg yolk.

Bake 10 minutes in the preheated oven. Lower the heat to 350 degrees and bake 35 minutes more, or until the crust is lightly browned.

Schnitz un Knepp

*Dried apples are traditional in Pennsylvania Dutch
cooking. Their frequent inclusion in meat recipes
such as this one produces a tasty variant to
meat and potatoes. This recipe is an updated version
of an old favorite.*

HAM

5 *pounds butt end of ham, cooked, country cured, or ready to eat*	*4 cups dried sweet apples*
¼ *cup brown sugar*	

DUMPLINGS

2 *cups all-purpose flour*	1 *egg*
4 *teaspoons baking powder*	4 *tablespoons butter, melted*
1½ *teaspoons salt*	*Milk*
¼ *teaspoon black pepper*	2 *tablespoons granulated sugar*

SERVES EIGHT

Preheat the oven to 350 degrees.

Score the ham fat with a sharp knife and rub the brown sugar in on all sides. Bake the ham in the preheated oven for 2 hours, or until heated through.

One hour before the ham is ready to serve, cover the dried apples with cold water and soak for 30 minutes. Discard the fat in the bottom of the roasting pan. Pour the apples and their soaking water into the pan, and continue baking for 30 minutes.

Sift together the flour, baking powder, 1 teaspoon salt, and pepper. Beat the egg lightly and add to the dry ingredients, along with the melted butter and enough milk to make a fairly stiff batter. Bring 1 quart of water to a boil in a large kettle, add the sugar and ½ teaspoon salt. Drop in the dumpling batter by table-spoonsful. Cover the kettle tightly and cook the dumplings at a low boil for 15 minutes.

Meanwhile, slice the ham. To make a thin gravy, you may thicken the apple mixture with a little flour mixed with a bit of water. To serve, arrange the ham slices on a platter and top with the apple gravy and dumplings.

Philadelphia Ham Slices with Red Currant Glaze

3 center ham slices, 2 inch thick
4 shallots, finely chopped
3 tablespoons vegetable oil
¾ cup currant jelly

¾ cup ketchup
2 tablespoons lemon juice
2½ teaspoons prepared English mustard

SERVES EIGHT

Score the fat on the edges of the ham slices to prevent the slices from curling. Broil the ham 8 minutes on each side, turning once. If the ham slices are the ready-to-eat variety broil only 4 minutes on each side.

Meanwhile, sauté the shallots in the oil for 3 minutes. Add the jelly, ketchup, lemon juice, and mustard, and cook 1 minute. Brush the ham slices with the mixture. Broil 7 minutes longer, turn the slices over, brush again with the glaze, and continue to broil for 5 minutes or until well done. Boil the remaining sauce over low heat for 4 to 5 minutes. Arrange the ham slices on a platter, top with the sauce, and serve immediately.

Ham with Mushrooms and Cream Sauce

4 center slices precooked ham,
  1-inch thick
6 tablespoons butter
1 cup applejack
24 medium mushrooms

4 tablespoons flour
1 cup Beef Stock (page 108) or
  canned beef bouillon
½ cup heavy cream

SERVES EIGHT

In a large skillet sauté the ham slices in 3 tablespoons butter over low heat, only long enough to brown each side. Add the applejack, and cook until most of the liquid evaporates, turning the ham slices once.

Wipe the mushrooms with a damp cloth and slice them. Sauté them gently in 3 tablespoons butter in a separate skillet.

When most of the applejack has evaporated, transfer the ham slices to a platter and keep them warm. Stir the flour into the juices remaining in the pan and mix in the stock. Simmer over low heat for 5 minutes, stirring constantly, while the mixture thickens. Add the cream and simmer for 3 minutes, or until the sauce reaches the desired consistency. Arrange the sautéed mushrooms on top of the ham slices, pour the sauce over all, and serve immediately.

Barbecued Suckling Pig

1 25-pound suckling pig, cleaned
  and dressed
  Juice of 2 oranges
  Juice of 1 lime
8 cloves garlic, crushed
¼ cup salt

2 teaspoons black pepper
2 tablespoons dried thyme
4 tablespoons butter, melted
¼ teaspoon powdered saffron

SERVES FIFTEEN

Gash the pig lightly on all sides with a sharp knife. Combine the fruit juices with the garlic, salt, pepper, and thyme. Rub this mixture in the cavity and over the outside surfaces of the pig. Refrigerate the pig overnight, covered with a dish towel.

When ready to cook, secure the pig so that it balances evenly on a revolving spit. Place a drip pan under it, and roast slowly over medium coals for 4 to 5 hours. Combine the melted butter and saffron and baste the pig frequently with the mixture.

To serve, carve into chops and slices, and accompany each serving with Sweet and Hot Barbecue Sauce (page 234).

Warning: Make a small cut at the joint and check to see that the meat is thoroughly cooked. Pork should never be eaten rare.

Roast Leg of Pork (Fresh Ham)

Leg of pork with skin left on *Thyme*
Sage

Preheat the oven to 350 degrees.

Score the skin by crisscrossing with a sharp knife in a diamond pattern.

Rub the skin of the roast lightly with sage or thyme. Place the leg of pork skin side up on a rack in a roasting pan. Bake in the preheated oven for 25 to 30 minutes per pound, or until well done. Increase the oven temperature to 425 degrees and brown the skin to a nice crispness. Skim off most of the fat in the pan and make Basic Brown Gravy (page 241).

Roast Loin of Pork with Maple Sugar Glaze

Loin of pork (about 8 pounds)
Salt and black pepper
¾ cup water
1 medium onion, chopped
2 stalks celery with leaves, chopped

1 cup orange juice
Juice of ½ lemon
¾ cup maple sugar or light brown sugar

SERVES EIGHT

Preheat the oven to 350 degrees.

Wipe the loin with a damp cloth, sprinkle it with salt and pepper, and place it fat side up in a roasting pan with the water. Add the onion, celery, orange juice, and lemon juice. Roast the pork in the preheated oven until well done, figuring 25 to 30 minutes per the pound. Pork must *never* be served pink or even slightly underdone.

Baste the loin frequently with the juices in the pan. During the last 20 minutes of baking raise the oven temperature to 450 degrees. Remove the roast and press the sugar into the top and sides with the back of a spoon. Return the roast to the oven for 15 minutes. Serve the pork hot accompanied, if you wish, by a sauceboat of Sweet and Hot Barbecue Sauce (page 234).

Old-Fashioned Pork Chops with Kraut and Cider***

*Fried sauerkraut sweetened with cider
is a wonderful accompaniment to pork chops.*

16 thick and meaty pork chops
Salt and black pepper
Flour

6 tablespoons butter
3 quarts sauerkraut
1 cup cider

SERVES EIGHT

[151]

Rub the chops with salt and pepper, then dredge them in flour.

Fry in melted butter over medium heat in 2 skillets until the chops are well done and golden brown on both sides. Remove the chops and set them aside to keep warm.

Drain the sauerkraut well and place 1½ quarts in each skillet. Add ½ cup of cider to each skillet and cook over medium heat until the cider boils away and the sauerkraut browns. Arrange the hot pork chops on a large platter, surround with the sauerkraut, and serve piping hot.

Shartlesville Roast Spareribs with Sauerkraut

9 pounds spareribs

3 quarts sauerkraut

4 McIntosh apples, peeled, cored, and sliced

3 tablespoons dark brown sugar

2 teaspoons caraway seeds

¾ cup honey

⅓ cup ketchup

SERVES EIGHT

Preheat the oven to 375 degrees.

Place the ribs in a large roasting pan and bake for 1½ hours in the preheated oven. Remove the ribs and discard the fat in the roasting pan. Raise the oven heat to 425 degrees.

Drain the sauerkraut, reserving ¼ cup sauerkraut juice. Spread the kraut and the apple slices on the bottom of the roasting pan, sprinkle with ¼ cup sauerkraut juice, brown sugar, and caraway seeds, and replace the ribs in the pan.

Brush the ribs with ¼ cup honey and bake for 45 minutes. Lift the ribs and stir the kraut with the juices in the pan. Replace the ribs and brush with ½ cup honey mixed with the ketchup. Bake at 500 degrees for 15 minutes. Stir the kraut and arrange it on the platter around the ribs. Serve immediately.

Salt Pork, Beans, and Hominy

*Up-North beans and down-South hominy
get together in this unusual dish.*

½ pound navy or pea beans

1 teaspoon marjoram

⅛ teaspoon black pepper

⅓ pound salt pork

2 sweet red peppers

2 green peppers

¾ cup chopped onion

1 20-ounce can hominy

SERVES EIGHT

Rinse the beans, cover with water, and let stand overnight. Drain the beans and place them in a large kettle. Add fresh water to cover. Stir in the marjoram and pepper. Cut the salt pork into strips and arrange on the top. Bring the mixture to a boil, lower the heat, and cook, covered, for 3½ to 4 hours. Add water if necessary to keep the beans from scorching.

Wash the peppers, discarding the stems, seeds, and white fibers. Cut into ½-inch strips. Remove the salt pork from the kettle and discard. Stir the pepper strips, chopped onion, and well-drained hominy into the beans and continue to cook over very low heat for 35 to 40 minutes. Most of the liquid will evaporate. Serve very hot.

Berks County Pickled Pigs' Feet

16 pigs' feet

2 teaspoons baking soda

   Boiling water

1 teaspoon salt

1 green pepper, seeded and chopped

5 stalks celery, chopped

5 medium carrots, chopped

3 small bay leaves

1 teaspoon whole black peppercorns

2¼ cups white vinegar

1 cup dry white wine

2 egg whites with their shells

SERVES EIGHT

[153]

Scrub the pigs' feet well in several changes of water, then soak them for 15 minutes in enough cold water mixed with the baking soda to cover.

Drain the pigs' feet, pat them dry, and cover with boiling water and salt. Bring the water to a rolling boil, lower the heat, and simmer for 1½ to 2 hours, skimming from time to time to remove the scum that rises to the surface.

Add the green pepper along with the celery, carrots, bay leaves and peppercorns to the pigs' feet. Raise the heat and boil for 30 minutes. Add the vinegar and wine. Cover the pot, lower the heat, and simmer for 1½ hours.

Strain the broth and refrigerate it and the pigs' feet separately. After several hours the fat in the broth will rise to the surface and harden. It can then be easily removed. To clarify the broth after the fat has been removed, bring it to a boil with the lightly beaten egg whites and the egg shells. Boil several minutes, then lower the heat and simmer for 25 minutes. Add salt to taste and strain the broth through a clean dish towel.

Chill the broth and serve it cold with the chilled pigs' feet.

How to Render Lard

Fresh or leaf lard is obtained from the leaf fat taken from the main portions of a freshly killed hog. After butchering and splitting the hog in half, remove the thin skin from the sides and slice the fat away from each set of ribs. Cut the fat into small pieces and wash it well. Drain the pieces and press out as much water as possible.

You will need a very large pot, at least 4 gallons in capacity, to cure the fat. Place 4 quarts of water in the pot, add the fat pieces, and cook at a rolling boil until the solid part of the fat (or cracklings) begins to crisp or turn light brown. Lower the heat and continue to cook until the cracklings sink to the bottom of the pot. Strain out these cracklings and use them as flavoring, crumbled in sliced fried potatoes, or hot between slices of bread as a sandwich. Drain off the water, place the lard in crocks or pans, and refrigerate.

Spit-Roasted Rib Eye of Beef

1 8-pound boneless rib eye of
  beef
⅓ cup coarsely cracked black
  peppercorns
½ teaspoon ground cardamom

¾ cup lemon juice
¾ cup soy sauce
¼ cup ketchup
4 garlic cloves, crushed

SERVES EIGHT

Trim all fat from the beef. Combine the cracked peppercorns with the cardamom and press this mixture against all sides of the beef, making sure that as much adheres as possible. Prepare a marinade by blending the lemon juice, soy sauce, ketchup, and garlic. Marinate the beef overnight in this mixture, turning occasionally. Balance the roast evenly on a spit and rotate over coals until medium rare, about 2 hours.

Country Beef Slice Casserole***

3 pounds rump of beef
  Salt and pepper
3 tablespoons butter
2 tablespoons vegetable oil
2 large onions, coarsely chopped
4 stalks celery, coarsely chopped
10 large mushrooms, coarsely
  chopped
1 medium bay leaf
  Flour

Dried sage
Dried thyme
Grated zest of 1 small lemon
2½ tablespoons cider vinegar
1¼ cups beer
3½ cups Clarified Beef Stock
  (page 110) or canned beef
  bouillon
2½ tablespoons tomato paste
1½ teaspoons granulated sugar

SERVES EIGHT

Cut the beef into ¼-inch slices and flatten with a mallet or the side of a rolling pin. Season each flattened slice with salt and pepper. Heat 1 tablespoon butter and 2 tablespoons oil in the bottom of a large dutch oven and brown the beef, a few slices at a time. Transfer the meat to a platter as each is browned. Heat the remaining 2 tablespoons butter in a skillet and gently sauté the chopped onions, celery, and mushrooms for 2 minutes. Remove from the heat.

Place the bay leaf in the bottom of a large casserole with a tight-fitting cover. Arrange a layer of beef slices in the casserole, and top with a layer of sautéed vegetables. Sprinkle ½ teaspoon of flour, a pinch each of sage and thyme, and a little grated lemon zest over the vegetables. Continue building layers in this manner until these ingredients are used.

Preheat the oven to 325 degrees.

Pour off any fat left in the dutch oven and add the vinegar to the pot, stirring well to scrape up any brown particles sticking to the sides. Add the beer, stock, tomato paste, and sugar. Bring the mixture to a boil, and simmer over low heat for 5 minutes. Pour this hot sauce over the meat and vegetables. Cover the casserole, and bake for 2 hours in the preheated oven.

Lehigh County Stuffed Beef Rolls***

2 pounds rump of beef
Salt and black pepper
2 medium potatoes, peeled and cubed
¼ pound sausage meat
1 medium onion, chopped
3 tablespoons dry bread crumbs
5 tablespoons butter
1 egg

Bacon
1 tablespoon oil
1 stalk celery, chopped
4 small carrots, thinly sliced
1 cup dry red wine
2–3 cups beef consommé
24 medium mushrooms
16 small white onions, peeled

SERVES EIGHT

Cut the beef into slices ¼ inch thick and flatten each slice with a wooden mallet or the side of a rolling pin. Season the slices with salt and pepper. Place the cubed potatoes in a saucepan and cover with water. Bring to a boil and cook until tender. Meanwhile, crumble the sausage meat and brown it lightly in a skillet over medium heat. Add the chopped onion to the skillet, and cook until the sausage is crisp and the onions are golden. Mix in the bread crumbs and continue to cook 3 minutes more.

Remove the skillet from the heat. Drain the potatoes and mash them with 1 tablespoon butter, then add to the sausage mixture. Beat the egg lightly and blend it into the sausage and potatoes. Season with salt and pepper to taste.

Arrange 1 tablespoon of potato-sausage stuffing on each flattened piece of beef. Roll up each beef slice and secure it with a strip of bacon. Heat 2 tablespoons butter and 1 tablespoon oil in an oven-proof casserole, and brown the beef rolls on all sides, taking care when you turn them that they stay tightly closed. When the beef rolls are browned, add the celery and carrots to the casserole. Add the wine and enough consommé to cover the beef. Bring to a boil and cook, covered, over very low heat for 2 to 2½ hours, or until the beef is tender but not falling apart.

Sauté the onions in 2 tablespoons of butter until lightly browned. Add the mushrooms and sauté the vegetables 5 minutes. Add these to the casserole during the last 30 minutes of cooking. Just before serving, skim off any excess fat from the top of the casserole.

Potted Rump Roast
with Tomato–Sour Cream Gravy

*Partially prepare this tasty dish the day before
your party and refrigerate it overnight for a minimum
of work on dinner-party day.*

1 slice salt pork, 2 by 3 inches

2 tablespoons vegetable oil

2 medium onions, sliced

5 pounds rump roast, tied in a roll

⅛ teaspoon ground cloves

¼ teaspoon ground ginger

1 cup water

1½ tablespoons bottled beef concentrate

1 10¾-ounce can tomato soup, undiluted

1 tablespoon granulated sugar

1 tablespoon lemon juice

¼ cup sour cream

SERVES SIX TO EIGHT

Fry the salt pork in the oil for 3 minutes in a deep, heavy kettle. Separate the onion slices into rings, and sauté them with the salt pork until the vegetable is soft and translucent. Rub the roast with the cloves and ginger, then place it on top of the onions in the kettle. Add the water, cover tightly, and cook over a low flame for 4½ to 5 hours, or until the meat is very tender

Remove the roast from the kettle, wrap it in aluminum foil, and set aside. Remove and discard the salt pork. Allow the gravy in the kettle to cool, then refrigerate overnight until the fat congeals. Remove the fat and measure 1 cup of gravy. Reserve remaining gravy for later use in seasonings or stews. Mix the cup of gravy in the kettle with the bottled beef concentrate, tomato soup, sugar, and lemon juice. Bring to a low boil, reduce the heat to very low, then stir in the sour cream. Cut the meat into ½-inch slices, return to the kettle, and simmer over very low flame in the thickened gravy for 1 hour, covered. Adjust the seasonings. Serve hot, accompanied by noodles or fluffy Potato Pancakes (page 300).

Aunt Hannah's Brisket
with Sauerkraut and Dumplings

3 tablespoons butter	3 quarts sauerkraut
2 large onions, thinly sliced	2 cups all-purpose flour
4½ pounds brisket of beef	1¼ teaspoons baking powder
3½ teaspoons salt	Milk
¼ teaspoon black pepper	

SERVES EIGHT

Melt 2 tablespoons butter in a large heavy kettle or dutch oven and brown the onion slices. Rub ½ to ¾ teaspoon salt and the pepper into the meat, and brown on all sides with the onions.

Drain the sauerkraut, reserving ½ cup of liquid. Spread the sauerkraut around the brisket, pour in the reserved liquid, and cook over low heat for 2 hours, or until the meat is tender.

Sift together the flour, baking powder, and remaining ¾ teaspoon of salt. Work in the remaining 1 tablespoon butter with your fingers and add just enough milk to make a stiff batter. Turn the dough onto a heavily floured board and roll out ½ inch thick. Cut into 2-inch squares, triangles, or rounds. Bring 1½ quarts water, to which 2 teaspoons salt have been added, to a boil, and drop in the dumplings. Reduce the heat and cook the dumplings at a low boil for 20 to 25 minutes.

While the dumplings are cooking, remove and slice the meat. Sauté the sauerkraut over a medium flame until browned. Do not scorch. To serve, arrange the sauerkraut on a platter, place slices of meat on top, and surround with the dumplings.

Nine-Day Beef

This unique beef dish takes 9 days to prepare
but requires very little time each day.
Wrapped in aluminum foil and refrigerated,
it will keep for several weeks.

6–8 *pounds rump of beef*	*2 tablespoons whole allspice*
1 *cup dark brown sugar*	⅛ *teaspoon ground cloves*
¾ *cup coarse (Kosher) salt*	1½ *cups water*
1 *cup dried juniper berries*	*Onions*
2 *tablespoons whole black peppercorns*	

SERVES EIGHT

Rub all sides of the meat with the brown sugar, using the fingertips to work it in. Place the meat in a large covered dish and store it in the refrigerator for 2 days. Put the salt, juniper berries, peppercorns, allspice, and cloves into a mortar. Use the pestle to pound the ingredients until the peppercorns and allspice are finely crushed.

For the next 9 days, work 2½ tablespoons of this spice mixture into all sides of the meat each day. On the tenth day, rinse the beef under cold, running water. Place the beef in a covered casserole, add 1½ cups water, and bake in a 275-degree oven for 5 hours, or until the meat is tender. Remove from the oven, cool, and wrap well in aluminum foil. Place a weight on top of the foil-wrapped meat and refrigerate for 12 hours. To serve, cut this spicy beef into thin slices and surround with very thinly sliced raw onion.

How to Make Jerky

If you have access to a smokehouse, or have your own smoker, excess game or beef may be preserved as jerky, which has excellent keeping qualities and needs no refrigeration. Jerking means smoking or sun-drying meats, and in pioneer days was the method most commonly used for preservation of deer meat, the traditional source of jerky for our pioneer forefathers.

Cut the meat into thin 12-inch strips, about ½ inch thick and 1 inch wide. Follow the instructions that come with your smoker. Use hickory or maple sticks whenever available. Aspen leaves added to the fire also lend good flavor to the meat. Keep the fire smoldering for at least 12 hours, adding more wood from time to time as needed. Jerky made this way will last indefinitely and may be used in several ways. Eat it just the way it is, or soak it in water for 4 or 5 hours, cut it up, then boil it for soup or stew meat for an additional 2 to 3 hours. On a wilderness trip, nature will supply the vegetables to perk up the stew or soup. Use dandelion or violet leaves, grape leaves, wild onions, or juniper berries.

Pemmican, a traditional North American Indian and Eskimo staple, makes a nutritious snack for hiking or camping. Add hot fat, suet, raisins, and dried berries to the prepared and powdered jerky strips, and cut into cakes when cool.

Old-Fashioned Beef Stew with Dumplings

⅓ cup plus 3 tablespoons flour
¼ teaspoon black pepper
4 pounds lean stewing beef
¼ cup vegetable oil
8 cups Beef Stock (page 108) or canned beef bouillon
1 teaspoon salt
8 large potatoes, peeled and quartered

4 large onions, quartered
4 medium turnips, peeled
¼ teaspoon dried thyme
⅛ teaspoon powdered sage
¼ cup water
2 teaspoons bottled beef concentrate
Basic Dumpling Batter (page 227)

SERVES EIGHT

Work ⅓ cup flour and the pepper into the meat. Place in a heavy kettle and brown the meat in the oil over high heat. Stir in the stock and bring to a boil. Cover the kettle, lower the heat, and simmer for 3 hours.

Add the salt, vegetables, thyme, and sage and cook at a low boil for 20 minutes, or until the potatoes are nearly tender. Mix the remaining 3 tablespoons flour and water to a smooth paste, add a few tablespoons of the hot cooking liquid, and stir this rapidly into the stew along with the beef concentrate. Stir constantly until the liquid thickens. Adjust the seasonings and bottled concentrate to suit your taste.

Drop the Dumpling Batter by spoonsful into the bubbling stew. The dumplings should not touch each other. Cover the pot and boil gently for 2 minutes. Turn the dumplings, cover once again, and boil 2 minutes more. Serve immediately.

Sada Draper's Chuck Steak Stew***

2½ pounds lean chuck steak,
   1½ inches thick
3½ tablespoons vegetable oil
 18 large mushrooms
  1 large onion, chopped
  2 stalks celery, chopped
1¾ tablespoons flour
3–4 cups beef consommé
  2 tablespoons tomato paste
 ½ teaspoon granulated sugar
  2 cloves garlic

  1 bay leaf
  3 tablespoons minced parsley
 ¼ teaspoon dried thyme
   Pinch ground cloves
12 small white onions, peeled
  1 tablespoon butter
  6 small carrots, quartered
   lengthwise
  6 medium potatoes, peeled and
   cut into eighths

SERVES SIX

Sauté the chuck steak until browned on both sides in 2½ tablespoons vegetable oil in a large dutch oven. Rinse the mushrooms, chop the stems, and reserve the caps. Transfer the steak to a platter, and sauté the mushroom stems, onion, and celery in the oil until golden. Stir in the flour, and when it is thoroughly blended, gradually add 3 cups of consommé, stirring constantly until the gravy thickens. Stir in the tomato paste and sugar.

Stick toothpicks into the garlic cloves to make retrieval easy later, and add them, along with the bay leaf, to the gravy. Place the meat back in the dutch oven and sprinkle it with parsley, thyme, and cloves. Add as much of the remaining consommé as is necessary to cover the meat. Add more consommé if needed to keep the liquid at this level. Cover the dutch oven and cook the meat over low heat for 2½ hours or until tender.

In a large skillet, sauté the white onions in the butter and remaining 1 tablespoon oil until golden. Remove them with a slotted spoon, add the reserved mushroom caps, and sauté them until brown on both sides.

When the steak is tender, remove it from the dutch oven and place it in the skillet with the mushroom caps to keep warm. Add the white onions, carrots, and potatoes to the gravy, and cook, covered, over low heat until the potatoes are tender. To serve, arrange the mushroom caps over the steak on a large platter. Surround the steak with the white onions, carrots, and potatoes. Skim the fat from the gravy. Stir the mushroom juices from the skillet into the gravy and discard the garlic and bay leaf. Pour the gravy over the meat and serve.

Marinated Steak

1 medium onion, finely chopped

6 cloves garlic, crushed

3 tablespoons freshly grated horseradish

2 cups dry red wine

½ teaspoon black pepper

4 2-pound porterhouse steaks or 2 4-pound sirloins, trimmed of fat

2 tablespoons butter

SERVES EIGHT

Place the onion, garlic, horseradish, wine, and pepper in a dish large enough to hold the steaks. Marinate the steaks in this mixture for at least 4 hours, turning occasionally. Remove the steaks from the marinade, pat them dry, and spread butter on both sides of each steak. Broil the steaks to the degree of doneness you prefer, turning once. The steaks may also be prepared this way and broiled outdoors over charcoal, turning once.

Six-Layer Beef Dinner

2 cups sliced mushrooms

2 tablespoons butter

3 cups peeled and cubed potatoes

1½ pounds ground lean chuck

2 cups sliced onions

2 cups diced green pepper

1 10¾-ounce can tomato soup, undiluted, or 2 cups canned tomatoes, mashed

1 teaspoon oregano

1 teaspoon salt

SERVES EIGHT

Preheat the oven to 350 degrees.

Sauté the mushrooms in the butter until lightly browned; arrange them in a layer on the bottom of a casserole. Place the potatoes over the mushrooms, and cover them with the meat; cover the meat with the onions and peppers. Pour in the tomato soup or tomatoes and sprinkle with oregano and salt. Bake for 2 hours in the preheated oven.

Aunt Amanda's Meat Loaf

2 *tablespoons vegetable oil*
2 *medium onions, minced*
1 *large stalk celery with leaves, minced*
3 *slices soft white bread*
½ *cup milk*
3 *pounds ground lean chuck*
½ *cup ketchup*

4 *tablespoons Dijon mustard*
½ *teaspoon salt*
¼ *teaspoon black pepper*
½ *teaspoon powdered sage*
½ *teaspoon dried thyme*
2 *eggs*

SERVES SIX TO EIGHT

Heat the oil in a skillet and sauté the onions and celery gently until the onion is transparent. Trim the bread crusts and cut the slices into ½-inch cubes. Pour the milk over the bread cubes, soak thoroughly, and squeeze dry.

Crumble the meat into a bowl, add the onions, celery, bread, ketchup, mustard, and seasonings; mix lightly. Beat the eggs and add them to the meat mixture, stirring only enough to blend the ingredients.

Preheat the oven to 350 degrees.

Divide the meat mixture equally between 2 lightly oiled loaf pans. You may, if you wish, spoon ketchup and mustard in alternating stripes over the top of each meat loaf. Bake for 1 hour in the preheated oven. Pour off any excess grease, remove the loaves to a serving platter, cut into slices, and serve hot.

Pennsylvania Dutch Sauerbraten***

*A touch of the Deutsch lends old-world flavor to
this piquant potted dish featuring gravy thickened
with gingersnaps.*

5½ pounds rump or beef chuck	10 whole cloves
1 teaspoon salt	2 cups sliced carrots
¼ teaspoon black pepper	2½ cups chopped onions
2 cups white vinegar	3 tablespoons dark brown sugar
5 bay leaves	16 small gingersnaps
15 whole black peppercorns	

SERVES SIX TO EIGHT

Rinse the meat, wipe it with a damp cloth, and rub with salt and pepper. Place meat, vinegar, bay leaves, peppercorns, and cloves in an earthenware or enamel container. Add water to cover and let stand tightly covered for 6 days in refrigerator.

Remove the meat from the marinade, wipe it dry, and brown well. Add the carrots, onions, 1 tablespoon brown sugar, and 1 cup marinade, reserving the rest. Cover and cook over very low heat for 4 hours. Remove the meat and keep it hot. There should be about 1 quart of stock left in the pot. Add additional marinade if necessary to yield that amount before boiling the stock until it is slightly thickened and reduced. Add the crumbled gingersnaps and the remaining sugar to make a sweet and sour gravy. Adjust seasonings, slice the meat, and serve with hot gravy.

Farm-Corned Beef

This nineteenth-century recipe is a tradition in itself!

50 pounds freshly killed beef	¾ pound brown sugar
Water	½ ounce saltpeter (potassium nitrate)
7 cups salt	

Place the beef in a well-made, clean oak barrel. Cover with cold water to a level of several inches above the meat and let stand for 48 hours.

Drain off the water and measure it. Discard the 2-day old water. Draw an equal amount of fresh cold spring water. To every gallon of water used, add the above proportions of salt, sugar, and salt-peter. Boil the water and seasonings together for 15 minutes. Remove from heat, skim off the foam, and cool completely.

Pour over the meat in the barrel, then set a heavy weight on top to keep the meat beneath the surface of the brine. Store in a cool place such as a cellar or spring house for 10 days, after which it will be ready to use.

Glazed Corned Beef***

Corned beef is even more delicious when glazed with maple syrup.

6 pounds corned beef   ¾ cup maple syrup
  Whole cloves

SERVES EIGHT

Follow directions on the package if you buy corned beef. Otherwise, place the farm-corned beef in a kettle, add water to cover, and bring to a boil. Pour off this cooking water and add fresh water to cover. Bring to a boil, lower the heat, and simmer, covered, allowing about 40 minutes per pound.

Preheat the oven to 400 degrees.

Drain the corned beef, stud it with whole cloves, and set it on a rack in a roasting pan. Pour the maple syrup over it and bake for 15 minutes, or until nicely glazed, basting once or twice with the syrup. To serve, cut into thin slices.

Down East Corned Beef Hash

1¾ cups finely chopped cooked
   corned beef

1 small onion, minced

4 cups coarsely chopped cooked
   potatoes

¼ teaspoon powdered sage

3 tablespoons heavy cream

3 tablespoons butter

SERVES FOUR

Combine the corned beef, onions, potatoes, and sage. Stir in the cream. Heat the butter in a skillet and cook the hash over medium heat for 15 minutes on each side, or until crusty and brown, turning once. Remove from the heat, set a serving plate on top, and turn over so the hash slides out in one piece. Cut into 4 wedges and serve immediately.

Red Flannel Hash

Red Flannel Hash, a New England favorite,
combines corned beef, potatoes, and beets cooked in
the traditional manner. It is, if possible,
even more tasty than plain corned beef hash.

1⅓ cups finely chopped cooked
   corned beef

1 small onion, minced

3½ cups coarsely chopped cooked
   potatoes

1 cup coarsely chopped cooked
   beets

2 tablespoons heavy cream

3 tablespoons butter

SERVES FOUR

Mix the corned beef, onions, potatoes, and beets. Stir in the cream. Heat the butter in a skillet and cook the hash over medium heat for 15 minutes on each side, or until crusty brown, turning once. Remove from the heat, set a serving plate on top, and turn over so the hash slides out in one piece. Cut into 4 wedges and serve immediately.

Veal with Spinach Stuffing

3 tablespoons butter
1 medium onion, finely chopped
5 cups chopped spinach
1½ cups dry bread crumbs
1 egg
⅓ teaspoon salt
⅛ teaspoon celery salt

6 pounds breast of veal, with pocket
1 tablespoon oil
1 10¾-ounce can chicken broth diluted with ½ can water
1 pound mushrooms, sliced and sautéed in butter

SERVES EIGHT

Heat 1 tablespoon butter in each of 2 small skillets. Sauté the onion in one and the spinach in the other. Stir both vegetables from time to time. When the onions turn golden, mix in 1 tablespoon bread crumbs. Stir a bit while the bread crumbs brown, then mix the spinach, onions, and remaining bread crumbs together. Beat the egg lightly, and add to the skillet, along with the salt. Remove from the heat.

Pack the spinach-bread crumb stuffing into the veal pocket and sew closed. Heat 1 tablespoon each butter and oil in a large dutch oven over medium heat. Brown the veal on both sides. Add the diluted chicken broth, lower the heat, cover, and simmer until tender, about 2½ to 3 hours. Cut into slices and arrange the stuffed meat on a platter. Garnish with sautéed mushrooms and serve with Veal Gravy.

VEAL GRAVY

Remove the meat from the pan and keep it hot. Reduce the cooking liquid to 3 cups, thicken with 5 tablespoons cornstarch mixed with ¾ cup cold water and bring to a boil, stirring constantly.

Dutch Treat Veal Steaks with Green-Tomato Gravy

2 2½-pound veal slices or steaks each ¾-inch thick

Salt and black pepper

4 tablespoons plus 2 teaspoons flour

4 tablespoons butter

8 medium green tomatoes, peeled, seeded, and sliced

½ cup Clarified Beef Stock (page 110) or canned beef bouillon

½ cup light cream

SERVES EIGHT

Rub the steaks with salt and pepper and dredge them in 4 tablespoons flour. Sauté them in the butter in a large skillet until lightly browned on each side. Transfer the steaks to a broiling pan.

Add the tomato slices to the skillet and sauté until soft. Stir in the 2 teaspoons flour with a fork, mashing the tomatoes well. Add the stock and bring to a boil, stirring constantly. Lower the heat, stir in the cream and simmer, stirring, for about 4 minutes or until slightly thickened.

Broil the veal steaks for 4 minutes on each side, turning once, and transfer to a serving platter. Pour the green tomato gravy over the steaks and serve.

Veal Steaks with Tomato-Cream Sauce

2 2½-pound veal slices or steaks each ¾-inch thick

Salt and black pepper

4 tablespoons flour

4 tablespoons butter

6 medium tomatoes, peeled, seeded, and sliced

1 cup heavy cream

Pinch grated nutmeg

Pinch dried thyme

SERVES EIGHT

Rub the steaks with salt and pepper and dredge them in flour. Sauté them in the butter in a large skillet until lightly browned on each side. Transfer the steaks to a broiling pan.

Add the tomato slices to the skillet and sauté until soft. Add the cream, nutmeg, and thyme, and simmer the cream gravy slowly until slightly thickened, stirring occasionally with a fork to loosen all browned particles.

Broil the veal steaks for 4 minutes on each side, turning once and transfer to a serving platter. Pour the tomato cream over the steaks and serve.

Veal Steaks with Peppers and Mushrooms

2 2½-pound veal slices or steaks, each ¾-inch thick

Salt and black pepper

4 tablespoons flour

4 tablespoons butter

2 medium green peppers, cut into strips

2 medium sweet red peppers, cut into strips

15 large mushrooms, sliced

SERVES EIGHT

Rub the steaks with salt and pepper and dredge them in flour. Sauté them in the butter in a large skillet until lightly browned on each side. Transfer the steaks to a broiling pan.

Add the peppers and mushrooms to the skillet and sauté until barely tender.

Broil the steaks for 4 minutes on each side, turning once. Heap on the sautéed vegetables and broil 4 minutes more.

Mrs. Baird's Veal Steaks with Paprika

8 strips bacon

2 2½-pound veal slices or steaks, each ¾-inch thick

Salt and black pepper

4 tablespoons flour

1 large onion, finely chopped

2 teaspoons paprika

2 cups sour cream

¾ cup tomato sauce (page 237)

SERVES EIGHT

Cut the bacon into fine dice and fry in a large skillet until crisp and brown. Rub the steaks with salt and pepper and dredge them in flour. Sauté in the bacon fat until lightly browned on each side. Transfer the steaks to a broiling pan.

Add the onions to the skillet and sauté until golden. Sprinkle the paprika and ¼ teaspoon of salt over the onions and bacon, stir in the sour cream and tomato sauce, and heat gently over low flame, stirring occasionally.

Broil the veal steaks for 4 minutes on each side, turning once, and set on a serving plate. Pour the paprika cream over and serve piping hot.

Veal Steaks with Cider

2 2½-pound veal slices or steaks, each ¾-inch thick

Salt and black pepper

4 tablespoons flour

4 tablespoons butter

½ cup apple cider

1 cup heavy cream

⅛ teaspoon grated nutmeg

SERVES EIGHT

Rub the steaks with salt and pepper and dredge them in flour. Sauté them in the butter in a large skillet until lightly browned on each side. Transfer the steaks to a broiling pan.

Stir the cider into the skillet, loosening all brown particles with a fork. Boil vigorously until reduced by half, then add the cream and nutmeg and simmer the gravy until slightly thickened.

Broil the veal steaks for 4 minutes on each side, turning once and transfer to a serving platter. Pour the cream gravy over the steaks and serve.

Veal and Mushrooms in Onion Sauce***

16 veal scallops

11 tablespoons (1 stick plus 3 tablespoons) butter

5 medium onions, sliced

2¼ tablespoons flour

1½ cups Chicken Stock (page 111) or canned chicken broth

Salt and black pepper

¾ teaspoon granulated sugar

Pinch dried thyme

Pinch grated nutmeg

2 pounds mushrooms

¾ cup heavy cream

1 egg yolk

SERVES EIGHT

Ask the butcher to flatten the veal or do it yourself with a mallet or rolling pin. Heat 6 tablespoons butter in a large skillet, add the onion rings, and cook until soft but not brown. Stir in the flour, cook for 2 minutes, stir in the stock, salt and pepper to taste, sugar, thyme, and nutmeg. Continue to stir until the sauce thickens and comes to a boil. Cover the skillet and simmer over low heat for 40 minutes, stirring occasionally.

Wipe the mushrooms with a damp cloth; cut off and mince the stems. Slice the caps very thinly and set the mushrooms aside. Heat 3 tablespoons butter in a skillet and brown the veal scallops over medium heat on each side. Transfer the veal to a heatproof serving dish.

Add the remaining 2 tablespoons butter to the skillet. Add the mushroom caps and sauté them to a light golden before adding the minced stems. Add more butter if necessary to prevent sticking. Arrange the mushroom caps and minced stems over the veal.

Bring the cream to a simmer in a small saucepan. Simmer briefly, then stir in the egg yolk and continue to cook over low heat for 1 minute, stirring constantly. Force the onion sauce through a fine strainer, add the hot cream mixture, and mix well. Pour this sauce over the veal and mushrooms, place under the broiler for 2 or 3 minutes to glaze, and serve.

Dorothy Mead Evan's
Veal Ragout with Golden Sauce***

4½ pounds veal shoulder	*1 bay leaf*
16 small white onions, peeled	*Pinch dried thyme*
8 small carrots	*24 large mushrooms*
2 stalks celery, halved	*Juice of ½ lemon*
1 teaspoon salt	*3 egg yolks*
5 whole black peppercorns	*½ cup heavy cream*

SERVES EIGHT

Cut the veal shoulder into 1½-inch pieces. Place in a large kettle, add water to cover, and cook over medium heat for 5 minutes. Drain the meat, rinse well, and replace in the kettle. Add just enough water to cover and bring to a boil. Add the onions, carrots, celery, salt, peppercorns, bay leaf, and thyme. Simmer, covered, over low heat until tender, about 1 to 1½ hours.

Wipe the mushrooms with a damp cloth. Fresh mushrooms need not be peeled. "Turn" the mushrooms by cutting spiral notches with a sharp knife from the top of the cap to the edge, in a circular design all around the cap (see Broiled Mushroom Caps, page 282). Remove the veal, onions, and carrots from the kettle. Set on a serving platter and keep warm. Remove and discard the celery stalks and strain the stock into a large skillet. Add the lemon juice and mushrooms and cook the mushrooms in the stock over medium heat until barely tender. Transfer the mushrooms to the serving platter with the meat and continue to cook the stock until it is reduced to 2 cups. Beat the egg yolks lightly and stir into the cream. Gradually add 1 tablespoon of the reduced stock at a time to the cream and egg yolk mixture, beating constantly. Reheat the sauce if necessary, but do not let it boil or it will curdle. Pour the sauce over the veal and vegetables. Serve at once over rice.

Six-Layer Veal Dinner

2 cups sliced mushrooms	*1½ pounds ground veal*
2 tablespoons butter	*1 large green pepper*
2 cups dry bread crumbs	
¾ cup milk	*¾ teaspoon salt*
2 cups sliced onions	*⅛ teaspoon grated nutmeg*
3 medium tomatoes, peeled, sliced, and seeded	*1 cup heavy cream*

SERVES EIGHT

Preheat the oven to 350 degrees.

Sauté the mushrooms in the butter until lightly browned. Briefly soak the bread crumbs in the milk, then squeeze dry. Arrange the onion slices on the bottom of a large casserole and top with the mushrooms. Build the casserole with layers of the other ingredients in this order: tomato slices, bread crumbs, and meat.

Cut the green pepper into ½-inch-long strips, discarding the stem, seeds, and pith. Arrange the pepper strips in a latticework over the top. Season with salt and nutmeg and pour the cream over the casserole. Bake for 2 hours in the preheated oven.

Old-Farm Veal Loaf with Green-Pepper Topping

1 cup fine dry bread crumbs
1 egg, beaten
6 tablespoon butter, softened
1 cup minced onion
¾ teaspoon salt
⅛ teaspoon white pepper

⅛ teaspoon celery salt
⅛ teaspoon grated nutmeg
¼ cup apple cider
3¼ pounds ground lean veal
1 cup minced green pepper

SERVES SIX TO EIGHT

Preheat the oven to 350 degrees.

Use your fingers to work the bread crumbs, egg, 3 tablespoons butter, half the onion, salt, pepper, celery salt, nutmeg, and cider into the veal. Sauté the remaining onion and the green pepper in 3 tablespoons butter until the onion is transparent.

Press the veal mixture into a loaf pan, top with the sautéed onion and green pepper and bake for 1 hour in the preheated oven.

Broiled Butterflied Leg of Lamb

Lamb Marinade (page 216)

7½-pound leg of lamb, boned and butterflied

SERVES SIX

Set the meat in a flat glass baking dish and pour the Lamb Marinade over. Marinate in the refrigerator for 3 days, turning occasionally. Broil the meat until brown on the outside but still pink within and serve immediately.

Mint-Honey-Yoghurt Sauce (page 338) may be served separately in a sauceboat.

Roast Saddle of Lamb

1 saddle of lamb
  Salt
  Flour

4 tablespoons butter,
  melted
½ cup boiling water

SERVES EIGHT

Ask the butcher to trim and tie the saddle of lamb.

Preheat the oven to 400 degrees.

Wipe the roast well, sprinkle it with salt, and dredge in flour. Place on a rack in a lightly floured roasting pan.

Roast in the preheated oven, allowing 15 minutes to the pound. Mix the butter with the boiling water and baste the lamb every 5 minutes while it is cooking. Lamb is at its best when slightly underdone. Serve hot, accompanied by Currant Jelly Sauce (page 235).

Crown Roast of Lamb

1 16-rib crown roast of lamb
  Salt

Flour
Salt pork or bacon strips

SERVES EIGHT

Ask the butcher to prepare the roast by tying 2 loins of lamb together with the ribs outside. Be sure that the bones, which should be scraped down to where the meat begins, are not too long. The roast should be tied securely.

Preheat the oven to 400 degrees.

Rub the meat with salt and dredge in flour. Wrap each upright bone with a thin strip of salt pork or bacon. Sprinkle additional flour over the bottom of the roasting pan, set the roast on a rack, and place it in the preheated oven for 1¼ to 1¾ hours, or until the lamb is pink. Baste the meat every 15 minutes with the pan drippings.

To serve, place the roast on a serving platter and fill the center with Buttered Green Peas (page 249) and sautéed mushroom halves. The center of the roast may be filled with Sausage Stuffing (page 219) before roasting; increase the roasting time by 20 minutes.

Kidneys with Mushrooms

These kidney slices with sautéed mushrooms
and tomato-cream sauce are perfect fare
for a "little dinner."

4 pounds veal kidneys
3 tablespoons brandy
2 pounds mushrooms, sliced
4 tablespoons butter
4 tablespoons tomato paste

1 cup heavy cream
Pinch grated nutmeg
Large croutons sautéed in
butter or buttered toast

SERVES EIGHT

Trim the kidneys and slice them, reserving the fat. Render the kidney fat in a large skillet. Sauté the kidneys in the fat until they are lightly browned and barely cooked through. Drain the kidneys in a large strainer and pour off the fat left in the pan. Return the kidney slices to the skillet, sprinkle them with brandy, heat slightly, and set aflame. Using a slotted spoon, transfer the kidneys to a bowl.

Melt the butter in the pan in which the kidneys were cooked. Add the sliced mushrooms and sauté until lightly browned. Stir in the tomato paste, cream, and nutmeg. Stir until the sauce is smooth, well blended, and steaming hot. Add the kidneys, stir for a minute or two, and spoon over croutons or buttered toast.

Schnitz and Liver Loaf

2¼ pounds beef liver

4 strips bacon, minced

3 large onions, sliced

3 tablespoons minced onion

¾ cup dried bread crumbs

1 tablespoon butter

3 tablespoons peeled and minced apple

3 eggs

½ teaspoon salt

⅛ teaspoon black pepper

4 tablespoons flour

1 teaspoon baking powder

SERVES EIGHT

Preheat the oven to 350 degrees.

Use a sharp knife to trim the liver and chop it into very fine pieces. Brown the minced bacon in a large skillet. Add the onion rings and sauté until golden. Place the onion rings, bacon, and pan drippings on the bottom of a generously oiled loaf pan.

In a separate skillet, brown the minced onion and bread crumbs in butter. Add the minced apple. Beat the eggs lightly, combine with the minced liver, and mix with the onions, bread crumbs, and apple. Mix in the salt, pepper, flour, and baking powder, stir to blend all ingredients, then gently pack into the loaf pan over the onion rings.

Bake in the preheated oven for about 1 hour and 20 minutes, or until the center no longer feels mushy when lightly pressed with the fingers. Unmold the loaf onto a serving dish and serve immediately.

Poultry

How to Bone Chicken

ANY JOB becomes considerably easier when you have the proper equipment. A sharp boning knife makes boning a relatively simple procedure.

First remove the wings and first joint of the chicken and set them aside. Begin the actual boning by severing the drumstick at the joint where it meets the thigh. Slide your boning knife under the tendons and along the bone at both ends of the drumstick. With a bit of tugging and some further cutting, the bone can be pulled out and the meat left in one piece. Cut off the second drumstick and the thighs. Use the same cutting and tugging procedure to remove the bones. Pull the skin from the boned pieces with your fingers.

Next, flatten the breasts on a board, bone side down. Use your fingers and your knife, if necessary, to pull or cut away the skin. Cut down the back in two quick strokes to remove the neck and backbone, then turn the chicken over exposing the breastbone between the two rib cages. Break the ribs attached to either side of the breastbone, and lift the breastbone out, carefully severing any attached meat. By pulling up the rib bones with your fingers and holding your knife at a flat angle, you can easily slip the bones from the meat.

The wings, skin, and bones may be used to make chicken stock.

How to Sauté Chicken

Sautéing in a skillet is one of the most popular methods of preparing young chickens because of the relative ease of preparation and the numerous variations in sauces and garnishes.

Fryers weighing 2½ to 3 pounds are the most suitable for sautéing. Plan on 2 to 3 chickens to feed 8 people. Clean the birds, pluck all feathers from each, and singe off any bothersome fine feathers by briefly turning the chickens over a flame. Clean and wash the chickens, and pat them dry inside and out. Set each chicken breast down on a board. Remove the neck and backbone by cutting down the back in two quick strokes with a sharp knife, then flatten the bird, skin side down. The breast bone thus exposed between the two rib cages is removed first by breaking the ribs attached to each side, and then by using a sharp knife held at a flat angle to sever any attached meat.

Cut the breast in half and remove the first two joints of each wing, leaving the main wing bones in place. Sever the legs from the carcass, then bend each leg and cut between the drumsticks and thighs at the joint. The drumstick and thigh may be left in one piece if preferred.

Wipe off any loose bits of bone and season the chickens with salt and pepper. Dust the pieces lightly with flour and shake off any excess. Loose flour will scorch while the chickens cook and cause both the meat and the fat to have an unpleasant taste.

Use a large, heavy metal or cast-iron frying pan or skillet when sautéing chicken; thinner pans may cause the chicken to brown rapidly on the outside while remaining uncooked within. Sauté with just enough fat to keep the pieces from sticking to the pan. Butter or vegetable oil are both acceptable, but Clarified Butter (page 240) produces the finest taste by far.

Be sure that your frying pan or skillet is large enough to accommodate all the chicken pieces you wish to cook without overcrowding. Use two skillets if necessary, and take care that heat is evenly distributed under the cooking surfaces.

Chicken should be sautéed over medium-low heat until the meat is cooked through. If the butter or oil is too hot, the outside of the chicken will cook too quickly, or brown too much, while the inside will remain pink and inedible. Arrange the seasoned and floured chicken pieces in the skillet, skin side down, when the butter or oil is hot but not browned. Allow the skin to crisp and turn golden brown, then turn the pieces and sauté them long enough to brown the other side. Do not cover your skillet or the chicken skin will not be crisp and delicious.

The chicken is done when the juices run clear with no pinkish tinge when pierced in the thickest parts of each piece with a sharp fork. Transfer the cooked pieces as they are finished to an warm oven while you prepare a sauce or garnish.

How to Roast Chicken

A 4- to 5-pound roasting chicken will usually feed four people amply. Clean your bird, rub the cavities lightly with salt or lemon juice, and stuff. If the chicken isn't stuffed, reduce the roasting time by 3 to 5 minutes per pound. Mix softened butter with poultry seasoning and rub this mixture all over the skin, then truss the wings and drumsticks securely.

Place the chicken, breast side up, on a rack in a roasting pan, and set in an oven preheated to 425 degrees. After 15 minutes, reduce the heat to 350 degrees and continue to roast, basting frequently with the juices in the pan. Add water if necessary to keep the juices from scorching.

The chicken can also be prepared by roasting breast side down for the first 15 minutes at 425 degrees and then breast side up when the oven temperature is reduced to 350 degrees. Baste frequently as above.

Roasting time for chicken should be figured at 15 to 20 minutes per pound. Test for doneness by gently lifting one drumstick, or use a long fork to pierce the joint where the thigh joins the body. If the drumstick feels loose and the juices run clear, the chicken is ready.

Farm Fried Chicken

3 2½-pound chickens, quartered

⅔ cup flour

¼ teaspoon salt

⅛ teaspoon black pepper

3 tablespoons butter

3 tablespoons rendered chicken fat or additional butter

SERVES SIX TO EIGHT

Dry the chickens well and work the flour, salt, and pepper into the skin.

Heat the butter and chicken fat over medium heat in a large, heavy skillet, and add the chicken quarters, meat side down. Lower the heat to medium-low and fry, turning frequently, until tender and golden brown on all sides. Fry the chicken pieces slowly and don't let them burn.

Aunt Katie's Fried Chicken with Cream

2 3-pound chickens, cut into
  serving pieces
5 tablespoons butter
¼ cup flour
½ teaspoon marjoram

½ teaspoon salt
¼ teaspoon black pepper
1 tablespoon vegetable oil
1 cup heavy cream

SERVES EIGHT

Rub the chickens with 2½ tablespoons of softened butter, and refrigerate for 1 hour. Place the flour, marjoram, salt, and pepper in a brown paper bag. Drop the cold chicken pieces into the bag, close the top, and shake well.

Heat the remaining butter and the oil in a heavy skillet. Brown the chicken pieces on both sides and pour in the cream. Simmer, covered, for 15 minutes and then uncovered for 15 minutes more.

Southern Fried Chicken***

*If I had to choose just one fried chicken recipe,
this would be the one.*

2 3-pound chickens, quartered
1½ cups all-purpose flour
1 teaspoon poultry seasoning
4 cups cracker crumbs
  (approximately)

2 eggs
⅓ cup milk
Vegetable oil for
  frying
Salt and black pepper

SERVES EIGHT

[182]

Wash and dry the chicken pieces. Combine the flour and poultry seasoning and mound on a plate or wax paper. Make another mound of cracker crumbs. Beat the eggs lightly with the milk. Heat 1 inch of oil in a large skillet.

Dredge the chicken pieces first in the flour, shaking off the excess, then dip them in the egg mixture. Finish by rolling in the cracker crumbs, thoroughly coating all the surfaces. Fry the pieces to a rich golden brown on both sides, turning once.

Preheat the oven to 325 degrees.

Transfer each piece as it is done to an ovenproof dish. Take care not to break the crusts. Bake in the preheated oven for 20 to 30 minutes, or until the chicken is cooked through. Season with salt and pepper before serving hot with Southern-Style Cream Gravy (page 242).

Old-South Fried Chicken

2 3-pound chickens, quartered	2 eggs
3 cups all-purpose flour	⅓ cup milk
1 teaspoon poultry seasoning	Vegetable oil for frying
	Salt and black pepper

SERVES EIGHT

Wash the chicken pieces, but do not dry them. Instead, shake off the excess water. Divide the flour into two equal mounds, adding the poultry seasoning to one mound. Beat the eggs lightly with the milk. Heat 1 inch of oil in a large skillet.

Preheat the oven to 325 degrees.

Dredge the chicken pieces first in the seasoned flour, shaking off the excess, then in the egg mixture. Finish by dredging them in the second mound of flour. Fry the pieces to a rich golden brown on both sides, turning once.

Transfer each piece as it is done to an ovenproof dish. Take care not to break the crusts. Bake in the preheated oven for 20 to 30 minutes, or until the chicken is cooked through. Season with salt and pepper before serving hot with Southern-Style Cream Gravy (page 242).

Oatmeal Fried Chicken

2 3-pound chickens, quartered
1½ cups all-purpose flour
1 teaspoon poultry seasoning
4 cups rolled oats
  (approximately)

2 eggs
⅓ cup milk
Vegetable oil for
  frying
Salt and black pepper

SERVES EIGHT

Wash and dry the chicken pieces. Combine the flour and poultry seasoning and mound on a plate or wax paper. Make another mound of rolled oats. Beat the eggs lightly with the milk. Heat 1 inch of oil in a heavy skillet.

Dredge the chicken pieces first in the flour, shaking off the excess, then dip them in the egg mixture. Finish by rolling in the oats, thoroughly coating all surfaces. Fry the pieces to a rich golden brown on both sides, turning once.

Preheat the oven to 325 degrees.

Transfer each piece as it is done to an ovenproof dish. Take care not to break the crusts. Bake in the preheated oven for 20 to 30 minutes, or until the chicken is cooked through. Season with salt and pepper.

Anne Hackette's Fried Chicken with Walnuts

4 whole chicken breasts, boned
  and skinned
3 teaspoons cornstarch
2 egg whites, lightly beaten
  Vegetable oil for frying

16 scallions
1 cup walnut halves
  Salt

SERVES EIGHT

Cut the chicken into long ¼-inch-thick slices and pat dry with paper towels. Rub the cornstarch into the chicken slices and allow them to stand for a few minutes. Dip them in egg whites and fry in ½ inch of hot oil without letting the pieces touch.

Drain the chicken briefly on paper towels and transfer to an ovenproof platter. Keep hot.

Quickly sauté the whole scallions in the hot oil and transfer them to the hot platter. Sauté the nuts for 1 minute.

Arrange attractively on the platter. Sprinkle with salt. Serve immediately.

Sue-Ellen's Fried Chicken in Banana Batter

Banana batter and coconut may be a bit too sweet for some, but it does provide a nice change for the adventurous chicken connoisseur. This recipe provides an excellent way to use that too-ripe banana in the fruit bowl.

3 *2½–3-pound chickens, cut into serving pieces*

3 *tablespoons butter*

1 *banana*

2 *eggs*

1 *tablespoon flour*

Pinch baking powder

Pinch baking soda

Vegetable oil for frying

Shredded coconut (optional)

SERVES EIGHT

Rinse the chicken pieces and dry with paper towels. Heat the butter in a large skillet and fry the chicken pieces over medium-low heat until they are lightly browned on both sides and nearly cooked through. Transfer the chicken to a platter to cool to room temperature.

Mash the banana in a small bowl. Beat the eggs lightly and add to the banana, along with the flour, baking powder, and baking soda. Mix until smooth.

Heat ½ inch oil in the skillet. Dip each chicken piece in the banana batter and then in shredded coconut, if desired. Fry in the oil until crisp and golden brown on both sides. Drain briefly on paper towels. Serve very hot.

Curried Fried Chicken

2 3-pound chickens, cut into
serving pieces

3 tablespoons butter

¾ teaspoon curry powder

½ teaspoon salt

3 tablespoons vegetable
oil

1 cup slivered almonds

SERVES EIGHT

Wash the chicken pieces and dry them well. Rub the butter, curry powder, and salt into the chicken pieces.

Heat the oil in a heavy skillet and fry the chicken over medium heat until the pieces are crisp and brown on the outside and well done on the inside. Remove from the pan and keep warm.

Sauté the nuts in the oil remaining in the pan, adding more if necessary.

To serve, arrange the chicken on a heated platter, sprinkle with the toasted nuts, and decorate with Fried Parsley (page 288) or fresh parsley sprigs.

Mrs. Knittle's Fried Chicken
with Brandied Fruit Sauce

2 3-pound chickens, boned and
skinned

3 tablespoons cornstarch

½ teaspoon grated nutmeg

8 apricots, halved and pitted, or
16 dried apricot halves

16 pitted prunes

1–2 cups dry white wine

3 tablespoons granulated
sugar

Vegetable oil for frying

¼ cup brandy

SERVES EIGHT

Cut the chicken into 1½-inch pieces. Rub the chicken with cornstarch and nutmeg and let stand for 15 minutes or more.

Soak the apricots and prunes in 1 cup wine for 30 minutes, then simmer with the sugar until the fruit is barely tender, adding more wine if necessary. Fresh apricots will require only a few minutes cooking.

Fry the chicken in hot oil until the outside is crisp and the inside is well done. Drain briefly on paper towels, place on an oven-proof dish, and keep hot. Discard all but 3 tablespoons of oil.

Drain the fruit and measure the liquid. Add enough additional wine to make 1 cup. Stir liquid into the skillet, continuing to stir over medium heat until the sauce has thickened slightly. Add the fruit and heat for 2 to 3 minutes. Add the brandy, allow it to warm, and set aflame. Pour the flaming sauce over the chicken and carry to the table while still flaming.

Amanda Philpot's Chicken in Cream Sauce with Cheddar Cheese

2 2½-pound chickens, cut into
  serving pieces
  Salt and black pepper
5 tablespoons butter
3 tablespoons flour
⅓ cup heavy cream

⅔ cup milk
2 egg yolks
½ cup grated sharp cheddar
  cheese
½ cup dry bread
  crumbs

SERVES EIGHT

Rinse the chicken pieces, pat them dry, and sprinkle with salt and pepper. Heat the butter in a large skillet and gently sauté the chicken pieces over low heat, turning once, for about 15 minutes. Transfer the chicken to a large casserole.

Add the flour to the butter in the skillet, stirring well to loosen all brown particles. Mix the cream and milk together and add all at once to the skillet. Continue to cook, stirring constantly, until the mixture thickens. Remove the cream sauce from the heat and set it aside to cool a bit.

Preheat the oven to 350 degrees.

Beat the egg yolks lightly and stir them into the slightly cooled cream sauce. Carefully pour the cream sauce over the chicken. Combine the grated cheddar with the bread crumbs and sprinkle the mixture over the chicken and cream sauce. Bake in the preheated oven for 15 to 20 minutes or until the chicken is tender. Serve immediately.

Grossmutter's Deviled Chicken***

2 3-pound chickens, quartered	½ teaspoon black pepper
1 large onion	Pinch cayenne
1 teaspoon salt	2 teaspoons lemon juice
12 whole black peppercorns	2 teaspoons cider vinegar
1 bay leaf	2 tablespoons Worcestershire sauce
7–8 tablespoons butter	
7½ tablespoons flour	Dry bread crumbs
1 tablespoon prepared mustard	Butter

SERVES EIGHT

Place the chicken pieces in a large kettle and cover with water. Add the onion, salt, peppercorns, and bay leaf. Bring the water to a boil, and simmer the chicken, covered, until tender, about 1 hour, skimming off any scum which rises. Remove the chicken and strain the stock.

Return the stock to the kettle and cook over medium heat until it is reduced to 3 cups. Skim off any fat.

Melt 5 tablespoons butter in a large skillet and stir in the flour, continuing to stir until the flour is browned. Add the stock all at once and stir constantly until it thickens, then remove from the heat. Combine the mustard, black pepper, cayenne, lemon juice, vinegar, and Worcestershire sauce, blend well, and mix into the sauce.

Preheat the oven to 375 degrees.

Dry the chicken pieces and dip them into the seasoned sauce until all surfaces are coated, then dip them into the bread crumbs. Arrange the chicken on a greased baking sheet, dot each piece generously with butter, and bake in the preheated oven for about

20 minutes, or until the chicken is heated through and the bread crumbs are golden brown. Serve immediately, with the remaining reheated brown sauce.

Frau Moyer's Chicken Biscuit Pie

*Crusty cream biscuits on top of a creamy chicken pie
must be the ultimate in country cooking.*

3 2½–3-pound chickens, cut into serving pieces
3 cups water
2 tablespoons butter
2 tablespoons flour
1 cup heavy cream

¼ teaspoon dried chervil
1 tablespoon minced chives
⅛ teaspoon black pepper
½ teaspoon salt
1 recipe Whipped Cream Biscuits (page 355)

SERVES SIX TO EIGHT

Place the chicken pieces and the water in a large heavy kettle and bring to a boil. Partially cover the pot, lower the heat, and simmer for about 35 minutes, turning once and skimming any scum which rises to the surface.

Melt the butter in a skillet and use a fork to stir in the flour. Remove the pan from the heat, add the cream, and mix well, mashing out any lumps with the fork.

Preheat the oven to 425 degrees.

When the chicken is done, pull the meat from the bones in large pieces and set aside. Stir 1 cup of the chicken cooking liquid into the butter-cream mixture and cook over medium heat, stirring constantly, until the sauce bubbles and thickens. Mix the sauce, chicken, and spices, and place in a glass baking dish. Top with rounds of biscuit dough and bake for 25 minutes in the preheated oven.

Pennsylvania Dutch Chicken Pot Pie

*My grandfather made two kinds of pot pie—
one used squares of pie dough and the other
thick pot pie noodles. Both were delicious.*

2 *3½-pound chickens, cut into
serving pieces*

7 *large potatoes*

4 *large onions*

½ *recipe Pastry for 2-Crust Pie
(page 418)*

1 *teaspoon salt*

⅛ *teaspoon black pepper*

3 *tablespoons flour*

*Dried sage, thyme, and
chervil*

Water or chicken stock

SERVES EIGHT TO TEN

Rinse the chicken pieces and dry them with paper towels. Peel the potatoes and onions and cut them into ⅓-inch slices. Roll out the pie crust dough ⅓ inch thick and cut into 2-inch squares.

Place a layer of chicken in the bottom of a deep, heavy kettle or dutch oven, cover with a layer of potatoes, and top with a layer of onions. Mix together the salt, pepper, and flour, and sprinkle ⅓ of the mixture over the onions. Add generous pinches of sage, thyme, and chervil. Top with a layer of pie-dough squares. Continue to build alternate layers of chicken, potatoes, onions, seasonings, and pie-dough squares until the kettle is filled, ending with a layer of chicken. Pour in enough water or stock to fill the kettle ¾ of the way to the top. Bring to a boil. Reduce the heat, cover the kettle tightly, and simmer for 40 minutes, or until the chicken is tender. Serve piping hot.

Indiana Chicken Pie with Meatballs***

Make 2 of these pies for 8 people.
The proportions of chicken, meatballs, gravy, and
pie crust are more perfectly balanced than when
all ingredients are baked in one large pie.

5 tablespoons butter

1 3-pound chicken, boned (page 179)

Salt and black pepper

½ medium potato, cooked, peeled, and mashed

½ cup (5 ounces) lean ground chuck

1 chicken liver, minced

¼ teaspoon powdered sage

⅛ teaspoon black pepper

1 egg yolk

1 tablespoon vegetable oil

1 tablespoon flour

Water or chicken stock

Pastry for 2 Crust Pie (page 418)

1 tablespoon minced chives

SERVES FOUR

Heat 3 tablespoons butter in a large skillet and sauté the chicken pieces. When they are lightly brown on all sides, sprinkle with salt and pepper, cover, and cook for 15 minutes, or until the chicken is pearly white. Take care not to overcook the chicken or it will be dry.

Combine the mashed potato with the ground chuck and minced chicken liver. Season with sage and pepper. Bind with the egg yolk. Remove the cooked chicken from the skillet and pour off and reserve the pan juices.

Heat 1 tablespoon each butter and oil in the skillet. Shape the meat and potato mixture into walnut-size balls. Brown the meatballs on all sides in the hot fat. Remove from the skillet with a slotted spoon. Add these pan juices to the reserved chicken juices.

Melt the remaining tablespoon butter in the skillet and blend in the flour. Combine the reserved pan juices with enough water or chicken stock to make ¾ cup liquid, and stir it into the butter and flour, continuing to stir until the gravy is smooth and thick. Remove the pan from the heat and let the gravy cool.

Preheat the oven to 425 degrees.

Roll out the pie dough and line a 7½-inch glass pie plate with 1 crust. Cut the cooked chicken into bite-size pieces and arrange with the meatballs over the pastry. Carefully pour the cooled gravy over the chicken and meatballs and sprinkle with minced chives. Top with the second crust and flute the edges of the 2 crusts together. Cut a small hole the size of a dime in the center of the top crust to allow steam to escape.

Bake for 15 minutes in the preheated oven, then lower the heat to 375 degrees and bake for 30 minutes longer, or until the crust is well done and nicely browned. Serve immediately.

Old Dutch Chicken Cake***

2 3-pound chickens, cut into
   serving pieces
½ cup minced celery
2 tablespoons minced chives
   Potato Stuffing (page 221)
1 cup half and half

6 tablespoons flour
   Salt and black pepper
⅓ cup coarse dry bread crumbs
⅛ teaspoon grated nutmeg
2½ tablespoons butter

SERVES EIGHT

Place the chicken pieces in a large kettle, add water to cover, and cook over low heat until tender, about 30 minutes. Remove the chicken from the kettle, reserving the broth. Discard the chicken skin, pull the meat from the bones, and cut into 1-inch pieces. Mix the celery and chives into the Potato Stuffing, then spread a layer of this stuffing on the bottom of a well-greased large baking dish. Arrange pieces of chicken over the stuffing.

Preheat the oven to 350 degrees.

Combine 1 cup of the chicken broth with the half and half, and blend in the flour. Spoon half of this thickening mixture over the chicken, and season with a little salt and pepper. Build one more layer of stuffing, chicken, thickening, salt, and pepper, then top with remaining potato stuffing.

Sprinkle with the bread crumbs and nutmeg, and dot generously with butter. Bake for 40 to 50 minutes in the preheated oven. The bread crumbs should be a golden brown. Remove from the oven and serve immediately.

Baked Chicken with
Caraway–Sour Cream Sauce***

*Chicken is transformed into a luxurious company dinner
when smothered with mushrooms and
caraway-flavored sour cream sauce.*

*3 2½-pound chickens, skinned and
 cut into serving pieces*

8 tablespoons (1 stick) butter

5 tablespoons flour

4 cups sour cream

 Salt and black pepper

1⅓ tablespoons caraway seeds

1½ pounds mushrooms, sliced

 ¼ cup minced chives

 3 tablespoons minced parsley

SERVES EIGHT

Preheat the oven to 325 degrees.

Rinse the chicken pieces and pat dry. Melt the butter in a skillet, brown the chicken pieces, and transfer them to a fairly large casserole or other baking dish.

Stir the flour into the butter remaining in the pan, mixing until smooth. Add the sour cream and simmer for 3 or 4 minutes, stirring constantly. Stir in salt and pepper to taste, the caraway seeds, mushrooms, and chives, and spoon the sauce over the chicken. Bake for 30 to 35 minutes in the preheated oven. Serve immediately, sprinkled with parsley.

Country Chicken Baked in Cream

*3 2½-pound chickens, cut into
 serving pieces*

6 tablespoons butter

6 medium onions, sliced

2 cups heavy cream

½ cup dry sherry

 Salt and black pepper

 Pinch grated nutmeg

SERVES EIGHT

Preheat the oven to 350 degrees.

Rinse the chicken pieces and pat them dry. Heat the butter in a large skillet and sauté the chicken until all the pieces are lightly browned. Arrange the onion slices in the bottom of a greased baking dish. Place the chicken pieces on top of the onions.

Mix the cream and sherry together and pour over the chicken. Season with salt, pepper, and nutmeg. Use aluminum foil to cover and seal the baking dish, and bake in the preheated oven for 30 to 40 minutes, or until the chicken is tender.

India Sandidge's Herbed Chicken with Saffron

2 3-pound chickens, cut into serving pieces

Salt

3 tablespoons butter

3 tablespoons vegetable oil

1 large onion, coarsely chopped

3 medium tomatoes, peeled, seeded, and coarsely chopped

2 cloves garlic, crushed

½ teaspoon powdered saffron

½ teaspoon dried thyme

½ teaspoon dried tarragon

1 tablespoon minced chives

¼ teaspoon oregano

2 small bay leaves

10 stuffed green olives, thinly sliced

2 cups Chicken Stock (page 111) or canned chicken broth

1 cup dry white wine

1 tablespoon cornstarch

SERVES EIGHT

Rub all surfaces of the chickens with salt. Heat the butter and oil in a large skillet, and sauté the chicken a few pieces at a time to a golden brown on all sides adding more oil and butter as needed. Transfer the chicken to a large baking dish or casserole. Add the chopped onion and tomatoes to the skillet and cook over low heat for 3 or 4 minutes, stirring once or twice. Mix in the garlic, saffron, thyme, tarragon, chives, oregano, bay leaves, and olive slices. Add the stock and wine, and simmer over low heat for 5 minutes.

Preheat the oven to 350 degrees.

Mix the cornstarch with enough water to make a paste, stir in ½ cup of cooking liquid, then stir this cornstarch mixture into the skillet. Stir constantly until the sauce bubbles and thickens. Pour the sauce over the chicken, and bake for 1 hour in the preheated oven. Serve hot over rice.

Chicken with Watercress Sauce

5 tablespoons butter

2 3-pound chickens, skinned and
cut into serving pieces

1 bunch watercress

6 shallots, chopped

2 cups Chicken Stock (page 111)
or canned chicken broth

2 egg yolks

⅓ cup heavy cream

Salt and black pepper

3 tablespoons chopped pecans

SERVES EIGHT

Heat the butter in a large skillet over low heat and sauté the chicken, turning frequently, until cooked through but not brown. Wash the watercress in several changes of water, remove and discard the thick stems, and pat the leaves dry with paper towels before mincing finely.

Transfer the chicken to an ovenproof serving platter and put in a warm oven to stay hot. Lightly sauté the watercress and shallots in the butter left in the skillet. Cook for 3 or 4 minutes, stirring frequently. Add the stock and cook until the sauce reduces by half and thickens slightly, 15 to 20 minutes.

Mix the egg yolks with the cream, stir in a little of the hot watercress sauce, then return the mixture to the skillet and cook over low heat, stirring constantly, until the sauce is thick. Do not allow the sauce to boil or the egg yolks will curdle. Season with salt and pepper to taste. Pour the sauce over the chicken pieces, garnish with the chopped pecans, and serve piping hot.

Chicken with Parsley Sauce

Prepare the chicken in exactly the same way, substituting 1 bunch finely minced parsley leaves and 5 thinly sliced scallions for the watercress. Instead of Chicken Stock, make the sauce with 1 cup dry white wine.

New England Creamed Chicken and Oysters

3 1½–2½-pound chickens,
  skinned and quartered
Flour
¼ teaspoon salt
⅛ teaspoon white pepper
3 tablespoons butter

1 cup milk
1 quart shucked oysters
1 cup heavy cream
¼ cup minced chives

SERVES EIGHT

Preheat the oven to 375 degrees.

Rinse the chicken pieces, pat them dry, and dredge well with flour. Sprinkle with salt and white pepper. Heat the butter in a skillet and sauté the chicken pieces to a light brown on both sides. Transfer to an ovenproof dish, pour in the milk, cover the dish and bake for 1 hour. Baste the chicken pieces frequently while they are cooking.

Drain the oysters well and arrange them in the dish with the chicken. Heat the cream, add it to the dish and bake, uncovered, for 15 minutes longer.

To serve, arrange the chicken pieces on a serving platter, pour the oysters and cream sauce over, and sprinkle with chives.

Chicken or Turkey Croquettes

*If you don't have enough cooked chicken or turkey,
try combining your leftovers with enough chopped
hard-boiled eggs or minced cooked mushrooms
to make the necessary amount.*

3–4 cups finely minced cooked
  chicken or turkey
2¼ cups fine dry bread crumbs
  Salt and black pepper
  1 cup thick Easy White Sauce
  (page 238)

2 eggs
3 tablespoons grated mild cheddar
  cheese
  Vegetable oil for frying

SERVES EIGHT

Mix the chicken or turkey with ¾ cup bread crumbs, season with salt and pepper to taste, and bind the mixture with white sauce. Refrigerate for at least 2 hours.

Lightly flour your hands and shape the mixture into cone-shaped croquettes 2 inches across at the base and 2½ to 3 inches high. Beat the eggs lightly. Blend the cheese with the remaining 1½ cups bread crumbs. Dip each croquette first in the beaten eggs, then in the cheese and bread crumb mixture, and fry in 2 inches of hot oil until golden brown on both sides, turning once. Drain briefly on paper towels before serving.

How to Roast Turkey

Perhaps nothing represents a festive American meal as much as delicately browned roast turkey, carried triumphantly to the table amid "ahhhs" of admiration. A regal bird accompanied by chestnut stuffing, sweet potato–pumpkin soufflé, scalloped onions, and cranberry mold is a traditional meal brought to a peak of excellence.

To prepare the turkey for roasting, first rub the cavity lightly with salt or lemon juice, and fill with stuffing. Mix softened butter with poultry seasoning and rub all over the turkey skin. Truss the bird, place on a rack in a roasting pan, and set a very loose tent of aluminum foil over the bird. Arrange the aluminum foil cover so that it does not actually touch the turkey.

There are several methods for roasting turkey. One method is to roast the bird breast side down for the first 30 minutes, turning it first to one side and cooking for one hour, then turning it to the other side for another hour. Finish by turning the turkey breast side up for the remaining cooking time. Brush frequently with pan drippings.

Another method is to roast the turkey breast side down for one hour, then turn it and allow the bird to cook breast side up for the remainder of the cooking time, basting frequently throughout.

Most people find the old-fashioned way of roasting equally satisfactory. Season and stuff the bird, rub the skin with the seasoned butter as above, then truss, and place breast side up on the rack in the roasting pan. Arrange 6 to 8 strips of bacon, depending on the size of the bird, over the breast, and cover loosely with a tent of foil.

Roast at 450 degrees for 30 minutes, reduce the heat to 325 degrees and continue to cook, figuring 20 minutes to the pound. Lift the tent cover at frequent intervals and baste the bird with the pan drippings. If the breast gets too dark during the cooking, flatten the foil close to the bird to prevent excessive browning. Remove the foil 15 minutes prior to taking the bird from the oven.

Test for doneness by gently pulling one drumstick, or pierce the joint where the thigh joins the body. If the drumstick seems loose and the juices run clear when pierced, the turkey is ready. Allow the bird to rest 10 minutes before carving.

Spit-Roasted Turkey with Tarragon

2 6-pound turkeys	1 cup white wine vinegar
Juice of 1 lemon	¾ cup vegetable oil
Salt and black pepper	¼ cup granulated sugar
1 bunch fresh tarragon, chopped, or 2½ teaspoons dried tarragon	

SERVES EIGHT TO TEN

Rub the turkeys inside and out with lemon juice. Rub the inside of the turkeys with tarragon; reserve at least ¼ cup of fresh or 1 teaspoon dried for the sauce. Truss the turkeys and secure them so they balance evenly on a revolving spit. Roast over slow coals for 2 hours or until the drumsticks are loose and the juices no longer run pink.

Prepare the sauce while the birds revolve. Place remaining tarragon, vinegar, oil, and sugar in a small saucepan. Bring to a boil and cook for 5 minutes over low heat. Refrigerate until serving time.

To serve, remove the trussing string and cool the turkeys a bit before carving. Top each serving with a spoonful or two of the tarragon sauce, either cold or at room temperature.

Roast Guinea Hen

3 guinea hens
   Chestnut Stuffing (page 221)
3 tablespoons butter, softened

1 tablespoon dried juniper berries, crushed
12 strips bacon
2 cups dry white wine

SERVES EIGHT

Preheat the oven to 475 degrees.

Fill the birds with the stuffing and rub them well with softened butter into which has been mixed the crushed juniper berries. Arrange 4 strips of bacon over the breast of each bird, and set them in a large roasting pan. Pour the wine over the birds and roast for 20 minutes. Reduce the heat to 350 degrees and continue roasting, basting occasionally for 30 to 40 minutes, or until the birds test done.

Serve hot with Currant Jelly Sauce (page 235).

Berks County Duck with Kraut***

1 duck (about 4½ pounds)
1 quart sauerkraut
2 tablespoons granulated sugar

1 teaspoon grated orange zest
⅔ cup water

SERVES FOUR

Preheat the oven to 450 degrees.

Prepare duck for roasting. Place breast down on a rack in a roasting pan. Bake for 15 minutes in the preheated oven. Lower the heat to 350 degrees, turn the duck breast up, and bake for 20 minutes more. Pour off and discard the duck fat in the pan, remove the rack, and place the duck breast down in the pan.

Drain the sauerkraut, arrange it around the duck, sprinkle with the sugar and orange zest, and pour in the water. Bake for 45 minutes. Stir the sauerkraut in the pan. Turn the duck breast side up, raise the oven temperature to 450 degrees, and bake 15 to 20 minutes longer, or until the skin is brown and the breast meat slightly pink.

Remove the duck and keep it warm. Drain the sauerkraut of most of the fat and liquid and sauté over medium heat until brown. Serve the duck accompanied by sauerkraut and mashed potatoes.

Salmi of Duck

4 tablespoons butter

4 shallots, minced

2 cups Basic Brown Gravy (page 241) or leftover duck gravy

1 cup dry sherry

2 tablespoons lemon juice

4 tablespoons pâté de fois gras (optional)

Salt and black pepper

Pinch dried rosemary

Pinch dried thyme

4 cups thinly sliced cooked duck

10 stuffed green olives, thinly sliced

SERVES EIGHT

Melt the butter in a chafing dish pan and sauté the shallots until they are golden but do not allow them to brown. Stir in the gravy, sherry, lemon juice, pâté de fois gras if you have some available, and seasonings. Bring the sauce to a low boil, add the duck slices, and continue to simmer the sauce for 5 minutes, or until the duck slices are heated through. Garnish with olive slices. Serve over hot wild rice.

Game

How to Hang and Cut Deer

WHILE IT IS my feeling that wild creatures should be allowed to roam alive and free, there are, I suppose, circumstances in which the overpopulation of wild species in some rural areas makes it imperative that some be killed. In any case, here are general directions for hanging, cutting, and marinating a fresh-killed deer.

First, the carcass of a freshly killed deer must be eviscerated and drained of all blood, then hung in a cool place for at least a week. After hanging, cut the legs off at the knees. Skin the animal by first cutting the skin from the knees to the center of the eviscerated gut. Slit the skin from the top of the gut to the neck. Sever the head, then strip the skin completely away from the carcass.

Cutting the animal into manageable portions is the next step. Here the best bet is a butcher, who has the knowledge and skill necessary for cutting venison steaks, roasts, and chops. It's probably best to let him do the job unless you've had lots of practice.

In general, you can expect to get tenderloin steaks from the loin ends. The short loins will provide steaks and loin chops. The ribs will serve as standing or rolled rib roasts, may be cut into rib steaks, or, if cut double, into rib chops. The plates can be rolled or used for shortribs. From the chuck ends come pot roasts, blade steaks, and meat for stew or grinding into burgers. The shanks can be cut and used as soup bones; the flanks can be cut into steaks, stewing meat, or meat for grinding. The large hind shanks will provide round roasts, plus enough meat for stew or grinding. Slice any steaks cut from the larger portions not more than ½ inch thick. Unlike beef, venison steaks are not improved when thickly sliced.

Be sure to trim all fat from these cuts before marinating them—although most wild animals are leaner than domestic animals because they run more and their food supply is less certain, their fat tends to taste strong and unpleasant. Larding or other fat may be tied on later when the cuts are cooked or roasted.

The roasts, chops, and other cuts are marinated for 5 days. Place them in crocks, pour enough marinade (page 217) in each crock to bring the liquid level just above the meat, cover the crocks, and store in a cool place. The crocks may be set in the refrigerator for 5 days if other cool storage is unavailable. Allow the crocks and their contents to stand at room temperature for 2 hours each of the 5 days if refrigerator storage is necessary. Wipe the cuts dry after the marinating, then wrap them neatly in one thickness of cheesecloth, cover with freezer paper, and freeze whatever pieces you are not using immediately.

Hunter's Round Roast of Venison

Round roast of venison
2 cups Hunter's Marinade or
  Venison Marinade (page 217)
Salt

Salt pork
2 tablespoons butter
3 tablespoons vegetable oil

SERVES TWELVE

Marinate the haunch for at least 5 days (page 201). Wipe the meat dry and strain the marinade, reserving 2 cups. Remove the sinews from the roast and season the meat with salt to taste. Tie strips of salt pork securely to the roast.

Preheat the oven to 450 degrees.

Place the butter and oil in the bottom of a large roasting pan. Set the pan in the oven long enough to heat the butter and oil to sizzling. Place the roast in the pan, and roast for 20 minutes. Meanwhile, reduce the 2 cups of reserved marinade to 1 cup.

Lower the oven temperature to 350 degrees and continue to roast the meat, basting occasionally with the reduced marinade, for about 18 to 20 minutes per pound for rare to medium-rare meat. Slice and serve hot on heated plates, which will keep the portions from cooling too rapidly.

Spit-Roasted Venison

1 8-pound saddle of venison	Salt pork
Hunter's Marinade or Venison Marinade (page 217)	8 tablespoons (1 stick) butter, melted
Salt and black pepper	

SERVES EIGHT

Marinate the saddle for at least 5 days (page 201). Dry the meat and strain the marinade, reserving 2 cups. Sprinkle the meat with salt and pepper, pressing in as much of the seasonings as possible. Tie strips of salt pork to the venison, and balance the roast evenly on a spit.

Place the reserved marinade in a saucepan, bring to a boil, and cook until the liquid is reduced by half. Strain the marinade and mix with the melted butter. Roast the venison over very hot coals for 30 minutes, basting often with the marinade-butter mixture.

Lower the coals and continue to roast the venison for about 18 to 20 minutes per pound for rare to medium-rare meat, basting occasionally. Remove from the heat, cut into individual portions, and serve on heated plates with Horseradish Sauce (page 340).

Venison Steaks

¾ cup white vinegar	¾-inch slice beef suet, coarsely chopped
1½ cups dry red wine	Salt and black pepper
Juice of 2 lemons	4 tablespoons butter, at room temperature
¼ cup Worcestershire sauce	
¼ teaspoon ground allspice	
8 venison steaks, ½ inch thick	

SERVES EIGHT

Prepare a marinade by combining the vinegar, wine, lemon juice, Worcestershire sauce, and allspice. Arrange the steaks in a glass or enamel pan, and pour the marinade over them. Refrigerate overnight, turning the meat once or twice.

When ready to cook, render the beef suet pieces in a large skillet over medium heat until the cracklings turn crisp and brown. Remove and discard the cracklings.

Wipe the steaks dry and season with salt and pepper to taste. Fry in the fat until medium, since well-done or rare venison steaks may be tough. Turn the steaks from time to time until they reach the desired degree of doneness. Remove them from the skillet, brush with generous amounts of butter, and serve immediately on heated plates.

How to Dress and Hang Rabbit

Rabbit, like other small game, should always be dressed as soon as possible after the hunt and then hung for several days, skinned, and marinated before cooking.

Clean the rabbit by slitting the stomach and removing the entrails. Sprinkle the internal cavity with ⅓ cup salt immediately after the animal has been drawn. Hang the rabbit by its legs in a cool, shady spot outdoors or indoors. The temperature for hanging should never exceed 36 degrees. If the weather is too warm, hang your game as high as possible in a refrigerator where air can circulate freely.

After hanging the rabbit, cut off its head and feet. Skin it by first slitting the fur on the hind legs. This should enable you to pull the rest of the skin off easily. Cut the animal into serving pieces and, if desired, marinate for 2 to 3 days in Rabbit Marinade (page 216).

Country-Style Fried Rabbit

2 *rabbits, skinned, dressed, and cut into pieces*	3 *tablespoons butter*
⅓ *cup flour*	3 *tablespoons vegetable oil*
	Salt and black pepper

SERVES EIGHT

After rabbits have been hung and marinated, arrange the pieces in a large bowl, cover with lightly salted water, and soak for 8 to 10 hours. Drain the pieces, pat them dry on paper towels, then roll them in flour.

Heat the butter and oil in a large skillet. Fry the rabbit pieces, covered, over medium heat to a golden brown, turning frequently. Season to taste with salt and pepper, remove to a serving platter, and serve garnished with Fried Parsley (page 288).

Hasenpfeffer

2 rabbits, skinned, dressed, and cut into pieces

2 large onions, sliced

White vinegar

1 teaspoon salt

12 whole black peppercorns

8 whole cloves

4 bay leaves

5 tablespoons butter

1½ cups sour cream

SERVES EIGHT

Place the rabbit pieces in a large earthenware crock. Arrange the onion slices in layers between the pieces. Measure equal parts of water and vinegar and pour enough into the crock to barely cover the meat. Add the salt to the mixture. Tie the peppercorns, cloves, and bay leaves in a small cheesecloth bag and add to the liquid in the crock. Set the crock, covered, in a cold place for 3 days.

Remove the rabbit pieces from the crock, reserving the liquid. Pat the meat dry with paper towels. Heat the butter in a very large skillet, add the meat, and brown it on all sides, turning frequently. Add more butter if needed to keep the meat from sticking. Stir in 3 cups of the strained marinade, lower the heat, and simmer, covered, for 30 minutes, or until the meat is tender. Remove the meat to a serving platter and keep it warm. There should be about 2 cups of liquid left in the skillet. Add more, if necessary, to measure 2 cups; bring to a boil, then stir in the sour cream. Pour this gravy over the meat pieces and serve immediately.

Shartlesville Rabbit Pie***

This rewarding recipe should be tried;
if rabbit is not available, substitute young chickens.

2 rabbits, skinned, dressed, and
   cut into large pieces
Salt
1 tablespoon butter
5 large onions, sliced
Flour
2 teaspoons bottled beef
   concentrate

3–4 cups mashed potatoes
1 tablespoon minced parsley
1 tablespoon minced chives
1 clove garlic, crushed
1 egg

SERVES EIGHT

Place the rabbit pieces in a large kettle and barely cover with water. Bring to a boil, cover, lower heat, and simmer gently until the meat is tender, about ½–1 hour. Season the meat with salt when partially cooked.

Heat the butter in a skillet and gently sauté the onion rings until transparent.

Remove the rabbit pieces from the kettle and separate the meat from the bones, keeping it in large pieces. Measure the cooking liquid and mix it with 1 tablespoon of flour for each cup of liquid. Add the bottled beef concentrate and ½ teaspoon salt to the thickened gravy. Stir until well blended.

Place a layer of rabbit meat on the bottom of a large baking dish and top with a layer of onions. Continue to arrange alternate layers of meat and onions until the dish is filled. Pour in enough gravy to barely cover the meat and onions.

Preheat the oven to 350 degrees.

Mix the mashed potatoes with the parsley, chives, and garlic. Beat the egg lightly, then blend thoroughly with the mashed potatoes. Spread the potato mixture over the top of the casserole, or drop by tablespoonfuls around the edge. Bake in the preheated oven for 30 to 40 minutes or until the liquid is bubbling hot and thick and the potatoes are browned. Serve immediately.

Rabbit Cake

2 rabbits, skinned and dressed   Salt and pepper
  Potato Stuffing (page 221)   ⅓ cup coarse dry bread crumbs
6 tablespoons flour   2½ tablespoons butter

SERVES EIGHT

Cut the rabbits into serving pieces and place in a large kettle. Cover with water, and cook gently until tender, about ½ to 1 hour. Pull the meat from the bones and cut into 1-inch pieces. Reserve the cooking liquid. Spread a layer of Potato Stuffing on the bottom of a well-greased large baking dish. Arrange pieces of rabbit over the stuffing.

Preheat the oven to 350 degrees.

Mix the flour with 2 cups of the liquid in which the rabbit cooked, stir until thoroughly blended. Spoon half of this thickening mixture over the meat. Season with a little salt and pepper. Build one more layer of stuffing, meat, thickening, and seasonings, and top with Potato Stuffing. Sprinkle with bread crumbs and dot generously with butter.

Bake for 40 to 50 minutes in the preheated oven. When the top is golden brown, remove from the oven and carry, piping hot, to the table.

How to Dress and Hang Game Birds

All game birds, including partridge, quail, pheasant, dove, goose, and wild duck, should be properly dressed as soon as possible after the hunt, then hung, and plucked before preparations for cooking are begun.

First, clean your bird by cutting through the breast skin at the base of the neck. Cut out the windpipe and the crop, which lies just below the windpipe in front of the neck vertebrae. Make a slit in the skin over the keel bone, located at the junction of lower breast and tail. Break the keel bone away from the pelvis and pull the entrails completely out of the abdominal cavity. Save the liver and heart for making gravy. Drawing the bird in this way removes the blood and prevents tainting or spoilage. Shot should also be cut out at this point.

Sprinkle the internal cavity of each bird with salt immediately after it has been drawn. The bird must be hung for several days in order to age properly. Hang in a cool, shady place outdoors or indoors. The temperature for hanging should never exceed 36 degrees. If the weather is too warm, place in refrigerator, hung as high as possible where air can circulate around the bird freely.

After aging, the birds should be plucked. Melt paraffin wax in a large kettle. Dip each bird in the kettle, taking care to coat the entire body surface, then hang it in a cool place until the wax hardens. Pull the wax down from the body in strips, using quick, sure motions. This should remove most of the feathers and down. Repeat the dipping, hanging, and pulling procedures to get rid of any recalcitrant pinfeathers. Despite your care, the birds may need to be singed before cooking.

Now your birds are ready for cooking or for your home freezer. Game birds should be marinated or smoked before cooking. After hanging and plucking, marinate in Hunter's Marinade (page 217) for 2 to 3 days for large birds, 24 hours for small birds. Store in a cool place, or refrigerate while marinating. To smoke game birds, follow directions for using your own smoking unit, first soaking the bird in brine in a cool place for 2 days. Drain the bird, wipe it dry, and hang it for a few hours. Smoke as directed. Use immediately, or store in a cool, dry place (but do not refrigerate) until needed.

Spit-Roasted Small Game Birds

When small game birds are in season and plentiful,
this is the recipe you'll need.
Partridge are especially good
cooked outdoors this way.

4 small game birds, dressed, hung, and marinated (see above)

¼ teaspoon dried thyme

Black pepper

8–10 tablespoons butter

8 strips bacon

4 scallions (white part only), minced

4 game livers, halved

Salt

¾ cup dry sherry

8 slices toast

SERVES EIGHT

Rinse the birds with cold water, pat dry, then rub with thyme. Sprinkle pepper inside the cavity of each bird and rub the skins with butter. Crisscross 2 strips of bacon over each breast and truss the legs of each bird close to its body. Use extra string to secure the bacon slices.

Spit-roast the birds over fairly high heat for approximately 30 to 40 minutes, basting frequently with 2 tablespoons butter. The birds are ready to eat when the thigh is fully cooked but the breast is still pink. Do not overcook!

While the birds are roasting, melt 2 tablespoons butter in a skillet. Sauté the scallions in the butter for 3 minutes, stirring frequently. Sauté the liver halves until they are browned, with only a pinkish tinge at their centers. Remove the skillet from the heat, mash the livers, and season with salt and pepper. When the game bird juices no longer run pink, remove from the spit and set aside to keep warm.

Make a sauce by adding remaining 4 tablespoons butter and ¾ cup of sherry to the mashed liver. Return the skillet to medium heat and reduce the liquid, stirring frequently.

To serve, remove the trussing string and cut the game birds in half. Spread the toast with the seasoned liver-sherry mixture. Place half a game bird on each slice and garnish with the remaining sauce.

Frau Muller's Potted Pigeons

2 tablespoons vegetable oil

4 slices salt pork

8 medium onions, sliced

1 pound mushrooms

1 large head lettuce, shredded

8 pigeons, dressed, hung, and marinated (page 207)

1 cup Chicken Stock (page 111) or canned chicken broth

½ cup dry white wine

2 small bay leaves

¼ teaspoon grated nutmeg

¼ teaspoon dried thyme

1 cup heavy cream

3 tablespoons dry sherry

1 tablespoon flour

Salt and black pepper

SERVES EIGHT

Heat the oil in a skillet and render the salt pork, discarding the cracklings. Sauté the onions and mushroom slices for 4 minutes in the rendered fat.

Preheat the oven to 350 degrees.

Divide the onions, mushrooms, and lettuce between 2 oven-proof baking dishes. Truss the birds and arrange on the vegetables, 4 birds to each dish, and divide the stock between the baking dishes. Cover tightly and bake for 45 minutes without lifting the lids.

Mix the wine, bay leaves, nutmeg, thyme, and cream. Make a paste of the sherry and flour and blend well with the wine-cream mixture. Divide this between the 2 dishes, cover tightly and bake 45 to 55 minutes more. Season to taste and serve immediately.

Roast Wild Goose

1 young wild goose, dressed, hung, and marinated (page 207)
Salt and black pepper

Wild Rice Stuffing (page 226) or any other stuffing

Preheat the oven to 475 degrees.

After removing the goose from the marinade, cut off the neck. Place it in a saucepan, add water to cover, and simmer for 45 minutes.

Wipe the bird inside and out and pat the skin dry. Remove any remaining stubborn pinfeathers with tweezers. Fill the cavities with stuffing and truss the legs and wings close to the body. Season the goose with salt and pepper, and set it breast side up on a rack in a roasting pan. Cover the pan and place it in the preheated oven. Roast for 30 minutes, then lower the oven temperature to 325 degrees and continue to roast for 2 to 2½ hours more, or until the goose tests done.

After the first 30 minutes of roasting, baste the goose frequently as it cooks with goose-neck broth. From time to time pour off the goose fat which accumulates in the roasting pan.

Cook the goose uncovered during the last 30 minutes of roasting. Test for doneness by piercing the breast with a 2-pronged fork. If the fork slides in easily, the goose is ready to be taken from the oven.

Fish

How to Clean and Dress Fish

A FEW MINUTES of presoaking in cold water will make scaling easier. Using a sharp knife, scale the fish by holding it firmly down by the head on a flat surface. Begin at the tail and scrape toward the head, taking care to clean well around the gills and base of the head. Slit the entire underbelly and discard the entrails. Carefully remove the pelvic fins located underneath the head, and if desired cut off the head just above the collarbone. A large fish may need to have its backbone snapped in half before the head can be completely severed from the body. Next, cut away the pectoral fins which are situated behind the gills and the tail. Removing the large back dorsal fin and ventral fins on the back underside requires some finesse: make cuts on either side of each of these fins and then pull them forward with a quick movement to make sure that the small base bones come out along with the fins. Finally, wash the fish thoroughly in cold water to remove any clinging bits of innards or dark matter. Now you are ready to cook your fish whole, or to cut it into steaks or slice it into fillets.

Filleting

Use the same sharp knife to bone the fish if you are making fillets. First, split the fish along the length of its back. Lay the fish flat, and cut through to the backbone at the head end. Then angle your knife flat and slice the fillet away from the bones on this one side. The fillet can then be lifted intact from the bones. Reverse the fish, and follow the same procedure on the other side.

Skinning the Fillet

Lay the fillet on a flat surface, skin side down. Grip it by the tail and, beginning at the tail end, cut through just to the skin; then with your knife at a flat angle, slice the fillet completely away from the skin.

[211]

Fried Trout with Spicy Butter Sauce

8 medium brook trout
½ teaspoon salt
½ cup milk
¾ cup flour
5 tablespoons vegetable oil

6 tablespoons butter
3½ teaspoons Dijon mustard
2 tablespoons minced chives
3 tablespoons lemon juice
Pinch cayenne

SERVES EIGHT

Clean, wash, and dry the trout. Mix together the salt and milk. Dip each trout in the milk mixture, then roll in flour.

Heat the oil and 3 tablespoons of butter in a large skillet. Fry the trout until they are tender and crisp. Remove and keep warm. Quickly stir the mustard, chives, lemon juice, cayenne, and remaining butter into the pan. Bring to a boil, and pour the hot spicy butter over the fish.

Grandfather's Oatmeal-Fried Trout

8 medium brook trout
½ pound (2 sticks) butter
Salt and black pepper

2½ cups oatmeal
2 lemons

SERVES EIGHT

Clean, wash, and dry the trout. Heat the butter in a large skillet over medium heat. Season the trout with salt and pepper. Place the oatmeal on wax paper. Dip the fish in the butter and roll in the oatmeal, making sure the oatmeal adheres.

Arrange the fish in the hot butter in the pan. Sauté until golden brown on both sides, turning once. Cut the lemons into 8 wedges to garnish each serving.

Mushroom-Stuffed Trout in Crust***

3 tablespoons butter
6 shallots, minced
1 pound mushrooms, minced
1 cup dry bread crumbs
  Salt and black pepper

8 medium trout, cleaned and
  backbones removed
  Double recipe Pastry for 2-
  Crust Pie (page 418)
1 egg yolk
  Milk or cream

SERVES EIGHT

Heat the butter in a skillet and sauté the shallots and mush-rooms, stirring occasionally. When the mushrooms turn golden, stir in the bread crumbs and cook for 1 minute longer. Season the stuffing with salt and pepper and divide it equally to fill the cavities of the 8 fish.

Preheat the oven to 425 degrees.

Roll out the pastry and cut it into 8 pieces, each large enough to wrap one fish. Shape one piece of dough around each fish, molding it to shape, and place the pastry-wrapped fish on a baking sheet. Cut any extra bits of dough into small crescents shaped to resemble scales and arrange them attractively over the tail of each fish. Mix the egg yolk with a little milk or cream and use this mixture to glaze all of the dough-wrapped fish.

Bake the fish for 15 minutes in the preheated oven. Lower the heat to 350 degrees and bake for 20 to 25 minutes longer, or until the crust is crisp and browned. Serve immediately.

Trout with Sour Cream Sauce

8 medium brook trout
4 tablespoons butter
½ cup dry white wine
4 egg yolks

1 cup sour cream
4 tablespoons minced scallions or
  chives

SERVES EIGHT

Split and clean the trout, leaving the heads intact. Melt the butter in a skillet and sauté the trout 5 minutes on each side. Pour in the wine, cover, and simmer over low heat for 5 minutes, or until the fish are almost done.

In a small bowl, beat the egg yolks lightly and blend in the sour cream and the juices from the pan. Pour this mixture over the fish, and top with the scallions. Cover and cook over low heat 8 to 10 minutes longer, or until the fish is done.

Oyster Cake

Potato Stuffing (page 221)
½ *teaspoon dried thyme*
24 *oysters, shucked and with their liquid reserved*
Bottled clam juice

6 *tablespoons flour*
Salt and black pepper
⅓ *cup coarse dry bread crumbs*
2½ *tablespoons butter*

SERVES EIGHT

Prepare the Potato Stuffing according to directions, substituting ½ teaspoon thyme for the poultry seasoning. If your oysters are not bought out of their shells, shuck them and reserve the liquid. Arrange the oysters in a large saucepan, add enough of the oyster juices to barely cover, and simmer gently until the edges curl. Do not overcook. Remove from the heat and lift the oysters from the pan with a slotted spoon. Measure the juices in the pan and add as much bottled clam juice as necessary to make 2 cups liquid. Blend in the flour and mix thoroughly.

Preheat the oven to 350 degrees.

Spread a layer of Potato Stuffing on the bottom of a well-greased deep casserole. Arrange a layer of oysters over the stuffing. Spoon half the thickened cooking liquid over the oysters, and season with a little salt and pepper. Build one more layer of stuffing, oysters, thickening, and seasonings, then top with another layer of stuffing. Sprinkle with the bread crumbs and dot generously with the butter. Bake for 30 to 40 minutes in the preheated oven. The bread crumbs should be a golden brown. Remove from the oven and serve immediately.

Frogs' Legs with Sweet Peppers

24 medium or 32 small frogs' legs
8 tablespoons (1 stick) butter
　Salt and black pepper
　Generous pinch cayenne
1 cup dry white wine
1 green pepper, seeded and cut into ½-inch squares
1 sweet red pepper, seeded and cut into ⅓-inch squares

1 large onion, coarsely chopped
1 large tomato, peeled, seeded, and chopped
1 clove garlic, crushed
¼ cup minced parsley
1 hard-boiled egg
2 tablespoons minced chives

SERVES EIGHT

Sauté the frogs' legs a few at a time in the butter in a large deep skillet over medium heat for about 5 minutes, or until the meat turns pearly white. Sprinkle the legs with salt, pepper, and cayenne. Add the wine and simmer for 5 minutes more, turning the frogs' legs once.

Add the peppers, onion, tomato, garlic, and minced parsley. Simmer for 10 minutes, or until the vegetables are tender. Arrange the frogs' legs on a serving dish and pour the sauce over them. Force the hard-boiled egg through a fine sieve over the top of the sauce. Garnish with the minced chives, and serve immediately.

Meat and Game Marinades

Lamb Marinade

1 cup lemon juice
8 tablespoons honey
1 cup chopped mint

½ cup olive oil
4 bay leaves, crumbled

YIELDS TWO AND ONE HALF CUPS

Mix all ingredients together and pour over the meat. Marinate in the refrigerator for 1 to 3 days, turning occasionally. Broil the meat until brown on the outside but still pink inside, and serve hot.

Rabbit Marinade

Sliced onions
Water
Vinegar
1 teaspoon salt

12 peppercorns
8 whole cloves
4 bay leaves

Place the pieces of meat in an earthenware crock, and layer with slices of onion. Mix equal parts of water and vinegar to cover the rabbit pieces and add the salt, peppercorns, cloves, and bay leaves.

Cover the crock and place in a very cool place for 2 to 3 days. Be sure to turn the meat pieces each day. If refrigerated, allow the crock to stand at room temperature for 2 hours daily. Pat the rabbit pieces dry before cooking.

Venison Marinade

4 large onions, thinly sliced	2 tablespoons black pepper
4 large carrots, thinly sliced	5 large bay leaves
4 stalks celery, coarsely chopped	2 tablespoons dried thyme
10 cloves garlic, sliced	20 dried juniper berries
3 cups red wine vinegar	½ cup minced parsley
3 cups vegetable oil	8 cups dry red wine

YIELDS ENOUGH TO COVER TWENTY POUNDS OF GAME

Place all the vegetables in a large bowl and pour the wine vinegar and oil over them. Add the pepper, bay leaves, thyme, juniper berries, and parsley. Stir in the wine, and mix all ingredients thoroughly. Arrange cuts of game in a large crock and cover with the marinade. Marinate 5 days, turning several times a day.

Hunter's Marinade

8 cups dry white wine	20 bruised peppercorns
2½ cups tarragon vinegar	20 dried juniper berries
2½ cups olive oil	2½ teaspoons dried thyme
4 large onions, sliced	2½ teaspoons powdered sage

YIELDS ENOUGH TO COVER TWENTY POUNDS OF GAME

Mix all ingredients together. Arrange game in a large crock, and pour in marinade. Marinate 5 days, turning several times a day.

Stuffings, dumplings, noodles, and sauces

Stuffings

ALTHOUGH MANY farmers' wives still follow the Early American method of tightly packing the cavity to produce a dense, easily sliced stuffing, the proportions given in this book are for loosely packed cavities to allow room for expansion during roasting. Fill your bird in the method you prefer.

Two rules that must never be broken, however, are:

1. Always bring the stuffing to room temperature before filling the bird.
2. Always stuff the bird immediately before roasting to prevent spoilage.

Sadie's Cornbread and Sausage Stuffing

1 pound sausage meat

2 large onions, chopped

4 large stalks celery with leaves, chopped

5 cups stale cornbread cubes

4 cups stale white bread cubes

1 cup chopped nutmeats

1 tablespoon minced fresh sage or 1½ teaspoons powdered sage

1 tablespoon minced fresh thyme or 1½ teaspoons dried

1 tablespoon minced fresh tarragon or 1½ teaspoons dried

2 eggs, lightly beaten

Hot water

YIELDS ONE TO TWO CUPS

Fry the sausage for 4 minutes in a heavy skillet, stirring constantly and breaking up any large lumps with the back of a fork.

Add the onion and chopped celery. Stir over medium heat until the onions are very lightly browned. Toss the sausage-vegetable mixture with the bread cubes, nuts, and herbs. Mix the eggs into the stuffing and moisten slightly with hot water.

Sausage Stuffing

½ pound sausage meat

1 large onion, chopped

3 slices white bread

½ cup milk

1 cup fine dry bread crumbs

½ teaspoon salt

¼ teaspoon dried thyme

⅛ teaspoon marjoram

1 egg

YIELDS ABOUT THREE CUPS

Place sausage meat in a skillet and fry until brown, stirring occasionally. Use a slotted spoon to transfer the sausage to a large mixing bowl. Discard all but 2 tablespoons of fat.

Sauté the onion in the sausage fat until golden (do not brown).

[**219**]

Soak the bread slices in the milk and squeeze out the excess moisture. Use your fingers to crumble together the sausage, onion, bread crumbs, and bread slices. Season with the spices and stir in the egg.

Meat Stuffing

½ pound ground pork	½ teaspoon powdered sage
½ pound ground veal	½ teaspoon dried thyme
½ pound ground ham	½ teaspoon grated nutmeg
1 large onion, chopped	½ teaspoon black pepper
1 cup chopped celery with leaves	2 teaspoons salt
3 tablespoons butter	3 eggs
6 cups soft dry bread crumbs	¾ cup dry sherry

YIELDS ABOUT TEN CUPS

Mix the meats with your fingers until they are well blended. Sauté the onion and celery in the butter for 3 minutes. Add the crumbled meats and continue to cook for 5 minutes, stirring constantly and pressing out lumps with a fork.

Place the meat mixture, bread crumbs, and spices in a large bowl and mix well, breaking up any large lumps that remain. Beat in the eggs, one at a time, beating well after each addition. Moisten the stuffing with the sherry and mix again.

Ham and Fruit Stuffing

½ pound cooked ham, cut into ½-inch cubes	2½ cups dry bread crumbs
10 pitted prunes	⅛ teaspoon ground cloves
20 dried apricots	¼ teaspoon dried thyme
½ cup sweet sherry	½ teaspoon salt
1 cup currants	

YIELDS ABOUT TEN CUPS

Place the ham, prunes, apricots, and currants in a large bowl and toss with the sherry. Let stand for 1 hour. Mix the bread crumbs and spices with the ham and fruit. Sprinkle with additional sherry or hot water if the stuffing seems too dry.

Chestnut and Mushroom Stuffing

5 tablespoons butter

1 tablespoon finely chopped shallots

½ pound sausage meat, finely chopped

24 mushrooms, finely chopped

2 cups Chestnut Puree (page 269)

1 tablespoon minced parsley

Salt and black pepper

⅔ cup soft dry bread crumbs

24 boiled chestnuts (page 267)

YIELDS ABOUT SIX CUPS

Melt the butter in a large, heavy skillet, and sauté the shallots for 5 minutes. Add the sausage and mushrooms, allowing them to brown a bit before stirring in the chestnut puree. Simmer the mixture over low heat for 5 minutes. Mix in the parsley, seasonings, crumbs, and chestnuts. Cook for a minute or two, stirring constantly. Remove the stuffing from the heat, cool slightly, and stuff the bird.

Note: If this stuffing is used for chicken or a small turkey, any leftover mixture may be placed in a greased casserole, topped with several slices of bacon, then baked and served along with the chicken.

Miss Maud's Potato Stuffing***

5 large potatoes

¼ cup milk

4 tablespoons butter

5 cups stale bread cubes

2 eggs

1 large onion, minced

¾ cup diced celery

1¼ teaspoons salt

1 teaspoon poultry seasoning

Pinch black pepper

2 tablespoons minced chives

YIELDS ABOUT EIGHT CUPS

Peel the potatoes and boil until tender. Drain well, then mash with the milk and butter. Cool the mashed potatoes a bit. Soak the bread cubes in cold water and squeeze out the excess moisture. Beat the eggs and stir them, along with the bread cubes, minced onion, celery, salt, poultry seasoning, pepper, and chives into the potatoes. Stir thoroughly to blend all ingredients.

Sweet Potato Stuffing

1 medium sweet potato

3 cups dry bread crumbs (use sweet or cornbread crumbs for 1 of these cups)

⅓ cup hot water

1 large onion, finely chopped

3 stalks celery, finely chopped

¾ cup chopped pecans

1 teaspoon poultry seasoning

½ teaspoon salt

2 tablespoons butter

1 egg

YIELDS ABOUT SIX CUPS

Boil the sweet potato in its skin until very tender. Drain well, peel, and mash thoroughly. Place the bread crumbs in a large bowl and sprinkle with hot water. Stir in the mashed sweet potato.

Sauté the onion, celery, pecans, poultry seasoning, and salt in the butter. Beat the egg lightly and combine with the vegetable mixture. Stir into the sweet potato and bread crumb mixture.

Miss Melissa's Cranberry and Nut Stuffing

2 cups cranberries

5 tablespoons granulated sugar

2 tablespoons water

3 tablespoons butter

1 small onion, chopped

1 cup coarsely chopped pecans

3 cups dry bread crumbs

¾ teaspoon salt

½ teaspoon marjoram

YIELDS ABOUT SIX CUPS

Coarsely chop the cranberries and simmer them with the sugar and water for 5 minutes, stirring frequently. Melt the butter in a large skillet and sauté the onion for 2 minutes. Add the nuts and sauté 2 minutes more, stirring occasionally. Stir in the bread crumbs, salt, marjoram, and cranberries. Toss well.

Fruit and Nut Stuffing

8 fresh apricots or 16 dried	1 cup sweet wine
3 tart apples, peeled and cut into ½-inch slices	2 cups dry bread crumbs
½ cup golden raisins	3 tablespoons butter
½ cup currants	½ cup coarsely chopped almonds
	½ cup coarsely chopped pecans

YIELDS ABOUT SEVEN CUPS

Place the apricots, apples, raisins, and currants in a bowl and pour the wine over. Set aside for 1 hour.

Toast the bread crumbs in the butter, add the nuts, and sauté for 1 minute longer.

Toss all ingredients together.

Aunt Rose's Kasha Stuffing

2 cups kasha (buckwheat groats)	3 tablespoons butter
1 egg, lightly beaten	1 cup cornflake crumbs
2 cups water	1 cup currants
2 medium onions, chopped	1 cup chopped nutmeats

YIELDS ABOUT SEVEN CUPS

Place the kasha in a large heavy skillet. Stir in the egg until it disappears, then add the water and stir well. Cover and cook over low heat until the groats have absorbed all the water and are tender.

Sauté the onions in the butter until lightly browned. Toss all ingredients together.

Irene's Hazelnut Stuffing

1½ cups chopped hazelnuts
  6 shallots, chopped
  3 tablespoons butter

2 cups zwieback crumbs
⅛ teaspoon grated nutmeg

YIELDS ABOUT THREE AND ONE HALF CUPS

Sauté the nuts and shallots in the butter. Mix with remaining ingredients.

Mushroom and Dill Stuffing

2 pounds medium mushrooms
4 tablespoons butter
1 medium onion, chopped
3 cups soft dry bread crumbs

3 tablespoons minced dill
1 teaspoon salt
½ cup heavy cream

YIELDS ABOUT FIVE CUPS

Halve the mushrooms and sauté them in the butter for 4 minutes. Add the onion and sauté 2 minutes longer. Toss with the bread crumbs, dill, and salt and add the cream.

Electra Pritchett's Oyster Stuffing***

½ cup chopped shallots

2 tablespoons butter

2 cups oysters, shucked, with their liquid reserved

3 cups soft dry bread crumbs

½ teaspoon grated nutmeg

½ teaspoon dried thyme

½ teaspoon salt

2 tablespoons minced parsley

1 egg

3 tablespoons heavy cream

YIELDS ABOUT FIVE CUPS

Sauté the shallots in the butter until they begin to color. Add the oysters in their liquid and simmer until the edges curl. Stir in the bread crumbs, nutmeg, thyme, salt, and parsley. Beat the egg with the cream and stir all ingredients together.

Clam and Cracker Crumb Stuffing

1 cup littleneck clams, shucked, with their liquid reserved

1 cup sliced mushrooms

1 medium onion, chopped

3 tablespoons butter

1 cup cracker crumbs

2 tablespoons minced fresh sage

⅓ teaspoon salt

YIELDS ABOUT THREE CUPS

Simmer the clams in their liquid until the edges curl. Sauté the mushrooms and onion in the butter until the onion is golden. Toss all ingredients together.

Holiday Wild Rice Stuffing

1 cup wild rice
4 cups cold water
1½ teaspoons salt
½ cup chopped shallots
10 medium mushrooms, chopped
1 large onion, chopped

Liver from the bird, chopped
1 teaspoon poultry seasoning
4 tablespoons butter
1 cup coarsely chopped toasted almonds

YIELDS ABOUT FIVE CUPS

Wash the rice in several changes of cold water. Cover with 4 cups cold water. Stir in 1 teaspoon salt and bring to a boil. Boil uncovered for 35 to 40 minutes, or until tender. Drain the rice and dry out over very low heat for 5 minutes.

Sauté the shallots, mushrooms, onion, liver, and seasonings in the butter until the onion is transparent. Stir in the nuts and rice.

Bird Stuffing from the Orient

3 large stalks celery with leaves
½ pound mushrooms, sliced
1 large onion, coarsely chopped
4 tablespoons vegetable oil
1 cup blanched and slivered almonds

1 cup sliced water chestnuts
1 teaspoon cornstarch
½ teaspoon salt
1 cup Chicken Stock (page 111) or canned chicken broth
1 cup ground blanched almonds

YIELDS FOUR TO FIVE CUPS

Wash the celery well. Chop the celery leaves and cut the stalks into slivers ¼ inch wide by 1 inch long. Sauté the mushrooms, celery, celery leaves, and onion in the oil until the onion is transparent.

Stir the cornstarch and salt into the stock and pour this over the vegetables. Bring to a boil, stirring constantly, until the sauce is thick and clear. Stir in the ground nuts.

Dumplings

Basic Dumpling Batter

2 cups all-purpose flour

6 teaspoons baking powder

1 teaspoon salt

2 eggs

¾ cup milk

2 teaspoons butter, melted

¼ teaspoon dried dill

2–3 cups boiling liquid

YIELDS ABOUT TEN DUMPLINGS

Sift together all dry ingredients with the exception of the dill. Beat the eggs and milk together and stir into the dry ingredients. Add the melted butter and the dill and mix well. Drop by spoonfuls into 2 to 3 cups of boiling stock or into a bubbling stew. Cover immediately and cook for 2 minutes. Turn the dumplings, cover once again, and cook for 2 minutes more. Serve immediately.

Note: If the dumplings are dropped directly in a stew, be sure there is some liquid on top for the dumplings to poach in.

Old German Potato Dumplings***

*This recipe brings together the best qualities
of both potatoes and dumplings.*

7 medium potatoes, peeled	⅛ teaspoon black pepper
2 medium onions	¾ teaspoon dried dill
12 slices white bread	3 eggs
¾ teaspoon salt	1½ cups all-purpose flour

SERVES EIGHT TO TEN

Grate the potatoes coarsely, squeeze out as much water as possible, then press between paper towels to eliminate any remaining liquid. Grate the onions, place in a fine sieve, and press out all juices with the back of a spoon. Mix the onion juice and 3 tablespoons of onion pulp with the grated potatoes, reserving the rest of the onion pulp for future use, perhaps in a salad or soup.

Soak the bread slices in water. Squeeze out as much water as possible and place the bread in a bowl. Add the salt, pepper, and dill, stir in the grated potato and onion mixture, and mix in the eggs. Blend all ingredients thoroughly, then form into balls. Bring 4½ quarts of salted water to a low, rolling boil in a 6 quart kettle.

Spread a generous amount of the flour on a pastry board, roll the dumplings in it until they are thickly coated, and drop them into the boiling water. Cook, covered, for 15 minutes. Remove with a slotted spoon and serve piping hot.

Feather-Light Dumplings***

2 cups all-purpose flour
4 teaspoons baking powder
1 teaspoon salt
½ teaspoon black pepper
1 egg

4 tablespoons butter, melted
Milk
Water, stock, or thin gravy
2 tablespoons granulated sugar
½ teaspoon salt

YIELDS EIGHT LARGE DUMPLINGS

Sift the flour, baking powder, salt, and pepper into a large bowl. Beat the egg lightly and add to the dry ingredients along with the melted butter and enough milk to make a fairly stiff batter.

Bring 1 quart of water, stock, or thin gravy to boil in a very large kettle. If you are cooking the dumplings in water, add the sugar and salt. Drop the dumpling batter into the boiling liquid by tablespoonsful. Cover the kettle tightly and cook the dumplings at a low boil for 15 minutes. Do not remove the lid. Remove the dumplings with a slotted spoon when they are cooked through. Serve hot with stews, soups, or as a side dish.

Old-Fashioned Pot Pie Dumplings

2 cups flour
1¼ teaspoons baking powder
2¾ teaspoons salt

1 tablespoon butter
Milk
1½ quarts water

SERVES EIGHT

Sift the flour, baking powder, and ¾ teaspoon salt into a large bowl. Using your fingers, work the butter into the dry ingredients, then add enough milk to make a stiff batter.

Turn the dough out onto a heavily floured board and roll ½ inch thick. Cut into 2-inch squares or rounds. Bring the water to a boil, add 2 teaspoons salt, and drop in the dumplings. Lower the heat and cook the dumplings at a low boil, covered, for 20 to 25 minutes.

Soup Dumplings with Cheese

6 tablespoons butter
1 cup grated Swiss cheese
4 tablespoons flour

1 tablespoon minced chives
2 egg yolks

YIELDS SIXTEEN SMALL DUMPLINGS

Beat the butter until it is light. Add the cheese, flour, and chives. Stir in the egg yolks and blend thoroughly. Dust your hands with flour and shape the batter into balls ½ inch in diameter. Drop them into boiling soup. When the dumplings rise to the surface, boil for 1 minute longer. Serve immediately.

Soup Dumplings with Nuts

1 cup blanched almonds or brazil
    nuts
⅔ cup dry bread crumbs

½ teaspoon salt
3 egg whites
4 tablespoons vegetable oil

YIELDS SIXTEEN SMALL DUMPLINGS

Grind the nuts in a blender until they resemble coarse meal. If necessary, stop the blender several times, stir the nuts, and push them down against the blades. Place the bread crumbs in a small bowl and add the pulverized nuts and salt.

Beat the egg whites until frothy, and stir 1 tablespoonful into the nut mixture. Shape the mixture into small balls. Dip the balls into the remaining egg whites and fry half of them at a time in 2 tablespoons of hot oil. When the balls are golden brown all over, remove them with a slotted spoon and set aside to drain on paper towels. Add the remaining oil to the skillet and fry the rest of the nut balls. Serve immediately in hot soup.

Lancaster County Liver Dumplings

*Any hearty soup is transformed into a meal
when served with these dumplings and
thick slices of buttered, home-baked bread.*

1½ pounds beef liver

2 tablespoons butter

3 tablespoons minced onion

6 tablespoons dry bread crumbs

2 eggs

¼ teaspoon salt

4 tablespoons flour

1 teaspoon baking powder

Milk

YIELDS TWELVE TO FOURTEEN DUMPLINGS

Coarsely chop the liver and fry until well done in 1 tablespoon butter. Remove from pan and mince finely. Heat the remaining butter in a separate skillet, add the onions and bread crumbs and sauté until the onions are transparent. Beat the eggs lightly, combine with the minced liver, and mix in the onions and bread crumbs. Add the salt, flour, and baking powder, plus just enough milk to make the mixture easy to roll into 1½-inch balls. Roll the dumplings in additional flour and drop into lightly boiling soup. Cook, covered, for 25 to 30 minutes.

Noodles

Soup Noodles

4 eggs
2 egg yolks
4 tablespoons water
Pinch salt

3 cups hard flour
2 teaspoons vegetable oil
2 quarts water

SERVES EIGHT

Place the eggs, egg yolks, water, salt, and 1½ cups flour in a blender. Whirl for 2 minutes on high speed. The mixture should be smooth. Use a spatula to scrape the paste into a large bowl. Set it aside for 10 to 15 minutes.

Knead in the remaining flour, forming a solid ball of dough. Work the oil into this with your fingers, shape the dough, and allow it to rest for 10 minutes. Form the dough into a long roll about 1 inch in diameter, then divide it into 3-inch pieces. Dust a pastry board and rolling pin with flour, and roll each piece into a long, thin strip, about 14 inches wide and 2 inches thick. Set each of these strips of dough aside for 35 minutes to dry slightly. Cut them into noodles approximately ¼ inch wide, then arrange them on towels and set them in a warm place for 1½ to 2 hours to dry out and turn brittle.

Bring 2 quarts water to a boil in a saucepan, add the noodles and boil gently for 10 minutes before adding to your soup.

Pennsylvania Dutch Pot Pie Noodles for Stew

*These chewy square noodles require
an ample amount of liquid and cooking room, so be sure
to use a large pot and a stew recipe with lots of gravy.*

2 cups all-purpose flour
1 teaspoon baking powder
Pinch salt

1 tablespoon vegetable
shortening
1 egg
¾–1 cup milk

SERVES EIGHT

Sift the flour, baking powder, and salt together into a large bowl. Cut in the shortening with 2 knives or a pastry blender until the mixture resembles coarse meal. Beat the egg lightly and stir into the dry mixture, along with as much milk as necessary to make a stiff dough.

Divide the dough into 4 pieces for easy handling. Roll out each piece on a well-floured board, incorporating flour into the dough as you work. Cut each portion of rolled-out dough into 2-inch squares. Layer these pot pie noodles into your stew, about 1 hour before the stew is ready to serve. Take care that the pot pie noodles do not overlap.

Sauces

Sweet and Hot Barbecue Sauce***

4 cloves garlic, crushed

2 cups soy sauce

1 tablespoon crushed hot red peppers

6 tablespoons molasses

1 cup drained crushed pineapple

YIELDS ABOUT TWO CUPS

Mix all ingredients together. Refrigerate for at least 1 hour. Serve with ham, chicken, pork or shrimp, or use as a marinade.

Hot 'n' Delicious Texas Barbecue Sauce

1 medium onion, finely chopped

1 small green pepper, finely chopped

3 cloves garlic, crushed

½ cup ketchup

½ cup vegetable oil

⅓ cup wine vinegar

¼ cup water

1½ teaspoons salt

1 tablespoon chili powder

1 teaspoon oregano

¼ teaspoon Tabasco

YIELDS TWO AND ONE HALF CUPS

Place the onion, green pepper, and garlic in a saucepan. Stir in the remaining ingredients. Cook for 10 to 12 minutes over low heat, stirring occasionally. Serve hot or at room temperature with pork, chicken, or lamb. The flavor of this sauce is improved when refrigerated for a day or two before serving.

Bread Sauce

Bread Sauce is traditionally served with game or fowl.

3 cups milk

1 medium onion, peeled and
 studded with whole cloves

Salt

Pinch cayenne

1½ cups soft bread crumbs or ½
 inch pieces of fresh bread

2 tablespoons butter

YIELDS FOUR CUPS

Place the milk and onion in a saucepan, season with salt and cayenne, and bring to a boil. Lower the heat and simmer for 5 minutes. Remove and discard the onion and stir the bread crumbs and butter into the hot milk.

Currant Jelly Sauce

*This sauce was often served with roast lamb
around the turn of the century.*

1 cup currant jelly

½ cup granulated sugar

1 cup water

2 teaspoons arrowroot

4 tablespoons sweet sherry

YIELDS ABOUT TWO CUPS

Place the currant jelly and sugar in a saucepan, stir in the water, and bring to a boil. Cook over medium heat for 7 minutes. Mix just enough cold water into the arrowroot to make a mixture that will pour easily, and add it, a bit at a time, to the boiling syrup. Continue to cook the sauce for 5 minutes, stirring constantly, until the sauce thickens. Remove from the heat, stir in the sherry, and serve hot.

Mint Jelly Sauce

Substitute mint jelly for the currant jelly. The result is a refreshingly different mint sauce.

Curry Sauce

3 tablespoons butter
1 small onion, finely chopped
1¼ teaspoons curry powder
    Pinch dried thyme
2 tablespoons flour

3¼ cups Chicken Stock (page 111) or canned chicken broth
    Pinch white pepper
    Salt
¼ cup heavy cream

YIELDS TWO CUPS

Melt 2 tablespoons butter in a saucepan and sauté the onion until it is transparent. Blend in the curry powder, thyme, and flour. Cook, stirring, for 2 or 3 minutes. Add the broth all at once, beating well with a wire whisk until smooth. Sprinkle with white pepper and salt to taste and cook the sauce, stirring constantly, until it comes to a boil. Simmer for 15 minutes. Skim the sauce occasionally as it thickens and reduces in volume.

Stir in the heavy cream, reheat, and serve hot over vegetables, fish, or stuffed eggs (page 92).

Herb Sauce

¼ cup chervil
¼ cup parsley
½ cup watercress
3 scallions, minced
⅓ cup boiling water

2 small cloves garlic, crushed
¾ cup mayonnaise
½ cup yoghurt
1 teaspoon lemon juice
    Salt

YIELDS ABOUT TWO AND ONE HALF CUPS

Place the herbs and scallions in a small saucepan, cover with the boiling water, and steep for several minutes. Set the mixture in a blender container, add the garlic and mayonnaise, and blend for 30 seconds. Add the yogurt, lemon juice, and salt, and blend 10 seconds more. Chill thoroughly. Use as a dip for fresh vegetables or as a sauce for cold meats and fish.

Tomato Sauce

15 medium tomatoes, quartered
3 tablespoons oil or butter
2 small cloves garlic, sliced
1 large onion, coarsely chopped

2½ cups Chicken Stock (page 111) or water
Salt and black pepper

YIELDS THREE AND ONE HALF TO FOUR AND ONE HALF CUPS

Remove the seeds from the tomatoes but do not peel them. Heat the oil or butter in a heavy skillet. Coarsely chop the tomatoes and add them, with the garlic and onion, to the oil in the pan. Mash the tomatoes with a fork over medium heat until they are quite soft.

Add the stock or water and simmer for about 20 minutes, or until the sauce thickens somewhat. Rub the sauce through a sieve and return it to the pan. Season to taste. Simmer the sauce until it is fairly thick.

Tomato-Cream Sauce***

15 medium tomatoes, quartered
3 tablespoons butter
1 large onion, coarsely chopped

Salt and black pepper
2 cups heavy cream

YIELDS ABOUT FIVE TO SIX CUPS

Remove the seeds from the tomatoes but do not peel them. Heat the butter in a heavy skillet. Sauté the onion for 1 minute. Coarsely chop the tomatoes and sauté with the onions over medium heat for 5 minutes. Mash well with a fork and continue to cook for 5 minutes more, stirring occasionally. Rub through a sieve and return the puree to the pan.

Gradually stir in the cream and simmer over low heat until the sauce is fairly thick. Serve hot with eggs, fish, vegetables, or meat.

Mint Sauce

1 cup cider vinegar　　　　　　　3 tablespoons granulated sugar
½ cup finely chopped mint

YIELDS ONE AND ONE HALF CUPS

Combine all ingredients and mix well. Serve with lamb.

Easy White Sauce

This recipe makes a medium-thick sauce.
If you want a thicker sauce,
reduce the amount of milk by ½ cup.
For a thinner sauce, increase the milk by ½ cup.

4 tablespoons butter　　　　　1 cup heavy cream or ¾ cup
¼ cup flour　　　　　　　　　　　milk
1 cup milk　　　　　　　　　　½ teaspoon salt
　　　　　　　　　　　　　　　White pepper

YIELDS TWO CUPS

Melt the butter in a heavy skillet over medium heat, add the flour, and stir until the mixture forms a smooth paste. Remove the skillet from the heat and add the cold milk all at once, stirring well. Mix in the cream and stir with a fork until the sauce is smooth and free of lumps. Return the skillet to medium heat and cook the white sauce, stirring constantly, until it thickens. Season with salt and white pepper.

Béchamel Sauce

3 tablespoons butter	Pinch white pepper
2 tablespoons finely chopped onion	Pinch grated nutmeg
4 tablespoons flour	Pinch fresh thyme or dried
2 cups cold milk	1 egg yolk
2 ounces chopped lean veal*	

YIELDS TWO CUPS

Melt 2 tablespoons butter in a heavy skillet and sauté the onions until they are transparent but not brown. Blend in the flour, add the cold milk all at once, and stir *constantly* until the mixture is smooth and thick. Place the remaining tablespoon of butter in another skillet and add the veal, pepper, nutmeg, and thyme. Cook over very low heat for 5 minutes. Do not brown the veal.

Stir the veal into the cream sauce and cook the mixture over very low heat for 20 minutes, stirring occasionally. Beat the egg yolk lightly, add a little of the hot sauce to the egg, beat again, then stir this mixture into the sauce. Cook for 1 minute longer, then strain the sauce through a fine sieve. Dot with tiny bits of butter to prevent any surface film.

* Cooked or raw veal may be used in this sauce. If you have no veal, substitute 1 cup chicken broth for 1 cup milk to give the sauce a slight meat flavor.

Hollandaise Sauce

½ pound (2 sticks) butter   Salt
6 egg yolks   White pepper
4 teaspoons lemon juice

YIELDS TWO CUPS

Melt the butter in a saucepan over low heat. Warm a blender container by keeping 1 cup of hot water in it for several minutes. Empty and dry the container and add the egg yolks, lemon juice, and seasonings. Blend at high speed for a few seconds, then shut the motor off. The butter should be very hot when adding it to the egg yolk mixture. Partially cover the blender container, turn the blender on high, and add the butter in a thin, steady stream. The sauce will be ruined if you become impatient and add the butter too quickly. As soon as all the butter has been incorporated, shut off the blender. Serve the sauce immediately.

Clarified Butter

To clarify butter, place the amount you will need in a saucepan over low heat. Skim off the foam as it rises. Remove the pan from the heat and cool the butter slightly. The sediment will remain at the bottom and the oil that floats on top can be used for any recipe that calls for Clarified Butter.

How to Make Perfectly Smooth Gravy

No matter how many recipes you have read or tried, there is only one sure-fire way to make lump-free gravy. The secret is adding *cold* liquid all at once, to the blend of flour and drippings in the pan.

Begin by placing several tablespoons of pan drippings in a saucepan over low heat, adding butter if there is not enough drippings. Blend 2 tablespoons of flour into the drippings to make a smooth paste. Add your cold liquid (stock or water or vegetable juices) all at once to the pan. Stir the mixture *constantly* and blend it well, pressing out all lumps with the back of a spoon. Continue to stir over medium-low heat until the gravy boils and thickens.

Basic Brown Gravy

4 tablespoons pan drippings
3 tablespoons flour

3 cups Beef Stock (page 108) or canned beef bouillon
Salt and black pepper

YIELDS ABOUT THREE CUPS

Heat the pan drippings and stir in the flour until it forms a smooth paste. Allow the mixture to brown slightly, then add the cold stock all at once. Stirring constantly with a fork, scrape loose all brown bits in the bottom of the pan and bring the gravy to a boil. Season to taste and simmer for 5 to 10 minutes. Strain if desired and serve hot.

Piquant Brown Gravy

3 tablespoons butter
1 tablespoon minced onion
2 tablespoons cider vinegar

2 teaspoons dry mustard
1 tablespoon water
1 cup Basic Brown Gravy (above)

YIELDS ONE AND ONE QUARTER CUPS

Heat the butter in a saucepan, add the onion, and sauté until golden. Stir in the vinegar, reduce the heat, and simmer for 5 minutes. Mix the dry mustard with the water to form a thin paste and blend into the onion-vinegar mixture. Add the Basic Brown Gravy, simmer for 3 minutes, strain, and serve immediately.

Southern-Style Cream Gravy

3 tablespoons flour
6 tablespoons pan drippings from
    baked or fried chicken

1¼ cups milk
1¾ cups heavy cream
    Salt and black pepper

YIELDS ABOUT THREE CUPS

Add the flour to the pan drippings and mix to a smooth paste. Stir in the milk and bring to a boil over medium heat, stirring constantly and scraping the bottom of the pan to loosen any remaining brown bits. Add the cream and bring the gravy to a boil once more. Season to taste. Strain and serve hot.

Red-Eye Ham Gravy

This old-time recipe has an interesting flavor and provides a nice change, especially when leftover ham is being served. It is, however, not to everyone's taste, so try it before you serve it to guests.

2 cups weak black coffee
6 tablespoons pan drippings

1 cup heavy cream
    Salt and black pepper

YIELDS THREE CUPS

Add the coffee to the pan drippings and barely simmer for 7 or 8 minutes. Pour in the cream and continue to simmer for about 10 minutes, or until the gravy is the thickness you desire. Season with salt and pepper. Serve hot over ham slices or ham sandwiches.

Fine Herb Gravy

6 tablespoons pan drippings from
  a veal roast

3 tablespoons flour

1 tablespoon minced parsley

1 tablespoon minced fresh thyme
  or 1½ teaspoons dried

1 tablespoon minced fresh tarragon or 1½ teaspoons dried

3 cups Chicken Stock (page 111)
  or canned chicken broth

Salt and black pepper

YIELDS ABOUT THREE CUPS

Stir the flour into the pan drippings and mix to a smooth paste. Cook over medium heat until the mixture is light brown.

Stir in the herbs and stock and bring to a boil; stir constantly until the gravy thickens. Season to taste with salt and pepper. Serve hot.

Shallot Gravy

6 shallots, minced

1 tablespoon minced parsley

6 tablespoons pan drippings

3 tablespoons flour

3 cups Beef Stock (page 108) or
  Chicken Stock (page 111)

Salt and black pepper

YIELDS ABOUT THREE CUPS

Sauté the shallots and parsley in the pan drippings for 3 or 4 minutes. Stir in the flour and blend to a smooth paste. Add the stock, salt and pepper to taste, and cook over medium heat, stirring constantly, until the gravy boils and thickens. Serve hot.

Vegetables

Artichokes

ALTHOUGH ARTICHOKES are not standard farmhouse fare they make a delicious addition to vegetable dinners and company lunches.

Prepare artichokes for boiling or steaming by snipping off the thorny tip on each of the outer leaves with scissors. Slice off the stalk at the base of each so it will sit level on a plate. Rinse the artichokes well and place in a very large kettle.

To boil, add water to cover, salt, and the juice of ½ lemon. Bring the water to a boil, and cook the artichokes, covered, over low heat for 35 to 45 minutes, or until tender. Drain before serving.

To steam the artichokes, place a small amount of water in a deep, heavy kettle, add 1 teaspoon salt and the juice of ½ lemon, and turn the trimmed artichokes on all sides in the water. Set the artichokes upright. Cover the kettle tightly and cook over very low heat until they are tender, about 45 to 60 minutes. Remove from the heat and drain. Serve the artichokes with hot Clarified Butter (page 240) or cold with French Dressing (page 333) or Your Own Mayonnaise (page 334).

Stuffed Artichokes

SERVES EIGHT

After 8 artichokes have been cooked and drained (above), cut away and discard the soft center leaves and carefully dig out the chokes with a spoon, leaving the bottoms intact. Fill the cavity with one of the following stuffings. Place 4 artichokes in each of 2 casseroles, pour 1½ cups of Beef Stock (page 108) into each casserole, and cover tightly with aluminum foil. Bake for 30 minutes in a preheated 350-degree oven. If you wish to brown the artichokes, sprinkle the stuffing with bread crumbs and broil briefly before serving.

Bread Crumb and Garlic Stuffing

Mix together 2⅔ cups dry bread crumbs, 8 tablespoons (1 stick) melted butter, and 3 crushed garlic cloves. Stuff and bake as above.

Almond Stuffing

Sauté until golden 1 finely chopped onion and 15 chopped mushrooms in 8 tablespoons butter. Stir in 1 cup dry bread crumbs, 1 cup ground almonds, and ½ cup ketchup. Stir over low heat for 2 or 3 minutes. Stuff and bake as above.

Mushroom Stuffing

Chop 1 pound of mushrooms, reserving 8 caps. Sauté until golden the chopped mushrooms and 1 chopped onion in 4 tablespoons butter. Stir in 1 cup dry bread crumbs and cook for 2 or 3 minutes. Add 2 tablespoons heavy cream. Stuff and bake artichokes; top each with mushroom cap, stem side up. Brush with melted butter and broil for 2 or 3 minutes. Turn the mushroom caps, brush again with melted butter, and broil 2 or 3 minutes longer.

Ham and Tomato Sauce Stuffing

Boil the artichokes for only 15 minutes. Sauté until golden 1 finely chopped onion in 8 tablespoons butter. Add 1 cup finely chopped cooked ham, brown a bit, then stir in 1 cup dry bread crumbs, and ¾ cup Tomato Sauce (page 237). Stuff the artichokes and tie each with string. Crisscross 2 slices of bacon over each artichoke. Bake as above, adding, if desired, ¼ cup each chopped onion and celery to the stock in each casserole.

Meat Stuffing

Sauté until golden 3 tablespoons finely chopped onion in 3 table-spoons butter. Add 1½ cups finely chopped cooked chicken or veal, ¾ cup dry bread crumbs, and enough Easy White Sauce (page 238) to moisten the stuffing. Stuff and bake as above.

How to Prepare Artichoke Bottoms

Artichoke bottoms may be prepared by following directions for cooking whole artichokes (page 244), and then removing the leaves and chokes. Scrape the pulp from the leaves after removing them; use in Cream of Artichoke Soup (page 117), or arrange the chilled leaves attractively on a platter surrounding a dipping bowl of French Dressing (page 333).

There is an alternate method of preparation, one generally used in French cooking. This method, although more complicated, produces admirable results and should be attempted at least once by every enthusiastic cook.

First cut or break off the stem of the whole artichoke by bending it back. Hold the artichoke upright and bend and snap off the leaves just beyond the point where the meaty section of each begins, moving in circular fashion over the whole artichoke. When you reach the soft inner leaf structure, the rest of leaves may be cut off with a knife or scissors. The choke remains until the artichoke bottoms are cooked, when it may be easily removed with a spoon.

As you work, rub the exposed parts of the artichoke bottoms with lemon juice to prevent discoloration. Set each bottom as you finish its cutting into a quart of water to which a tablespoon of lemon juice has been added.

Cooking Artichoke Bottoms

Bring to a boil 6 cups water, 2 tablespoons flour, 1½ tablespoons salt, and 2 tablespoons lemon juice. Add 8 artichoke bottoms and cook over medium heat for 35 to 45 minutes, or until tender. Add more boiling water if necessary to cover the artichoke bottoms.

Turn the bottoms upside down to drain. The artichokes may also be kept in their liquid and refrigerated if not used immediately. Remove and discard the chokes carefully with a spoon, and garnish or fill the bottoms when hot or cold with any of the preparations which follow.

Pâté and Périgourdine Sauce

3 tablespoons butter
2 tablespoons finely chopped onion
1 tablespoon flour
1 10¾-ounce can beef bouillon
3 tablespoons tomato sauce

3 tablespoons dry sherry
1 teaspoon bottled beef concentrate
2 slices Country Pâté (page 102)

Heat the butter in a skillet, and sauté the onions over low heat until just golden. Stir in the flour, and cook long enough to brown the flour. Add the stock, tomato sauce, sherry, and beef concentrate. Stir constantly until the sauce is thickened, but do not allow it to burn.

Cut the pâté slices in quarters and place a quarter in each artichoke. Top immediately with spoonfuls of périgourdine sauce, and serve at once. Pass extra sauce on the side.

Creamed Chicken

2 tablespoons butter
1 small onion, minced
2 large whole chicken breasts,
  minced

2 cups Béchamel Sauce (page
  239)

Heat the butter in a skillet, and sauté the onions until golden. Stir in the minced chicken breasts, and cook only until the chicken is pearl white. Remove from the heat, and use 1 cup of the sauce to bind the chicken and onion mixture. Heap the artichoke bottoms with the chicken mixture and top each with 1 tablespoon of the remaining sauce. Place the filled artichokes under the broiler for 2 or 3 minutes to glaze them. Serve immediately.

Creamed Crabmeat

¾ pound cooked crabmeat
⅛ teaspoon dry mustard

2 cups Béchamel Sauce (page
  239)

Flake the crabmeat carefully to eliminate all shell. Mix the mustard into 1 cup of the sauce and stir this into the crabmeat. Divide the crabmeat mixture equally among the artichoke bottoms. Top each with 1 tablespoon of the remaining sauce, and place the filled artichokes under the broiler for 2 or 3 minutes to glaze them. Serve immediately.

Creamed Mushrooms

1 pound mushrooms
2 tablespoons butter

2 cups Béchamel Sauce (page
  239)

Wipe or rinse any sand from the mushrooms and slice them very thin. Heat the butter in a skillet, and sauté the mushrooms over low heat until golden. Place 1½ tablespoons of sauce in each of the artichoke bottoms. Divide the sautéed mushrooms among the artichokes, and spread 2 tablespoons of the remaining sauce over each. Glaze under the broiler for 2 or 3 minutes and serve at once.

Buttered Green Peas

2 cups shelled green peas
2 or 3 lettuce leaves
¼ cup water
1 teaspoon granulated sugar

4 tablespoons butter
Salt
½ cup Béchamel Sauce (page 239)

Place the peas and lettuce in a large saucepan with the water, sugar, and butter. Simmer, covered, for 8 to 12 minutes, or until tender. Discard the lettuce leaves and season the peas with salt to taste.

Place an equal amount of peas in each artichoke bottom. Top each serving with 1 tablespoon sauce; glaze under the broiler for 2 or 3 minutes. Serve immediately.

Shrimp and Hard-Boiled Eggs

1 cup mayonnaise
8 hard-boiled eggs

24 cooked whole shrimp
Black olives

Spread 1 tablespoon mayonnaise over the inside of each chilled artichoke bottom. Shell and slice the eggs thinly, and arrange 3 or 4 slices over each artichoke bottom. Top with 3 shrimp and 1 teaspoon mayonnaise for each serving and garnish each with a slice of black olive. Serve cold.

Fish Salad

2 cups cooked flaked fish
¾ cup mayonnaise

2 tablespoons chopped fresh dill

Mix the fish with as much mayonnaise as necessary to bind it, and divide the salad equally among the chilled artichoke bottoms. Serve cold, garnished with fresh dill.

Chicken Salad

2 cups cooked minced chicken *4 hard-boiled egg yolks, sieved*
1 cup mayonnaise *2 tablespoons minced parsley*

Mix the cooked chicken with enough mayonnaise to bind it. Place equal amounts in each chilled artichoke bottom. Top with sieved egg yolk and garnish with parsley. Serve cold.

Meat Salad

2 cups minced cooked veal or *¾ cup mayonnaise*
other meat *1½ tablespoons minced chives*

Mix the cooked meat with enough mayonnaise to bind it. Place equal amounts in each chilled artichoke bottom. Garnish with chives.

Vegetable Salad

2 cups cooked vegetables *2 tablespoons minced chives*
¾ cup mayonnaise

Mix the vegetables with enough mayonnaise to bind. Place equal amounts of vegetable salad in each of the artichoke bottoms and garnish with chives. Serve cold.

Buttered Asparagus

4 pounds asparagus *Salt*
10 tablespoons butter, melted

SERVES EIGHT

Asparagus is freshest when the bud ends are tightly closed and compact. Rinse all asparagus carefully to eliminate the sand.

Cut or snap off any thick, woody stems, and use a vegetable peeler to trim the lower portions of the stalks if the asparagus is not particularly young and/or freshly picked.

The vegetable may be either steamed or boiled. To steam, place upright in a deep kettle or coffee pot; or lay flat in a saucepan with the tips propped up on a small heatproof glass jar; or cook in an asparagus cooker. Add a very little boiling salted water, and cook over very low heat, covered, until tender, about 12 to 15 minutes. To boil, cover all but the tips with boiling salted water, bring to a boil again, and cook until tender, about 12 to 18 minutes, depending upon the thickness of the asparagus stalks.

Drain the steamed or boiled stalks, toss with melted butter, and season with salt to taste. Cooked asparagus may be served warm or cold with French Dressing (page 333), or hot with Hollandaise Sauce (page 240).

Shaker Asparagus in Egg-Cream Sauce

*Asparagus tastes even more delectable
when served with this delicate cream sauce
freshened with mint.*

4 pounds asparagus

2 tablespoons butter

1 cup heavy cream

½ teaspoon salt

⅛ teaspoon granulated sugar

1½ teaspoons chopped fresh mint
or ½ teaspoon dried

2 egg yolks

Pinch grated nutmeg

SERVES EIGHT

Wash the asparagus, cut off the thick white ends, and use a vegetable peeler to trim the lower stalks. Steam the asparagus in a little water until tender.

Melt the butter in a large saucepan over low heat. Stir in the cream, salt, sugar, and mint, and allow the mixture to simmer slowly for 8 to 10 minutes. Beat the egg yolks together lightly, slowly add to the cream sauce, and heat gently for 1 minute more. Do not allow to boil.

[251]

Drain the asparagus, arrange on a serving plate, pour the cream sauce over, and grate a bit of nutmeg over the top. Serve immediately.

Deep-Fried Asparagus

3–4 pounds asparagus	*Flour*
2 eggs	*2 cups dry bread crumbs*
½ teaspoon salt	*Vegetable oil for frying*

SERVES EIGHT

Trim the asparagus and cut into 4½- to 5-inch lengths. Cook according to directions given in Buttered Asparagus (page 250). Drain the spears and dry them on paper towels.

Beat the eggs lightly with the salt. Dip each spear first in flour, then in the egg, and finally in bread crumbs. Fry to a golden brown, a few at a time, in hot oil to cover, transferring them as they are finished to an ovenproof platter. Set the platter in the oven to keep the vegetable warm. Serve hot as soon as all the asparagus have been fried.

Asparagus with Buttered Crumbs

4 pounds asparagus	*Grated zest and juice of 1 lemon*
½ pound (2 sticks) butter	*Salt and black pepper*
1 cup dry bread crumbs ·	

SERVES EIGHT

Trim and wash the asparagus. Cook them in a small amount of simmering water, tightly covered, over low heat. Just before the spears are tender (after about 10 minutes of cooking) melt the butter in a large skillet, add the bread crumbs, and allow them to brown lightly. Sprinkle the bread crumbs with the grated lemon zest and salt and pepper to taste.

Drain the asparagus and arrange on serving plates. Top with the buttered crumbs. Stir the lemon juice into the butter remaining in the pan and pour over the asparagus. Serve immediately, garnished with thin slices of lemon if desired.

Sister Lettie's Green Bean Stew

¼ pound slab bacon

1 tablespoon butter

4 medium onions, finely chopped

4 large potatoes, peeled and cut into ½-inch cubes

4 medium tomatoes, peeled, seeded, and chopped

½ teaspoon salt

Black pepper

3 cups Clarified Beef Stock (page 110) or canned beef bouillon

1 pound green beans

1 teaspoon bottled beef concentrate

2½ tablespoons flour

½ cup water

SERVES EIGHT

Discard the bacon rind and cut the bacon into ½-inch cubes. Heat the butter in a heavy kettle and sauté the bacon cubes until they are lightly browned on all sides. Remove and reserve the bacon. Add the onions to the kettle, sauté them until golden, then add the potatoes, tomatoes, salt, and pepper. Simmer the mixture over low heat for 10 minutes.

Stir in the stock, and bring to a boil. Trim the green beans, pulling off strings if necessary, and add them whole to the kettle along with the reserved bacon. Lower the heat and simmer the vegetables, covered, until just tender. Do not overcook. Just before serving, stir in the beef concentrate.

Combine the flour and water, blend well and add ½ cup of the liquid from the kettle to it. Stir this mixture back into the stew, and stir constantly until thick and bubbling. Serve the stew piping hot.

Buttered Green Beans

2½ pounds green beans   *Salt and black pepper*
7 tablespoons butter

SERVES EIGHT

If the beans are not from your garden, be sure they are young and fresh by snapping one or two. If they snap crisply they are young slightly immature green beans that are at the peak of good taste. The beans may be left whole after rinsing and tearing off the strings with only the stem ends cut off, or they may be trimmed and cut into 1½-inch lengths. To French cut the beans, slice them lengthwise into thin strips after trimming the ends.

Place the green beans in a little boiling salted water, cover tightly, and bring the water to a second boil. Lower the heat, cover, and steam until barely tender and still crisp, about 10 to 12 minutes. Drain the beans in a colander and add the butter to the pan. Replace the beans and shake the pan to thoroughly soak the beans with butter. Transfer the buttered beans to a serving dish, season with salt and pepper, and serve immediately.

Green beans may also be boiled in the following way. Bring salted water to a boil, and add the beans a few at a time. Cook the beans over medium heat for about 10 to 12 minutes. They should be crisp but tender. Drain off the water, add the butter to the beans, and cook, covered, over low heat, shaking the pan frequently, until all the beans are coated. Transfer to a serving dish, season with salt and pepper to taste, and serve at once.

Buttered Lima Beans

4 pounds lima beans

4 tablespoons butter, melted

Black pepper

SERVES EIGHT

Shell lima beans immediately before cooking to prevent vitamin and flavor loss. The beans will be easier to shell if the rounded ends of the pods are broken first.

Place the shelled beans in a small amount of boiling salted water, cover the kettle tightly, lower the heat, and steam for 15 to 20 minutes, or until barely tender. Take care not to overcook or the beans will be soggy. Drain well, return the beans to the cooking pan, and place the pan over very low heat to dry the beans slightly. Add the butter and toss until the beans are well coated. Season with black pepper to taste and serve immediately.

Buttered Wax Beans

Wax beans, while not as widely used as green beans, may be prepared and cooked in most of the same ways.

2½ pounds yellow wax beans

4 tablespoons butter, melted

Salt and black pepper

SERVES EIGHT

Rinse the beans well, remove any strings, and trim the stem ends. Cut into short lengths, cut them lengthwise, or leave them whole. Steam the beans in a tightly covered kettle in a little boiling salted water until they are tender, or boil them for 12 to 15 minutes in water to cover. Drain thoroughly after steaming or boiling, and toss with melted butter until all the beans are coated. Season with salt and pepper before serving.

Buttered Beets

16 to 18 small young beets   3 tablespoons lemon juice
5 tablespoons butter   Salt and black pepper

SERVES EIGHT

Leave the skin, root end, and 1 inch of stem on the beets, and rinse carefully without breaking the skins. Place them in a large kettle with about 1 inch of boiling salted water, cover the kettle tightly, and simmer gently until tender. This should take about 30 minutes for small beets, up to 1½ hours for large ones.

When the beets are cooked through, drain them, slip off the skins, and trim off the root ends and stems. The beets may be left whole if small, or sliced. Melt the butter in the kettle, add the beets, sprinkle with lemon juice, and cook over low heat, shaking the kettle frequently, until all the beets are coated with butter. Turn out into a serving dish, sprinkle with salt and pepper to taste, and serve immediately.

Abigail's Harvard Beets

16–18 small beets   ¼ teaspoon salt
    ½ cup granulated sugar   1 cup cider vinegar
    1½ tablespoons cornstarch   4 tablespoons butter

SERVES EIGHT

Leave the skins and 1 inch of stem on the beets. Scrub them well under running water and place them in a saucepan with water to cover. Cook as directed in Buttered Beets (above).

When the beets are tender, drain them and reserve the liquid. Peel and cut the beets into slices. Combine the sugar, cornstarch, and salt in a saucepan, stir in the vinegar and ½ cup of the reserved beet liquid. Cook the mixture over medium heat until it thickens. Add the sliced beets and butter, and cook long enough to heat the beets through. Serve hot.

Broccoli with Lemon Butter

3 pounds (2 bunches) broccoli
6–8 tablespoons butter

Juice of 1 lemon
Salt and black pepper

SERVES EIGHT

The freshest broccoli has tightly compressed, gray green flowers and slender stalks. Thick, woody stalks should be trimmed, halved and quartered lengthwise so that a shorter cooking time will be required.

Rinse the broccoli, drain it well, then pull off and discard the leaves. Cut off a few inches of the bottoms of the stalks and discard. Tie the broccoli together and stand upright in a deep kettle. Pour boiling salted water to a depth of 1 inch into the kettle, cover with a tight lid, or with tightly secured aluminum foil if the broccoli flowers rise over the rim of the kettle, and cook over low heat until the stalks are tender, about 12 to 15 minutes.

Melt the butter in a separate saucepan and add the lemon juice. Drain the broccoli well and toss gently with the lemon butter. Season with salt and pepper to taste. Serve immediately. If desired, broccoli may be steamed and served with Hollandaise Sauce (page 240).

Broccoli with Buttered Crumbs

3 large bunches broccoli
½ pound (2 sticks) butter
1 cup dry bread crumbs

Grated zest and juice of 1 lemon
Salt and black pepper

SERVES EIGHT

Prepare and cook the broccoli as directed in Broccoli with Lemon Butter (above). Heat the butter and sauté the bread crumbs until lightly browned. Sprinkle the bread crumbs with the grated lemon zest and salt and pepper to taste.

Drain the broccoli, arrange on serving plates, and top with the buttered crumbs. Stir the lemon juice into the butter remaining in the pan and pour over the broccoli and crumbs.

Fried Broccoli with Shrimp

3 large bunches broccoli,
   quartered
2 pounds shrimp
½ cup vegetable oil
1 large clove garlic, minced

10 scallions chopped
2 tablespoons cornstarch
⅛ teaspoon ground ginger
½ cup cold water
   Salt and black pepper

SERVES EIGHT

Cook the broccoli in water to cover until barely tender. Meanwhile, peel and devein the shrimp and cut them in half lengthwise. Heat the oil in a large pan and add the minced garlic.

Drain the broccoli, reserving the cooking liquid, and trim the tough stalks. Add the broccoli, scallions, and shrimp to the oil, and sauté until the broccoli is tender and the shrimp turn bright red, turning the pieces frequently.

Remove the broccoli and shrimp from the pan with a slotted spoon and set them aside. Mix the cornstarch and ginger with the cold water until smooth, add 1½ cups of reserved cooking liquid, and stir this mixture into the oil remaining in the pan.

Continue to stir as the sauce thickens and becomes clear, then return the shrimp and broccoli to the pan to heat through. Season with salt and pepper to taste and serve hot over rice.

Deep-Fried Broccoli

3 large bunches broccoli
2 eggs
½ teaspoon salt

Flour
2 cups dry bread crumbs
Vegetable oil for frying

SERVES EIGHT

Separate the broccoli into medium-size stalks. Cook according to directions given in Broccoli with Lemon Butter (page 257). Drain when tender and dry thoroughly on paper towels.

Beat the eggs lightly with the salt. Dip each broccoli piece first in flour, next in the eggs, and then in the bread crumbs. Fry the broccoli pieces, a few at a time, to golden brown in hot oil to cover. Drain them briefly on paper towels as you finish each batch, and set them aside to keep warm until they all are ready. Serve hot.

Brussels Sprouts with Lemon Butter

2 pounds brussels sprouts
6–8 tablespoons butter

Juice of ½ lemon
Salt and black pepper

SERVES EIGHT

Pick over the brussels sprouts and discard any wilted leaves. Make a crisscross gash in the bottom of each sprout after trimming the stems with a sharp knife.

Bring a small amount of salted water to a boil in a large saucepan. Drain the sprouts well, and add them to the saucepan. Lower the heat, cover tightly, and steam for 12 to 15 minutes, or until barely tender. Take care not to overcook brussels sprouts or they will be soggy and unpalatable.

Heat the butter in a saucepan and add the lemon juice. Drain the sprouts and pour the lemon butter over them, tossing gently until all are lightly coated. Transfer to a serving dish, season with salt and pepper, and serve immediately.

Buttered Cabbage

1 medium head cabbage
8 (1 stick) tablespoons butter

Salt and black pepper

SERVES EIGHT

Pull off and discard the limp outer leaves of the cabbage, and cut the head into quarters. Cut away and discard the tough inner core, and slice the cabbage into ¼-inch shreds. Cover the shredded cabbage with lightly salted cold water and soak for 30 minutes.

Bring ½ inch lightly salted water to a boil in a large saucepan. Drain the cabbage thoroughly, add to the saucepan, and steam the cabbage, tightly covered, over low heat for 5 minutes, or until tender but still a bit crunchy. Shake the pan occasionally while the cabbage is cooking to make sure all the shreds are steaming.

Drain the cooking water from the cabbage and discard it.

Melt the butter in the saucepan over low heat, add the drained cabbage, stir, cover, and shake the pan over low heat for 1 minute. Add salt and pepper to taste, and serve immediately.

Edna's Rolled Cabbage with Sausage Stuffing

1 large head cabbage
½ pound sausage meat
2 medium onions, chopped
½ pound ground beef
⅓ cup bread cubes (cornbread is best)
⅓ cup fine dry bread crumbs
½ teaspoon salt
¼ teaspoon poultry seasoning

⅓ cup warm water
1 egg
1½ cups Clarified Beef Stock (page 108) or canned beef bouillon
1 cup tomato sauce
Lemon juice
Granulated sugar

SERVES FOUR

Core the cabbage, carefully break off the leaves, wash them well, and place them in a large kettle with cold water to cover. Bring the water to a boil, remove from the heat, and allow the cabbage leaves to stand for 15 minutes. Meanwhile, prepare the stuffing.

Crumble the sausage and fry until light brown. Pour off all but 2 tablespoons of fat. Add the onions and sauté for 5 minutes. Reserve the sausage meat and onions in a bowl. Crumble the beef and fry until very lightly browned. Pour off the fat and add the beef to the sausage along with the bread cubes, bread crumbs, seasonings, and water. Mix well with your fingers, breaking up any large meat pieces. Beat the egg lightly and stir into the stuffing.

Remove the cabbage leaves from the water and drain them well. Place a cabbage leaf in front of you on a flat surface with the stem side to your right. Arrange 1 tablespoon of stuffing on the edge of the leaf closest to you. Roll up the leaf, folding the sides inward to form a small, neat envelope. Continue this procedure until all the leaves are stuffed. Arrange these stuffed leaves, one tightly against the other, seam side down in a large kettle. Mix the stock and tomato sauce with as much water as needed to yield enough liquid to barely cover the cabbage rolls.

Cover the kettle and simmer gently over low flame for 1½ hours, or until the cabbage leaves are tender. Carefully remove the rolls from the kettle and place on a serving dish. Reduce the liquid until it is slightly thickened. Adjust the seasonings, adding lemon juice and sugar to taste if a sweet and sour flavor is desired. Pour the sauce over the cabbage rolls and serve immediately.

Down East Scalloped Cabbage

*This is an old-time country recipe
that turns an ordinary vegetable into a hearty
and deliciously filling luncheon dish.*

1 *large head cabbage*

5 *strips bacon, minced*

3 *medium onions, coarsely chopped*

2 *cups Easy White Sauce (page 238)*

1 *teaspoon caraway seeds (optional)*

1 *cup dry bread crumbs*

2 *tablespoons butter*

8 *slices buttered toast*

SERVES EIGHT

Preheat the oven to 350 degrees.

Discard the tough outer leaves and hard core of the cabbage and finely chop the vegetable. Sauté the bacon, add the onions, and cook them until they are slightly limp. Add the cabbage and stir over medium heat for 5 minutes.

Spoon the cabbage, onion, and bacon into a glass baking dish, cover with white sauce, sprinkle with caraway seeds, and top with the bread crumbs. Dot with the butter and bake for 20 minutes in the preheated oven. Serve hot over toast.

Hanna's Stuffed Cabbage

1 *medium head cabbage*	1 *egg*
1 *tablespoon olive oil*	¼ *teaspoon dried thyme*
6 *strips lean bacon, minced*	*Salt and black pepper*
1 *large onion, minced*	1 *cup consommé*
5 *slices white bread*	1 *cup tomato sauce*
Milk	¼ *cup heavy cream* (*optional*)

SERVES SIX

Remove the limp outer leaves, cut off the stem flush with the base of the cabbage, then hollow out the center to form a 1-inch-thick outer shell. Reserve the scooped-out center. Parboil the hollow outer shell for 8 minutes, then drain well by turning upside down on a drain board.

Separate and discard the hard core from the scooped-out inner leaves. Mince these tender inner leaves. Heat the oil in a skillet and sauté the bacon until it is crisp but not burned. Remove the bacon and add the onion. Cook for 3 minutes over medium-low heat, stirring constantly, then add the minced cabbage. Continue to cook and stir for 10 minutes longer.

Preheat the oven to 350 degrees.

Cut the bread slices into ½-inch cubes. Moisten the bread with milk, squeeze dry, and add to the cabbage and onion mixture. Beat the egg lightly, and mix it into the stuffing, along with the crumbled bacon, thyme, and salt and pepper to taste. Heap the stuffing into the cabbage shell and wrap a single layer of cheesecloth over the outside of the shell.

Place the wrapped cabbage shell in a deep glass baking dish. Mix the stock with the tomato sauce and spoon the mixture carefully around the cabbage. Cover the baking dish with aluminum foil and bake in the preheated oven for 50 minutes. Remove the foil and the cheesecloth and baste the cabbage with the sauce. Bake for 30 minutes more, basting the stuffed cabbage with the sauce several times.

Cut the cabbage into wedges at the table. If you like you may add ¼ cup of heavy cream to the sauce in the baking dish, simmer it briefly, and serve in a sauceboat along with the stuffed cabbage.

Dorothy Foresman's Dutch Cabbage

Here's another recipe with Pennsylvania Dutch origins.

4 strips bacon, minced	¾ teaspoon salt
1 large head cabbage	1¾ cup milk
2 tablespoons flour	3 tablespoons white vinegar
1 tablespoon granulated sugar	

SERVES EIGHT

Sauté the bacon until crisp. Remove with a slotted spoon and set aside. Remove the tough outer leaves and hard core of the cabbage and chop medium-fine. Add the cabbage to the bacon fat and fry over medium heat, stirring occasionally until the cabbage is tender and brown-flecked, about 15 minutes.

Stir the flour, sugar, and salt into the cooked cabbage. Mix the milk and vinegar and stir it into the cabbage. Stir constantly over medium heat until thick and smooth. Sprinkle with bacon bits and serve hot.

Dutch Uncle Red Cabbage

1 medium head red cabbage

3 strips lean bacon, minced

2 tart apples, peeled, cored, and coarsely chopped

1 small onion, finely chopped

⅓ cup tarragon vinegar

2 tablespoons lemon juice

2 cups water

½ cup granulated sugar

¼ teaspoon salt

4 whole cloves

1 bay leaf

1 tablespoon flour

SERVES EIGHT

Quarter the cabbage, discard the limp outer leaves, and cut away the hard core. Shred the cabbage quarters as thinly as possible. Rinse the cabbage and drain it thoroughly.

Sauté the minced bacon until fairly crisp, add the apples and onions, and sauté for 4 minutes longer. Sir the vinegar, lemon juice, and water into the apple-onion mixture, add the sugar, salt, cloves, and bay leaf and mix well. Bring the mixture to a boil, add the cabbage, and simmer, covered, over low heat for 1 hour, stirring every 10 minutes. Additional water should be added during the cooking if necessary to keep the cabbage from sticking.

Preheat the oven to 300 degrees.

Sprinkle the flour over the top of the cabbage, let stand for 2 or 3 minutes, then stir well. The red cabbage may be served at this point, but to mellow its flavor and texture, bake it uncovered in the slow oven for an additional 45 minutes, stirring occasionally.

Buttered Carrots

2½ pounds young, tender carrots

6 tablespoons butter

Salt and black pepper

SERVES EIGHT

Remove the feathery tops from the carrots and set them aside to use in making soup stock. Scrub the carrots with a stiff vegetable brush, peeling them only if they are very large.

Leave the carrots whole, or slice or dice them if preferred. Melt the butter in a large heavy skillet over very low heat. Add the carrots, cover tightly, and allow the vegetable to cook until tender. This will take about 20 minutes for whole carrots, 15 minutes or less for cut carrots. Take care not to overcook or to brown the vegetable. Shake the skillet occasionally while the carrots are cooking to coat them on all sides with butter. Transfer to a deep serving dish, and season with salt and pepper.

Steamed Carrots

Place the carrots in a kettle with a very small amount of boiling salted water. Cover tightly, cook 15 minutes for whole carrots, 10 to 12 minutes for cut carrots. Toss gently with the butter and season with salt and pepper to taste. Serve hot.

Herbed Carrots

Prepare Dilled Carrots, Minted Carrots, or Parsleyed Carrots by adding 2 tablespoons minced fresh dill, mint, or parsley to the vegetable after preparing according to preference.

Nanna Hannah's Baked Carrot Pudding***

Serve this delectable carrot ring with fresh,
young green peas in the center.

1 pound carrots, sliced	1 ¼ teaspoons salt
1 large onion, coarsely chopped	3 eggs
2 ½ cups Chicken Stock (page 111) or canned chicken broth	½ cup matzo meal

SERVES SIX TO EIGHT

Place the carrots, onion, and stock in a saucepan and bring to a boil. Lower the heat to medium, cover tightly, and cook until the vegetables are tender.

Preheat the oven to 375 degrees.

Drain the vegetables and save the cooking liquid. Mash the carrots and onion with the salt. Beat the eggs and add the matzo meal, mixing well. Gradually stir the cooking liquid into the egg–matzo meal mixture. Beat until smooth and stir in the vegetables. Pour into a well-greased 5-cup ring mold and bake for 45 minutes, or until firm. Unmold onto a platter and fill the center hole with a cooked green vegetable or vegetable puree.

Buttered Cauliflower

1 medium head cauliflower   Salt and black pepper
6 tablespoons butter, melted

SERVES FOUR

Cauliflower is at its freshest when the head is firm and the flowerets tight and compact. Rinse the cauliflower, remove the green outer leaves, and trim the heavy part of the stem. Break the cauliflower into flowerets, or leave the vegetable whole and score the stem with a knife to shorten the cooking time.

Place the cauliflower in a large saucepan, add boiling salted water to a depth of 1 inch, and allow the vegetable to steam, tightly covered, until tender. Whole cauliflower should take 25 to 30 minutes; flowerets should be tender in 10 to 15 minutes. Take care not to overcook. The cauliflower should be slightly crisp.

Reserve the cooking liquid in your stock jar and return the cauliflower to the saucepan to heat briefly over very low flame. Transfer to a serving dish, pour the butter over, and season with salt and pepper to taste.

Celery in Cream Sauce

1 small bunch celery
2 cups Chicken Stock (page 111)
or canned chicken broth
1 tablespoon flour

¼ cup heavy cream
Salt and black pepper

SERVES EIGHT

Trim the leaves and roots from the celery and wash the stalks thoroughly. Remove any strings and cut the celery into ½-inch dice, or into strips ½ inch wide and 1 or 2 inches long.

Bring the Chicken Stock to a low boil in a deep, heavy skillet, add the celery, and braise over medium heat, tightly covered, until the celery is tender but still crunchy, 10 to 12 minutes. Remove the celery from the stock with a slotted spoon and set it in a serving dish to keep warm.

Reduce the stock until it measures 1½ cups, then blend in the flour. Add the cream and stir constantly over medium heat until the sauce boils and is smooth and thick. Season with salt and pepper, pour the sauce over the celery, and serve immediately.

How to Prepare Chestnuts

Roasting

Roasted chestnuts have a sweeter and nuttier taste than boiled chestnuts, although either method may be used unless otherwise specified.

With a sharp knife cut a small cross on the flat side of the chestnut shells to allow steam to escape. Arrange the nuts on a cookie sheet, cut side up, and bake for 15 minutes in an oven preheated to 350 degrees. Remove shells and inner skins while still hot.

Boiling

Use a sharp knife to slit a cross on the flat side of the chestnut shells. Place the nuts in a saucepan, add water to cover, and bring to a boil over medium heat. Cook for 15 minutes, then drain. The outer shell and inner brown skin will come off much more easily if removed while the chestnuts are still hot.

Creamed Chestnuts

*Start with creamed chestnuts and use your imagination
to create delectable vegetable dishes,
meat pies, stuffings, and omelets.*

4 tablespoons butter

3 tablespoons flour

1½ cups milk

1½ cups heavy cream

3½ cups (1½–2 pounds) boiled
and coarsely chopped
chestnuts

½ teaspoon salt

1 teaspoon dried tarragon

⅛ teaspoon grated nutmeg

SERVES EIGHT

Melt the butter in a heavy skillet over medium heat. Blend in
the flour. Gradually add the milk and cream, stirring constantly until
the sauce thickens. Lower the heat and gently stir in the chestnuts,
salt, tarragon, and nutmeg. Heat through.

Sunday Dinner Mushrooms and Chestnuts

4 tablespoons butter

3 cups sliced mushrooms

3 tablespoons flour

1½ cups milk

1½ cups heavy cream

2 cups boiled and chopped
chestnuts

½ teaspoon salt

1 teaspoon dried tarragon

½ teaspoon grated nutmeg

SERVES EIGHT

Melt the butter in a heavy skillet and cook the mushrooms,
stirring occasionally, until lightly browned. Sprinkle the flour over
the mushrooms, stir until well blended, then add the milk and cream
gradually, stirring constantly until the sauce thickens. Lower the
heat and gently stir in the chestnuts, salt, tarragon, and nutmeg.
Heat through. Serve very hot.

Chestnut Balls

5 cups peeled chestnuts (pre-
    pared by the boiling method,
    page 267)
3 tablespoons butter, softened
1 egg plus 1 egg yolk
2 tablespoons heavy cream

1 tablespoon dark rum
½ teaspoon salt
Pinch black pepper
Flour
Vegetable oil for frying

SERVES EIGHT

Force the chestnuts through a fine sieve. Mix the butter into the puree. Beat the egg and egg yolk together and add them to the chestnuts, along with 1 tablespoon cream and the rum. The remaining tablespoon of cream should be added only if the mixture is too thick to handle. Add salt and pepper to taste.

Shape the mixture into 1-inch balls and roll the balls in flour. Fry the chestnut balls in 1-inch of hot oil until crisp and golden brown. Drain briefly on paper towels before serving.

Chestnut Puree

*A small dollop of chestnut puree brings out the best
in any meal centering around poultry or game.*

2 pounds chestnuts
    Milk
1 small onion, peeled

2 small stalks celery with leaves
    Salt and black pepper
3 tablespoons butter

YIELDS TWO CUPS—SERVES SIX TO EIGHT

Prepare the chestnuts for peeling by boiling or roasting method (page 267), reducing the boiling time to 8 minutes, or roasting only long enough for the skins to come off easily. Shell and peel the chestnuts and place in a large saucepan. Pour in enough milk to barely cover, and add the whole onion and celery. Cook the chestnuts over medium heat for 10 to 15 minutes or until tender, then drain, reserving the milk they were cooked in. Discard the onion and celery. Force the chestnuts through a fine sieve to puree them, season with salt and pepper to taste, and mix in the butter. Add as much reserved cooking milk as necessary to give the chestnuts the consistency you desire.

Holiday Glazed Chestnuts

1½ pounds chestnuts

1½ cups Clarified Beef Stock (page 110) or canned beef bouillon

SERVES EIGHT

Prepare the chestnuts for peeling by the boiling method (page 267), but boil only for 8 minutes. Remove the shells and dark skins, and place the chestnuts in a large skillet. Add the stock and simmer over low heat, shaking the skillet from time to time until the chestnuts are tender and the stock has evaporated. Serve immediately.

How to Cook Corn

Corn is at its freshest, most tender, and has the best flavor when the husks are green, the silks are brown, and the kernels are very milky when pierced with a fingernail. The natural sugar in corn is rapidly converted to starch after the ears are picked. If you have grown your own corn, put the water on to boil ten minutes before you're ready to eat, pick your corn and run back to the stove. You'll be amazed at how delicious corn can taste. If there is any delay between picking and cooking keep the corn in the refrigerator to prevent flavor loss. Remove the husks and silks after the water comes to a boil and plunge the corn immediately in rapidly boiling water to cover. One tablespoon sugar may be added to the water if desired.

Cover the cooking pot tightly, and allow the corn to cook for 5 minutes, or until barely tender. Do not overcook.

Remove the corn from the water and serve immediately with melted butter and lots of salt and freshly ground pepper. For best results, cook only as much corn as you will need for one serving apiece, then cook another batch for second helpings.

Oven-Roasted Ears of Corn

Nothing could be easier to prepare or more pleasing to eat than this corn. The corn silk lends a delicate sweetness acquired in no other way.

16 ears corn with husks   Salt and black pepper
  Butter

SERVES EIGHT

Preheat the oven to 300 degrees.

Arrange the ears just as you pick or purchase them on the middle rack and roast for 30 minutes. To serve, strip off the husks and silk, brush the corn with butter, and sprinkle with salt and pepper. Serve immediately.

Pennsylvania Dutch Dried Stewed Corn***

2 cups Pennsylvania Dutch dried   1 tablespoon granulated sugar
  corn   Salt
1 quart boiling water
2 tablespoons butter   1 cup heavy cream or half and
                                           half

SERVES EIGHT

Place the dried corn in a large saucepan, cover with boiling water, and set aside to soak for 1½ hours. Add the butter, sugar, and salt to taste, bring the mixture to a boil, and allow it to simmer for 45 minutes. Just before serving, stir in the cream and cook over low heat for 10 minutes longer. Serve hot.

Pennsylvania Dutch Dried-Corn Fritters***

These corn fritters are served as a vegetable
to accompany ham or poultry, or dished forth
on their own drowned in maple syrup.

2½ cups milk
  2 cups Pennsylvania Dutch
    dried corn
  2 eggs
  1 teaspoon granulated sugar

1 teaspoon salt
2 teaspoons baking powder
¾–1 cup all-purpose flour
  Vegetable oil for frying

SERVES EIGHT

Stir the milk into the dried corn and allow the mixture to stand for at least 45 minutes. Beat the eggs lightly and add to the corn and milk, along with the sugar and salt. Mix the baking powder with ½ cup of flour and stir this into the corn, adding enough additional flour to produce a fairly stiff batter. Heat ⅓ inch of oil in a large skillet. Drop the batter by tablespoonfuls into the hot oil and fry to a golden brown on both sides, turning once. Drain the fritters briefly.

Grandmother Margaret's Boiled Green Corn***

8 ears very young corn
  Water
  Milk

Salt and black pepper
Melted butter

SERVES EIGHT

Husk the corn and remove all the silks. Place equal amounts of water and milk in a large kettle (enough to cover the corn by 1 to 2 inches) and bring to a boil. Drop in the corn and cook for about 10 minutes, or until the corn is tender. Cooking the corn in milk keeps the kernels white and the flavor sweet.

Serve at once, with salt, pepper, and melted butter.

Lillie Bower's Deviled Corn Custard Pie

4 ears corn	*Salt*
½ sweet red pepper, seeded and minced	*Pinch mace*
	¼ teaspoon Tabasco
½ green pepper, seeded and minced	*4 tablespoons sweet sherry*
1 cup water	*1 cup heavy cream*
3 eggs	*½ recipe Pastry for 2-Crust Pie (page 418)*
1 teaspoon granulated sugar	

SERVES FOUR TO SIX

Husk the corn and remove the silks. Finely grate the kernels into a saucepan. As you finish grating each ear, run a knife over the cob to extract any remaining milk. Add the peppers and water to the corn.

Cook the vegetables over medium heat, stirring occasionally, until most of the water evaporates. Remove saucepan from heat and cool slightly. Beat the eggs lightly and add them to the vegetables, along with the sugar, salt, mace, Tabasco, sherry, and cream.

Preheat the oven to 425 degrees.

Roll out the dough and use it to line a 7½-inch pie plate. Spoon the seasoned corn mixture into the crust, and bake for 15 minutes in the preheated oven. Reduce the heat to 350 degrees, and bake for 30 minutes longer, or until a knife blade inserted in the center of the pie comes out clean. Cut into wedges and serve piping hot.

Honeyed Corn on the Cob

16 small ears corn
½ cup honey

2½ teaspoons salt

SERVES EIGHT

Gently pull the husks down from the corn but do not tear them off. Remove the silks. Place the honey and salt in a small saucepan, bring to a boil, and simmer gently for 1 minute. Brush the corn with this syrup, pull the husks up around the ears, and wrap each ear with aluminum foil. Place the wrapped corn in the coals of a charcoal fire or bake in a hot oven. Turn frequently until the corn is tender, about 20 to 25 minutes.

My Own Sautéed Cucumbers***

*Few people cook cucumbers,
but these are perhaps the most delicious
cooked vegetable of all.*

8 medium cucumbers, peeled
3 tablespoons butter
1 teaspoon granulated sugar

Salt
1 teaspoon chopped chives

SERVES EIGHT

Cut the cucumbers in half lengthwise and use a spoon to remove the seeds. Slice the cucumber halves into 1-inch pieces, cover with boiling salted water, and boil for about 5 minutes.

Heat the butter in a large skillet. Drain the cucumbers thoroughly, and sauté in the melted butter until they are nicely golden on all sides. Sprinkle sugar over the pieces as they cook. When all pieces are sautéed, transfer the vegetable to a serving dish, season with salt, and sprinkle with chopped chives.

Country-Baked Cucumbers with Sour Cream

6 large cucumbers, peeled

2 tablespoons white vinegar

1½ teaspoons salt

¼ teaspoon granulated sugar

4 tablespoons butter, melted

2 tablespoons sour cream

4 scallions, chopped

1 teaspoon minced dill

Pinch white pepper

SERVES EIGHT

Cut the cucumbers in half and remove the seeds. Cut the cucumber halves into thin strips, about 2 or 3 inches long and ¼ inch wide. Place them in a bowl and sprinkle with a mixture of vinegar, salt, and sugar. Allow the cucumber strips to stand in this mixture for 1 hour, then drain them thoroughly and pat them dry with paper towels.

Preheat the oven to 375 degrees.

Arrange the vegetable in a baking dish. Combine the melted butter and sour cream, pour over the cucumbers, and sprinkle with the scallions and dill. Season with the pepper and bake the cucumbers for about 30 minutes, stirring occasionally. The cucumber strips should be tender but still a bit crunchy.

Shrimp and Eggplant Casserole

2 medium eggplants, peeled

Salt

Vegetable oil for frying

1 pound shelled raw shrimp

2 tomatoes, peeled, seeded, and chopped

2 leeks, cut into ½-inch slices

2 tablespoons butter

1½ cups thick Easy White Sauce (page 238)

¾ cup dry bread crumbs

½ cup grated Swiss or parmesan cheese

SERVES EIGHT

Cut the eggplants into ½-inch slices, arrange them in a single layer on a flat surface, and sprinkle lightly with salt. Allow the eggplant to drain for 30 minutes; pat dry with paper towels. Pour oil to a depth of ¾ inch into a large skillet and sauté the eggplant slices until tender and golden brown on both sides. Meanwhile, sauté the shrimp, tomatoes, and leeks in the butter in a separate skillet until the shrimp turn bright pink and the vegetables are tender.

Preheat the oven to 400 degrees.

Drain the eggplant slices on paper towels and arrange a layer of them in the bottom of a lightly buttered baking dish. Spread ⅓ of the white sauce over the eggplant slices, top with a layer of shrimp and vegetables, then sprinkle with ¼ cup of the bread crumbs. Build 2 more layers of eggplant, white sauce, shrimp and vegetables, and bread crumbs, top with grated cheese, and bake for 25 minutes.

Charcoal-Broiled Eggplant

2 large eggplants, peeled *⅓ cup olive oil*
3 large cloves garlic *¼ teaspoon oregano*
1 tablespoon salt *1 tablespoon wine vinegar*

SERVES EIGHT

Cut each eggplant lengthwise into 4 equally thick slices. Place the garlic cloves and salt in a mortar and crush with a pestle to a fine paste. Add the oil and oregano to the garlic, stir briefly, then mix in the vinegar. Brush the eggplant slices on both sides with this dressing, and arrange on a broiler rack.

Set the rack several inches from the heat and broil the eggplants to a golden brown on both sides. Turn the slices often and brush with the dressing after each turn.

To cook over a charcoal fire, prepare in the same manner and broil over slow coals, turning and basting frequently.

Batter-Fried Eggplant***

3 medium eggplants, peeled	*3 eggs*
Salt	*1 cup milk*
1½ cups all-purpose flour	*Vegetable oil for frying*
⅛ teaspoon salt	

SERVES EIGHT

Cut the eggplants into ¼-inch-thick slices. Arrange them on a flat surface and sprinkle them lightly with salt. Allow them to stand for 15 minutes.

Meanwhile, sift the flour with the salt into a bowl. Beat the eggs into the flour mixture and add the milk, stirring long enough to thoroughly moisten the batter.

Dry the eggplant slices between paper towels, then dip them into the batter. Fry them in 1 inch of hot oil until golden brown on both sides, turning once. Drain briefly on paper towels before serving hot.

Note: Almost any vegetable can be transformed into a tempting and mouth-watering specialty when prepared this way.

How to Cook Greens

Greens of various varieties—beet greens, chard, chicory, collards, escarole, mustard, and turnip greens—can be delicious as well as nutritious when steamed and flavored with butter and seasonings.

Always wash greens well in several changes of water. Drain them briefly, and steam over medium heat in a tightly covered heavy saucepan with ¼ inch water. Cook only long enough to wilt the leaves, stirring occasionally. The greens may then be drained and chopped, tossed with melted butter, and seasoned according to your taste.

Margaret Young's Kale with Chestnuts***

4 pounds kale
2½ quarts boiling salted water
7 tablespoons butter
3 tablespoons flour
3 cups Clarified Beef Stock (page 110) or canned beef bouillon

½ teaspoon salt
½ teaspoon black pepper
⅓ teaspoon grated nutmeg
1½ cups peeled and chopped boiled chestnuts
½ cup heavy cream

SERVES EIGHT

Remove the tough stems and ribs from the kale and wash thoroughly in several changes of cold water. Shake off excess water. Place in a large kettle, cover with the boiling salted water, and cook the kale until tender, about 30 minutes. Drain and finely chop the leaves.

Heat the butter in a large skillet and blend in the flour. Add the stock and the seasonings and stir constantly until slightly thickened. Add the kale and let the mixture simmer over low heat until most of the liquid is absorbed, about 20 minutes. Stir in the chestnuts and cream and heat slightly before serving.

Kohlrabi with Cream Sauce

16 small to medium kohlrabi
2 cups Chicken Stock (page 111) or canned chicken broth
2 tablespoons butter
2 tablespoons flour

Salt and black pepper
Pinch grated nutmeg
Heavy cream (optional)

SERVES EIGHT

Small, tender kohlrabi roots need not be peeled, but it is best to peel if the roots are more than 2 to 2½ inches in diameter.

Slice or dice the kohlrabi. Steam it in the stock, in a tightly covered saucepan, until tender. Melt the butter in a separate saucepan and blend in the flour. Drain the kohlrabi, reserving the cooking liquid, and place the vegetable in a serving dish to keep warm.

Add 1 cup cooking liquid to the butter and flour mixture, season with salt, pepper, and nutmeg, and stir over medium heat until the sauce is well blended and fairly thick. Thin the sauce with a little cream, if desired. Serve the vegetable hot, covered with the sauce.

Braised Leeks

16 large or 24 small leeks   *4 tablespoons butter*
  Water or chicken broth   *Salt and black pepper*

SERVES EIGHT

Trim the leeks, leaving at least 2 inches of green leaves. Sand tends to hide away in the intricate layers of the leeks, so wash them carefully. Use a sharp knife to cut a little more than halfway through each leek, flatten slightly, and hold under running water to rinse away the sand.

Place the leeks in a large saucepan, barely cover with water or chicken broth, and simmer, covered, until tender but firm, about 15 minutes. Drain quickly, toss with butter until thoroughly coated, and season with salt and pepper to taste.

Leeks with Lemon Butter

16 large or 24 small leeks   *3½ tablespoons lemon juice*
  Water or chicken broth   *Salt and black pepper*
5 tablespoons butter   *Pinch grated nutmeg*

SERVES EIGHT

Prepare and cook the leeks as directed in Braised Leeks (above). Melt the butter and mix in the lemon juice. Drain the leeks when they are tender and cover with the lemon butter. Season with salt, pepper, and nutmeg, and serve immediately.

Leeks with Lemon-Clam Sauce

16 large or 24 small leeks
    Water or chicken broth
5 tablespoons butter
3½ tablespoons lemon juice

1 cup minced clams including
    their liquid
Salt and black pepper

SERVES EIGHT

Prepare and cook the leeks as directed in Braised Leeks (page 279). Melt the butter in a skillet, stir in the lemon juice, clams, and clam liquid, and simmer the mixture until it is slightly reduced, about 5 minutes.

Drain the leeks when tender, and arrange on a serving dish. Pour the clam sauce over and serve piping hot.

Scallions with Lemon-Clam Sauce

Scallions can be prepared and served in the same manner. Braise 40 scallions in water to cover for 5 or 6 minutes. Drain, season with salt and black pepper, and pour the lemon-clam sauce over them.

Baked Leeks

16 large or 24 small leeks
    Water or chicken broth
5 tablespoons butter

2 tablespoons heavy cream
Salt and black pepper

SERVES EIGHT

Preheat the oven to 350 degrees.

Prepare the leeks as directed in Braised Leeks (page 279). Place in a large saucepan, add water or chicken broth to barely cover, and simmer, covered, for 5 to 7 minutes. Drain the leeks and transfer to a baking dish.

Add the butter and cream, and bake, turning occasionally, for 15 minutes. Season with salt and pepper to taste and serve immediately.

Mrs. Moss' Baked Lettuce with Potato-Sausage Stuffing

2 heads Boston lettuce

2 medium potatoes, peeled and cubed

¼ pound sausage meat

1 medium onion, chopped

3 tablespoons dry bread crumbs

2 tablespoons butter

1 egg

Salt and black pepper

1 medium carrot, thinly sliced

2 medium onions, sliced

½ cup heavy cream

6 strips bacon

SERVES EIGHT

Pull the center of each lettuce head apart slightly and carefully remove enough center leaves to form an outer shell 1 inch thick. Reserve center lettuce for salads. Rinse the hollowed shells and turn them upside down to drain. Place the cubed potatoes in a saucepan and cover with water. Bring to a boil and cook until tender.

Preheat the oven to 350 degrees.

Crumble the sausage into a skillet and set over medium heat to brown. Add the chopped onion and cook until the sausage is crisp and the onions are golden. Mix in the bread crumbs and continue to cook 3 minutes more. Remove the skillet from the heat.

Drain and mash the potato cubes with 1 tablespoon butter, then add to the sausage mixture. Beat the egg lightly and stir into the sausage and potatoes, blending well. Season with salt and pepper. Fill the hollow lettuce heads with this stuffing and secure the heads with string.

Arrange the carrot and onion slices in a deep casserole. Place the 2 stuffed lettuce heads in the casserole, pour the cream over them, and top each with 3 strips of bacon. Dot the tops with the remaining tablespoon of butter and seal the casserole with aluminum foil. Bake for 50 to 60 minutes.

To serve, cut the lettuce heads into 4 portions each, and pour the pan drippings and vegetables over them.

Broiled Mushroom Caps

24 very large mushrooms   *Salt and black pepper*
4 to 5 tablespoons melted butter

SERVES EIGHT

Wipe the mushroom caps with a damp cloth to remove any sand, or wash them if they are particularly sandy and pat them dry. You do not need to peel fresh, tender mushrooms. Remove the entire stem from each and reserve for future use. Place the mushrooms stem side down on an oiled broiling pan and brush with melted butter. Set the broiling pan about 4 inches from the heat, and broil for 2 to 3 minutes or until very lightly browned. Turn the caps over, brush with additional butter, and broil for 2 to 3 minutes more. The caps should be tender. Sprinkle with salt and pepper after removing from the broiler, and serve immediately.

These caps may be served as a vegetable, on toast, or as a garnish. When used as a garnish they may also be fluted by cutting long, V-shaped notches, one after another, in a spiral design from the top of the cap to the edge.

Broiled mushroom caps may be filled with any of the stuffings which follow.

Sour Cream and Caviar Stuffing

Sour cream   *Black or red caviar*

Immediately after removing mushroom caps from broiler place a dab of sour cream in the center, top with a bit of caviar, and serve.

Cherry Tomato and Sour Cream Stuffing

24 cherry tomatoes   ½ cup sour cream

After turning the mushroom caps, broil 1 minute, remove from the heat, and place a cherry tomato and a dab of sour cream in the center of each mushroom. Broil about 1 minute longer.

Bacon Stuffing I

4 ¼-inch strips cut from a slab   1 medium onion, chopped
 of lean bacon

Cut the bacon strips into squares and sauté only until partially cooked. Drain on paper towels. Sauté the onion in the bacon fat until golden. After turning and brushing with butter, place a bit of onion and bacon in each stem center. Broil 2 to 3 minutes longer, or until the bacon is done. Serve hot.

Bacon Stuffing II

8–10 strips lean bacon, finely   ¼ cup dry bread crumbs
 diced   Salt and black pepper
1 medium onion, finely chopped   ⅛ teaspoon oregano
½ green pepper, finely chopped   2 tablespoons butter

Sauté the bacon for a few minutes in a large frying pan, then add the onion and pepper and continue to sauté until the bacon and vegetables are lightly browned. Stir in the bread crumbs, add the seasonings, and mix well. Remove from the heat. After turning and brushing with butter, fill the mushroom caps with stuffing. Dot with butter, and broil 2 to 3 minutes longer.

Almond Stuffing

4 tablespoons butter
1 small onion, finely chopped
½ cup dry bread crumbs
½ cup ground almonds

¼ cup ketchup
2–3 strips bacon, minced and
    partially cooked (optional)

Heat the butter in a skillet over medium heat and sauté the onion until transparent. Add the bread crumbs and almonds and stir briefly, then mix in the ketchup. Remove from the heat. After turning and brushing with butter, fill the mushroom caps with stuffing. Broil for 2 to 3 minutes longer. Top while broiling with a bit of partially cooked bacon, if desired.

Chicken and Almond Stuffing

1 chicken breast, boned and
    diced
2 tablespoons butter
½ cup ground almonds

2 tablespoons heavy cream
Salt and black pepper
2–3 strips bacon, minced and
    partially cooked (optional)

Sauté the chicken breast in the butter until cooked through and tender. Place the chicken in a mortar and crush it to a paste with the pestle, or puree in an electric blender. Mix in the ground almonds and cream, and season with salt and pepper.

After turning and brushing with butter, fill the mushroom caps with stuffing. Broil for 2 to 3 minutes longer. Top while broiling with a bit of partially cooked bacon, if desired. Serve at once.

Chopped Chicken Liver Stuffing

4 tablespoons butter
1 small onion, finely chopped
½ pound chicken livers

Pinch grated nutmeg
2–3 strips bacon, minced and
    partially cooked (optional)

Heat the butter in a skillet and sauté the onion until transparent. Add the chicken livers and cook until the livers are browned outside but still slightly pink at the center. Remove from the heat and mash the livers with a fork, taking care to discard any tough tendons. Season with nutmeg.

After turning and brushing with melted butter, fill the mushroom caps with the liver paste. Broil for 2 to 3 minutes longer. Top before broiling with a bit of partially cooked bacon, if desired.

Bulgur Stuffing

1 tablespoon butter
1 small onion, minced
1 strip lean bacon, minced
1 cup bulgur (cracked wheat)
⅛ teaspoon salt
   Pinch grated nutmeg

Pinch dried rosemary
2½ cups Chicken Stock (page 111) or canned chicken broth
2–3 strips bacon, minced and partially cooked

Heat the butter in a large skillet and sauté the onion, bacon, and bulgur until golden. Sprinkle with the seasonings. Stir in the Chicken Stock and bring to a boil. Lower the heat and continue to cook, covered, until the bulgur is tender, about 15 minutes. After turning and brushing with butter, fill the mushroom caps with the bulgur mixture. Top before broiling with a small piece of partially cooked bacon, if desired. Broil for 2 to 3 minutes longer.

Sautéed Mushroom Caps

2 pounds mushrooms (or 4 large per serving)
4 tablespoons butter

½ teaspoon lemon juice
   Salt and black pepper

SERVES EIGHT

Wipe the mushrooms well with a damp cloth, or wash them if they are particularly sandy. Fresh, tender mushrooms need not be peeled. Cut off the stems and reserve for another use. Melt the butter in a large skillet, add the mushroom caps, and sauté over medium heat, covered, for about 6 to 8 minutes. Shake the skillet frequently while the mushrooms absorb the butter. Uncover and allow to brown lightly. Sprinkle with the lemon juice, season with salt and pepper, and transfer to a warm serving dish.

Mushroom quarters or slices may also be prepared this way, as may fluted mushrooms to use as a garnish. To flute, use a sharp knife to cut long, V-shaped notches, one after another, from the top of the cap to the edge in a spiral design.

Sue Ellen's Okra with Lemon Butter

2 pounds okra
  Juice of 1 lemon

8 tablespoons (1 stick) butter
  Black pepper

SERVES EIGHT

Pick or choose okra pods under 2 inches long as these are the most tender. Wash the okra well and carefully trim off the stems. Place ¼ inch of lightly salted water in a large saucepan. Bring to a boil, add juice of half the lemon, and the okra. Cover the saucepan and steam over very low heat until okra is tender, 8 to 10 minutes. Take care not to overcook or the okra will be soggy and unpalatable.

Melt the butter in a small saucepan over low heat and stir in the remaining lemon juice. Drain the okra, place it in a serving dish, and pour in the lemon butter. Sprinkle with black pepper and serve immediately.

Sister Content's Scalloped Onions

9 large onions
7 tablespoons butter
½ cup fine dry bread crumbs
½ teaspoon salt

⅛ teaspoon grated nutmeg
¼ cup heavy cream
3 tablespoons grated cheddar cheese

SERVES EIGHT

Preheat the oven to 450 degrees.

Peel the onions and cut them into slices ⅓ inch thick. Separate the onion rings and sauté them in the butter until they just begin to brown. Stir frequently. Place the sautéed onions in a deep glass baking dish.

Mix together the bread crumbs, salt, and nutmeg. Stir half this mixture into the onions in the dish. Sprinkle the cream over all and top with the remaining crumbs and the cheese. Bake until the crumbs and cheese are brown and the onions are hot. Serve immediately.

Glazed Onions

32 small white onions
½ teaspoon granulated sugar
¼ teaspoon salt
3 tablespoons butter

1½ tablespoons vegetable oil
⅔ cup Chicken Stock (page 111) or canned chicken broth

SERVES EIGHT

Blanch and peel the onions. Sprinkle them with a mixture of sugar and salt. Heat the butter and oil in a very large skillet, and sauté the onions over medium heat until golden. Add the stock, cover, and simmer over low heat until the onions are tender, about 30 to 40 minutes. Remove the cover and tilt the pan gently back and forth to glaze the onions on all sides. Serve immediately.

Onions and Fried Apple Slices

6 tablespoons butter
3 Spanish onions, sliced into rings

8 medium apples, cored
¼ cup dark brown sugar

SERVES EIGHT

Heat 4 tablespoons butter in a large skillet and sauté the onion rings until lightly browned on the edges. Cut thin slices from the stem and blossom ends of the apples. Leave the skins intact, and cut the apples into ½-inch-thick slices.

Transfer the onion rings to a heatproof serving dish and place in a low oven to keep warm. Add the remaining 2 tablespoons butter to the skillet and brown the apple rings lightly on one side. Sprinkle the tops of the apple rings with sugar and turn them to brown and glaze the other side. Top the onion rings with the glazed apples and serve immediately.

Fried Parsley

1 bunch parsley   Salt
  Vegetable oil for deep frying

SERVES EIGHT

Rinse the parsley well, drain, and dry thoroughly. Cut off any long stems, and fry the parsley sprigs, a few at a time, in deep hot oil. Fry only long enough for the sprigs to crisp. Drain the sprigs on paper towels and sprinkle with salt. Use as a garnish.

Clara Whitcher's Fried Parsnips

8 parsnips   Vegetable oil for frying
  Flour   Salt and black pepper
1 egg, lightly beaten

SERVES EIGHT

Place the whole parsnips in a saucepan, cover with salted water, bring to a boil, and cook until barely tender. Drain the parsnips and scrape off the skins. Cut into ½-inch slices and dredge with flour.

Dip the floured parsnips into the egg and fry in ½ inch of hot oil until crisp and very brown. Drain briefly on paper towels. Season with salt and pepper before serving hot.

Parsnip Fritters

8 parsnips
2 teaspoons granulated sugar
¼ teaspoon salt

2 teaspoons flour
2 eggs
Vegetable oil for frying

SERVES EIGHT

Peel the parsnips and cut them into 1-inch pieces. Bring salted water to a boil, stir in the sugar, and cook the parsnip pieces in water to cover until they are tender, but not mushy. Drain and mash the parsnips, making sure to break up any lumps, then mix in the salt and flour.

Separate the eggs, beat the yolks lightly with a fork, and add them to the parsnip mixture. Beat the whites until they form stiff peaks, and fold into the parsnips. Pour oil to a depth of ½ inch into a skillet and drop the parsnip batter by tablespoonsful into the hot oil. Fry until crispy brown on both sides. Drain briefly before serving hot.

Anne Brightbill's Parsnip Croquettes

8 parsnips
½ teaspoon salt
1 teaspoon granulated sugar
3 tablespoons light cream or
  half and half
2 tablespoons butter
3 egg yolks, lightly beaten

Salt and black pepper
Bread crumbs
2 eggs
1½ tablespoons milk
Flour
Vegetable oil for frying

SERVES EIGHT

Peel the parsnips and cut them into 1-inch lengths. Bring water to a boil, stir in the salt and sugar, and cook the parsnips until tender but not mushy. Drain the parsnips, then rub them through a fine sieve with the back of a spoon. Heat the light cream and add to the vegetable, along with the butter. Beat the egg yolks into the parsnip mixture. Add salt and pepper to taste, plus enough bread crumbs to make the mixture hold its shape when formed into croquettes. Refrigerate until well chilled.

Mix 2 eggs with the milk. Shape the batter into 1 inch by 2 inch croquettes. Dip each in flour, then in the eggs and milk, and, finally, roll them in additional bread crumbs. Fry in 2 inches hot oil until golden brown on both sides, turning once. Drain briefly and serve immediately.

Buttered Green Peas

6 cups shelled green peas (about 6 pounds in the shell)	4 tablespoons butter
¼ cup water	2 or 3 lettuce leaves
2 teaspoons granulated sugar	Salt

SERVES EIGHT

Place the peas in a large saucepan with the water, sugar, and butter. Arrange well-washed lettuce leaves over the peas, and cook, covered, over low heat for about 8 to 12 minutes, or until tender. Cooking time will vary according to the size and age of the peas. Discard the lettuce leaves and season the peas with salt to taste.

Beef-Stuffed Green Peppers

1 large onion, coarsely chopped	¼ teaspoon powdered sage
1 tablespoon butter	1 egg
2 pounds ground beef	1 cup tomato soup, undiluted
1 cup cooked rice	8 medium green peppers
1½ cups soft dry bread crumbs	Boiling water
½ teaspoon salt	½ cup cold water
¼ teaspoon dried thyme	

SERVES EIGHT

Preheat the oven to 300 degrees.

Sauté the chopped onion in the butter until soft and transparent. Mix together the onion, beef, rice, bread crumbs, salt, thyme, and sage. Beat the egg lightly and stir well into the meat mixture, along with ⅓ cup of undiluted tomato soup.

Rinse the green peppers, cut away the stems, seeds, and inner white pith, and place in a large kettle. Cover with boiling water and let stand for 7 minutes. Drain the peppers well and stuff them with the meat mixture.

Mix the remaining tomato soup with ½ cup water in the bottom of a large baking dish and arrange the peppers upright in the dish. Bake for 1 hour.

Sautéed Sweet Peppers

4 medium green peppers	2 medium onions, sliced
4 medium sweet red peppers	4 tablespoons French Dressing (page 333)
2 tablespoons vegetable or olive oil	Pinch dry mustard
2 tablespoons butter	

SERVES EIGHT

Wash, stem, and seed the peppers, then slice them into 1-inch strips and place on paper towels to dry. Heat the oil and butter in a large skillet. Sauté the pepper strips and onion rings only long enough for the onions to become translucent.

Transfer the vegetables to a serving dish. Beat the mustard into the dressing and toss gently with the vegetables until well mixed.

Serve hot or cold.

New Potatoes with Lemon-Zest Sauce

40 *small new potatoes*
8 *tablespoons (1 stick) butter*
2½ *teaspoons grated lemon zest*

6 *scallions, minced*
Coarse salt
Black pepper

SERVES EIGHT

Scrub the potatoes well but do not peel. Plunge them into a kettle of rapidly boiling salted water and cook until they are just tender, but not mushy, about 20 minutes.

Melt the butter in a heavy skillet, add the lemon zest and the scallions and sauté for 2 minutes. With a sharp knife cut an X across the top of each potato and serve with the hot lemon-zest sauce.

Baked Potato Slices with Lemon

6 *cups peeled and thinly sliced*
  potatoes
6 *tablespoons butter, melted*

4 *tablespoons lemon juice*
½ *teaspoon salt*
¼ *teaspoon paprika*

SERVES EIGHT

Preheat the oven to 350 degrees.

Cut the potatoes into slices ⅛ inch thick. Cover them with cold water and allow to stand for 15 minutes. Drain the slices, place them in a saucepan, and cover with boiling salted water. Cook for 2 minutes over medium heat. Drain again and spread the slices in a buttered baking dish.

Bake for 50 minutes, or until the potatoes are soft. Combine the melted butter with the lemon juice, salt, and paprika, and baste the potatoes with the mixture two or three times while they are baking.

Farmhouse Creamed Potatoes***

*These rich and creamy potatoes are
as delectable as any I've ever tasted.*

4 tablespoons butter

1½ cups heavy cream

1½ cups milk

10 medium potatoes, peeled and
thinly sliced

1 teaspoon salt

¼ teaspoon black pepper

SERVES EIGHT

Melt the butter in a large, heavy skillet, taking care not to brown it. Add the cream and milk and heat over the lowest possible flame. Do not boil. Slip the potato slices into the hot cream one at a time until evenly distributed. The liquid should barely cover the potatoes. Season with half the salt and pepper. Simmer for 30 minutes.

Turn the potatoes carefully, season with the remaining salt and pepper, and simmer for 30 minutes more.

Mame's Potatoes Fried with Salt Pork

½ pound salt pork, sliced

3 tablespoons vegetable oil

8 cups peeled and sliced boiled
potatoes

1 teaspoon chopped fresh sage
or 1 teaspoon powdered

SERVES EIGHT

Wipe the salt pork with a damp cloth and fry it in the oil. Discard the meat, season the potato slices with the sage, and fry in the drippings in the pan. Turn once.

Potato-and-Mushroom Pie***

Serve this tasty potato pie with meats and stews.

6 *large potatoes, peeled*

2 *tablespoons butter*

⅓ *cup milk*

½ *teaspoon salt*

6 *strips bacon*

3 *tablespoons flour*

1 *10¾-ounce can undiluted beef bouillon*

4 *cups small mushroom caps or sliced large mushrooms*

½ *recipe Pastry for 2-Crust Pie (page 418)*

2 *tablespoons heavy cream*

1 *egg yolk*

SERVES EIGHT

Boil the potatoes until tender, then drain and mash them with butter, milk, and salt. Mince the bacon, sauté until crisp, drain well and set aside. Reserve the bacon fat.

Preheat the oven to 425 degrees.

Blend the flour and undiluted bouillon into the reserved bacon fat and bring to a boil, stirring constantly. Remove from heat. Spread the mashed potatoes in a buttered 10-inch glass pie plate, heap the mushrooms onto the potatoes, and cover with the cooled liquid. Sprinkle with crumbled bacon pieces.

Top the pie with the crust. Slash it in several places to allow steam to escape. Mix the cream and egg yolk and brush the pastry with it. Bake for 10 minutes and lower the heat to 350 degrees. Continue to bake until the crust is cooked through and golden brown, about 15 minutes.

Potato Slices Baked with Salt Pork

2 *large onions, sliced*

8 *large potatoes, peeled and sliced*

Butter

Salt and black pepper

2 *¼-inch slices salt pork (about 2 by 3 inches), cut in strips*

SERVES EIGHT

Preheat the oven to 300 degrees.

Arrange the onion and potato slices in alternate layers in a large, well-buttered casserole. Sprinkle with salt and pepper, and add just enough water to barely cover the top layer. Arrange the strips of salt pork over the top. Bake for 2½ hours.

Hanoverdale Scalloped Potatoes

7 medium potatoes, peeled and thinly sliced

4 tablespoons flour

Salt and black pepper

Sage or thyme (optional)

5 tablespoons butter

3–4 cups milk

Paprika

SERVES FOUR TO SIX

Preheat the oven to 350 degrees.

Cover the bottom of a 2-quart baking dish with ¼ of the potato slices. Sprinkle with 1 tablespoon flour and a sprinkling of herbs and seasonings. Dot with 1 tablespoon butter. Repeat this layering process, ending with the potatoes.

Pour enough milk over the potatoes to fill the dish ⅔ full. Dot with the remaining butter and sprinkle with paprika. Cover the dish with aluminum foil and bake for 45 to 50 minutes. Remove the foil and raise the heat to 425 degrees. Bake until the potato slices are tender and the top is brown.

French Fried Potatoes***

8 large potatoes

3 cups vegetable oil

Salt

SERVES EIGHT

Peel the potatoes, dropping them into a bowl of cold water as you proceed. Slice each potato into strips ½ inch thick and about 3½ inches long, dropping the strips back into the cold water. Place the strips in a large saucepan, add just enough water to cover, and place over medium heat. Cook only until the water comes to a boil.

Remove from the heat and drain the potatoes immediately. Arrange the strips on paper towels and dry thoroughly. The potatoes must be dry before frying. Fry the potatoes in hot oil until crispy brown. Do not crowd the strips in the fryer; frying too many at once will lower the oil temperature and the potatoes will not brown properly. Drain briefly, season with salt, and serve immediately.

Country-Style Hash Browns

8 medium potatoes, peeled
8 strips lean bacon
3 medium onions
⅓ teaspoon salt

⅛ teaspoon black pepper
⅛ teaspoon powdered sage
⅛ teaspoon dried thyme

SERVES EIGHT

Grate the potatoes coarsely onto several thicknesses of paper towels to absorb any liquid. Blot excess moisture from the top of the grated potatoes with additional paper towels. Place the bacon strips in a large skillet and sauté over medium heat until crisp and brown. Remove the bacon and reserve, along with half the bacon fat. Spread the potatoes in the bacon fat remaining in the skillet and brown lightly on one side. Peel and grate the onions, reserving the onion juices. Use a spatula to flatten the potatoes, then scatter the onions, onion juice, seasonings, and herbs over them.

When the potatoes are crisp and brown on the underside, cut the pancake into 8 wedges. Lift each wedge carefully from the skillet and set it on a plate. Add the reserved bacon fat to the skillet, turn the wedges over carefully, and return them to the skillet, uncooked side down. Top each wedge with a strip of bacon and cook until the underside is brown. Serve immediately.

Home Fried Potatoes

8 medium potatoes
½ cup vegetable oil

Salt

SERVES EIGHT

Boil the potatoes in their skins until they are tender. Peel the potatoes (or leave the skins on if you prefer) and cut into ⅓-inch-thick slices. Heat half the oil in a large heavy skillet. Arrange 1 layer of potato slices in the hot oil and fry until golden brown. Turn the slices carefully and brown on the other side. Keep these potatoes warm while you fry the remaining slices, adding oil as necessary to prevent sticking and/or burning. Sprinkle with salt and serve hot.

Cubed Potato with Pimiento and Green Pepper

2 large onions, coarsely chopped
1 large green pepper, seeded and cut into ½-inch dice
4 tablespoons vegetable oil
1 6-ounce can pimiento, drained and cut into ½-inch dice

8 medium potatoes, peeled and cut into ½-inch cubes
Salt

SERVES EIGHT

Sauté the onions and green pepper in 2 tablespoons oil until the green pepper pieces are lightly browned. Add the remaining oil to the pan and sauté the pimiento for 2 minutes. Remove the onion, green pepper, and pimiento with a slotted spoon, place in a small bowl, and set aside.

Fry the potato cubes in the oil until each cube is well browned on several sides, turning frequently and adding more oil if necessary to prevent sticking. Sprinkle the potatoes with salt, cover the pan, and cook over low heat until the potatoes just tender.

Add the reserved vegetables and stir until hot. Serve immediately.

Potato Balls

9 large potatoes

5 tablespoons butter

Dried or fresh minced herbs

Salt

SERVES EIGHT

Peel the potatoes, dropping each into a bowl of cold water as you proceed. One by one, with the large end of a melon baller, scoop out balls and drop them into the cold water as you cut them, soaking them for at least 15 minutes. Drain off the water, cover with fresh water, and boil gently until the potato balls are tender but not mushy, about 10 to 12 minutes. Drain and carefully toss well with the butter and herbs. Season with salt and serve immediately.

Dilled Potato Balls

Toss the potato balls with ⅓ cup minced dill and serve accompanied with sour cream.

Minted Potato Balls

Toss the potato balls with ⅓ cup minced mint. Serve with lamb.

Fried Potato Balls

Prepare the potato balls as above, soaking them for 30 minutes in the cold water. Drain and dry well with paper towels. Heat ½ inch of vegetable oil in a large skillet and fry the potato balls until they are crisp and brown outside and soft inside. Drain briefly, season with salt, and serve.

Minted Mashed Potatoes

10 *large potatoes, peeled*
3 *tablespoons butter*
⅓ *cup hot milk*

Salt
¼ *cup minced fresh mint*

SERVES EIGHT

Cover the potatoes with water and boil until tender. Drain and mash them well. Blend in the butter and milk and whip vigorously until fluffy and light. Salt to taste. Stir in the mint and serve piping hot.

Mary MacLean's Potato Soufflé

4 *medium potatoes, peeled and quartered*
1½ *cups heavy cream*
Salt
Generous pinch cayenne

½ *cup grated parmesan cheese*
½ *teaspoon oregano*
6 *egg yolks*
8 *egg whites*
Butter

SERVES EIGHT

Place the potatoes in a large saucepan, cover with salted water, and bring to a boil. Cook over low heat, covered, until the potatoes are tender. Drain the potatoes, mash them well, and stir in ½ cup of cream. Season with salt and cayenne. Place the mashed potatoes in a saucepan, add the remaining cup of cream, and cook over low heat, stirring constantly, until the mixture is heated through. Remove from the heat and stir in the cheese and oregano.

Preheat the oven to 375 degrees.

Beat in the egg yolks one at a time, beating after each addition until well blended. Cool to room temperature. Beat the egg whites until they are stiff but not dry and fold them into the potato mixture. Divide the soufflé mixture between 2 well-buttered 1 quart soufflé dishes. Fill each ⅔ full. Bake the soufflés 30 minutes, or until they are high and golden. Serve immediately.

Note: An interesting variation on this recipe is to substitute 1 tablespoon minced fresh dill for the oregano.

Mother's Own Potato and Cheese Croquettes

4 cups hot mashed potatoes (mashed with a small amount of hot milk)

2 cups grated cheddar cheese

1 teaspoon salt

Pinch cayenne

½ teaspoon onion juice, pressed through a garlic press or available bottled in the supermarket

¼ cup heavy cream

2 eggs

Dry bread crumbs

Vegetable oil for frying

SERVES EIGHT

Place the mashed potatoes in a bowl, add the cheese, salt, cayenne, onion juice, and cream; mix well. Separate one of the eggs, beat the yolk slightly, and add it to the potatoes. Beat the egg white until stiff, and fold it into the potato mixture until well incorporated. Shape the mixture into croquettes, 2½ inches long and 1½ thick, and roll first in bread crumbs, then in the remaining egg which has been lightly beaten, and then in bread crumbs again. Fry in hot oil to a crisp golden brown on both sides, turning once. Drain briefly on paper towels before serving hot.

Great-Aunt Katie's Potato Pancakes

6 medium potatoes, peeled

4 eggs, separated

3 tablespoons flour

1¼ teaspoons salt

1 teaspoon baking powder

Vegetable oil for frying

SERVES SIX TO EIGHT

Coarsely grate the potatoes into cold water. Squeeze out as much moisture as possible, then place between paper towels to press out any remaining liquid. Mix the egg yolks with the potatoes. Thoroughly blend in the flour, salt, and baking powder. Beat the egg whites until they form stiff peaks. Fold them into the potato mixture.

Heat 1 inch of vegetable oil in a large skillet. Drop the batter by large tablespoonsful into the oil. Fry to a golden brown on both sides, turning only once. Drain before serving hot.

Valley-of-God's-Pleasure Squash Pie***

3–4 medium squash, stems removed

1 cup water

3 eggs

1 teaspoon granulated sugar

½ teaspoon salt

Pinch mace

Pinch black pepper

⅛ teaspoon ground cinnamon

⅛ teaspoon grated nutmeg

⅛ teaspoon ground ginger

4 tablespoons sherry

1 cup heavy cream

½ recipe Pastry for 2-Crust Pie (page 418)

SERVES FOUR TO SIX

Preheat the oven to 425 degrees.

Rinse the squash well under running water, and slice. Place the slices in a large saucepan, add water, and cook over medium heat, stirring occasionally, until most of the water evaporates. Puree the squash in an electric blender or by forcing it through a fine sieve with the back of a spoon. Beat the eggs lightly and add to the pureed squash, along with the sugar, salt, and spices. Stir in the sherry and cream.

Roll out the pie pastry and line a 7½-inch pie plate with it. Spoon the seasoned squash mixture into the pie crust, and bake for 15 minutes. Reduce the oven heat to 350 degrees and bake for 30 minutes longer, or until a knife blade inserted in the center of the pie comes out clean.

Caramelized Green-Tomato Slices***

*8 large or 16 small green
  tomatoes*
5 tablespoons butter
Flour

¾ cup light brown sugar
Heavy cream (optional)
Salt (optional)

SERVES EIGHT

Cut large tomatoes into ½-inch slices, removing the tops and bottoms. If small tomatoes are used, cut them in half crosswise. Heat the butter in a large skillet, press both sides of the tomato slices into the flour, and sauté the slices until brown on one side. Sprinkle the tomatoes with the sugar, then turn them gently and allow them to caramelize on the other side. Remove from the heat and serve immediately, caramelized side up.

If desired, stir a bit of cream and a pinch of salt into the pan drippings, blend over medium heat for a minute or two, and serve with the tomatoes.

Fried Tomatoes with Cheese

8 medium, ripe tomatoes
Salt and black pepper
Flour

4 tablespoons butter
Toast
Grated parmesan cheese

SERVES EIGHT

Cut the tomatoes in ½-inch-thick slices and sprinkle each slice with salt and pepper. Dredge the slices in flour, then sauté in the butter until golden on each side, turning once. Cut slices of toast into rounds, top each round with a tomato slice, and sprinkle with cheese. Serve immediately.

Grilled Tomatoes

8 large firm, ripe tomatoes
   Salt
1 clove garlic, minced
1 tablespoon butter

1 tablespoon olive oil
⅓ cup dry bread crumbs
   Black pepper
   Parsley sprigs

SERVES EIGHT

Cut a ½-inch slice from the stem-end of each tomato. Shake the tomatoes gently to remove some of the seeds and sprinkle with a little salt. Drain the tomatoes, cut side down, for 5 minutes.

Combine the garlic, butter, and olive oil with the bread crumbs, and spread this mixture over the tops of the tomatoes. Season with salt and pepper. Place the tomatoes on a broiling rack set on the middle shelf of the oven. Broil for 4 to 5 minutes, then raise the pan closer to the heat to brown the bread crumbs. Garnish each tomato with a small parsley sprig before serving.

Variations

With cheese: Add 4 tablespoons grated parmesan cheese to the bread crumb mixture, eliminating the garlic.
With herbs: Add 2 tablespoons minced fresh tarragon or dill to the bread crumb mixture.
With mushrooms: Sauté 8 minced mushrooms in 1½ tablespoons butter until lightly browned. Add to the bread crumb mixture, eliminating the garlic.

Miss Clymena's Scalloped Turnips

3 large yellow turnips, peeled and
   grated
5 tablespoons butter

2 cups Easy White Sauce (page 238)
1 cup fine dry bread crumbs

SERVES SIX TO EIGHT

Preheat the oven to 325 degrees.

Place turnips in a well-buttered baking dish, dot with 3 table-spoons butter, spread with white sauce, and sprinkle with bread crumbs. Dot with the remaining 2 tablespoons butter. Bake 30 to 40 minutes.

Sautéed Yellow Turnips***

You won't believe how simply delicious turnips
can be until you prepare them like this.

3 large yellow turnips, peeled and grated	5 tablespoons butter
	Salt and black pepper

SERVES SIX TO EIGHT

Melt the butter in a large skillet and sauté the turnips until they are soft and deep yellow in color. Serve hot.

Yellow Turnips with Bacon

Fry 7 strips bacon until crisp. Drain the bacon on paper towels and reserve the fat. Sauté the grated turnip as directed above. Serve hot topped with crumbled bacon.

Zucchini Pancakes

3 medium zucchini	Dry bread crumbs
1 small onion	Butter or vegetable oil for frying
2 eggs	
4 tablespoons flour	Sour cream
½ teaspoon salt	

SERVES SIX

Grate the zucchini and onion, squeeze out the liquid and re-serve it for stock if desired. Press the grated vegetables between paper towels to remove as much liquid as possible. Mix the vegeta-bles, eggs, flour, and salt well and add enough bread crumbs to make a fairly firm batter. Heat ⅛ inch butter in a 10- to 12-inch skillet. Place the batter, by the tablespoonful, in the hot fat and press flat with the back of the spoon. Fry the pancakes until lightly browned on both sides, turning once. Serve hot or cold with sour cream.

Charcoal-Cooked Vegetables

All fresh summer vegetables can be prepared outdoors quickly and easily by this charcoal method. Rinse, peel, and/or seed the vegeta-ble as you would for indoor cooking.

Cut as follows:

> Carrots, squash, celery—bite-size pieces
> Broccoli spears, eggplant fingers—serving-size pieces
> Eggplant, potatoes, squash—slices
> Acorn squash—halves
> Tomatoes, squash, onions may be halved, brushed with butter
>   and grilled in a wide-wire barbecue basket.
> Corn, new potatoes, onions—leave whole.

Leave the vegetables with just the water that clings to them after washing. Sprinkle with salt or other spices and dot them generously with butter. Wrap the vegetables in a double thickness of aluminum foil.

When steaming, fold the foil tightly so that no steam will escape; to bake them (as for acorn squash and potatoes), leave a small hole in the top for the steam to escape.

Broil over medium coals until the package and the vegetable may be pierced easily with a skewer or fork (from 15 to 30 minutes for cut vegetables; 30 to 60 minutes for whole vegetables). Be care-ful not to overcook vegetables.

Curried Vegetables

4 *large potatoes, peeled and cut*
into balls

2 *medium carrots, cut into ½-inch*
dice

2 *cups shelled green peas*

2 *cups Curry Sauce (page 236)*

2 *tablespoons minced parsley*

SERVES EIGHT

Bring to a boil enough salted water to cover the potato balls and carrots. Cook the vegetables over medium heat for 10 minutes. Add the peas and cook for 10 minutes more, or until all the vegetables are tender. Drain (reserving the cooking liquid for use in soups or sauces) and mix the vegetables with hot Curry Sauce. Serve immediately, garnished with parsley.

Vegetables in Cream

If you think all creamed vegetables come to the table
in a sticky sauce, these delicately flavored vegetables
will change your mind.

8 *carrots*

2 *tablespoons butter*

3 *leeks, cut into ½-inch pieces*

3 *6-inch yellow squash, sliced*

½ *cup heavy cream*

¼ *teaspoon salt*

Pinch each sugar and nutmeg

Black pepper

1 *tablespoon minced chives*

SERVES EIGHT

Slice the carrots thinly, and sauté them in the butter until nearly tender. Add the leeks and squash to the carrots, and sauté for 5 minutes, or until the squash is tender but not soggy. Remove the squash slices from the skillet with a slotted spoon and set them aside.

Stir the cream, salt, sugar, nutmeg, and pepper into the vegetables in the pan, and cook over medium heat until the cream thickens and clings to the vegetables. Carefully stir the squash into the rest of the vegetables, adjust the seasoning, and cook only long enough to reheat the squash. Serve hot, sprinkled with chives.

Hattie Barrow's Steamed Vegetable Pudding

½ cup chopped cooked spinach

½ cup chopped cooked zucchini

8 tablespoons (1 stick) butter

6 eggs

¾ cup minced mushrooms, sautéed in 1 tablespoon butter

6 slices bread

Heavy cream

2 tablespoons grated parmesan cheese

2 tablespoons minced parsley

½ cup dry bread crumbs

Salt and black pepper

SERVES EIGHT

Be sure to press the cooking liquid from the spinach and zucchini before measuring. Beat the butter until light and fluffy. Separate the eggs, reserving the whites in a mixing bowl. Add the egg yolks to the butter and beat until the mixture is light and smooth, then stir in the spinach, zucchini, and sautéed mushrooms.

Place the bread slices in a bowl, add enough cream to thoroughly moisten the slices. Squeeze the bread as dry as possible and mix it into the spinach mixture, along with the cheese, parsley, bread crumbs, salt, and pepper. Beat the egg whites until they hold stiff peaks, and fold into the vegetable pudding.

Pour the pudding into a well-greased tubular pudding mold and tightly cover with a layer of aluminum foil. Place the lid over the foil and set the mold in a deep kettle. Arrange crushed circles of aluminum foil around the top and bottom of the mold to keep it upright. Pour in enough boiling water to reach ¾ up the outside of the mold. Cover the kettle and allow the mold to steam for 1½ to 2 hours. Add more boiling water if necessary to keep the water level constant. The pudding is done when the top springs back when lightly pressed with the fingers.

To unmold, loosen the edges of the pudding including the area around the center of the mold. Set a serving plate over the mold, turn upside down and shake once. Serve immediately, garnished with Sautéed Mushroom Caps (page 285) or Buttered Peas (page 290).

Sour Cream–Potato Pancakes

8 medium potatoes, peeled	½ teaspoon salt
1 large onion	Pinch granulated sugar
2 eggs	4 tablespoons sour cream
2 tablespoons flour	⅓ cup vegetable oil

SERVES EIGHT

Grate the potatoes into cold water, drain them well, then squeeze between paper towels to remove all moisture. Place the potatoes in a bowl and grate the onion into them.

Beat the eggs lightly, and add to the potatoes and onions along with the flour, salt, and sugar. Mix well, then beat in the sour cream.

Heat the oil in a skillet and fry small pancakes to a crispy brown on both sides, turning once. Serve plain or with applesauce.

Baked Pumpkin

This was recommended in an old New England cookbook as "a proper supper dish" for a growing child.

A small and very ripe pumpkin with a hard shell was selected. Its stem end was sliced off to form a cover with a handle. Next the seeds and stringy fibers were scooped out until only the solid meat remained. The shell was then filled with "new milk," the cover was set on, and the pumpkin was popped into the tin baker or the brick oven to roast for 6 to 7 hours. When ready to serve, milk was added to the brim, and the pumpkin was eaten straight from the shell.

Pumpkin Puree

1 ripe pumpkin, about 3 to 4 pounds

Butter

Pinch cloves

Pinch salt

YIELDS ABOUT THREE TO FOUR CUPS PUREE

Preheat the oven to 350 degrees.

Cut the pumpkin in half and scoop out the seeds and stringy fibers. If the pumpkin is large, slice it into quarters. Arrange the pumpkin pieces in a large roasting pan filled to a depth of ½ inch with hot water. Bake in the preheated oven for 1½ to 2 hours, depending on the size of the pumpkin pieces. The pulp should be tender.

Scrape the pulp from the rind and puree in a blender or force it through a sieve with the back of a spoon. Season to taste with butter, cloves, and salt, or use in pumpkin pie recipes.

If you wish, you may cook the pumpkin with water to cover until tender. In this case, peel the pumpkin after removing the stringy fibers and seeds, and cut into large dice. Puree the cooked pumpkin as directed above.

Ratatouille

3 large onions, sliced

½ cup olive oil

3 small eggplants, peeled and cut into ½-inch cubes

4 green peppers, seeded and chopped

6 medium tomatoes, peeled, seeded, and chopped

6 small zucchini, cut into ½-inch slices

2 cups chopped celery

2 cloves garlic, crushed

Salt and black pepper

1 tablespoon minced fresh marjoram or 1½ teaspoons dried

1 tablespoon minced fresh basil, or 1½ teaspoons dried

SERVES EIGHT

Sauté the onions gently in the oil in a large skillet until they are soft but not browned.

Stir the eggplants and peppers into the onions, and sauté over low heat for 5 minutes. Combine the tomatoes, zucchini, and celery with the other vegetables in the skillet, and simmer, covered, for about 50 minutes. Add the garlic, salt and pepper, marjoram, and basil during the last 5 minutes of cooking. Serve the ratatouille hot or chilled.

Fried Salsify

4 pounds salsify (oyster plant)
6 tablespoons butter, softened
Milk
4 eggs

Salt and black pepper
Flour
3 tablespoons vegetable oil

SERVES EIGHT

Scrape the salsify roots and cut them into pieces, taking care to place them in cold water as soon as they are cut to prevent discoloration. Boil the salsify for 10 to 12 minutes, or until tender. Drain and puree by forcing through a fine sieve with the back of a spoon to remove any tough fibers.

Mix the pureed salsify with half the butter. Stir in just enough milk to produce a thick mixture. Beat the eggs lightly and add to the salsify, along with salt and pepper and a little flour to bind, if necessary. Heat the remaining butter and oil in a skillet and drop in the batter by tablespoonfuls. Fry to a golden brown on both sides, turning once. Drain briefly on paper towels and serve piping hot.

Pennsylvania Dutch Sautéed Sauerkraut

3 medium onions, sliced
4 tablespoons butter

2 pounds sauerkraut
1 teaspoon dark brown sugar

SERVES EIGHT

Separate the onions into rings and sauté them in the butter until they are limp. Drain the sauerkraut and add it to the onions. Sauté until lightly browned. Sprinkle with sugar, cover, and cook over very low heat for 15 to 20 minutes. Stir and serve.

Early American Spinach
Stewed with Cream

Early American recipes often called for
a small amount of confectioners' sugar to be added
to the spinach with the salt and pepper.
Try this for an unusual variation.

3–4 pounds spinach
2 tablespoons butter
Pinch confectioners' sugar

Salt and black pepper
Pinch grated nutmeg
Heavy cream or half and half

SERVES EIGHT

Wash the spinach thoroughly in several changes of cold water, picking off and discarding any thick stems or wilted leaves. Drain the spinach leaves, shaking off the excess water, and cook over low heat in the water clinging to the leaves for 2 to 3 minutes, or until tender. Remove from the heat.

Force the spinach through a fine sieve, or puree in a blender. Melt the butter in a large skillet, add the pureed spinach, and season with the sugar and spices. Cook over low heat, stirring constantly. Gradually stir in enough cream to reach the consistency you prefer. Serve hot.

Buttered Spinach

3–4 pounds spinach
6 tablespoons butter

Salt and black pepper
Pinch grated nutmeg

SERVES EIGHT

Wash the spinach thoroughly in several changes of cold water, picking off and discarding any thick stems or wilted leaves. Drain the spinach leaves, shaking off the excess water and cook over low heat in the water clinging to the leaves for 2 to 3 minutes, or just long enough to wilt the leaves.

Remove from the heat, drain well, and add the butter. Toss gently until the leaves are well coated. Season with salt and pepper and a pinch of nutmeg.

Creamed Spinach with Hard-Boiled Eggs

3–4 pounds spinach
1 cup boiling salted water
½ teaspoon granulated sugar
2 tablespoons butter

1 tablespoon flour
½ cup heavy cream
4 hard-boiled eggs, sliced
Fried Bread (page 359)

SERVES EIGHT

Wash the spinach thoroughly in several changes of cold water, picking off and discarding any thick stems or wilted leaves. Place in a large kettle containing the boiling water to which the sugar has been added. Cook the spinach for 4 minutes, drain well, and chop the leaves coarsely. Puree the spinach by forcing it through a fine sieve with the back of a spoon.

Heat the butter in a large skillet, add the pureed spinach, and cook for 3 minutes. Stir in the flour and continue to cook for 2 minutes more. Add the cream, mix well, and serve immediately, garnished with slices of hard-boiled egg and Fried Bread.

Garden-Fresh Spinach Soufflé

¾ pound spinach

1 tablespoon butter

½ teaspoon salt

5 eggs

1 cup hot Easy White Sauce
(page 238)

Pinch grated nutmeg

2 tablespoons grated parmesan
cheese

4 poached eggs

SERVES FOUR

Preheat the oven to 375 degrees.

Rinse the spinach in several changes of cold water. Drain, remove the tough stalks, and mince the leaves. Heat the butter in a skillet and cook the spinach over low heat, stirring occasionally. Season with salt. When all the liquid has evaporated, remove the spinach from the heat and set it aside.

Separate the 5 eggs, reserving the whites in a mixing bowl. Beat the yolks lightly, and slowly mix in 2 or 3 spoonsful of the white sauce. Stir these thickened yolks into the remaining white sauce, add the spinach, nutmeg, and cheese. Mix thoroughly and allow the mixture to cool.

Beat the 5 reserved egg whites just long enough to form stiff peaks, then fold them thoroughly into the spinach mixture. Arrange half of the spinach soufflé in a buttered 6 cup soufflé dish. Set the poached eggs on top, and cover with the rest of the soufflé. Fill the dish only ¾ full. Bake for about 30 minutes. When the soufflé is golden, remove it from the oven and cut it into quarters to include a poached egg in each portion.

Succotash

2½ cups shelled lima beans

1 1-inch cube salt pork

2 cups corn kernels scraped
from the cob

1 tablespoon butter

Salt and black pepper

⅓ cup heavy cream

SERVES EIGHT

Place the lima beans in a large saucepan; add the salt pork and enough boiling water to cover. Cover the saucepan and cook the beans until they are nearly tender. Stir in the corn and continue to cook for 15 minutes, or until the corn is tender. Most of the cooking liquid will have evaporated. Remove and discard the salt pork. Blend in the butter, salt and pepper to taste, and the cream. Simmer until the cream is thick. Serve piping hot.

Scalloped Sweet Potatoes and Apples

*Apples and sweet potatoes are perfectly compatible,
especially if the sweets are the home-cooked variety
and sugar is added with restraint.*

6 *medium to large sweet potatoes*	¼ *teaspoon grated nutmeg*
4 *McIntosh apples*	⅛ *teaspoon mace*
3 *tablespoons dark brown sugar*	4 *tablespoons butter*
½ *teaspoon salt*	

SERVES EIGHT

Preheat the oven to 350 degrees.

Boil the sweet potatoes in their jackets until tender, drain, peel, and cut them into ¼-inch slices. Peel and core the apples and cut them into ¼-inch slices. Place a layer of potato slices on the bottom of a large buttered casserole. Cover with a layer of apples. Combine the sugar, salt, nutmeg, and mace, and sprinkle some of this mixture over the apples. Dot with bits of the butter. Continue to build alternating layers, ending with a layer of apples. Bake for 50 minutes.

Sweet Potato–Pumpkin Soufflé***

½ cup plus 2 tablespoons milk
5 tablespoons butter
4 tablespoons orange liqueur
1⅓ cups cooked, mashed sweet potatoes
1⅓ cups cooked or canned pumpkin

5 eggs
1¼ teaspoons grated lemon zest
¾ teaspoon salt
Pinch mace
Pinch grated nutmeg

SERVES EIGHT

Preheat the oven to 400 degrees.

Heat the milk, remove from the flame, and stir in the butter and orange liqueur. Place the sweet potatoes and pumpkin in a large bowl, add the milk mixture, and beat until smooth. Separate the eggs, setting aside the whites. Beat the egg yolks into the sweet potato and pumpkin mixture and continue to beat while adding the lemon zest, salt, mace, and nutmeg.

Beat the egg whites until they form stiff peaks and gently fold them into the potato-pumpkin mixture. Pour into a well-buttered soufflé dish and bake for 30 to 40 minutes. The soufflé should be lightly browned and puffy on top before removing from the oven. Serve immediately.

Sweet Potatoes Baked with Applesauce

4 large sweet potatoes
2 tablespoons butter
2¼ cups applesauce

4 tablespoons light brown sugar or honey

SERVES EIGHT

Preheat the oven to 375 degrees.

Boil the sweet potatoes in their jackets until tender but not mushy. Drain, cool a bit, peel, and cut into ⅓-inch-thick slices.

Butter a glass baking dish with 1 tablespoon butter. Spoon ¾ cup applesauce into the bottom of the dish. Arrange sweet potato slices over the applesauce and cover with another ¾ cup applesauce. Sprinkle 2 tablespoons brown sugar over the applesauce. Continue with the remaining sweet potatoes, and top with the last ¾ cup of applesauce. Sprinkle with 2 tablespoons of brown sugar and dot with the rest of the butter. Bake for 25 to 30 minutes. Serve hot.

Baked Sweet Potato

SERVES EIGHT

Rinse and peel 8 medium sweet potatoes. Parboil the potatoes in water to cover for 8 minutes. Drain and slice in half. About 30 to 40 minutes before roast turkey or chicken is scheduled to be done, arrange the potato halves around the bottom of the pan in which the bird is roasting. Baste the potatoes occasionally with the pan drippings while baking.

Summer Squash in Lemon Butter

3 pounds summer squash
8 tablespoons (1 stick) butter, melted

Juice of ½ lemon
Black pepper

SERVES EIGHT

Use yellow crookneck, zucchini, or pattypan squash, singly or in combination. In any case, pick squash from your garden or buy it when it is small, as these young ones will be the most tender.

If the squash are small, leave them whole. Otherwise, slice or quarter them lengthwise. Large yellow crooknecks will need to be peeled before slicing. Bring a small amount of salted water to a boil, add the squash, and steam, tightly covered, until the vegetable is tender but still firm.

Drain thoroughly, place in a serving dish, and pour the melted butter over. Sprinkle with lemon juice and freshly ground black pepper. Serve at once.

Salads
and
dressings

Salads

Leafy Green Salad

SERVES EIGHT

2 quarts of the following greens, alone or in combination:

Leaf, butterhead, romaine, or iceberg lettuce;
Endive or escarole;
Beet, turnip, Swiss chard, spinach, dandelion, collard, or kale
greens.
¼ cup minced fresh chives, chervil, parsley, tarragon, mint, or
any combination of these
French Dressing (page 333)

Be sure to use only the freshest and most perfect greens. Wash
them well, drain, and dry carefully on paper towels. No water should

cling to the leaves. Tear, do not cut, into bite-size pieces and re-frigerate until very cold. Just before serving, toss with dressing.

Mushroom and Romaine Salad

½ *pound mushrooms*
1 *large head romaine lettuce*
2 *green peppers, cut into ½-inch dice*

¼ *cup chopped scallions*
French Dressing, Variation 3 (page 333)

SERVES EIGHT

Wipe the mushrooms with a damp cloth to remove any lingering sand; slice very thinly. Wash the romaine leaves well, dry them thoroughly, and tear into bite-size pieces. Combine the mushrooms, romaine, peppers, and scallions in a salad bowl and chill well. Toss gently with dressing just before serving.

Miss Maud's Lettuce Salad

2 *heads lettuce*
7 *hard-boiled eggs*
⅛ *teaspoon dry mustard*
Salt and black pepper

1 *tablespoon vegetable oil*
¼ *cup white vinegar*
2 *scallions, including 3 inches green top*

SERVES EIGHT

Rinse and dry the lettuce, discarding any limp or damaged outer leaves. Arrange the lettuce on individual salad plates. Remove the yolks from 3 of the hard-boiled eggs. Chop and reserve the whites. Thinly slice the 4 remaining eggs, and divide among the lettuce leaves on each plate.

[319]

Mash the 3 egg yolks thoroughly, then blend in the mustard, salt and pepper. Add the oil, mix well, and stir in the vinegar. Pour this dressing over the lettuce and eggs, top with the chopped egg whites, and the scallions. Serve cold.

Summer Vegetable Salad

*A fresh-from-your-own-garden salad
is one of summer's best treats.*

1 small yellow summer squash, trimmed

1 small zucchini, trimmed

1 sweet red pepper, seeded

1 green pepper, seeded

16 scallions, with 3 inches green top

16 radishes

3 cups lettuce, or beet or turnip greens

2 small cucumbers, peeled and sliced

16 cherry tomatoes, halved

4 small carrots, cut into thin strips

French Dressing (page 333)

SERVES EIGHT

Cut the squash into ¼-inch slices and the peppers and scallions into ½-inch slices. Cut off a flat piece from the root end of each radish and make thin, petal-shaped cuts around the radishes to create a rose effect. Arrange the lettuce or greens in the bottom of a large salad bowl, top with squash and cucumber slices, and decorate with carrot and pepper strips radiating outward from the center of the salad. Set the radish roses and cherry tomato halves around the edge of the bowl and sprinkle the scallion pieces over all. Refrigerate. Toss with French Dressing just before serving.

Summer Vegetable Bowl

Prepare all vegetables as directed above, omitting the lettuce or greens and leaving the scallions whole.

Arrange the vegetables attractively over cracked ice. Serve with French Dressing (page 333) on the side.

Hunter's Cattail Salad

This was a favorite salad even in Indian days. Early spring is the time to gather the tiny new ivory-colored cattail shoots that grow so abundantly in swamps. Cut the shoots when they are no more than 3 inches high, and trim off everything but the ivory shoot itself.

Wash the shoots thoroughly in several changes of water, pat them dry with paper towels, and cut them into 1-inch pieces. Add salt to taste and toss with French Dressing (page 333), or any other dressing you wish.

Country Kitchen Coleslaw***

1 medium head cabbage	3 tablespoons lemon juice
3 tablespoons granulated sugar	¼ cup milk
¾ teaspoon salt	1 cup mayonnaise
1 teaspoon poppy seeds	

SERVES EIGHT

Remove the tough outer leaves from the cabbage, cut it in half, and remove the hard core. Cut each half into quarters and rinse. Allow to drain thoroughly, then shred into very fine strips with a sharp knife. Combine the sugar, salt, poppy seeds, lemon juice, and milk, blend into the mayonnaise, and pour over the cabbage. Toss well and refrigerate for at least 4 hours before serving.

Coleslaw in a Cabbage Shell

1 medium head cabbage	6 cherry tomatoes
1 cup Boiled Dressing (page 339)	Parsley sprigs

SERVES SIX

Remove the tough outer leaves from the cabbage and cut off the stalk close to the base. Slice a 1-inch piece from the top of the cabbage and set it aside. Use a sharp knife to cut out the center leaves of the cabbage, leaving a 1-inch-thick shell. Finely shred the center leaves. Rinse the hollow shell and top, and turn the shell upside down to drain. Soak the shredded cabbage in hot water for 1 hour, drain, and dry by rolling in paper towels.

Moisten the shredded cabbage with Boiled Dressing and refill the cabbage shell. Decorate the top of the salad with a circle of 5 halved cherry tomatoes. Set the reserved cabbage top on the salad, and top this with a cherry tomato secured with a thick wooden toothpick. Refrigerate the cabbage salad for at least 3 hours before serving. To serve, place the whole cabbage on a platter, and surround with parsley sprigs. Cut the cabbage into 6 wedges. Serve with additional dressing in a sauceboat, if desired.

Calico Cabbage Salad

1 large head green cabbage, shredded	2 Golden Delicious apples, cored and chopped
2 medium carrots, shredded	¾ cup granulated sugar
½ large Spanish onion, minced	1 cup mayonnaise
1 small sweet red pepper, finely diced	1 cup white vinegar
1 small green pepper, finely diced	¾ teaspoon salt
	2 teaspoons poppy seeds

SERVES EIGHT

Place the shredded cabbage and carrots in a large bowl with the onion, the peppers, and apples. Mix the sugar, mayonnaise, vinegar, salt, and pepper. Toss the vegetables and fruit with the mayonnaise and vinegar mixture. Refrigerate at least 6 hours or overnight, stirring occasionally. Drain if desired.

Cream Cheese-Filled Celery

16 tender, inside stalks celery
8 ounces cream cheese, softened
1 tablespoon butter, softened

1 tablespoon sour cream
1 tablespoon mayonnaise
Paprika

SERVES EIGHT

Trim the leaves and roots from the celery, rinse the stalks well, and pat dry with paper towels.

Thoroughly blend together the cream cheese, butter, sour cream, and mayonnaise. Force through a fluted nozzle of a pastry tube into the celery stalks. Chill before serving. To serve plain, sprinkle with paprika; or stuff with one of the following tasty and decorative cream cheese preparations.

Shrimp and Dill Filling

Top each filled celery stalk with 3 tiny shrimp and garnish with snips of fresh dill and bits of 6 chopped black olives.

Hard-Boiled Egg and Anchovy Filling

Add 1 teaspoon onion juice to the cream cheese filling and mix thoroughly. Force the filling through a pastry tube into the celery stalks. Cut 8 flat anchovy fillets into ½-inch pieces. Rub 2 hard-boiled egg yolks through a fine sieve. Arrange the anchovy pieces on the celery filling and garnish with sieved egg yolk.

Blue Cheese and Walnut Filling

Mix 2 tablespoons softened blue cheese into the cream cheese filling. Force the filling through a pastry tube into the celery. Before serving top with ¼ cup finely chopped walnuts.

Spicy Chicken Filling

Add ¼ cup finely minced cooked chicken and 6 or 7 drops Tabasco to the cream cheese filling and mix thoroughly. Heap the filling into the celery stalks with a fork. Garnish with strips of pimiento and capers before serving.

Cucumber Ribbons

8 large cucumbers, peeled *French Dressing (page 333)*

SERVES EIGHT

Beginning at one end of each cucumber, cut long strips ¼-inch thick from all sides. Reserve the centers and save for use in salads or to flavor consommé. Place the strips in a large bowl with sloping sides and then set a plate directly on top of the cucumber ribbons. Weight the plate with a heavy pot or jar. Allow the ribbons to stand for 2 hours, pouring off any liquid that accumulates. Gently toss the cucumber ribbons with French Dressing and refrigerate for several hours. Toss gently again before serving.

Jenny Jane's Cucumber Aspic

4 large cucumbers, peeled and sliced
1 cup white wine vinegar
2 cups water
2 envelopes unflavored gelatin

1 tablespoon bottled onion juice or juice from onion squeezed in a garlic press
Pinch cayenne
Salt and black pepper
Green vegetable coloring

SERVES SIX TO EIGHT

Place the cucumber slices in a saucepan, add the vinegar, and 1 cup water; bring to a boil. Simmer over low heat until the cucumber is tender. Puree the cucumber mixture by forcing it through a fine sieve with the back of a spoon.

Sprinkle the gelatin over the remaining cup of water to dissolve. Add the dissolved gelatin to the cucumber puree, along with the onion juice, cayenne, and salt and pepper. Mix in a few drops of food coloring to achieve an attractive green color. Stir over very low heat for 3 to 4 minutes. Pour the aspic mixture into a well-oiled ring mold. Cool to room temperature, then refrigerate until the aspic is set.

To serve, unmold on a serving plate and fill the center with meat, vegetable, or egg salad. Garnish with peaks of mayonnaise forced through a pastry tube.

Old-Country Carrot and Chestnut Salad

4 cups sliced carrots

2 cups boiled and peeled chestnuts (page 267)

¼ cup minced chives

1 cup Unboiled Dressing (page 339)

SERVES SIX

Simmer the carrots in water to cover until tender, drain well, and chill. Chop the chestnuts, mix with the carrot slices and chives, and toss with the dressing. Serve cold.

Sadye's Cauliflower Salad

This attractive cauliflower dish will enhance
any summer meal. It tastes somewhat like a pickle,
looks like a vegetable,
and serves as an easy, make-ahead salad.

1 large head cauliflower

MARINADE

1½ cups granulated sugar
2 cloves garlic, minced
1 tablespoon mustard seed or
½ teaspoon dry mustard
1½ teaspoons celery seed or ½
teaspoon celery salt

1½ teaspoons whole allspice or
½ teaspoon ground allspice
1½ teaspoons whole cloves or ½
teaspoon ground cloves
1½ teaspoons turmeric
White vinegar and water

GARNISH

1 small head Bibb lettuce
2 hard-boiled eggs, finely chopped

4 tablespoons minced scallions
Piquant Mayonnaise (page
335)

SERVES EIGHT

Rinse the cauliflower and trim the stem so the whole vegetable stands upright on a plate. Cut a slim triangular notch 2 inches deep from the core of the cauliflower. Place the sugar, garlic, and spices in a deep kettle slightly larger than the cauliflower. Add equal portions of vinegar and water to completely immerse the cauliflower. Bring the marinade to a boil, add the cauliflower, cover, and simmer until tender, about 20 minutes.

Refrigerate the cauliflower in the marinade until cold, about 3 hours. To serve, arrange Bibb lettuce leaves on a plate. Drain the cauliflower thoroughly and stand it stem down in the center of the plate. Sprinkle with the hard-boiled eggs and top with scallions. Divide into 8 wedges and serve cold with Piquant Mayonnaise (page 335).

Old-Fashioned Potato Salad I***

20 small potatoes, boiled, peeled, and cubed

6 hard-boiled eggs

10 scallions, including several inches green top, chopped

1 cup chopped celery

⅔ cup chopped sweet pickle

3 tablespoons mild yellow mustard

5 tablespoons pickle juice

1 tablespoon cider vinegar

1 teaspoon granulated sugar

¾ teaspoon salt

¾ teaspoon poppy seeds

1½ cups commercial mayonnaise or Your Own Mayonnaise (page 334)

Pimiento strips

¼ cup finely minced parsley

SERVES EIGHT

Boil the potatoes in their skins until tender. Coarsely chop the hard-boiled eggs, reserving 1 yolk. Combine the eggs, scallions, celery, sweet pickle, mustard, pickle juice, vinegar, sugar, salt, poppy seeds, and mayonnaise. Lightly toss the potatoes in the mayonnaise mixture until the cubes are well coated. Turn the salad into a serving bowl and decorate the top with thin strips of pimiento and finely minced parsley. Garnish the center of the salad with the reserved egg yolk which has been pressed through a sieve. Chill for at least 4 hours, or overnight, before serving.

Old-Fashioned Potato Salad II

*The mustard-flavored tartness of Unboiled Dressing
makes this potato salad with ham
particularly piquant.*

10 medium potatoes, boiled in
    their skins

3 hard-boiled eggs, sliced

1 medium onion, minced

2 stalks celery, trimmed and
    finely minced

3 tablespoons finely minced
    chives

½ teaspoon salt

¼ teaspoon black pepper

½ cup finely minced cooked ham

1 cup mayonnaise

½ cup Unboiled Dressing (page
    339)

SERVES EIGHT

Drain the potatoes, cool them slightly, and peel. Cut the potatoes
into ½-inch cubes. Combine the potatoes, eggs, onion, celery, chives,
salt, pepper, and minced ham. Mix together the mayonnaise and Unboiled Dressing until well blended. Pour this dressing over the
potato salad and toss the mixture gently until the potatoes are well
coated. Refrigerate for several hours or overnight before serving.

Potato Salad with Blue Cheese Dressing

5 strips lean bacon, minced

1 tablespoon butter

3 medium onions, coarsely
    chopped

7 medium potatoes, boiled, peeled,
    and sliced ¼-inch thick

2 stalks celery, chopped

4 ounces blue cheese, at room
    temperature

1 cup heavy cream

½ cup tarragon vinegar

    Salt and black pepper

1 tablespoon minced fresh chervil
    or 1½ teaspoons dried

1 tablespoon minced fresh tarra-
    gon or 1½ teaspoons dried

1 tablespoon finely chopped
    chives

SERVES EIGHT

Sauté the minced bacon in a large skillet until crisp. Add the butter and sauté the onions until they are transparent but not too soft—they should retain a bit of crunch. Mix gently with the potato slices and celery.

Mash the cheese well with a fork, add the cream, and blend the mixture until very smooth. Mix in the vinegar, salt, pepper, chervil, and tarragon. Pour the blue cheese dressing over the potato salad, toss lightly to coat well, and refrigerate for at least 1½ hours. Just before serving garnish with chopped chives and Brown Bread Croutons (page 361).

German Hot Potato Salad

7 medium potatoes

8 strips lean bacon, minced

2 small onions, sliced

¾ cup tarragon vinegar

¾ cup beef consommé

1 teaspoon granulated sugar

½ teaspoon salt

1 teaspoon cornstarch

3 egg yolks

SERVES EIGHT

Boil the potatoes in their skins until tender but not mushy. Drain them and cool a bit before peeling and slicing them at least ¼-inch thick. Sauté the bacon in a large skillet until crisp. Add the onion rings and cook until they are transparent but still slightly crunchy.

Mix in the vinegar, stock, sugar, salt and cornstarch. Bring to the boil and immediately remove from the heat. Beat the egg yolks lightly, add a little of the boiled dressing, then stir the egg mixture into the dressing, mix well, and pour over the potato slices. Toss the salad gently and serve.

Hot Dandelion Salad

8 *cups dandelion greens*
8 *strips lean bacon, minced*
1 *large onion, chopped*
1 *teaspoon flour*

3 *tablespoons white vinegar*
1 *tablespoon granulated sugar*
   Salt and black pepper
1 *tablespoon butter*

SERVES EIGHT

Use only the young, tender dandelion leaves you find in early spring. Wash the leaves thoroughly in several changes of water, drain, and dry thoroughly with paper towels.

Sauté the minced bacon until brown. Remove the bacon from the skillet with a slotted spoon and set it aside to drain. Add the onion to the bacon fat and sauté until golden brown. Stir in the flour, vinegar, sugar, and seasonings.

Heat the butter in a separate skillet and toss the dandelion greens for 30 seconds. Pour the hot onion and vinegar mixture over the greens, sprinkle the reserved bacon bits on top, and toss gently. Serve immediately.

Dutch-Treat Wilted Lettuce Salad

This salad is also tasty if a few small,
tender dandelion leaves are tossed with the lettuce.

2–3 *heads leaf lettuce*
6 *strips lean bacon, minced*
3 *tablespoons lemon juice*

3 *teaspoons granulated sugar*
½ *teaspoon salt*
¼ *teaspoon dry mustard*

SERVES EIGHT

Wash the lettuce leaves, drain, dry thoroughly, and tear into shreds. Sauté the minced bacon until crisp; drain on paper towels.

Add the lemon juice, sugar, salt, and mustard to the bacon fat remaining in the skillet. Heat for 2 or 3 minutes until the sugar is dissolved. Arrange the lettuce leaves in a salad bowl, pour the hot dressing over, and toss gently. Serve immediately, topped with the crumbled bacon.

Anne Petrie's Strawberry Salad

2 heads lettuce
2 pints strawberries
4 tablespoons confectioners' sugar

½ cup Strawberry Mayonnaise
(page 334)
2 limes, quartered

SERVES EIGHT

Rinse, drain, and dry the lettuce leaves. Rinse, dry, and hull the strawberries. Arrange the lettuce leaves attractively on 8 salad plates. Roll the strawberries in confectioners' sugar and place equal amounts of fruit on top of each portion of lettuce. Top each serving with 1 tablespoon Strawberry Mayonnaise. Garnish each plate with lime wedges and serve very cold.

Greengage Plum and Melon Salad

2 cantaloupes, cut into balls
15 greengage plums, peeled and pitted
1 cup sauterne

3 tablespoons lemon juice
8 lettuce leaves, well chilled
Confectioners' sugar (optional)

SERVES EIGHT

Toss the cantaloupe balls with the quartered plums, sauterne, and lemon juice. Refrigerate for at least 1 hour, tossing at least once again.

Arrange the fruit on lettuce leaves and dust with confectioners' sugar, if desired.

Mrs. Revere's Cranberry Mold

4 cups cranberries

2 cups granulated sugar

1 cup boiling water

4 oranges (optional)

SERVES EIGHT

Place the cranberries in a saucepan with the sugar, add the boiling water, and cook over medium heat for 15 minutes, or until cranberries have popped and are tender. Puree the cranberry mixture by forcing it through a fine sieve with the back of a spoon. Fill 8 small, attractively shaped glasses with the puree. Refrigerate for several hours before removing from the glasses and setting on a serving plate.

The shells of orange halves make unusual containers for serving cranberry mold. Cut 4 oranges in half, scoop out the pulp, and add it to the cranberries before cooking. Scrape the inside of the reserved orange skins. Chill and serve the mold in the hollow orange halves.

Dressings

French Dressing

¼ teaspoon salt
⅛ teaspoon black pepper

¼ cup wine, cider, or tarragon vinegar
¾ cup olive oil

YIELDS ABOUT TWO CUPS

Mix the salt and pepper into the vinegar, then slowly beat in the oil. Alternatively, place all ingredients in a screw-top jar and shake vigorously until well blended.

Variations

(1) For a more assertive dressing, add ¼ teaspoon dry mustard to the vinegar before beating in the oil.

(2) For a milder dressing, suitable for such delicate greens as Bibb, Boston, or field lettuce, substitute lemon juice for all or part of the vinegar.

(3) For cold or hot boiled beef, chicken, fish, or vegetables, or an aggressive combination salad, add to the French Dressing in a screw-top jar 1 teaspoon paprika, ½ teaspoon dry mustard, 2 halved garlic cloves, 1 teaspoon oregano, ¼ cup minced green pepper, ¼

cup minced pimiento, and 3 tablespoons minced onion. Close the jar and shake vigorously until well blended. Discard the garlic cloves before serving.

(4) For a dressing in the Italian manner substitute 2 chopped and mashed anchovy fillets for the salt.

Your Own Mayonnaise

2 egg yolks, at room
   temperature
2 teaspoons vinegar
½ teaspoon dry mustard

½ teaspoon salt
White pepper
1 cup olive oil
½ cup vegetable oil

YIELDS ABOUT TWO CUPS

Place the egg yolks and 1 teaspoon vinegar in the small bowl of an electric mixer after the bowl has been rinsed in hot water and dried. Add the mustard, salt, and white pepper to taste. Beat at low speed until well blended. Combine the olive and vegetable oil and gradually beat into the yolks, one or two drops at a time. When ¼ cup of oil has been added, add the second teaspoon of vinegar, continuing to beat all the while. Gradually pour in the rest of the oil in a thin stream. Watch carefully to see that the oil is well absorbed. Do not add too quickly.

Strawberry Mayonnaise

Crush 6 large, hulled strawberries with 1 tablespoon confectioners' sugar. Stir into 1 cup Mayonnaise and serve with fruit salads.

Piquant Mayonnaise

Reduce 1 cup Cauliflower Marinade (page 326) until it measures ¼ cup. Cool and stir into 1 cup Mayonnaise. Garnish with 2 minced scallions and chill.

Herb Mayonnaise

This thick mayonnaise is served with
cold cooked vegetables, hard-boiled eggs,
fish, meat, or seafood.

2 hard-boiled eggs	*⅓ teaspoon salt*
1 egg yolk	*¼ teaspoon black pepper*
⅓–½ cup olive oil	*½ teaspoon dry mustard*
1 tablespoon finely minced mixed herbs (chives, parsley, tarragon, thyme)	*Pinch grated nutmeg*
	2 tablespoons white vinegar

YIELDS ONE CUP

Separate the hard-boiled yolks from the whites and set the whites aside. Force the yolks through a fine sieve and place in the bowl of an electric mixer. Add the raw egg yolk and mix well.

Begin to add the oil a few drops at a time. Gradually increase the amount of oil added to the egg yolks from ½ teaspoon to 1 full teaspoon, until the mixture will not absorb any more oil. If the mixture begins to separate, beat 1 egg yolk and ½ teaspoon vinegar together in another bowl; beat in the mayonnaise, slowly at first, then gradually increase the beating tempo until thoroughly incorporated.

Reduce the beater speed to low, and continue to beat as you add the herbs, salt, pepper, mustard, nutmeg, and vinegar. When the dressing is well blended, chop and stir in the reserved egg whites. Refrigerate until needed. Serve cold.

Tartar Sauce

3 egg yolks
1 teaspoon prepared mustard
1 teaspoon salt
Pinch cayenne
1 cup olive oil
1 tablespoon while vinegar
1½ teaspoons lemon juice

½ small onion, minced
1 tablespoon finely chopped capers
1 tablespoon finely chopped sweet pickles
1 tablespoon finely chopped stuffed olives
1 tablespoon minced parsley

YIELDS ONE AND ONE HALF CUPS

Place the egg yolks in a bowl and stir in the mustard, salt, and cayenne; mix well. Add the oil a bit at a time, beating constantly, until all the oil is worked in and the mixture is thick. Add the vinegar, beating it in well, and then beat in the lemon juice. Chill the sauce thoroughly. Just before serving, stir in the onion, capers, pickles, olives, and parsley.

Celery Seed Dressing

Use this as a dip for fresh vegetables
or shrimp as well as a dressing for
lettuce wedges and tomato slices.

2 teaspoons celery seed
1½ teaspoons dry mustard
¾ teaspoon salt
White pepper

1 large clove garlic, crushed
3 tablespoons lemon juice
1 cup sour cream
1 cup mayonnaise

YIELDS ABOUT TWO CUPS

Combine the celery seed, mustard, salt, pepper, and garlic in a bowl. Stir in the lemon juice, sour cream, and mayonnaise. Mix thoroughly and refrigerate for 30 minutes before serving.

Mrs. Fegan's Cumberland Spread

This recipe was contributed by Mrs. Milton S. Fegan.
It is a favorite of the Pennsylvania Dutch families
in and around Cumberland County, Pennsylvania.

¼ *pound dried beef*   1 *green pepper*

¼ *pound sharp cheddar cheese**   1 *egg*

1 *cup undiluted canned tomato*
  soup or canned tomatoes

YIELDS TWO CUPS

Put all ingredients except the egg through a food mill. Place in a saucepan and cook until the cheese is melted. Beat the egg and add it to the ingredients in the pan. Stir oven medium heat for 2 minutes.

Store in a covered jar in the refrigerator. Serve on toast points or crackers.

* Use mild cheddar cheese for a milder and less salty spread.

Your Own Yoghurt

4 *cups milk*   ½–1 *cup commercial yoghurt, at*
                                 room temperature

YIELDS FOUR CUPS

Pour the milk into a glass pot and heat it as you would a baby's bath so that a few drops on the wrist feel lukewarm. Remove the milk from the heat and stir in commercial yoghurt. Wrap a warm towel around the mixture and set it in a warm place, such as the oven if it has a pilot light or a sunny window sill. Yoghurt must remain undisturbed for 8 hours, or overnight.

When the allotted time has passed and the yoghurt is tangy and thick, refrigerate immediately.

Yoghurt Dressing

Use this healthful dressing as a substitute for
mayonnaise or any dressing high in oil.

2 tablespoons butter	1 tablespoon granulated sugar
4 tablespoons whole wheat flour	¾ teaspoon dry mustard
1 cup milk	½ teaspoon salt
1 egg yolk	1 cup yoghurt
Juice of ½ lemon	

YIELDS TWO CUPS

Melt the butter in a skillet and stir in the flour. Add the milk all at once and stir over medium heat until the sauce is thick and smooth. Remove from heat and beat in the egg yolk, lemon juice, sugar, mustard, and salt. Stir in the yoghurt and cool. Refrigerate.

Mint-Honey-Yoghurt Sauce

This yoghurt sauce is a delicious dressing
for fruit salads or lamb—cool and exotic.

3 tablespoons honey	¼ cup apple or orange juice
2 tablespoons chopped mint	1 cup yoghurt

YIELDS ABOUT ONE AND ONE HALF CUPS

Simmer the honey, mint, and fruit juice for 1 or 2 minutes. Cool and stir in the yoghurt. Chill.

Boiled Dressing

2 teaspoons prepared mustard
2 teaspoons salt
4 teaspoons flour
3 tablespoons granulated sugar
  Pinch cayenne

2 teaspoons butter, melted
2 egg yolks
⅔ cup hot white vinegar
1 cup heavy cream

YIELDS ABOUT TWO CUPS

Place the ingredients in the top of a double boiler in the order given. Cook over hot water, stirring constantly, until the dressing thickens. Remove from the heat, strain, and cool.

Unboiled Dressing for Salads

2 eggs
1 teaspoon salt
1½ teaspoons dry mustard
  Pinch cayenne

2 tablespoons butter
¾ cup white vinegar
3 tablespoons honey

YIELDS ABOUT ONE CUP

Beat together all ingredients and stir over a very low flame until slightly thickened. Do not boil or dressing will curdle. Chill well.

Fresh-Cooked Horseradish Sauce

*Horseradish is so easy to grow
that there is no excuse for depriving yourself
of its appetite-stimulating zestiness. Try this sauce
with beef or game.*

1¾ cups grated fresh horseradish	¼ teaspoon ground allspice
2¼ cups dry red wine	Salt
¾ teaspoon ground cinnamon	Black pepper
¼ teaspoon grated nutmeg	1½ cups red currant jelly

YIELDS ABOUT FOUR CUPS

Use a blender or a mortar and pestle to pulverize the grated horseradish. Drain well and set aside. Bring the wine and spices to a boil in a large saucepan, lower the heat, and cook until the liquid is reduced to about 1½ cups. Remove from the heat and stir in the horseradish and currant jelly. Serve hot. The sauce will keep in the refrigerator for a week. Reheat before serving.

Horseradish Cream

This unique sauce is sweet and sour, hot and cold.

1 horseradish root	2 cups yoghurt
4 apples, peeled and cored	⅛ teaspoon salt
2 tablespoons honey	

YIELDS ABOUT THREE CUPS

Grate the horseradish and apples. Mix with honey, yoghurt, and salt. Place in a glass bowl and freeze until mushy. Stir the cream with a fork and refreeze. To serve, arrange cold meat or fish on a platter and decorate with watercress. Allow the cream to soften slightly, scoop out in balls, and place on the meat. Serve immediately.

Cucumber Dip

*Use this refreshing dip with fresh vegetables,
boiled potatoes, or cottage cheese. Stir a
tablespoon or two into egg salad for added zest.*

2 medium cucumbers	⅓ teaspoon salt
1 medium onion	⅔ cup sour cream
3 tablespoons plus 2 teaspoons white vinegar	⅛ teaspoon black pepper

YIELDS ABOUT ONE AND ONE HALF CUPS

Peel the cucumbers and grate them into a large shallow bowl. Grate the onion into the cucumbers. Add 3 tablespoons vinegar and the salt. Stir briefly to mix, then fit a small plate into the bowl so that it rests directly on top of the cucumber mixture. Place a heavy jar or pot on top of the plate to weight it. Allow the cucumber mixture to stand for 1 hour, then press down on the plate and pour off the liquid in the bowl, continuing to press down and pour off every 15 or 20 minutes for about 2 hours or until most of the liquid has been removed.

Remove the plate and jar, and mix in the sour cream, pepper, and remaining vinegar. The dip may be covered and kept for several days in the refrigerator if desired.

Breads and muffins

Country Brown Bread***

*This recipe makes a hearty, crusty, country-style bread
which may be flavored with either
shallots or currants.*

4½ cups whole wheat flour

3 cups all-purpose flour

3 teaspoons baking soda

1 teaspoon salt

⅓ cup granulated sugar

½ pound (2 sticks) plus 2
teaspoons butter

2 eggs

2¼ cups buttermilk

3 tablespoons minced shallots

4 tablespoons currants

YIELDS TWO LOAVES

Preheat the oven to 400 degrees.

Combine the flours, baking soda, salt, and sugar in a large bowl.
Cut in ½ pound (2 sticks) butter with 2 knives until the mixture
resembles coarse meal. Beat the eggs lightly, then add the buttermilk
and beat again. Make a well in the center of the flour mixture, and

add the eggs and buttermilk, a little at a time, mixing well with your fingers after each addition. The result should be a stiff dough.

Brown the shallots lightly in the remaining 2 teaspoons butter.

Place the dough on a lightly floured board, knead for 8 to 10 minutes, then divide the dough in half. Knead the currants into one half and the shallots into the other. Shape each half into a rounded loaf. Set the loaves on a well-greased cookie sheet, and use a sharp knife to make a crisscross cut about ½-inch deep on the top of each loaf. Bake in the preheated oven for 50 to 60 minutes, or until baked through. Cool on wire racks.

Mrs. Young's Raisin Graham Bread

2 cups golden raisins	3 tablespoons butter
6 tablespoons applejack	⅓ cup granulated sugar
Juice of 2 oranges	2 teaspoons salt
2 teaspoons ground cinnamon	1 cup graham flour
2 cups milk	5–6 cups all-purpose flour
1 package dry-active yeast	

YIELDS TWO LOAVES

Place the raisins in a saucepan; stir in the applejack, orange juice, and cinnamon. Cook the mixture over low heat until most of the liquid is absorbed. Set aside.

Heat the milk to lukewarm. Place the yeast in a small bowl, and mix in ¼ cup of warm milk. Set aside for 10 minutes until the yeast dissolves. Place the remaining milk in a large bowl. Add the butter, sugar, and salt. Stir in the yeast, the graham flour, and 2 cups of the white flour. Blend well. Stir in as much additional flour as necessary to make a fairly stiff dough.

Spread a generous amount of flour on a board, and knead the dough until it is smooth and elastic, about 8 to 10 minutes. Place the dough in a greased bowl, turning once to grease the top. Cover with a dish towel and set the bowl in a warm, draft-free place until the dough doubles in bulk. This should take about 2½ hours.

Punch the dough down and turn out on a lightly floured board.

Knead gently for 5 minutes. Replace the dough in the bowl, cover it again, and set it in a warm, draft-free place for 40 minutes.

Divide the dough in half, and roll each half into a rectangle. Spread half the reserved raisin mixture over the top surface of each rectangle. Roll each rectangle up from the narrow end, tucking the ends in and under as you go. Place in 2 well-buttered 9¼-by-5¼-by-2¾-inch loaf pans, cover, and set in a warm, draft-free place to rise for 1 hour.

Uncover the loaves, place them in a cold oven, set the oven to 350 degrees, and bake for 1 hour, or until they are nicely browned on top. Cool the breads for 10 minutes in the pans, then turn them out, and cool on wire racks.

Orange Juice Bread

This makes a nice breakfast bread.
Serve it slightly warm with butter and marmalade.

3 tablespoons granulated sugar

1 package dry-active yeast

¼ cup warm water

½ cup orange juice

½ cup milk

4 tablespoons butter, melted

1½ teaspoons salt

Grated zest and juice of 1 large orange

4½–5 cups all-purpose flour

½ cup currants

2 tablespoons candied citron

3 tablespoons dark brown sugar

¼ teaspoon grated nutmeg

YIELDS ONE LOAF

Place 1 tablespoon granulated sugar and the yeast in the warm water; let the mixture stand for 15 minutes. Combine the remaining sugar with ½ cup orange juice, milk, butter, salt in a small saucepan. Grate the zest, or skin, of the whole orange, and set the orange aside. Add the zest to the orange juice mixture in the saucepan and heat over low flame to wrist temperature, no hotter. Stir 1 cup flour along with the yeast mixture into the warmed orange juice mixture. Mix in as much of the remaining flour as needed to make a rather stiff dough.

Turn the dough out onto a heavily floured surface, and knead for 10 minutes. Place the dough in a greased bowl, turning once to grease the top. Cover with a dish towel, and set to rise in a warm, draft-free place or until the dough doubles in bulk. This should take about 2 hours.

Place the juice from the whole orange in a saucepan with the currants, citron, 1 tablespoon dark brown sugar, and nutmeg. Bring to a boil. Stir the mixture for 1 minute over medium heat, then stand it at room temperature until the loaf is ready to be formed.

When the dough has doubled in bulk, punch it down and turn it out on a floured board. Knead it for several minutes, then roll it into a rectangle. Sprinkle the top surface with 2 tablespoons brown sugar and the reserved fruit mixture. Roll into a loaf, beginning at the short end. Turn the ends under as you go. Place the rolled dough in a greased 9¼-by-5¼-by-2¾-inch loaf pan. Cover with a light cloth and set in a warm, draft-free place to rise for 1 hour and 15 minutes, or until the top of the dough rises above the pan.

Preheat the oven to 375 degrees.

Bake the bread for 1 hour. Remove the loaf from the pan and set on a wire rack to cool.

Whole Wheat Carrot Bread***

*It would be difficult to find a bread
more nourishing or flavorsome than this one.*

¼ cup Irish oatmeal

1 cup grated carrots (about 4 medium)

1½ cups water

½ cup cornmeal

¼ cup molasses

½ cup honey

½ cup cooking oil or 8 tablespoons (1 stick) butter

¾ cup buttermilk or whole milk

1 teaspoon ground cinnamon

½ teaspoon salt

2 packages dry-active yeast

½ cup water, at wrist temperature

2½ cups whole wheat flour

3–4 cups all-purpose flour

YIELDS TWO LOAVES

Cook the oatmeal according to package directions. Simmer the carrots in 1½ cups water until tender. Reserve the cooking liquid. Place the cooked oatmeal and carrots, 1 cup carrot cooking liquid, the cornmeal, molasses, honey, oil, buttermilk, cinnamon, and salt in a very large mixing bowl, and cool to room temperature.

Sprinkle the yeast over the ½ cup of water at wrist temperature and let stand for 5 minutes. Stir the yeast and the whole wheat flour into the carrot mixture, cover, and set in a warm, draft-free place for 35 minutes to rise.

Stir 1 cup white flour into the soft risen dough. Place 1 cup white flour on a kneading board and turn the dough onto it. Knead the loose flour into the dough and, when this flour has been incorporated, knead in 1 more cup. Continue to knead in flour until the dough is fairly stiff and easy to handle (about ½ to 1 cup more should be enough). Knead vigorously for 8 minutes. Place the dough in a well-oiled bowl, turning once to grease the top. Cover with a dish towel and set to rise in a warm, draft-free place until the dough doubles in bulk. This should take about 45 to 50 minutes.

Punch the dough down, turn it over, cover, and let rise again for 45 minutes. Punch the dough down, divide in half, and roll each half into a long rectangle 8 inches wide. To form a loaf, begin at the short end and roll up tightly to produce an 8-inch loaf. Turn the ends under, and place each loaf in an oiled 9¼-by-5¼-by-2¾-inch loaf pan. Cover and set in a warm, draft-free place until double in bulk, about 50 minutes.

Preheat the oven to 325 degrees.

Bake for 1 hour. Remove from the oven and use a sharp knife to loosen the sides of the loaves. Remove from the pans and place on wire racks to cool.

Sweet Carrot Bread***

1 cup grated carrots (about 4 medium)

1½ cups water

¾ cup cornmeal

¼ cup molasses

½ cup honey

¼ cup light brown sugar

½ cup cooking oil or 8 table-spoons (1 stick) butter

¾ cup buttermilk or whole milk

½ teaspoon salt

1 teaspoon ground cinnamon

¼ teaspoon grated nutmeg

⅛ teaspoon ground cloves

Grated zest of 2 medium oranges

2 packages dry-active yeast

½ cup water, at wrist temperature

2½ cups whole wheat flour

3–4 cups all-purpose flour

¾ cup currants

YIELDS TWO LOAVES

Simmer the carrots in 1½ cups water until they are tender. Drain and reserve the cooking liquid. Place the carrots, 1 cup of carrot cooking liquid, the cornmeal, molasses, honey, brown sugar, oil, buttermilk, salt, cinnamon, nutmeg, cloves, and zest in a very large mixing bowl. Cool to room temperature.

Sprinkle the yeast over ½ cup water at wrist temperature and set aside for 5 minutes. Stir the yeast and the whole wheat flour into the carrot mixture, cover with a dish towel, and set in a warm, draft-free place for 35 minutes to rise.

Stir 1 cup white flour into the soft risen dough. Place 1 cup white flour on a kneading board and turn the dough onto it. Knead the loose flour into the dough and, when this flour has been incorporated, knead in 1 more cup. Continue to knead in flour, along with the currants, until the dough is fairly stiff and easy to handle (about ½ to 1 cup more should be enough). Knead vigorously for 8 minutes.

Place the dough in a well-oiled bowl, turning once to grease the top. Cover and let rise to double in bulk in a warm, draft-free place, about 45 to 50 minutes.

Punch the dough down, turn it over, cover, and let rise again for 45 minutes. Punch the dough down, divide in half, and roll each half into a long rectangle 8 inches wide. To form a loaf, begin at the short end and roll the dough tightly to produce an 8-inch loaf. Turn the ends under, and place each loaf in an oiled 9¼-by-5¼-by-2¾-inch loaf pan. Cover and set in a warm, draft-free place until double in bulk, about 50 minutes.

Preheat the oven to 325 degrees.

Bake for 1 hour. Remove from the oven and use a sharp knife to loosen the sides of the loaves. Remove from the pans and place on wire racks to cool.

Potato Sweet Bread

*This is a bread, not a cake, but it serves
as a coffee cake when sliced and spread
thickly with butter and apple butter.
Leftover bread may be dipped in beaten egg
and milk and fried in butter.*

BREAD

1 large potato, peeled and sliced

1 cup heavy cream

½ package dry-active yeast

¼ cup water, at wrist temperature

¼ cup vegetable shortening

½ cup granulated sugar

1 egg

5 cups all-purpose flour

½ teaspoon salt

⅛ teaspoon grated nutmeg

1 teaspoon butter, melted

TOPPING

½ cup light brown sugar

¼ cup flour

2 tablespoons butter

YIELDS ONE LOAF

Place the potato slices in a saucepan, add just enough water to cover, and boil until tender. Remove from the heat and drain the slices, reserving the cooking liquid. Mash the potato carefully to remove all lumps, then beat the mixture and set aside.

Mix the cream with the potato water, using additional water if necessary to make 1½ cups liquid in all. Stir the yeast into the warm water at wrist temperature and set aside.

Cream the shortening and sugar together. Beat the egg lightly, and add to the creamed mixture, mixing well. Add the yeast, potatoes, cream mixture, 3 cups flour, salt, and nutmeg to produce a rather stiff dough. Cover with a dish towel and let rise in the refrigerator overnight.

Next day, knead the 2 remaining cups flour into the batter, cover, and allow to rise again for 1½ hours, or until doubled in bulk. Spread the dough over a well-greased 9-by-13-inch baking pan, and let rise again, about 1¼ hours. Brush the top with melted butter.

Preheat the oven to 400 degrees.

To make the topping, combine the light brown sugar with the flour. Cut in the butter until the mixture resembles coarse meal. Sprinkle over the top of the bread and bake for 40 minutes, or until the baking pan sounds hollow when lightly tapped with a fingernail. Remove from the oven and cool on a wire rack before cutting.

Anadama Bread***

7½–8½ cups all-purpose flour

1¼ cups yellow cornmeal

2¾ teaspoons salt

2 packages dry-active yeast

8 tablespoons (1 stick) butter, softened

2¼ cups warm water (about 130 degrees)

¾ cup molasses

YIELDS TWO LOAVES

Combine 2½ cups flour with the cornmeal, salt, and yeast in a large bowl and mix thoroughly. Stir in the butter. Add the water and molasses, a little at a time, blending well. Beat with an electric mixer at medium speed for 2 minutes, scraping the bowl occasionally.

Stir in ½ cup flour and beat at high speed for 2 minutes more, scraping the bowl occasionally. Stir in enough additional flour to form a stiff dough. Turn out onto a lightly floured board. Knead the dough for 8 to 10 minutes, until it is smooth and elastic. Place the dough in a large greased bowl, turning once to grease the top. Cover the bowl with a dish towel, and allow the dough to rise in a warm, draft-free place until it doubles in bulk, about 1 to 1¼ hours.

Punch the dough down and divide in half. To shape the dough, roll each piece into a rectangle, 14 by 9 inches. Roll the dough from its short upper end and seal the sides with the fingers, folding the sealed ends under. Place the loaves, seam side down, in 2 greased 9¼-by-5¼-by-2¾-inch loaf pans. Cover with a dish towel and allow the dough to rise again in a warm, draft-free place until double in bulk, about 45 minutes.

Preheat oven to 375 degrees.

Bake the bread for about 45 minutes. Remove from pans and cool on a wire rack.

Whole Wheat Corn Bread***

1 cup whole wheat flour	1 teaspoon salt
1 cup yellow cornmeal	1 egg
2 tablespoons granulated sugar	1 cup sour cream
1 teaspoon baking soda	5 tablespoons milk
1 teaspoon cream of tartar	1 tablespoon vegetable oil

YIELDS ONE LOAF

Preheat the oven to 425 degrees.

Combine the whole wheat flour, cornmeal, sugar, baking soda, cream of tartar, and salt in a large mixing bowl. Rub the mixture well to eliminate lumps. Beat the egg lightly and add to the dry ingredients along with the sour cream, milk, and oil. Stir until thoroughly moistened and well blended.

Grease an 8-inch-square baking pan, pour in the batter, and bake for 20 minutes. Remove the pan from the oven and set it on a wire rack to cool slightly before serving.

Farm Country Spoon Bread

1 cup cold water	4 tablespoons butter
1 cup white cornmeal	6 eggs
1 teaspoon salt	1¼ cups milk
1 cup boiling water	½ cup heavy cream

YIELDS ONE LOAF

Preheat the oven to 350 degrees.

Stir the cold water into the cornmeal and salt until well blended. Add the boiling water and cook over medium-low heat, stirring constantly, for 2 minutes. Remove from the heat and mix in 2 tablespoons butter.

Place 5 eggs in the large bowl of an electric mixer, beat until light and fluffy. Blend in 1 cup milk. Stir the cornmeal mixture into the eggs and milk, and beat until the batter is free of lumps. Put the 2 remaining tablespoons butter in a 9-inch-square baking pan and place the pan in the oven. As soon as the butter sizzles pour in the batter and bake for 15 minutes.

Combine the remaining ¼ cup milk with the cream and beat in the remaining egg. Pour over the bread and bake for 25 minutes longer, or until the top is lightly browned and puffy. Serve immediately, spooned onto plates.

Johnnycake

1½ cups milk	3 tablespoons butter
1 tablespoon lemon juice	3 tablespoons vegetable shortening
2 cups yellow cornmeal	1 egg, separated
1 cup all-purpose flour	1 teaspoon baking soda
1½ tablespoons granulated sugar	2 tablespoons hot water
½ teaspoon salt	

YIELDS ONE LOAF

Preheat the oven to 350 degrees.

Mix the milk with the lemon juice and set in a warm oven for a few minutes to sour. Combine the cornmeal, flour, sugar, and salt; cut in the butter and shortening.

Stir the egg yolk into the dry ingredients along with the soured milk. Dissolve the baking soda in the hot water and add. Mix well.

Beat the egg white until stiff and fold into the batter. Pour the batter into a greased 8-inch cake pan, and bake for 35 minutes or until lightly browned. Cut into squares and serve hot, dripping with butter.

Graham Gems***

*Gem pans are similar in shape to muffin pans
but the depressions are half the size.
Small spoonfuls of batter bread in these pans
produce delicious bite-size "gems."*

2 teaspoons lemon juice

1 cup milk

½ teaspoon baking soda

1 large egg

3 tablespoons molasses

2 tablespoons honey or
additional molasses

2 tablespoons butter, melted

2 cups plus 2 tablespoons
graham flour

½ teaspoon salt

YIELDS TWO DOZEN

Preheat the oven to 400 degrees.

Mix the lemon juice with the milk and set in a warm oven for a few minutes to sour. Stir the baking soda into the sour milk.

Beat the egg lightly in a large bowl; add the molasses, honey, melted butter, and the soured milk. Blend in the flour and salt, mixing just enough to thoroughly moisten the dry ingredients.

Spoon the batter into well-greased gem pans, and bake for 12 to 15 minutes. Serve warm or at room temperature with lots of butter.

Graham Muffins with Currants

Stir ⅓ cup currants into the Graham Gem batter. Spoon into 16 well-greased muffin tins and bake for 25 minutes.

Oatmeal Gems***

2 teaspoons lemon juice

1½ cups milk

1 teaspoon baking soda

2 cups rolled oats

2 eggs

6 tablespoons molasses

1½ cups all-purpose flour

⅛ teaspoon salt

YIELDS TWO DOZEN GEMS OR
SIXTEEN TWO-AND-ONE-HALF-INCH MUFFINS

Add the lemon juice to the milk and set in a warm oven for a few minutes to sour. Stir the baking soda into the sour milk. Place the rolled oats in a bowl, add the milk, and let stand for 2 to 3 hours.

Preheat the oven to 400 degrees.

Mix the eggs, molasses, flour, and salt into oats and milk. Blend just long enough to thoroughly moisten the dry ingredients. Spoon the batter into well-greased gem pans or muffin tins and bake for 12 to 15 minutes for the gems and 25 minutes for the muffins. Serve warm with lots of butter.

Mrs. Hampton's Sweet Blueberry Muffins***

1 cup blueberries

4 tablespoons butter

⅓ cup granulated sugar

½ teaspoon lemon extract

1 cup all-purpose flour

1 teaspoon baking powder

Salt

½ cup milk

2 egg whites

YIELDS ONE DOZEN

Preheat the oven to 325 degrees.

Wash and pick over the blueberries; dry on paper towels. Beat the butter until fluffy, cream in the sugar, and continue to beat until the mixture is light and lemon colored. Blend in the lemon extract.

Sift together the flour, baking powder, and a pinch of salt. Add the dry ingredients alternately with the milk to the butter and sugar mixture. Beat the egg whites with ⅛ teaspoon salt until they form stiff peaks, and fold carefully into the batter.

Dust the blueberries with flour and stir them into the batter. Grease the muffin tins and fill each cup ⅔ full with the blueberry mixture. Bake for 25 to 30 minutes. Cool on wire racks.

Wheat and Cornmeal Muffins

1¼ cups whole wheat flour	1 teaspoon baking powder
¾ cup yellow cornmeal	1 egg
2½ tablespoons granulated sugar	1 cup sour cream
¾ teaspoon salt	5 tablespoons milk
1 teaspoon baking soda	1 tablespoon vegetable oil

YIELDS TWO DOZEN

Preheat the oven to 425 degrees.

Place the flour in a large mixing bowl, add the cornmeal, sugar, salt, baking soda, and baking powder. Work the mixture with your fingers to eliminate lumps.

Beat the egg lightly and add it, along with the sour cream, milk, and oil, to the dry ingredients. Mix thoroughly. Butter the muffin tins, lining them with buttered paper baking cups if you wish, and fill each cup ⅔ full. Bake for about 15 minutes, or until the tops of the muffins are golden brown. Cool slightly. Serve spread lavishly with butter.

Shortbread Biscuits

3 cups all-purpose flour	9 tablespoons butter
⅓ cup granulated sugar	1 egg
2 tablespoons baking powder	⅓ cup milk
¾ teaspoon salt	

YIELDS EIGHTEEN

Preheat the oven to 400 degrees.

Combine the flour, sugar, baking powder, and salt, and sift together into a large bowl. Cut the butter into the dry ingredients until the mixture resembles coarse meal. Beat the egg lightly, mix with the milk, and add to the dry ingredients. Blend thoroughly. The result should be a soft dough.

Lightly flour a pastry board, turn the dough onto it, and pat into a circle about ½-inch thick. Cut out the biscuits with a 2½-inch cookie cutter or the edge of a glass, and arrange on a well-greased cookie sheet. Leftover dough may be patted out and cut into additional biscuits. Bake for 15 minutes or until golden brown. Serve directly from the oven, split in half and lavishly buttered.

Whipped Cream Biscuits

Serve these tender, golden biscuits with butter,
jam, honey, or as a topping for a chicken or beef pie.

1 cup heavy cream   3 teaspoons baking powder
2 cups all-purpose flour

YIELDS ABOUT EIGHTEEN

Preheat the oven to 450 degrees.

Whip the cream until stiff and set aside. Sift together the flour and baking powder. Fold the whipped cream into the dry ingredients, turn the dough out onto a lightly floured surface, and knead for 1 minute.

Roll out lightly ½ inch thick and cut into 2- to 2½-inch rounds, using a cookie cutter or the edge of a glass dipped in flour. Place on a cookie sheet and bake for 10 to 12 minutes or until golden brown.

Buttermilk Biscuits

Lighter, more tender biscuits than these
would be difficult to imagine,
but handle the dough gently
or it may toughen.

2 cups sifted all-purpose flour	*3 tablespoons butter*
3 teaspoons baking powder	*¾ cup buttermilk*
½ teaspoon baking soda	*3 tablespoons butter, melted*
½ teaspoon salt	

YIELDS EIGHTEEN

Preheat the oven to 450 degrees.

Combine the flour with the baking powder, baking soda, and salt, and sift together into a large bowl. Using 2 knives, cut the butter into the dry ingredients until the mixture resembles coarse meal. Blend in the buttermilk.

Turn out onto a floured board and knead lightly for a minute or two. Roll the dough ¾ inch thick. Cut into small rounds and arrange on a cookie sheet. Brush the tops with melted butter and bake for 12 minutes. Serve hot.

Cloverleaf Raisin Rolls***

2 cups milk	*5–6 cups all-purpose flour*
1 package dry-active yeast	*½ cup raisins*
3 tablespoons butter	*2 tablespoons orange liqueur*
½ cup granulated sugar	*Juice of 1 orange*
2 teaspoons salt	*½ teaspoon ground cinnamon*
1 cup graham flour	*2 tablespoons light brown sugar*

YIELDS SIXTEEN LARGE ROLLS

Heat the milk to lukewarm. Place the yeast in a small bowl, stir in ½ cup of the warm milk, and set aside while the yeast softens.

Place the remaining warm milk in a large bowl, add the butter, sugar, and salt; mix well. Stir in the yeast. Add the graham flour and 2 cups of white flour a little at a time, stirring well after each addition. Gradually add as much of the remaining flour as necessary to make a stiff dough.

Generously flour a pastry board, turn out the dough, and knead until the dough is smooth and elastic, about 8 to 10 minutes. Set the dough in a greased bowl, turning once to grease the top. Cover lightly with a dish towel, and place the bowl in a warm, draft-free place for about 2½ hours, or until the dough doubles in bulk.

Place the raisins in a saucepan, stir in the orange liqueur, orange juice, cinnamon, and sugar. Cook over low heat until all the liquid has been absorbed by the raisins. Remove from the heat and set aside. When the dough has doubled in volume, punch it down, cover it, and refrigerate the dough and the raisins in separate bowls overnight.

To prepare the rolls, break off a piece of cold dough, and roll it between your hands into a small ball about ¾ inch in diameter. Insert 3 of the prepared raisins in the ball and re-form the ball. Continue to break off, shape, and insert raisins into pieces of dough until all the dough and raisins have been used.

Butter 2 muffin tins and place 3 balls of dough in each cup. Make sure the seams of each ball face the center of the cup. Cover the muffin tins with a dish towel and place in a warm, draft-free place for 2 hours, or until they double in bulk.

Preheat the oven to 375 degrees.

Bake the rolls for 12 to 15 minutes, or until the tops are golden brown. Serve warm, dripping with butter.

Yorkshire Pudding***

If the Yorkshire Pudding is to be served with jam,
use butter. If it is to be served with roast beef,
use the pan drippings.

2 cups sifted all-purpose flour	*1 cup light cream*
1 teaspoon salt	*4 eggs*
1 cup milk	*8 tablespoons butter or pan drippings from roast beef*

SERVES FOUR TO SIX

Combine the sifted flour and salt, and sift again. With an egg beater, gradually blend in the milk and cream, beating after each addition until the mixture is smooth. Add the eggs, one at a time, beating at least 1 minute for each. Set the liquid batter in the refrigerator, covered with a cloth or aluminum foil, for at least 2 hours.

Preheat the oven to 450 degrees.

Melt the butter in a shallow baking pan and place it in the oven. Beat the batter again briefly with an egg beater and pour over the sizzling butter to a depth of ½ inch. Bake for 15 minutes, or until the pudding rises; lower the temperature to 375 degrees and bake an additional 10 to 15 minutes. When the pudding turns crisp and brown and light in texture, cut into squares and serve immediately.

Popovers

2 cups sifted all-purpose flour	*1 cup milk*
½ teaspoon salt	*1 cup light cream or half and half*
4 eggs	

YIELDS SIXTEEN

Preheat the oven to 450 degrees.

Combine the flour and salt and sift again. Beat the eggs lightly, mix with the milk and cream, and blend thoroughly with the dry ingredients. Set popover or muffin pans in the oven briefly to heat; remove and butter the cups well.

Pour the batter into the pans, filling each cup ½ full. Bake the popovers for 20 minutes, then reduce the heat to 375 degrees and bake about 20 to 25 minutes longer, or until the popovers are puffy and nicely browned. Serve with lavish helpings of butter.

Fried Bread

Fried Bread can be served with jam at breakfast,
eggs at lunch, or vegetables at dinner.

8 slices white bread, crusts
   removed

5 tablespoons butter
   Salt or granulated sugar

SERVES EIGHT

Cut the bread slices into triangles. Sauté in butter until crisp and golden on both sides. Sprinkle with a bit of salt when serving with vegetables, eggs, or meat, and a bit of sugar when served alone or with sweet dishes.

Breakfast Scones

1½ cups all-purpose flour
1 teaspoon baking soda
2 teaspoons baking powder
¼ teaspoon salt
2 tablespoons butter, at room temperature

⅔ cup rolled oats
½ cup milk
1 egg yolk
1 teaspoon water

YIELDS SIXTEEN

Preheat the oven to 425 degrees.

Sift together into a large bowl the flour, baking soda, baking powder, and salt. With your fingers, blend in the butter and rolled oats. Add the milk and mix until the dough has a soft consistency. Knead the dough quickly, until it is smooth and elastic.

Roll out ½ inch thick and cut into 2-inch circles. Place on a lightly-greased cookie sheet. Brush the tops with the egg yolk mixed with 1 teaspoon water. Bake for 10 minutes, or until brown on top. Cool on a wire rack, or butter immediately and serve hot.

Egg Bread or "Hootsla"

6 eggs
1 cup milk

24 slices day-old bread
8 tablespoons (1 stick) butter

SERVES EIGHT

Beat the eggs lightly, add the milk, and beat once more. Dip the bread slices in the egg mixture until fairly well soaked. Fry until brown in the butter, turning only once. Serve immediately with jam, jelly, cinnamon, Farmhouse-Favorite Brown Sugar Syrup (page 473), or Shaker Cider Sauce (page 473).

White Bread Croutons

3 slices white bread, crusts removed

3 tablespoons butter or oil

YIELDS ONE CUP

Cut the bread slices into ½-inch cubes. Heat the butter in a large skillet and sauté the bread cubes to a golden brown on all sides, stirring frequently.

Brown Bread Croutons

6 large slices pumpernickel or other brown bread, crusts removed

2½ tablespoons butter
1½ tablespoons vegetable oil

YIELDS ABOUT TWO CUPS

Cut the bread into ½-inch squares. Heat the butter and oil together in a heavy skillet, add the bread, and brown the squares on all sides, stirring from time to time. Serve with soups or salads.

Desserts and sweetmeats

Fruits

Apple Dumplings***

*These apple dumplings are probably
the best ever baked. The apples are succulent,
the pie dough is dripping with slightly caramelized
maple syrup, and the flavor is superb.*

8 tart apples

Double recipe Pastry for 2-
Crust Pie (page 418)

⅔ cup granulated sugar

3 tablespoons heavy cream

¼ teaspoon almond extract

1 cup maple syrup

Heavy cream

SERVES EIGHT

[362]

Preheat the oven to 450 degrees.

Peel and core the apples without breaking through the bottom. Roll out the pastry and cut into squares large enough to partially envelop the apples. Set 1 apple on each pastry square.

Mix together the sugar, cream, and almond extract, and divide the mixture among the apples, pouring some in each hollowed core. Moisten the 4 corners of each pastry square and bring them up around each apple but not covering the hollowed-out centers, pressing lightly to make the dough stick together. Prick each pastry shell with a fork.

Set the apples in a large baking dish. Bake for 15 minutes, then baste the centers of each apple with 1 tablespoon maple syrup. Bake for 10 minutes more and baste again. Lower the heat to 350 degrees and bake an additional 20 minutes, basting every 5 minutes with the remaining maple syrup, plus any syrup in the bottom of the baking dish. Be sure to baste the crust as well during the last 20 minutes of baking. Serve hot with cold heavy cream.

Apple Fritters

1¼ cups all-purpose flour

4 tablespoons confectioners' sugar

1¾ teaspoons baking powder

¼ teaspoon salt

1 egg

⅓ cup plus 1 tablespoon milk

3 small tart apples, peeled, cored, and chopped

Vegetable oil for frying

Additional confectioners' sugar

SERVES EIGHT

Combine the flour, sugar, baking powder, and salt, and sift into a large bowl. Beat the egg until frothy, mix with the milk, and add to the dry ingredients, stirring well. Stir the apples into the batter.

Pour oil to a depth of ½ inch in a large skillet, heat over medium flame, and drop the batter by half teaspoonful into the sizzling oil. Fry to a crispy golden brown, turning once, and remove from the pan with a slotted spoon. Drain for a moment on paper towels. Serve immediately, sprinkled with additional confectioners' sugar.

Apple Brown Betty

5 cups peeled and thinly sliced
    McIntosh apples
3 cups coarse dry bread crumbs
1 cup dark brown sugar
⅓ cup molasses

3 tablespoons butter
½ teaspoon ground cinnamon
⅛ teaspoon ground cloves
⅓ cup hot water

SERVES EIGHT

Preheat the oven to 350 degrees.

Butter a pudding mold or glass baking dish. Arrange a layer of sliced apples on the bottom, cover with a cup of bread crumbs, sprinkle with ¼ cup sugar and 2 tablespoons molasses, and dot with 1 tablespoon butter.

Build alternate layers of apples and bread crumbs, sprinkle each with molasses and sugar, and dot with butter. End with a layer of apples sprinkled with ¼ cup of sugar and the spices. Add the hot water, cover the mold or baking dish with aluminum foil and bake for 35 to 45 minutes. If desired, brown lightly under the broiler. Remove from the mold and serve hot or warm with Hard Sauce (page 471).

Baked Apples with Dates and Nuts

8 large McIntosh apples
24 dates, pitted
24 pecans

⅓ cup light brown sugar
⅛ teaspoon ground cloves
8 teaspoons butter

SERVES EIGHT

Preheat the oven to 400 degrees.

Using a paring knife, carefully core the apples without cutting through the bottom. Scoop some of the pulp from each apple and chop it along with the dates and nuts. Sprinkle this filling with the sugar and cloves and mix well.

Fill the hollow of each apple with the date-nut mixture, and top each with 1 teaspoon butter. Pour warm water into an oven-proof dish to a depth of ½ inch. Place the apples in the water and bake for 40 minutes. The apples should be soft but not mushy. Serve hot or cold.

Jelly-Baked Apples

8 McIntosh apples	½ cup granulated sugar
¼ cup raspberry jelly	1 cup heavy cream, whipped
¾ cup finely chopped almonds	Banana liqueur

SERVES EIGHT

Preheat the oven to 350 degrees.

Using a paring knife, carefully core the apples without cutting through the bottom. Peel the skin from the top ⅓ of each apple. Place the apples in a baking dish and fill with a mixture of jelly and chopped nuts. Sprinkle the tops of the apples liberally with sugar. Bake slowly for 45 minutes or until the apples are tender but not mushy. Serve warm, topped with whipped cream lightly sweetened with banana liqueur.

Spiced Apple Meringue

8 McIntosh apples	3 egg whites
1 cup granulated sugar	6 tablespoons confectioners' sugar
1¼ teaspoons ground cinnamon	
⅛ teaspoon salt	½ teaspoon vanilla extract
3 tablespoons heavy cream	Granulated sugar
Water	Heavy cream

SERVES EIGHT

[365]

Preheat the oven to 350 degrees.

Peel and core the apples without breaking through the bottom. Place in a large baking dish. Mix the sugar, cinnamon, and salt with the cream. Divide the mixture among the hollowed cores of the apples. Pour in enough of the water to cover the bottom of the baking dish, and bake for about 30 to 35 minutes, or until soft but not mushy. Baste the apples frequently while baking with the syrup in the dish. Remove from the oven and cool slightly.

Beat the egg whites until they form stiff peaks; continue to beat while gradually adding the confectioners' sugar. Beat in the vanilla, and heap meringue on top of each apple. Return to the oven and bake 8 minutes longer. Refrigerate before serving with sugar and heavy cream.

Your Own Applesauce***

8 large McIntosh apples	½ teaspoon ground cinnamon
3 cups water or cider	⅛ teaspoon ground cardamom
6 tablespoons honey	⅛ teaspoon grated nutmeg

SERVES EIGHT

Core but do not peel the fruit. Cut the apples into ½-inch-thick slices and place them in a large saucepan. Cover with water and cook over medium heat for 15 minutes, or until the apple slices are soft.

Lift the fruit from the water with a slotted spoon and puree by forcing the pulp through a fine sieve. Stir the honey, cinnamon, cardamom, and nutmeg into the cooking liquid, and simmer over low heat until the liquid is reduced to ¾ cup. Mix this syrup into the pureed apples. Serve hot or cold, topped with a bit of cinnamon.

Berries Chantilly

6 cups mixed berries, or 1 kind only

1 teaspoon vanilla extract

¾ cup confectioners' sugar

3 cups heavy cream

SERVES EIGHT

Rinse the berries carefully and dry on paper towels. Put the fruit in a serving bowl and sprinkle with vanilla and confectioners' sugar. Whip the cream and stir it gently into the sweetened fruit. Refrigerate for at least 2 hours.

Miss Whitehall's Raspberry Trifle

You may substitute for the raspberries, strawberries, blackberries, or any other berries that are plentiful in your area. The resulting dessert is sure to be creamy, cooling, and delectable.

1½ cups plus 2 tablespoons granulated sugar

4 egg yolks

¾ cup milk

¾ cup light cream

2-inch piece vanilla bean

3 cups raspberries

6 tablespoons raspberry, grape, or apple jelly

3 cups Old-Fashioned Vanilla-Custard Ice Cream (page 453)

¼ cup kirsch

¼ cup orange juice

2 Spongecake layers (page 389*)

¾ cup heavy cream

SERVES EIGHT TO TEN

Place 6 tablespoons sugar in the top of a double boiler. Beat the egg yolks together a bit and add to the sugar, stirring until the mixture is fluffy and light. Combine the milk and cream in a

* This recipe makes 3 sponge layers. Freeze the remaining layer for later use.

[367]

saucepan with the vanilla bean and heat to scalding. Gradually add this to the sugar and egg yolks, stirring constantly. Continue to stir while the custard cooks over hot water. Do not allow to boil or the custard will curdle. When the custard thickens enough to coat the spoon, remove it from the heat, strain it, and cool, stirring from time to time. The vanilla bean retrieved by straining may be washed and returned to its original container for re-use.

Gently wash the raspberries and allow the excess water to drain off. Set 1 cup of the berries aside. Take the 2 remaining cups and mix with ¾ cup of sugar. Allow this mixture to stand for 30 minutes. Rub it through a strainer with the back of a spoon and stir in the jelly.

Allow the ice cream to soften a bit before adding the kirsch. When assembling the trifle, work fast so that the ice cream does not melt.

Sprinkle the orange juice over the sponge layers. Cover the bottom of a glass serving bowl with half of the sugar, berry, and jelly mixture. Place a sponge layer over, spread the layer with the ice cream, and top with half the custard. Repeat the process, ending with the custard, and place the trifle immediately in the freezer for 1 hour.

Just before serving, whip the heavy cream with 2 tablespoons granulated sugar. Take the trifle from the freezer, swirl whipped cream over the top, and garnish with the reserved whole raspberries. Serve immediately.

Mrs. Metz's Berries with Berry Sauce

6 cups mixed berries, or 1 kind only   *2 cups plain yoghurt*
½ cup honey (approximately)

SERVES EIGHT

Wash and hull or pick over the berries if necessary. Divide 5 cups of the berries among 8 sherbet glasses. Place the remaining cup of berries in a blender, add the yoghurt and honey to taste, and blend until the mixture is smooth. Spoon the sauce over the berries and refrigerate until serving time. Serve cold topped with a few whole berries.

Strawberries and Cream

8 cups hulled strawberries   Heavy cream or sour cream
   Granulated, confectioners', or
   maple sugar

SERVES EIGHT

Arrange the strawberries in a deep glass serving bowl and chill well. Serve accompanied by bowls of granulated, confectioners', or maple sugar, and whipped or sour cream.

Strawberries and Sugar

8 cups hulled strawberries   2 cups orange liqueur
   Confetti sugar*

SERVES EIGHT

Heap the berries in a large serving bowl and serve with 2 smaller bowls of sugar and 2 bowls of orange liqueur. Let your guests dip the strawberries first in the orange liqueur and then in the sugar.

* Confetti sugar is usually available in grocery stores. It is used here to give an interesting texture. So-called natural sugar may be substituted.

Frozen Strawberry Cream

Excellent with a fruit salad or as a creamy dessert.

4 cups hulled strawberries	*2½ cups cottage cheese*
½ cup honey	*4 ounces cream cheese*

SERVES EIGHT

Blend all ingredients at low speed in an electric blender until well mixed and smooth. Divide the cream equally among 8 small glass dishes. Freeze until slushy, stir with a fork, and refreeze. Remove the cream from the freezer a few moments before serving time. Unmold and serve immediately.

Fresh Fruit with Whipped Cream

5 peaches	*¼ cup confectioners' sugar*
5 bananas, cut into ½-inch slices	*½ cup orange liqueur*
6 purple plums, pitted and coarsely chopped	*1 cup heavy cream*
3 cups seedless white grapes	*3 tablespoons granulated sugar*
2 cups hulled strawberries	*½ teaspoon almond extract*

SERVES EIGHT

Dip the peaches in scalding water for a few seconds and slip off the skins. Slice the peaches, discarding the pits. Place all the fruit in a serving bowl and add the confectioners' sugar and orange liqueur. Toss the fruit lightly and refrigerate for 1 hour.

Just before serving, whip the cream with the granulated sugar and the almond extract. Serve the whipped cream in a separate bowl along with the fresh fruit.

Fresh Fruit Compote

4 large peaches, peeled and sliced
6 purple plums, peeled and sliced
2 cups quartered strawberries
1 cup blueberries
1 honeydew melon

¾ cup honey
1 cup orange liqueur
¼ cup lime juice
2 cups pitted and halved sweet cherries

SERVES EIGHT

Place the peaches, plums, strawberries, and blueberries in a large serving bowl. Cut the melon flesh into balls with a melon baller and add to the fruit bowl.

Combine the honey, liqueur, and lime juice in a saucepan. Bring to a boil and cook at low boil for 2 to 3 minutes. Cool the syrup and pour it over the fruits in the bowl. Refrigerate for at least 1 hour. At serving time, toss the cherry halves with the other fruit. Serve cold.

Up North Frozen Fruit Salad

1¾ cups granulated sugar
1¼ cup water
9 egg yolks
2-inch piece vanilla bean
3½ cups heavy cream
1¼ teaspoons vanilla extract

2 cups peeled and finely chopped peaches
1 cup pitted and quartered cherries
1 cup coarsely chopped strawberries
3 tablespoons orange liqueur

SERVES EIGHT

Combine the sugar and water in a saucepan and bring to a boil, stirring constantly. Simmer this syrup for 5 minutes, remove from heat, and cool.

Place the egg yolks in the top of a double boiler over hot water. Use an electric beater to beat them until they are thick and pale yellow. Add the sugar syrup in a thin stream, beating constantly. Split the vanilla bean and scrape the fine seeds into the egg yolk mixture. Continue to beat over hot, but not boiling, water until the custard is thick and creamy. Set a bowl over cracked ice and strain the custard. Let the custard cool over the ice, stirring occasionally.

Whip the heavy cream until stiff, add the vanilla extract, and fold the whipped cream into the cooled custard. Sprinkle the peaches, cherries, and strawberries with the liqueur. Carefully fold into the whipped cream-custard mixture. Pour into a chilled 2½-quart tubular mold and freeze overnight.

When ready to serve, unmold by dipping for a second in hot water. Turn the salad onto a serving plate. Fill the center with additional fresh fruits and decorate with swirls of whipped cream piped through a decorative tube of a pastry bag.

Sugar-Frosted Grapes

8 small bunches grapes   *Granulated sugar*
2 egg whites, lightly beaten

SERVES EIGHT

Wash and thoroughly dry the grapes. Dip them, bunch by bunch, first into the egg whites and then into a plate of sugar. Allow the sugar to dry and serve the frosted grapes with a plate of home-baked cookies.

Melon Balls and Cherries with Kirsch

2 *honeydew melons*	*3 teaspoons lemon juice*
2 *large cantaloupes*	½ *cup kirsch*
1½ *pounds dark cherries, pitted*	1½ *cups sour cream*
1 *cup honey*	

SERVES EIGHT

Halve and seed the melons. With a melon baller, scoop balls of pulp from them. Reserve and refrigerate the melon shells. Place the melon balls in a large bowl with the pitted cherry halves.

Combine the honey, lemon juice, and all but 1 tablespoon of kirsch. Pour this marinade over the fruit and stir thoroughly. Chill the fruit for several hours and stir it from time to time.

At serving time, smooth the sides of the melon shells and pile an equal amount of fruit into each. Mix the sour cream with the remaining tablespoon kirsch and serve in a separate dish.

Fruit Mincemeat***

½ *cup seedless dark raisins*	1 *teaspoon ground cloves*
½ *cup golden raisins*	1 *teaspoon ground allspice*
1 *cup chopped blanched, toasted almonds*	1 *teaspoon grated nutmeg*
	¼ *teaspoon mace*
6 *medium McIntosh apples, peeled, cored, and finely chopped*	1¼ *teaspoons salt*
	3½ *cups granulated sugar*
½ *cup orange marmalade*	½ *cup lemon juice*
½ *cup chopped candied orange peel*	¼ *cup dry sherry*
	¼ *cup brandy*
1 *teaspoon ground cinnamon*	

MAKES TWO QUARTS

Mix together all ingredients except the brandy. Toss lightly. Place the mincemeat in quart jars, seal tightly, and refrigerate for 24 hours. Turn the jars at least twice. Stir in the brandy and use the mincemeat for pie (page 429).

Old-Fashioned Orange Salad

9 oranges

3 tablespoons confectioners' sugar

3 tablespoons finely chopped mint

3 tablespoons sweet sherry

2 tablespoons lemon juice

Currant jelly

Mint sprigs

SERVES EIGHT

Peel the oranges, taking care to remove all the bitter white underskin. Remove the sections from the membranes. Chill the pulp for several hours, then divide into 8 champagne glasses. Combine the sugar, mint, sherry, and lemon juice. Pour a bit of this mixture over the fruit in each glass. Top the fruit with a bit of currant jelly and garnish with mint sprigs.

Poached Oranges

This makes a pleasing change of pace from the standard orange juice for breakfast, or it may be served as a luncheon dessert.

8 oranges

4 cups granulated sugar

2 cups water

¼ cup shredded coconut

SERVES EIGHT

Carefully peel off, the thin outer skin, or zest of 3 of the oranges and set aside. Cut away the thick white inner pith of these oranges, and the skins and piths of the remaining oranges. Slice all the oranges in half and place in a low-sided glass bowl.

[374]

Put the sugar and water in a saucepan, bring to a boil, and cook at low boil for 5 minutes. Sliver the reserved orange zest and cook in the boiling water for 4 minutes. Pour the syrup over the orange halves, sprinkle with shredded coconut, and serve.

Mrs. Simpson's Peach and Plum Compote

16 large peaches

16 greengage plums

1½ cups honey

¾ cup water

½ cup orange or banana liqueur

⅓ cup lemon juice

Mint leaves

SERVES EIGHT TO TEN

Skin the peaches and plums by dipping them briefly in boiling water and then cold water. The skins should loosen easily. Leave the fruit whole and place in a glass bowl.

Combine the honey and water in a small saucepan, bring to a boil, and boil for 5 minutes. Cool. Mix in the liqueur and lemon juice and pour over the fruit. Turn the peaches and plums gently in the syrup until all sides are coated. Refrigerate the compote, covered, for several hours before serving. Garnish each serving with mint leaves.

Broiled Peaches

8 freestone peaches

Butter

Light brown sugar

Candied ginger

¼ cup brandy

SERVES EIGHT

Slip the peaches into boiling water for a few seconds to loosen the skins, then peel, and halve, discarding the pits. Place them cut side down on aluminum foil on a broiling pan and broil for 2 minutes.

Turn and broil for another minute. Remove from the heat, dot with bits of butter, and sprinkle lightly with brown sugar and candied ginger. Return the peach halves to the broiler for 2 or 3 minutes, or until lightly browned. Heat the brandy slightly. Arrange the peach halves in a flameproof serving dish after taking from the oven. Pour the brandy over, ignite, and carry flaming to the table.

Poached Peaches

8 *freestone peaches*
2 *cups granulated sugar*
  1-inch piece vanilla bean

2 *cups water*
  Heavy cream

SERVES EIGHT

Peel the peaches by placing them in boiling water for a few seconds, then slip off the skins and halve. Place the sugar and vanilla bean in a large skillet, add the water, and bring to a boil. Cook at low boil for 5 minutes, stirring once or twice. Remove from heat. Place fruit in the syrup with a slotted spoon and poach over low heat until fruit is barely tender. Ladle the syrup over while the peaches cook and turn them once. Remove the skillet from the heat and cool the fruit in the syrup. Serve at room temperature or chilled, topped with heavy cream, plain or whipped.

Variations

With jelly and cream: Poach the peaches in simmering syrup of 1½ cups water, 1½ cups granulated sugar, and 1-inch piece vanilla bean. Heat 1 cup raspberry or grape jelly to liquid consistency and ladle over the warm peaches, removed from the poaching liquid.

In maple syrup: Poach the peaches in a simmering syrup of 2 cups water, 1 cup granulated sugar, 1-inch piece vanilla bean, and 1 cup maple syrup. Cool in the syrup.

In brandied syrup: Poach the peaches in a simmering syrup of 1½ cups water, 1½ cups granulated sugar, and 1-inch piece vanilla bean. Just before adding the peaches, stir in ¼ cup brandy. Cool in the syrup.

Poached Pears

8 *firm, ripe pears*
2 *cups granulated sugar*
 1-inch piece vanilla bean

2½ *cups water*
 Heavy cream

SERVES EIGHT

Peel, halve, and core the pears. Bring the sugar, vanilla bean, and water to a boil in a large skillet. Simmer for 5 minutes, add the pear halves, and poach over low heat, basting with syrup once or twice, until the fruit is tender but not soft. Cool the pears in the syrup. Serve at room temperature or chilled, with heavy or whipped cream.

Pears Hélène

8 *Poached Pears (above)*
1 *quart homemade Old-Fashioned Vanilla-Custard Ice Cream (page 453) or commercial vanilla ice cream*

2 *cups Grandmother's Chocolate Sauce (page 470)*
 Candied Violets (page 466)

SERVES EIGHT

Place 2 pear halves in each dessert dish, add a scoop or two of ice cream, and top with chocolate sauce. Garnish with Candied Violets.

Miss Pritt's Baked Rhubarb

2 pounds rhubarb, cut into
  2-inch pieces
1½ cups granulated sugar
Pinch salt

Juice of ½ lemon
⅓ cup water
Heavy cream (optional)

SERVES EIGHT

Preheat the oven to 350 degrees.

Place the rhubarb in a baking dish, sprinkle with sugar, add a pinch of salt, lemon juice, and water. Bake, covered, until tender, about 25 to 30 minutes. Remove from the oven and cool to room temperature. Chill, if desired. Serve with heavy cream, plain or whipped, if desired.

Sunday Picnic Watermelon Basket***

SERVES EIGHT TO TEN

To prepare the Watermelon Basket, place the melon lengthwise on the table in front of you. Form a handle by making 2 vertical cuts, about 3 or 4 inches apart, about halfway down into the meat of the melon. The handle should run crosswise, not lengthwise, across the melon. Next, slice through horizontally from both ends, bringing your knife just to the points where you made the cuts. Lift off these top 2 sections leaving the melon with its handle intact. Slide your knife down between the flesh and rind of the basket, taking care not to break the handle. Scoop out all the red flesh with a melon ball cutter, including the part of the melon remaining under the handle. Don't forget that melon balls may also be made from the cutaway top sections. Use a knife to smooth the insides of the basket and the underside of the rind handle, and make V-shaped notches all around the sides of the basket. The Watermelon Basket is ready to be filled.

Decorate it attractively after filling with small bunches of green grapes and whole mint leaves secured to the handle and sides with toothpicks.

Red and Green Fruit Filling

Watermelon balls
1 honeydew melon, cut into balls
3 cups green grapes, halved
12 greengage plums, pitted and quartered

2 cups gooseberries
1 cup mint leaves
Confectioners' sugar
Kirsch

Combine the fruits and mint leaves. Sprinkle lightly with confectioners' sugar and kirsch. Toss carefully several times and fill the Watermelon Basket. Refrigerate for several hours before serving.

Red Fruit Filling

Watermelon balls
3 cups pitted and halved Bing cherries
Several cups raspberries, if available

4 cups hulled and quartered strawberries
Confectioners' sugar
Madeira or sauterne

Sprinkle the fruits with confectioners' sugar and madeira or sauterne and toss lightly. Arrange the fruits attractively in the Watermelon Basket. Refrigerate for several hours before serving.

Mixed Fruit Filling

Watermelon balls
2 small cantaloupes, cut into balls
2 cups hulled and quartered strawberries

10 peaches, pitted and sliced
2 cups blueberries
Confectioners' sugar
Kirsch or sauterne

Mix the fruits together gently, sprinkle with confectioners' sugar and kirsch or sauterne, and toss lightly. Fill the Watermelon Basket and refrigerate for several hours.

Brandied Watermelon

1 watermelon   *Brandy*

SERVES EIGHT

Use a sharp knife to cut a good-size plug about 6 to 7 inches deep from one end of the watermelon. Reserve the plug. Poke a skewer or any other long, thin, sharp object through the hole into the watermelon flesh. Pour in as much brandy as the watermelon will absorb, then reinsert the plug. Small skewers inserted through both the plug and melon rind will hold the plug in place, or freezer tape may be used. Place the brandied melon, plug side up, in the refrigerator for at least 24 hours, turning from time to time, so that the brandy reaches all the melon flesh.

Cakes, cookies, and icings

Old-Fashioned Shortcake***

2⅓ cups all-purpose flour

⅓ cup granulated sugar

1½ teaspoons baking powder

½ teaspoon salt

7 tablespoons butter

⅓ cup milk

2 eggs

SERVES EIGHT GENEROUSLY

Preheat the oven to 375 degrees.

Sift together the flour, sugar, baking powder, and salt. Cut the butter into the dry ingredients until the particles are the size of small peas. Beat the milk and eggs together and stir them into the flour mixture to form a soft dough.

Place the dough on a heavily floured surface and pat it into a 10-inch circle. Grease a 10 inch skillet or dutch oven and turn the dough into it. Place in the preheated oven and bake until golden brown, 25 to 30 minutes. Cool for 5 minutes on a wire rack, then split the cake into 2 layers and butter the inside surfaces.

Strawberry Shortcake

10 cups strawberries
1 cup plus 2 tablespoons
  granulated sugar
2 teaspoons lemon or lime juice

1 cup heavy cream
½ teaspoon almond extract
Old-Fashioned Shortcake
  (page 381)

SERVES EIGHT

Rinse, stem, and slice 6 cups of berries. Mix these with 1 cup sugar and the citrus juice and refrigerate. Rinse, stem, and cut the remaining berries in half. Whip the cream slightly, add 2 tablespoons sugar and the flavoring, and continue to beat until stiff. Refrigerate the halved berries and the cream.

To serve, spread the bottom layer of shortcake with the sliced berries and half of the whipped cream. Top with the remaining shortcake layer and the rest of the whipped cream. Decorate with the halved berries and serve immediately.

Peach Shortcake

8 cups sliced peeled peaches
¾ cup plus 2 tablespoons
  granulated sugar
2 teaspoons lemon or lime juice

1 cup heavy cream
1 teaspoon vanilla extract
Old-Fashioned Shortcake (page
  381)

SERVES EIGHT

Mix the peach slices, ¾ cup sugar, and citrus juice. Whip the cream slightly, add 2 tablespoons sugar and the flavoring, and continue to beat until stiff. Refrigerate the peach slices and the cream.

To serve, spread the bottom layer of the shortcake with half of the sliced peaches and half of the whipped cream. Top with the other layer of shortcake and the remaining whipped cream, and decorate with the rest of the peach slices. Serve immediately.

Apple Shortcake

9 large McIntosh apples,
  peeled, cored, and quartered
1 tablespoon lemon juice
2¾ cups water
2¾ cups plus 2 tablespoons
  granulated sugar
¼ teaspoon ground cinnamon
  Large pinch grated nutmeg

1 cup heavy cream
  Old-Fashioned Shortcake (page
  381)
1 quart Old-Fashioned Vanilla-
  Custard Ice Cream (page 453)
3 tablespoons maple sugar
  (optional)

SERVES EIGHT

Toss the apple quarters with lemon juice. Place the water, 2¾ cups sugar, cinnamon, and nutmeg in a saucepan and boil for 6 or 7 minutes, stirring occasionally. Add the apple quarters and poach them over low heat until barely tender. Remove the fruit with a slotted spoon and set aside. Reduce the remaining apple syrup to 1½ cups. Cool to room temperature. Whip the cream with 2 tablespoons granulated sugar.

To serve, spread the bottom layer of the shortcake with ice cream and top with half of apples and the syrup. Place the top layer of the cake on the apples, swirl the whipped cream over, top with the remaining apples, and sprinkle with maple sugar. Serve immediately.

Sweet 'n' Spicy Pumpkin Cake

3 cups all-purpose flour
1¼ teaspoons baking soda
2½ teaspoons baking powder
½ teaspoon ground allspice
½ teaspoon ground cinnamon
½ teaspoon ground cloves
½ teaspoon grated nutmeg
10 tablespoons butter
1¼ cups granulated sugar

½ cup light brown sugar
2 eggs
½ cup milk
¼ cup orange juice
¾ cup canned pumpkin
1 teaspoon vanilla extract
  Orange Butter-Cream Icing
  (page 415)

SERVES EIGHT

Preheat the oven to 350 degrees.

Sift together the flour, baking soda, baking powder, and the spices. Cut the butter into small pieces, place in a mixing bowl, sprinkle in the sugars, and beat until fluffy. Add the eggs, one at a time, beating well after each. Mix the milk and the orange juice and let stand for 5 minutes: then stir in the pumpkin and vanilla extract. Add the milk-pumpkin mixture to the creamed butter alternately with the sifted dry ingredients, beating until smooth after each addition.

Grease and flour a tube pan, spoon the batter into it, and bake the cake for 40 to 45 minutes in the preheated oven. The cake is done when it springs back when pressed lightly with the fingers. Cool the cake in the pan for 15 minutes. Turn onto a rack and cool to room temperature. Frost with Orange Butter-Cream Icing.

Applesauce Cake with Apple Slices

4 tablespoons butter

4 tablespoons shortening

1 cup granulated sugar

2 eggs

1 cup sweetened applesauce

½ cup coarsely chopped golden raisins

½ cup coarsely chopped dark raisins

⅓ cup chopped pecans

¼ cup chopped walnuts

2¼ cups sifted all-purpose flour

1 teaspoon baking powder

¾ teaspoon baking soda

1 teaspoon salt

1 teaspoon ground cinnamon

½ teaspoon ground cloves

½ teaspoon grated nutmeg

4 medium McIntosh apples, peeled, cored, and sliced

3 tablespoons dark brown sugar

Whipped cream

SERVES EIGHT

Beat the butter and shortening together until light and fluffy, then thoroughly cream in the sugar. Lightly beat the eggs and stir them into the creamed mixture. Mix in the applesauce, raisins, pecans, and walnuts.

Preheat the oven to 375 degrees.

Sift the flour with the baking powder, baking soda, salt, cinnamon, cloves, and nutmeg. Stir these dry ingredients into the fruit and nut mixture.

Generously butter an 8-by-12-inch baking dish. Arrange the apple slices in a decorative pattern over the bottom and sprinkle with the brown sugar. Spoon the batter over the apples. Bake in the preheated oven for 40 to 50 minutes, or until the top of the cake springs back when lightly pressed. Cool for 15 minutes and turn the cake onto a serving plate. Serve warm with whipped cream.

Superior Chocolate Cake***

½ cup grated semisweet chocolate

1 cup milk

8 tablespoons (1 stick) butter

1½ cups granulated sugar

3 eggs

1 teaspoon baking soda

2 cups all-purpose flour

1½ teaspoons baking powder

1 teaspoon vanilla extract

Supermoist Chocolate Frosting (page 417)

SERVES EIGHT

Stir the grated chocolate into ½ cup milk and bring the mixture to a boil. Remove from the heat and set aside to cool. Beat the butter until light and fluffy. Cream in the sugar, blending well. Separate the eggs, placing the whites in a mixing bowl and adding the yolks to the butter-sugar mixture, mixing well. Stir the baking soda into the remaining ½ cup of milk, allow to fizz a bit, then add to the butter, sugar, and egg yolks.

Preheat the oven to 350 degrees.

Sift the flour together with the baking powder. Beat the egg whites until they form stiff peaks. Add the sifted flour and baking powder alternately with the beaten egg whites to the creamed mixture, folding in completely after each addition. Stir the vanilla into the cooled milk and chocolate, then fold it thoroughly into the batter.

Grease and lightly flour 2 9-inch cake pans, pour half the batter into each, and bake in the preheated oven for 25 to 35 minutes. Test for doneness by pressing the centers of the layers lightly with the fingers. If the tops spring back, remove from the oven and cool on wire racks before frosting with Supermoist Chocolate Frosting.

Miss Maud's Apple Gingerbread

2 *cups sifted all-purpose flour*	⅓ *cup granulated sugar*
1½ *teaspoons ground ginger*	1 *egg*
1¼ *teaspoons ground cinnamon*	¾ *cup milk*
¼ *teaspoon ground cloves*	¾ *cup molasses*
2 *teaspoons baking powder*	2½ *tablespoons butter*
¼ *teaspoon baking soda*	2 *medium apples, peeled, cored, and sliced*
½ *teaspoon salt*	
5 *tablespoons vegetable shortening or butter*	

SERVES EIGHT

Preheat the oven to 350 degrees.

Sift together the flour, ginger, cinnamon, cloves, baking powder, baking soda, and salt. Place the shortening in a large bowl and beat it lightly, then cream in the sugar. Mix in the egg and beat until light and fluffy. Combine the milk and molasses. Add the dry ingredients and the milk-molasses mixture alternately in small amounts to the creamed shortening. Stir after each addition only until blended.

Butter a 9-inch skillet, then dot it with the remaining 2 tablespoons of butter. Arrange the apple slices over the bottom and spoon the batter over the fruit. Bake in the preheated oven for 45 minutes, or until a toothpick inserted in the center comes out clean. Place a large serving plate over the skillet when it comes from the oven, and turn the gingerbread onto it so that the apples are on top. Serve warm or cold.

Apple Upside-down Cake

4 medium apples, peeled and cored

1 tablespoon lemon juice

2¼ cups granulated sugar

3 cups all-purpose flour

1 tablespoon baking powder

¼ teaspoon salt

4 eggs

1 cup vegetable oil

1 tablespoon vanilla extract

¼ cup orange juice

2 tablespoons butter

½ cup chopped nutmeats

1 teaspoon ground cinnamon

1½ cups heavy cream, whipped

SERVES EIGHT

Preheat the oven to 350 degrees.

Thinly slice 2 of the apples. Sprinkle the slices with lemon juice and set aside. Chop the 2 remaining apples. Combine 2 cups sugar, the flour, baking powder, and salt, and sift together into a bowl. Beat the eggs lightly and add to the dry ingredients, along with the oil, vanilla, and orange juice. Beat until the batter is smooth and free of lumps.

Grease the bottom of a heavy skillet with ½ tablespoon butter. Arrange the apple slices on the bottom, dot with the remaining butter, and pour half the batter over the fruit in the pan. Mix together the chopped apples and chopped nuts and place them over this layer of batter. Combine the remaining sugar and cinnamon and sprinkle half of this mixture over the nuts and apples. Pour in the remaining batter and top with the remaining sugar and cinnamon. Bake in the preheated oven for 55 minutes, or until a toothpick comes out clean when inserted in the center of the cake. Set a large serving plate over the skillet and turn upside down, so that the sliced apples are on top. Serve the dessert with whipped cream.

Note: If the cake does not turn out of the pan neatly and in one piece, serve it topped with the whipped cream and no one will be the wiser.

Margaret Young's Carrot Cake

1 cup finely grated carrots	1 cup finely grated blanched almonds
9 eggs	
1⅔ cups granulated sugar	⅛ teaspoon ground cinnamon

SERVES EIGHT TO TEN

Preheat the oven to 275 degrees.

Squeeze some of the liquid out of the grated carrots with paper towels. Separate the eggs. Combine the egg yolks with the sugar and beat until the mixture is thick and creamy. Stir in the carrots, almonds, and cinnamon. Beat the egg whites until stiff but not dry, fold them into the carrot mixture and turn the batter into a lightly buttered 9-by-13-inch baking pan.

Bake for 1¼ to 1½ hours in the preheated oven. Cool in the pan before cutting into squares.

Angel Food Cake

1½ cups egg whites	1 teaspoon vanilla extract
¼ teaspoon baking powder	½ teaspoon almond extract
1½ cups granulated sugar	1 cup cake flour

SERVES EIGHT

Preheat the oven to 375 degrees.

Beat the egg whites until they are foamy, add the baking powder, and continue to beat until the whites are stiff but not dry. Carefully fold ¼ cup sugar at a time into the egg whites. Fold in the flavorings.

Sift the cake flour 3 or 4 times, then fold it into the sweetened egg whites, ¼ cup at a time, incorporating each addition before adding the next. Take care not to overmix.

Carefully spoon the batter into an ungreased 10-inch tube pan, and bake for 35 to 40 minutes in the preheated oven. The cake is done when the top springs back when lightly pressed with the fingers.

Remove the cake from the oven, turn it upside down, and cool it in the pan on a wire rack, making sure the top of the cake is not resting directly on the rack. Prop up the edges of the pan if necessary. When the cake is cool, loosen with a knife or spatula and turn out onto a serving plate. Serve with fresh fruit and whipped cream, or trickle Maple Glaze (page 416) over the top and sides of the cake.

Spongecake

¾ cup granulated sugar	6 tablespoons ground almonds
8 eggs	1 tablespoon lemon juice
6 tablespoons flour	5 drops almond extract

MAKES THREE LAYERS

Preheat the oven to 375 degrees.

Place the sugar in a large bowl. Separate the eggs, reserving 5 of the whites. The 3 remaining egg whites may be kept for another use. Lightly beat the 8 egg yolks with a fork, then stir into the sugar until well creamed. Blend in the flour and ground almonds. Whip the 5 egg whites until they are stiff and gently fold them into the creamed mixture. Carefully stir in the lemon juice and almond extract.

Butter 3 9-inch cake pans and pour an equal amount of batter into each. Bake for 20 to 25 minutes in the preheated oven. Test for doneness by pressing each layer lightly with your fingers. If the center springs back, remove from the oven and cool.

Grandmother's Raspberry Jam Cake

12 tablespoons (1½ sticks) butter
1½ cups dark brown sugar
6 eggs
3 cups sifted all-purpose flour
1½ teaspoons baking soda
1 teaspoon ground allspice
½ teaspoon ground cinnamon
½ teaspoon grated nutmeg
¼ teaspoon ground cloves
½ teaspoon lemon juice
4 tablespoons heavy cream
1½ cups sieved raspberry jam
1 cup currants
Raspberry jam
Double recipe Lemon Icing (page 415)

SERVES EIGHT

Preheat the oven to 375 degrees.

Beat the butter until light and fluffy, and cream in the sugar. Separate the eggs, reserving the whites. Beat the yolks until lemon colored and beat them into the butter and sugar. Combine the sifted flour with the baking soda, allspice, cinnamon, nutmeg, and cloves, and sift again. Stir the lemon juice into the cream, and set the mixture in the oven for a few minutes to allow the cream to curdle. Remove and blend with the sieved jam.

Add the dry ingredients and the jam mixture alternately to the creamed mixture, stirring well after each addition. Sprinkle the currants with a little flour and mix them into the batter. Beat the reserved egg whites until they are stiff but not dry, then gently fold them into the batter.

Lightly grease 2 8-inch cake pans. Divide the batter between them and bake in the preheated oven, for about 30 minutes, or until the top of each layer springs back when lightly pressed with the fingers. Cool in the pans for 15 minutes, then turn out to cool further on wire racks. Spread additional raspberry jam between the layers before frosting with Lemon Icing.

Oat Torte***

APRICOT CREAM

⅔ cup granulated sugar
2 teaspoons cornstarch
2 egg yolks
1 cup orange juice
1 cup milk

2 envelopes unflavored gelatin
½ cup cold water
1 cup peeled and chopped apricots

SERVES EIGHT

Beat together the sugar, cornstarch, and egg yolks. Stir in the orange juice and milk a bit at a time. Cook in the top of a double boiler over boiling water, stirring constantly, until the mixture thickens. Sprinkle the gelatin over the cold water, let stand for 5 minutes, and then stir, along with the fruit, into the hot cream. Chill until partially set.

OAT LAYERS

8 tablespoons (1 stick) butter
1½ cups rolled oats
½ teaspoon ground cinnamon
1½ tablespoons flour

1¼ teaspoons baking powder
1 egg
¾ cup granulated sugar

Preheat the oven to 350 degrees.

Melt the butter in a large skillet. Stir in the oats, cinnamon, flour, and baking powder. Beat the egg and sugar until they are fluffy, add them to the dry ingredients, and beat well.

Invert 3 9-inch cake pans and butter and flour the backs. Spread the oat mixture over the buttered and floured surfaces to within 1 inch of the edges. Bake, batter side up, in the preheated oven. After 15 minutes, turn off the oven and remove 1 pan. Use a sharp knife to separate the layer from the pan. Set this layer on a flat surface to cool while you remove the other 2 layers, one at a time, by this same procedure.

TO ASSEMBLE

2 cups heavy cream	4 apricots, peeled, seeded, and halved Candied Violets (page 466)
¼ cup granulated sugar	

Beat 1 cup of the cream until it is stiff. Gently fold into it the partially set apricot cream and return to the refrigerator. When the mixture is almost set, spread it in equal portions between the torte layers. Smooth any excess apricot filling around the sides. Chill again, this time until the cream is completely set.

Beat the remaining cream with the sugar until stiff and swirl it over the top of the torte. Decorate with the apricot halves and Candied Violets. Refrigerate for 4 hours before serving.

Ground Nut Cake with Orange-Pecan Filling

*Here's a spongy nut cake
with a ½-inch-thick layer of orange-flavored
pecan icing.*

NUT CAKE

1 cup ground walnuts	2 cups confectioners' sugar
¾ cup ground pecans	2½ tablespoons cornstarch
½ cup ground blanched almonds	9 egg whites

SERVES TWELVE

Preheat the oven to 275 degrees.

Combine the nuts and mix thoroughly with the sugar and corn-starch. Beat the egg whites until they form stiff peaks. Gently fold the dry ingredients into the egg whites.

Butter and flour 2 9-inch cake pans. Divide the batter equally between the pans, and place in the preheated oven. Bake for 1½ to 1¾ hours, or until the cakes begin to pull away from the sides of the pans. Cool the cakes for 5 minutes in the pans, then remove, place on wire racks, and bring to room temperature.

ORANGE-PECAN FILLING

1½ cups confectioners' sugar	⅛ teaspoon orange extract
¾ pound (3 sticks) butter	1½ cups ground pecans
3 tablespoons orange juice	

Sift the sugar and combine with the butter, creaming together until light and fluffy. Stir in the orange juice and orange extract. Blend thoroughly. Set aside ½ cup of this mixture. Stir the nuts into the larger portion of this filling.

TO ASSEMBLE

2 tablespoons orange juice	1 egg white
12 walnut halves	¼ cup confetti sugar*

Mix the reserved ½ cup of the filling with the orange juice. Set aside. Spread the orange filling that contains the nuts over 1 cake layer. Carefully place the second layer on top of this filling. Use the ½ cup of filling thinned with the orange juice to frost the top of the cake. Dip the walnut halves in egg white then in confetti sugar, and arrange attractively around the top.

* This is a sugar used to decorate Christmas cookies and may be pur-chased in small glass bottles with shaker tops.

Honey Nut Loaf

Spread this with sweet butter or cream cheese.

1¼ cups honey	1 teaspoon salt
1 cup milk	1 teaspoon ground aniseed
¼ cup light brown sugar	¾ teaspoon ground cinnamon
6 tablespoons butter	¼ teaspoon ground nutmeg
2 egg yolks	1 cup coarsely chopped walnuts
2½ cups all-purpose flour	1 cup coarsely chopped pecans

SERVES EIGHT

Combine the honey, milk, and sugar in a saucepan and place over medium heat, stirring constantly, until the sugar dissolves. Remove from heat and allow the mixture to cool for 10 minutes. Add the butter, stirring well until it completely melts, and cool 10 minutes longer. Add the egg yolks and stir until thoroughly blended.

Preheat the oven to 325 degrees.

Sift the flour, salt, aniseed, cinnamon, and nutmeg into a bowl. Beat this dry mixture into the liquid ingredients and blend well. Fold in the chopped walnuts and pecans and pour the batter into a greased and floured 9¼-by-5¼-by-2¾-inch loaf pan. Bake in the preheated oven until the center of the loaf springs back when pressed with the finger, about 1¼ hours. Allow the loaf to cool in the pan for 15 minutes, then turn it onto a wire rack. Serve at room temperature, cut into thin slices.

New England Maple Nut Cake

½ cup shortening
4 tablespoons butter
¾ cup maple syrup
1½ teaspoons vanilla extract
3 eggs
2½ cups plus 2 tablespoons all-purpose flour

3¾ teaspoons baking powder
1½ teaspoons salt
⅓ cup milk
½ cup chopped pecans
½ cup chopped walnuts
Maple Frosting or Maple Glaze (page 416)

SERVES EIGHT

Preheat the oven to 375 degrees.

Beat the shortening and butter together until light and fluffy. Cream in the maple syrup, a bit at a time, blending after each addition until the syrup is completely absorbed. Mix in the vanilla extract. Beat the eggs to a lemony froth, then add to the shortening and syrup. Continue to beat until well blended.

Sift the flour and sift again together with the baking powder and salt. Add these dry ingredients to the creamed mixture alternately with the milk, stirring only long enough to moisten after each addition of flour. Mix in the chopped pecans and walnuts and pour the batter into 2 9-inch cake pans that have been greased and lightly floured. Bake for 25 to 30 minutes in the preheated oven. Test for doneness by pressing the tops lightly with the tips of the fingers. If the tops spring back, remove from the oven and let stand for 10 minutes before removing from the pans. Cool on wire racks to room temperature before frosting with Maple Frosting or Maple Glaze.

Vermont Maple Sugar Poundcake

4½ cups sifted all-purpose flour
½ teaspoon salt
1 pound (4 sticks) butter
2 cups maple sugar (or granulated sugar)

10 eggs (at room temperature)
1 teaspoon vanilla extract
½ teaspoon lemon extract

YIELDS TWO LOAVES

Preheat the oven to 300 degrees.

Combine the sifted flour with the salt, sift them together several times, and set aside. Beat the butter in the large bowl of your electric mixer until it is light and fluffy, then add the sugar a little at a time, creaming the mixture well after each addition.

Separate the eggs. With a rotary beater, beat the yolks until they are thick and pale yellow. Add the yolks to the creamed butter and sugar, and beat until the mixture is light.

Blend in the sifted flour a few tablespoons at a time, beating well after each addition. Stir in the flavorings. Beat the egg whites until they form stiff peaks, then gently fold them into the batter. Butter two 9¼-by-5¼-by-2¾-inch loaf pans, line them with buttered waxed paper, and divide the batter between them. Bake for about 1 hour and 35 minutes or until the cakes shrink from the sides of the pans and the top of each loaf springs back when lightly pressed with the fingers. Cool for 15 minutes in the pans before gently removing the cakes to a wire rack to cool further.

Miss Ravenna's Crumb Cake

2 cups golden raisins

6 tablespoons brandy

2¼ cups all-purpose flour

1½ teaspoons baking powder

½ pound plus 4 tablespoons
(2½ sticks) butter

1 cup granulated sugar

5 eggs

1¾ cups finely chopped almonds

1½ teaspoons almond extract

½ cup dark brown sugar

½ teaspoon ground cinnamon

3 cups crumbled macaroons

SERVES EIGHT

Place the raisins in a bowl, sprinkle them with brandy, and set them aside to plump for at least 30 minutes.

Meanwhile, prepare the cake batter. Combine 1¾ cups flour with the baking powder, sift together, and set aside. Beat ½ pound butter until light and fluffy. Cream the sugar, ⅓ cup at a time, into the butter, beating well after each addition. Beat the eggs, one at a time, into the butter and sugar mixture, incorporating each thoroughly before adding the next. Fold in 1½ cups nuts and the flour mixture.

To make topping, place brown sugar, ½ cup flour, ¼ cup chopped almonds, and cinnamon in a bowl. Cut in the remaining 4 tablespoons butter with 2 knives until the mixture is coarse and crumbly.

Preheat the oven to 350 degrees.

Butter a 9-inch springform pan, dust it lightly with flour, and spread half the cake batter over the bottom. Chop the raisins, sprinkle them over the batter, and top with the macaroons. Spoon the rest of the batter over the macaroons, and sprinkle the topping mixture over all.

Bake for 55 minutes in the preheated oven. Cool the cake in the pan. Remove the springform ring and serve warm or at room temperature.

White Christmas Fruitcake

1 cup golden raisins

½ cup coarsely chopped candied apricots

½ cup coarsely chopped candied citron

½ cup coarsely chopped candied lemon

½ cup coarsely chopped candied orange

½ cup coarsely chopped candied pears

½ cup coarsely chopped candied pineapple

½ cup coarsely chopped brazil nuts

½ cup coarsely chopped walnuts

1¼ cups sifted cake flour

¾ teaspoon baking powder

¼ teaspoon salt

5 tablespoons butter

⅔ cup granulated sugar

2 eggs

1 egg yolk

3 tablespoons brandy

2 tablespoons dry sherry

1 tablespoon lemon juice

Rum or brandy

MAKES TWO ONE-POUND LOAF CAKES

Place all the fruit and nuts in a large bowl. Sift the flour with the baking powder and salt. Sift these dry ingredients once more, this time over the fruits and nuts. Toss the fruit and nut mixture gently, or work the flour into the fruits and nuts with your fingers.

Preheat the oven to 300 degrees.

Beat the butter until light and cream in the sugar thoroughly. Lightly beat the eggs and egg yolk together and add to the creamed butter. Stir in the brandy, sherry, and lemon juice; blend thoroughly. Fold into the floured fruits and nuts.

Two 9¼-by-5¼-by-2¾-inch loaf pans, line them with buttered paper, and divide the fruitcake batter between them. Bake in the preheated oven 1½ to 2 hours, or until the cakes shrink from the sides of the pan. Allow the cakes to cool. Soak 5 or 6 layers of cheesecloth well in rum or brandy, wring the cheesecloth out slightly, and wrap it lightly around the fruitcake. Store in tin or plastic boxes for no less than a week and up to a month.

Candied Fruit and Nut Cake

½ cup candied pears, cut into
½-inch cubes

½ cup candied apricots, cut into
½-inch cubes

½ cup whole candied cherries

½ cup candied citron, cut into
¼-inch cubes

1 cup shelled whole hazelnuts

1 cup shelled whole brazil nuts

1 cup walnut halves

3 tablespoons finely chopped
pecans

½ cup all-purpose flour

1 tablespoon ground cinnamon

¼ teaspoon ground allspice

¼ teaspoon grated nutmeg

¾ cup granulated sugar

¾ cup honey

SERVES EIGHT TO TEN

Preheat the oven to 300 degrees.

Place the fruits and nuts in a large bowl. Add the flour and spices. Mix well. Bring the sugar and honey to a boil over medium heat. Reduce the heat to low, and continue to boil until the mixture reaches the soft-ball stage, 238 degrees on a candy thermometer. Or test by dropping a bit into cold water; if the ball holds its shape softly, the syrup is ready.

Remove the syrup from the heat and stir it into the fruit and nut mixture. Blend all ingredients thoroughly. Use well-buttered wax paper to line a 9-inch springform. Pour in the batter, and bake for 30 minutes in the preheated oven. Cool the cake in the pan for 30 minutes. Peel off the paper and serve the cake at room temperature.

Applesauce Cookies

4 tablespoons butter

4 tablespoons shortening

1 cup granulated sugar

2 eggs

1 cup sweetened applesauce

⅔ cup chopped walnuts

⅓ cup chopped pecans

½ cup coarsely chopped dark
raisins

½ cup coarsely chopped golden
raisins

2½ cups sifted all-purpose flour

1 teaspoon baking powder

¾ teaspoon baking soda

1 teaspoon salt

1 teaspoon ground cinnamon

½ teaspoon ground cloves

½ teaspoon grated nutmeg

YIELDS THREE AND ONE HALF TO FOUR DOZEN

Preheat the oven to 375 degrees.

Blend the butter and shortening until fluffy, then cream in the sugar. Beat the eggs lightly and beat them into the creamed mixture. Stir in the applesauce, nuts, and raisins. Resift the flour with the baking powder, baking soda, salt, cinnamon, cloves, and nutmeg. Thoroughly blend the dry ingredients into the moist ingredients. Drop the batter by tablespoons onto a buttered cookie sheet, and bake for 12 to 15 minutes. Cool the cookies for 1 minute before lifting each with a spatula and transferring to a wire rack to cool.

My Favorite Ginger Cookies***

*An improvisation on an inexact formula
for gingersnaps provided me with this
superior cookie recipe—my favorite.*

¼ cup molasses

¼ cup dark corn syrup

8 tablespoons (1 stick) butter

2 cups all-purpose flour

2 teaspoons baking powder

⅔ cup granulated sugar

1 teaspoon ground ginger

1 cup coarsely chopped walnuts

YIELDS ABOUT THREE DOZEN

[400]

Preheat the oven to 325 degrees.

Heat the molasses and corn syrup to just under a boil. Cut the butter into 1-inch pieces and stir it into the hot syrup. Sift together the flour, baking powder, sugar, and ginger. Stir these ingredients, a bit at a time, into the syrup-butter mixture. Add the nuts and mix well. Drop by teaspoonfuls 3 inches apart onto well-buttered cookie sheets. Bake 15 to 18 minutes.

Molasses-Pumpkin Cookies

5 *tablespoons butter*	½ *teaspoon salt*
¾ *cup granulated sugar*	1 *teaspoon ground cloves*
¾ *cup molasses*	1 *teaspoon grated nutmeg*
⅓ *cup canned pumpkin*	½ *teaspoon ground ginger*
1 *egg*	2 *teaspoons ground cinnamon*
3 *cups sifted all-purpose flour*	1 *cup hot water*
2 *teaspoons baking soda*	

YIELDS TWO DOZEN

Preheat the oven to 400 degrees.

Beat the butter until fluffy, then add the sugar, about 2 tablespoons at a time, creaming well after each addition. Stir in the molasses and pumpkin. Beat the egg lightly with a fork and add to the creamed mixture, blending all ingredients thoroughly.

Combine the sifted flour with the baking soda, salt, cloves, nutmeg, ginger, and cinnamon and sift again. Add these dry ingredients alternately with the hot water, a little of each at a time, to the creamed mixture, blending well after each addition. Drop the batter by tablespoonfuls onto a well-greased cookie sheet. Bake for 10 to 12 minutes. Cool for 3 minutes before loosening and removing to a wire rack.

Mother's Molasses Cookies

5 tablespoons butter
¾ cup granulated sugar
¾ cup molasses
1 egg
3 cups sifted all-purpose flour
2 teaspoons baking soda

2 teaspoons ground cinnamon
1½ teaspoons ground ginger
½ teaspoon ground cloves
½ teaspoon grated nutmeg
½ teaspoon salt
1 cup hot water

YIELDS TWO DOZEN

Preheat the oven to 400 degrees.

Beat the butter until creamy, add the sugar, about 2 tablespoons at a time, and continue to beat until the mixture is light and frothy. Stir in the molasses. Beat the egg a bit with a fork and add to the molasses mixture, mixing all ingredients thoroughly.

Combine the sifted flour with the baking soda, cinnamon, ginger, cloves, nutmeg, and salt and sift again. Blend the dry ingredients alternately with the hot water, a little of each at a time, into the molasses mixture. Stir thoroughly after each addition. Drop the batter by tablespoonfuls onto a well-greased cookie sheet. Bake for 7 or 8 minutes. Cool for 3 minutes before loosening and removing to a wire rack.

Sour Cream Cookies***

3 eggs
1 cup granulated sugar
1¼ cups sour cream

¾ teaspoon baking powder
3 cups all-purpose flour
1 teaspoon almond extract

YIELDS TWO DOZEN

Preheat oven to 400 degrees.

Beat together the eggs and sugar until creamy. Stir in the sour cream and the dry ingredients. Add the almond extract and beat well. Drop the batter by spoonsful onto a greased and floured cookie sheet. Bake for 15 minutes.

Chocolate Chip Cookies I

2 cups (firmly packed) light brown sugar
1 cup vegetable shortening
2 eggs
1⅔ cups sifted all-purpose flour
¼ teaspoon baking powder
½ teaspoon baking soda
½ teaspoon ground cinnamon
½ teaspoon salt
1½ cups semisweet chocolate bits
1½ cups rolled oats
½ cup raisins
¾ cup coarsely chopped walnuts

YIELDS ABOUT THREE DOZEN

Preheat the oven to 350 degrees.

Cream the sugar and shortening together until light and fluffy. Beat the eggs a bit with a fork, then add to the sugar-shortening mixture. Sift together the flour, baking powder, baking soda, cinnamon, and salt. Blend these dry ingredients thoroughly into the creamed mixture. Stir in the chocolate, rolled oats, raisins, and walnuts. Drop the batter by teaspoonfuls on an ungreased cookie sheet. Bake for 10 to 12 minutes. Cool for a minute and then loosen and place on a rack to cool.

Chocolate Chip Cookies II

8 tablespoons (1 stick) softened butter
½ cup light brown sugar
1 egg
½ teaspoon baking soda
1 tablespoon hot water
1¼ cups sifted all-purpose flour
½ teaspoon salt
1 teaspoon vanilla extract
1 6-ounce package chocolate bits
¾ cup coarsely chopped pecans

YIELDS ABOUT TWO DOZEN

Preheat the oven to 375 degrees.

Beat the butter until light and fluffy, then cream the sugar in well. Beat the egg to a lemony froth and beat it into the creamed mixture. Mix the baking soda with the water and add it, along with the flour, salt, vanilla, chocolate bits, and chopped pecans to the creamed mixture. Blend all ingredients thoroughly.

Drop by tablespoonfuls onto a lightly greased cookie sheet. Bake for 10 to 12 minutes, or until the cookies are light brown around the edges. Remove from the oven and transfer immediately to a wire rack to cool.

Chocolate-Nut Drop Cookies

1 cup granulated sugar

4 tablespoons butter, at room temperature

1 egg

½ cup milk

1½ cups all-purpose flour

½ cup cocoa

2 teaspoons baking powder

1 cup coarsely chopped walnuts

MAKES TWO DOZEN

Preheat the oven to 375 degrees.

Cream the sugar and butter together in a large bowl. Beat the egg until light and add, along with the milk, to the sugar-butter mixture. Sift the flour, cocoa, and baking powder together and combine with the liquid ingredients. Fold in the nuts. Drop the batter by spoonfuls onto a well-buttered cookie sheet and bake for 15 minutes. Loosen after taking from the oven and cool on a wire rack.

Filled Cookies

COOKIE DOUGH

2 teaspoons lemon juice

½ cup milk

½ pound (2 sticks) butter

1 cup granulated sugar

1 teaspoon baking soda

3½ cups all-purpose flour

1 teaspoon salt

YIELDS TWO DOZEN

Preheat the oven to 250 degrees.

Stir the lemon juice into the milk and set the mixture in the oven for 10 minutes to sour the milk. Beat the butter until light and cream in the sugar. Add the baking soda to the soured milk, stir until dissolved, then pour the milk into the butter and sugar. Add the flour and salt, mixing all ingredients thoroughly, and chill the dough for several hours in the refrigerator.

FRUIT AND NUT FILLING

½ *cup granulated sugar*
1 *teaspoon flour*
⅔ *cup finely chopped raisins*
⅔ *cup finely chopped dried apricots*

¼ *cup finely chopped pecans*
½ *cup water*

Place the sugar, flour, raisins, apricots, and pecans in a saucepan. Add the water and cook over low boil until the mixture thickens, stirring frequently. Cool.

TO ASSEMBLE

Preheat the oven to 400 degrees.

To roll out the chilled dough, use ample flour on your pastry board. The dough will be sticky, so handle it carefully. Roll out ¼ inch thick, and cut into 2½-inch rounds with a well-floured cookie cutter or glass edge. Place balls of filling the size of a small walnut on half of the cookie dough rounds, top each with another dough round, and use the tines of a fork to seal the edges all around. Arrange the filled cookies on a well-greased cookie sheet, and bake for 12 to 15 minutes. Remove the cookies from the pans with a spatula and set them on wire racks to cool after removing from the oven.

Mrs. Perkin's Pecan Cookies

½ pound (2 sticks) butter
1½ cups granulated sugar
3 eggs
1 teaspoon baking soda
1½ tablespoons hot water

1½ teaspoons ground cinnamon
½ teaspoon salt
3¼ cups all-purpose flour
1⅓ cups coarsely chopped pecans
¾ cup raisins

YIELDS THREE AND ONE HALF TO FOUR DOZEN

Preheat the oven to 350 degrees.

Cream the butter until light, then gradually add the sugar. Add the eggs one at a time, beating well after each addition. Soften the baking soda in the hot water.

Sift together the cinnamon, salt, and half the flour. Add the baking soda and the flour mixture to the creamed butter. Blend thoroughly then stir in the remaining flour, along with the pecans and raisins. Drop by tablespoonfuls about 1 inch apart onto well-buttered cookie sheets, and bake for 15 minutes. Loosen gently after removing from the oven, cool 1 minute on the cookie sheets, then set on wire racks.

Coconut Almond Cookies

*These tasty treats are as fat and crunchy
as the cookies Grandma used to bake.*

½ pound (2 sticks) butter
1½ cups granulated sugar
3 eggs
1 teaspoon baking soda
1½ tablespoons hot water
½ teaspoon salt
½ teaspoon grated nutmeg
3¼ cups all-purpose flour

1¼ cups coarsely chopped blanched almonds
¾ cup grated coconut
¾ cup currants
6 tablespoons finely chopped sour apple
1 teaspoon almond extract

YIELDS THREE AND ONE HALF TO FOUR DOZEN

Preheat the oven to 350 degrees.

Cream the butter until light, then gradually add the sugar. Add the eggs one at a time, beating well after each addition. Soften the baking soda in the hot water.

Sift together the salt, nutmeg, and half the flour. Add the baking soda and the flour mixture to the creamed butter. Blend thoroughly, then stir in the remaining flour, along with the almonds, coconut, currants, sour apple, and almond extract. Drop by tablespoonsful about 1 inch apart onto well-buttered cookie sheets, and bake for 15 minutes. Loosen gently after removing from the oven, cool 1 minute, then set on wire racks.

Ginger-Currant Cookies

*If you like ginger you will love these cookies—
they are ginger-flavored with a vengeance.*

½ *pound (2 sticks) butter*
1 *cup granulated sugar*
1 *egg*
1 *teaspoon baking soda*
⅓ *cup cider vinegar*

1 *cup molasses*
1 *teaspoon salt*
1 *tablespoon ground ginger*
4½ *cups all-purpose flour*
5 *tablespoons currants*

YIELDS ABOUT THREE DOZEN

Preheat the oven to 325 degrees.

Cream the butter and sugar together, then beat in the egg. Dissolve the baking soda in the vinegar. When it stops fizzing, stir the molasses into it and add to the creamed mixture. Blend in the salt, ginger, flour, and currants. The result should be a soft dough.

Drop by tablespoonsful 1½ inches apart on a well-buttered cookie sheet. Bake for 15 to 18 minutes. Use a spatula to remove the hot cookies to a buttered surface for a minute or two, then transfer to a wire rack to cool further. These cookies tend to stick together, even when cool, so place sheets of wax paper or plastic wrap on the serving plate and between the stacked layers.

Lemon Rounds

8 tablespoons (1 stick) butter
1 cup granulated sugar
2 eggs
1 teaspoon lemon extract
1 teaspoon grated lemon zest
2 teaspoons milk

Scant 1½ teaspoons baking powder
2⅔ cups all-purpose flour
Confetti sugar*
Walnut halves

YIELDS THREE AND ONE HALF DOZEN

Preheat the oven to 350 degrees.

Beat the butter in an electric mixer until it is fluffy. Work in the sugar, a bit at a time, creaming well after each addition. Beat the eggs lightly, then add to the butter-sugar mixture, along with the lemon extract, lemon zest, and milk. Mix well. Blend in the baking powder and flour.

Roll out ¼ inch thick on a lightly floured surface. Cut into rounds with a 2½-inch cookie cutter or a glass dipped in flour. Sprinkle with sugar, top each cookie with a walnut half, and place on a well-buttered cookie sheet. Bake for 13 to 14 minutes. Cool on wire racks.

* This is a sugar used to decorate Christmas cookies and may be purchased in small glass bottles with sprinkle tops.

Shrewsbury Cookies***

12 tablespoons (1½ sticks) butter
½ cup granulated sugar

1 egg
2 cups all-purpose flour
1 cup pecan halves

YIELDS ABOUT TWO AND ONE HALF DOZEN

Preheat the oven to 350 degrees.

Beat the butter until it is light and fluffy, then cream in the sugar a little at a time, beating well after each addition. Beat the egg to a lemony froth, add it to the creamed mixture, and work in the flour. Turn the dough out on a well-floured board, and knead for a minute or two, working in additional flour if the dough seems too sticky to handle.

Roll out the dough very thin. Use a 2½-inch cookie cutter or the edge of a glass dipped in flour to cut the cookies. Place them on a buttered cookie sheet. Top each cookie with a pecan half. Bake for 8 to 10 minutes or until lightly browned. Loosen the cookies with a spatula and set them on a wire rack to cool.

Crunchy Cinnamon Squares

Cinnamon Squares are a nice change for the cookie jar.
These spicy squares are decorated
with a sugar-nut-apple topping
that is delicious.

6 tablespoons butter	*¼ cup milk*
¾ cup granulated sugar	*¾ cup chopped nuts*
1¾ cups all-purpose flour	*3 tablespoons finely chopped*
1 teaspoon ground cinnamon	*sour apple*
1 teaspoon baking powder	*1 egg yolk*

YIELDS TWO TO THREE DOZEN

Whip 4 tablespoons butter in an electric mixer. Add ½ cup sugar and cream together. Sift the flour with the cinnamon and baking powder. Add the flour mixture and milk alternately to the butter and sugar, a little at a time, stirring well after each addition. Add more flour if necessary to form a fairly stiff dough. Roll out on a floured board and cut into 2-inch squares.

Preheat the oven to 375 degrees.

To make the topping, cream the remaining butter with the sugar, then mix in the nuts and apple. Beat the egg yolk lightly, and use your finger or a pastry brush to brush it over the tops of the cookies. Place ½ teaspoon of topping in the center of each cinnamon square. Arrange on well-buttered cookie sheets and bake for 10 to 12 minutes. Remove from the cookie sheets immediately and set on wire racks to cool.

Oatmeal Icebox Cookies

8 tablespoons (1 stick) butter
8 tablespoons vegetable shortening
1 cup granulated sugar
1 cup light brown sugar
2 eggs
1½ cups sifted all-purpose flour

1 teaspoon baking soda
1 teaspoon salt
3 cups rolled oats
1 teaspoon vanilla extract
1 cup chopped nutmeats
¾ cup chopped dried apricots

YIELDS THREE DOZEN

Beat the butter and shortening together until light and fluffy, then cream in the sugars. Add the eggs, and beat until the mixture is smooth. Blend in the flour, soda, salt, and oats. Add the vanilla and knead a bit on a floured board before dividing the dough in half.

Knead the nuts into one portion of the dough and the chopped apricots into the other. Shape each piece of dough into a long bar, wrap in wax paper, and refrigerate overnight.

Preheat oven to 375 degrees.

To bake, cut the bars of dough into slices ¼ inch thick, arrange on well-buttered cookie sheets, and bake for 10 to 12 minutes, or until nicely browned. Loosen with a spatula and cool on wire racks.

Christmas Sand Tarts***

½ pound butter, at room
   temperature
1½ cups granulated sugar
1 egg, at room temperature

2 cups all-purpose flour
1 egg white
   Granulated sugar
30 walnut or pecan halves

YIELDS TWO AND ONE HALF DOZEN

Whip the butter until light and fluffy, then cream it with the sugar. Beat the egg until frothy and stir it into the butter-sugar mixture. Add the flour, a little at a time, blending well after each addition. Cover the dough with wax paper and refrigerate overnight.

Preheat the oven to 350 degrees.

Work the dough a bit with your fingers to soften it. Divide the dough into 3 equal portions, and then divide each of these portions in half. Since the dough will be sticky, generously flour the pastry board and rolling pin as you roll out each of these small portions, one at a time. Cut the dough into rounds with a 2½-inch cookie cutter, or the edge of a glass dipped in flour. Brush the tops of the cookies with the egg white, sprinkle each with sugar, and set a nut half in the center. Arrange on cookie sheets and bake for 10 minutes. Remove the cookies from the baking sheet with a spatula immediately upon taking them from the oven. Set on a wire rack to cool.

Coconut Bars***

8 tablespoons (1 stick) butter
1¼ cups (firmly packed) light
   brown sugar
½ teaspoon salt
1 cup plus 2 tablespoons all-
   purpose flour
2 eggs

1 teaspoon vanilla extract
½ teaspoon baking powder
1¼ cups chopped pecans
1 6-ounce package semisweet
   chocolate bits
1 cup shredded coconut

YIELDS ABOUT TWO DOZEN

[411]

Preheat the oven to 325 degrees.

Cream the butter together with ½ cup sugar and the salt. Mix in 1 cup flour and blend well. Spread the mixture over the bottom of a well-buttered 9-by-9-inch baking pan and bake for 25 minutes. Remove from the oven and cool slightly.

Beat the eggs lightly, add the remaining ¾ cup sugar and the vanilla, and continue to beat for 3 minutes. Add the remaining ingredients and blend well. Spread this topping over the baked mixture and bake for 40 to 45 minutes longer. Cool in the pan and cut into small bars.

Basic Brownies

*This All-American favorite
has won friends around the world.*

2 1-ounce squares unsweetened
   chocolate

4 tablespoons butter

1 cup granulated sugar

2 eggs

¼ cup milk

¾ cup sifted all-purpose flour

1 teaspoon vanilla extract

⅓ teaspoon salt

1 cup coarsely chopped walnuts
   or pecans

YIELDS SIXTEEN

Preheat the oven to 350 degrees.

Melt the chocolate over hot water. Cream the butter and sugar. Add the melted chocolate and stir in the eggs. Gradually add the milk and the flour alternately, a bit at a time, beating well after each addition. Stir in the vanilla, salt, and nuts.

Pour the batter into an 8-inch-square pan that has been buttered and lightly dusted with flour. Bake for 15 minutes. Cut into squares when cool.

Fudge Brownies

2 1-ounce squares unsweetened chocolate, melted

8 tablespoons (1 stick) butter

1 cup granulated sugar

2 eggs

½ cup all-purpose flour

1 teaspoon vanilla extract

1 cup coarsely chopped walnuts or pecans

YIELDS SIXTEEN

Preheat the oven to 350 degrees.

Melt the chocolate over hot water. Beat the butter until light and cream in the sugar. Lightly beat the eggs and add to the creamed mixture, along with the flour, melted chocolate, vanilla, and nuts. Blend thoroughly. Turn the mixture into a buttered 8-by-8-inch pan and bake for 30 minutes. Cut into squares when cool.

Cake Brownies

1½ 1-ounce squares unsweetened chocolate

2 tablespoons butter

2 eggs

1 cup granulated sugar

⅔ cup all-purpose flour

¾ teaspoon baking soda

¼ cup milk

½ cup coarsely chopped walnuts

1 teaspoon vanilla extract

YIELDS SIXTEEN

Preheat the oven to 375 degrees.

Melt the chocolate and butter together over hot water. Beat the eggs lightly and mix in the sugar. Add the melted chocolate. Sift together the flour and baking soda. Add to the chocolate-sugar mixture alternately with the milk, a little at a time, stirring well after each addition. Blend in the chopped nuts and vanilla.

Lightly butter an 8-by-8-inch baking pan and pour in the batter. Top with a light sprinkling of additional granulated sugar. Bake for 30 minutes. Remove from the oven and cut into squares while still hot.

Lemon Gems or Cupcakes***

4 tablespoons butter	Pinch salt
½ cup granulated sugar	½ cup milk
½ teaspoon lemon extract	2 egg whites
1 cup all-purpose flour	⅛ teaspoon salt
1 teaspoon baking powder	½ recipe Lemon Icing (page 415)

YIELDS ABOUT TWO DOZEN GEMS OR
ONE DOZEN TWO-AND-ONE-HALF-INCH CUPCAKES

Preheat the oven to 325 degrees.

Beat the butter until fluffy, then cream in the sugar and continue to beat until the mixture is light and lemon colored. Add the lemon extract and mix well. Combine the flour, baking powder, and salt; sift them together into a small bowl. Add the dry ingredients alternately with the milk to the creamed mixture, stirring well after each addition.

Beat the egg whites with ⅛ teaspoon of salt until stiff, then carefully fold into the batter. Divide the mixture into buttered and floured gem* or cupcake pans, and bake until lightly browned. This should take about 15 to 20 minutes for the gems, and about 25 to 30 minutes for the cupcakes. Remove from the pans and allow them to cool on wire racks before frosting with Lemon Icing.

* Gem pans are small cupcake pans, with depressions of only half the size.

Icings

Orange Butter-Cream Icing

½ pound (2 sticks) butter
4 egg yolks
4 cups sifted confectioners' sugar

3 tablespoons orange juice
1 teaspoon orange zest
1 tablespoon lemon juice

ENOUGH FOR FOUR DOZEN CUPCAKES OR
ONE LARGE CAKE

Beat the butter until light and fluffy. Beat in the egg yolks. Blend in the sugar, orange juice, orange zest, and lemon juice. Continue to beat until all the ingredients are well blended and the icing is smooth. Spread on cooled cupcakes or cake. Refrigerate the icing if not used immediately.

Lemon Icing

8 tablespoons (1 stick) butter
2 egg yolks

2 cups sifted confectioners' sugar
2 tablespoons lemon juice

ENOUGH FOR TWO DOZEN CUPCAKES OR
ONE SMALL CAKE

Beat the butter until light and fluffy. Beat in the egg yolks. Blend in the sugar and lemon juice. Continue to beat until all the ingredients are well blended and the icing is smooth. Spread on cooled cupcakes or cake. Refrigerate the icing if not used immediately.

Maple Glaze

4 tablespoons butter
¼ cup heavy cream

1 ½ cups maple syrup

ENOUGH FOR TWO NINE-INCH LAYERS

Place all the ingredients in a saucepan and bring to a boil. Stir briefly and cook at full boil for at least 2 minutes. Cool slightly, then beat with a rotary beater until the glaze thickens, fluffs, and reaches spreading consistency.

Maple Frosting

1 ½ cups maple syrup
3 egg whites

⅛ teaspoon salt
1 ½ teaspoons vanilla extract

ENOUGH FOR TWO NINE-INCH LAYERS

Cook the syrup in a saucepan until it reaches the soft-ball stage when a bit is dropped in cold water (238 degrees on a candy thermometer). Remove from heat and cool slightly.

Beat the egg whites until they form stiff peaks, sprinkling in the salt as you beat. Pour the maple syrup into the egg whites in a thin stream, beating constantly at high speed with an electric mixer until the syrup is well blended and the frosting holds a stiff peak. Beat in the vanilla and frost the cake immediately.

Supermoist Chocolate Frosting***

2 1-ounce squares unsweetened
   chocolate

½ *cup granulated sugar*

2 *teaspoons cornstarch*

½ *cup milk*

1 *egg yolk*

ENOUGH FOR TWO NINE-INCH LAYERS

Place the chocolate, sugar, cornstarch, and milk in a saucepan, and boil over medium heat until the mixture thickens, stirring constantly. Cool slightly, then beat in the egg yolk. Allow the frosting to cool a bit more before icing the cooled layers.

Pies

Do's and Don'ts of Perfect Pie-crust–Making

Do use ice cold water.

Do use a fork and mix lightly.

Don't overmix.

Don't work the dough too much by rolling and rerolling with your rolling pin.

Don't flour the board too heavily.

Do roll the dough out large enough to more than cover the pie plate.

Don't stretch the dough when fitting it in the plate.

Pastry for 2-Crust Pie

2½ cups all-purpose flour
1¼ teaspoons salt

15 tablespoons vegetable shortening
8–10 tablespoons ice water

Mix the flour and salt and sift into a large bowl. Use 2 knives blade against blade to cut in the shortening. When the mixture resembles coarse meal, add 8 tablespoons ice water and stir with a fork until the dough comes clean from the sides of the bowl. If the pastry will not hold together and form a ball, stir in the 2 remaining tablespoons ice water. Chill the pie dough for at least 15 minutes before rolling out on a lightly floured surface.

This recipe may be halved if a 1-crust pie is called for. A work-saving device is to prepare the whole recipe, divide the dough in half, and freeze the unused portion.

To bake one pie shell, use only half the ingredients called for. Mix, chill, and roll out as indicated. Line the pie plate with the pastry, crimp the edges, prick the sides and bottom with a fork, and bake in a preheated 400 degree oven until nicely browned, about 10 to 15 minutes. To keep the crust from blistering or shrinking, line with aluminum foil, fill with uncooked rice, and bake as directed, or set a smaller pie plate within the larger one.

Apple Pie***

What could be better than a really superb apple pie?

8 large McIntosh apples, peeled and cored

1 cup granulated sugar

1¼ teaspoons ground cinnamon

1 teaspoon grated nutmeg

⅛ teaspoon ground cardamom

Pastry for 2-Crust Pie (page 418)

Juice of 1 lemon

2 tablespoons butter

1 egg yolk

Heavy cream

2 tablespoons maple sugar or light brown sugar

SERVES EIGHT

Preheat the oven to 450 degrees.

Cut the apples into ½-inch slices and toss them with the sugar and spices. Roll out the dough into 2 circles and use one to line a 9-inch pie plate. Fill with apple slices. Sprinkle the apples with lemon juice, and dot with butter. Cover the pie with the second crust and crimp the edges. With a knife, slit the top crust in several places to allow steam to escape.

Place the pie in the preheated oven and bake for 15 minutes. Reduce the heat to 375 degrees and bake for 30 minutes. Meanwhile, mix the egg yolk with a little cream. Remove the pie from the oven and brush the top crust with the glaze, taking care not to brush the edges of the crust if they are already brown. Sprinkle the maple or brown sugar over the top and return the pie to the oven to bake for 10 minutes more. Serve warm or at room temperature.

Apple Pudding Pie

This recipe makes 2 7½-inch or 1 10-inch pie.

8 eggs
1½ cups granulated sugar
1¼ cups (2½ sticks) butter, melted
2 cups milk
4½ cups peeled, cored, and chopped McIntosh apples

Juice of 1 lemon
Pastry for 2-Crust Pie (page 418)
¼ teaspoon ground cinnamon
Whipped cream

SERVES EIGHT

Preheat the oven to 425 degrees.

Beat the eggs lightly in a large bowl. Stir in the sugar, butter, milk, apples, and lemon juice. Roll out the pastry crust and line 2 7½-inch or 1 10-inch glass pie plate, crimping the edges of the crusts all around. Spoon the pudding mixture into the crust and sprinkle with cinnamon. Bake for 25 minutes in the preheated oven, then lower the heat to 350 degrees and bake 25 to 30 minutes longer for the small pies or 40 to 50 minutes longer for the large pie. The pie is done when a knife inserted in the center comes out clean. Serve warm topped with whipped cream.

Apple Tart***

5 tablespoons butter, softened
9 tablespoons granulated sugar
4 medium apples, peeled, cored, and sliced

½ recipe Pastry for 2-Crust Pie (page 418)
Heavy cream

SERVES FOUR

Preheat the oven to 400 degrees.

Spread 3 tablespoons softened butter over the bottom and sides of a 7½-inch glass pie plate. Sprinkle 6 tablespoons of sugar over the butter, taking care that it is well distributed. Arrange the apples in layers over the sugar, and dot the top with the remaining 2 tablespoons butter. Roll out the dough, cut a neat circle slightly smaller than the pie plate, and lay it over the apples. Do not fasten the crust to the edge of the pie plate.

Bake the tart in the preheated oven for 45 to 55 minutes, or until the crust is golden brown and the apples, as seen through the glass pie plate, are caramelized.

Remove the tart from the oven and loosen the crust. Place a serving plate somewhat larger than the pie plate over the tart. Hold the serving plate firmly and quickly turn the tart and the plate over so that the tart falls neatly onto the dish. Serve hot, accompanied by a bowl of whipped heavy cream or a pitcher of unwhipped heavy cream.

Applesauce Apple Pie

6–8 *McIntosh apples, peeled and cored*

½ *recipe Pastry for 2-Crust Pie (page 418)*

2¼ *cups Your Own Applesauce (page 366)*

½ *teaspoon flour*

2½ *tablespoons dark brown sugar*

1 *tablespoon butter*

⅓ *cup currant jelly*

SERVES EIGHT

Preheat the oven to 425 degrees.

Cut the apples into thin slices. Roll out the pastry and line a 10-inch pie plate with it. Spread ¾ cup of applesauce over the pie crust. Arrange a layer of apple slices over the applesauce, and top with a bit of the flour and about 1½ teaspoons brown sugar. Build 2 more layers of applesauce and apples, sprinkling each with flour and brown sugar. Dot the top layer with butter.

Bake for 15 minutes in the preheated oven. Reduce the heat to 350 degrees and bake for 30 to 40 minutes longer, or until the apples are tender and the crust is lightly browned. Remove from the oven and glaze while still hot with the currant jelly. Serve warm or at room temperature.

Maple Sugar Apple Pie

Waste not, want not.
Use the apple parings left over from this pie
to make Apple Parings Sauce (page 469).

Pastry for 2-Crust Pie (page 418)

7 large McIntosh apples, peeled and cored

3 tablespoons maple sugar

1 tablespoon all-purpose flour

1 tablespoon butter

Milk or cream

Granulated sugar

SERVES EIGHT

Preheat the oven to 400 degrees.

Cut the apples into ¾-inch slices and toss them with the sugar and flour. Roll out the dough into 2 circles and use one to line a 9-inch pie plate. Fill with apple slices, dot with butter, and cover with the top crust. Crimp the edges of the crusts and cut 6 gashes in the top for the steam to escape.

Bake for 10 minutes in the preheated oven. Lower the heat to 375 degrees and continue to bake for an additional 30 minutes. Remove the pie from the oven, brush the top with milk or cream, sprinkle with sugar, and bake 10 minutes longer.

Schnitz Pie

Dried apples were a staple item in farmhouse cooking.
The interesting flavor takes a bit of getting used to,
but familiarity breeds respect. Serve with cream
or ice cream for best results.

½ pound dried sour apples

½ pound dried sweet apples

2 quarts water

1 cup granulated sugar

½ cup raisins

¼ cup candied orange peel

Juice of 1 orange

1 tablespoon flour

2 tablespoons ground cinnamon

⅛ teaspoon grated nutmeg

Pastry for 2-Crust Pie (page 418)

¼ cup plus 1 tablespoon heavy cream

½ cup maple syrup

SERVES EIGHT

Put the dried apples in a pan, cover with 2 quarts water, and simmer until the pulp is soft. Remove from the heat, and add the sugar, raisins, orange peel, orange juice, flour, cinnamon, and nutmeg. Mix well and set aside to cool.

Preheat the oven to 450 degrees.

Roll out the dough into 2 circles and use one to line a 10-inch pie plate. Spoon in the apple mixture. Use the spoon to lightly swirl in the ¼ cup heavy cream and the maple syrup. Cut the second crust into strips and lay it over the filling to make a lattice top. Crimp the pastry edges together.

Bake for 10 minutes in the preheated oven. Lower the temperature to 350 degrees and bake for 30 minutes more. Remove the pie from the oven, brush the top with the remaining cream, and return to the oven for 5 minutes. Serve with ice cream or heavy cream.

Blackberry Pie

4 cups blackberries	*2½ tablespoons butter*
4 tablespoons flour	*3 tablespoons orange juice*
1¼ cups granulated sugar	*Sour cream*
½ teaspoon grated orange zest	*Brown sugar*
Pastry for 2-Crust Pie (page 418)	

SERVES EIGHT

Pick over the blackberries and set them in a strainer or colander. Rinse them gently by placing the strainer in a large bowl of water, and carefully stirring the water while the berries float. Lift the strainer out of the water and allow the berries to drain, then arrange them carefully on paper towels to dry.

Preheat the oven to 425 degrees.

Place the drained berries in a bowl and sift the flour and sugar over them. Add the orange zest and toss the berries gently.

Roll out the dough into 2 circles and line a 9-inch pie plate with one. Add the berries, dot with butter, pour the orange juice over, and top with a lattice crust. Bake for 15 minutes in the preheated oven. Lower the heat to 325 degrees and bake for 20 minutes longer, or until the crust is nicely browned. Serve warm, topped with dollops of sour cream, and sprinkled with brown sugar.

Blueberry Pie

3½ cups blueberries

¾ cup granulated sugar

1½ cups light brown sugar

4 tablespoons plus ⅔ cup all-purpose flour

¼ teaspoon salt

3 tablespoons orange juice

1¾ cups sour cream

1 teaspoon vanilla extract

1 egg

½ recipe Pastry for 2-Crust Pie (page 418)

3 tablespoons finely chopped almonds

1 teaspoon ground cinnamon

¼ teaspoon grated nutmeg

8 tablespoons (1 stick) butter

SERVES EIGHT

Preheat the oven to 450 degrees.

Pick over and rinse the blueberries, then set aside to dry on paper towels. Combine the granulated sugar, ½ cup brown sugar, 4 tablespoons flour, and salt. Beat in the orange juice, sour cream, vanilla, and egg.

Roll out the dough and use it to line a 10-inch pie plate. Fold the blueberries gently into the sour cream mixture and spoon the filling into the pie shell. Bake for 35 minutes in the preheated oven.

In the meantime, prepare a topping for the pie by mixing together the remaining brown sugar, ⅔ cup flour, nuts, cinnamon, and nutmeg. Cut in the butter until the mixture resembles coarse crumbs. When the pie has baked for 35 minutes, remove it from the oven, arrange the topping evenly over the filling, and bake for 10 to 15 minutes more, or until the topping is nicely browned. Cool and serve at room temperature.

Brown Sugar Pie

12 tablespoons (1½ sticks)
    butter
4½ cups light brown sugar
¾ cup heavy cream

4 eggs
½ recipe Pastry for 2-Crust Pie
    (page 418)
Juice of 1 small lemon

SERVES EIGHT

Preheat the oven to 425 degrees.

Melt the butter over hot water. Place the sugar in a bowl, and stir in the melted butter and cream. Beat the eggs and add them to the sugar mixture, blending well.

Roll out the dough and line a 10-inch pie plate with it. Pour in the sugar filling carefully. Sprinkle the top with lemon juice. Bake in the preheated oven for 15 minutes, then lower the heat to 350 degrees and bake for 30 to 40 minutes longer, or until a knife inserted in the center comes out clean. Cool after removing from the oven. Serve at room temperature or chilled.

Butterscotch Meringue Pie

4 cups light brown sugar
8 tablespoons (1 stick) butter
1 cup all-purpose flour
8 eggs, separated

5 cups milk
1 teaspoon vanilla extract
½ recipe Pastry for 2-Crust Pie
    (page 418)

SERVES EIGHT

Beat the sugar and butter together in a heavy saucepan over medium heat until the mixture becomes thick and waxy, then remove pan from heat. Combine the flour with the egg yolks and milk. Beat thoroughly to blend the mixture and add to the sugar and butter. Return the saucepan to medium heat and cook, beating constantly, until the pudding is thick and smooth. Stir in the vanilla and cool to room temperature.

Preheat the oven to 325 degrees.

Pour the cooled pudding into the baked pie shell. Beat the egg whites until they form stiff peaks, and spread the meringue over the top of the pudding. Bake the pie in the preheated oven until lightly browned on top, about 10 minutes. Cool, chill, and serve cold.

Sweet Carrot Pie

7 medium carrots	1 tablespoon cornstarch
1½ plus 3 tablespoons cups water	½ cup heavy cream
2 cups granulated sugar	½ recipe Pastry for 2-Crust Pie (page 418)
2 egg yolks	
Juice and grated zest of 2 lemons	Whipped cream (optional)

SERVES EIGHT

Preheat the oven to 425 degrees.

Use a very fine blade to grate the carrots directly into 1½ cups water. Add the sugar, egg yolks, lemon juice and zest. Blend these ingredients thoroughly.

Mix the cornstarch with 3 tablespoons water until a smooth paste is formed. Add the cream to the cornstarch paste and stir this into the carrot mixture.

Roll out the dough and line a 10-inch pie plate. Spoon the carrot filling into the pie shell. Bake in the preheated oven for 20 minutes, then reduce the heat to 350 degrees and bake about 1½ hours more. The pie is done when bits of carrot removed from the center of the pie are tender and cooked through and most of the liquid has cooked away. Serve at room temperature with whipped cream, if desired.

Cherry Pie Like Mother Used to Make***

4 cups pitted sour cherries
1½ cups granulated sugar
5 tablespoons flour
⅛ teaspoon ground cloves

⅛ teaspoon grated nutmeg
¼ teaspoon ground cinnamon
2 tablespoons butter
Pastry for 2-Crust Pie (page 418)

SERVES EIGHT

Preheat the oven to 425 degrees.

Toss the cherries with a mixture of the sugar and flour. Sprinkle with the spices and toss lightly again. Roll out the pastry and use half to line a 10-inch pie plate. Spoon the cherries into the pie shell and dot with bits of butter. Top with a lattice crust cut from the remaining pie dough, and bake for 15 minutes in the preheated oven. Reduce the heat to 350 degrees and continue to bake for 25 to 30 minutes more. Serve cold or at room temperature.

Chess Pie

2¼ cups granulated sugar
2 tablespoons cornmeal
2 tablespoons flour
2 tablespoons grated lemon zest
Generous pinch salt
6 eggs

½ cup lemon juice
8 tablespoons (1 stick) butter, melted
⅓ cup milk
½ recipe Pastry for 2-Crust Pie (page 418)

SERVES EIGHT

Preheat the oven to 350 degrees.

Combine the sugar, cornmeal, flour, lemon zest, and salt. Beat in the eggs, lemon juice, butter, and milk in the order given.

Roll out the dough and use it to line a 9-inch pie plate. Carefully pour in the filling, and bake in the preheated oven for 60 to 70 minutes, or until the pie no longer looks moist in the center. Set the pie plate on a wire rack to cool. Serve at room temperature or chilled.

Cider Pie

For an unusual and tangy old-fashioned pie, try this.

½ recipe Pastry for 2-Crust Pie
(page 418)

1 cup Grandfather's Boiled
Down Cider (page 479)

1¾ cups maple syrup

1½ tablespoons butter

Pinch salt

4 eggs, separated

SERVES EIGHT

Preheat the oven to 400 degrees.

Roll out the pastry and place it in a 10-inch pie plate.

Simmer the reduced cider, maple syrup, butter, and salt for 3 minutes and then cool to lukewarm. Beat the egg yolks into the warm syrup. Beat the egg whites until they are stiff and fold them thoroughly into the egg yolk–cider mixture. Pour into the pastry shell and bake for 70 minutes. Serve at room temperature or chilled.

Fried Fruit Turnovers

YIELDS EIGHT FOUR-INCH TURNOVERS

These fried pies or turnovers may be made with any of the following fillings. Prepare Pastry for 2-Crust Pie (page 418). Roll out the dough and cut into 4-inch rounds. Place a generous tablespoonful of filling on each round. Moisten the edges of the dough, fold over, and press firmly together with the tines of a fork. Fry in ½ inch hot oil, turning once, until golden brown on both sides. Drain briefly on paper towels and serve.

Applesauce Filling

Place 2 cups applesauce, 3 tablespoons apple butter, 2 tablespoons maple syrup, and ⅛ teaspoon grated nutmeg in a small saucepan. Simmer until the mixture is quite thick—the filling should not seep out of the crusts.

Apricot Filling

Place 1 cup (about 30 small) dried apricots, ⅓ cup granulated sugar, 2 tablespoons lemon juice, ¼ teaspoon ground allspice, and 2½ cups water in a saucepan. Simmer until the fruit is tender and the liquid reduced to a thick syrup.

Prune Filling

Place 1 cup pitted prunes, ⅓ cup granulated sugar, 2½ tablespoons lemon juice, ⅛ teaspoon ground cloves, and 2½ cups water in a saucepan. Simmer until the fruit is tender and the liquid is reduced to a thick syrup.

Fruit Mincemeat Pie***

Pastry for 2-Crust Pie (page 418)

1 quart Fruit Mincemeat (page 373)

3 tablespoons butter, melted

2 tablespoons lemon juice

SERVES EIGHT

Preheat the oven to 425 degrees.

Roll out the pie dough, and use one crust to line a 9-inch pie plate. Spoon the mincemeat into the crust, and add the melted butter and lemon juice. Cover with the top crust, slashed in several places to allow steam to escape. Crimp the edges of the crust.

Bake for 20 minutes in the preheated oven, then lower the heat to 350 degrees and bake for 30 to 40 minutes more, or until the crust is golden brown. Serve hot.

Meringue Topped Ice Cream Pie

3 pints homemade or commercial ice cream

½ recipe Pastry for 2-Crust Pie (page 418)

7 egg whites

1 cup plus 1 tablespoon granulated sugar

2 teaspoons vanilla extract

SERVES EIGHT

Allow the ice cream to soften slightly, then pack it carefully into the pie shell and refreeze for at least 2 hours. To serve the pie, beat the egg whites until they form soft peaks. Beat in the sugar a little at a time until it is all absorbed, and add the vanilla. The egg whites should be smooth, glossy, and stiff. Heap this meringue over the top of the ice cream, brown briefly under the broiler until the meringue turns golden brown, and carry immediately to the table.

Pecan Pie

2 cups dark corn syrup

4 tablespoons flour

2½ tablespoons granulated sugar

5 eggs

2 tablespoons butter, melted

1¼ teaspoons vanilla extract

¾ teaspoon salt

½ recipe Pastry for 2-Crust Pie (page 418)

¾ cup chopped pecans

Whipped cream

SERVES EIGHT

Preheat the oven to 375 degrees.

Measure the corn syrup into a bowl, and stir in the flour and sugar, blending well. Beat the eggs until they are light and frothy, then beat them into the corn syrup mixture. Add the butter, vanilla, and salt.

Roll out the dough and line a 9-inch pie plate with it. Crimp the edges. Spoon the filling into the pie shell. Distribute the pecans evenly over the top. Place the pie in the oven, and immediately lower the heat to 350 degrees. Bake for 40 to 45 minutes. The pie is done when the center is set, but not firm.

Cool the pie to room temperature before chilling. Serve with sweetened whipped cream.

Grandmother's Mock Pineapple Pie***

Don't disclose the secret ingredient
in the filling of this superb pie
until after it has been devoured to the last crumb.

2 cups water

4 medium potatoes, peeled

2 cups granulated sugar

2 egg yolks

Juice and grated zest of 2 lemons

½ cup heavy cream

½ recipe Pastry for 2-Crust Pie (page 418)

Whipped cream (optional)

SERVES EIGHT

Preheat the oven to 425 degrees.

Place the water in a large bowl and, using a very fine grater, grate the potatoes directly into the water. This will prevent discoloration. Stir the sugar and egg yolks into the potatoes and water. Add the lemon juice and grated zest to the potato mixture. Blend all ingredients thoroughly before mixing in the heavy cream.

Line a 10-inch pie plate with pastry. Spoon the pudding mixture into the pie shell and bake for 20 minutes in the preheated oven; lower the heat to 350 degrees and bake about 1½ hours more. The pie is done when a few bits of potato removed from the center of the pie are no longer tough. Serve at room temperature with whipped cream, if desired.

Aunt Tizzie's Sliced Potato Pie

If you are feeling adventurous,
try this unusually tasty Early American dessert.

4 medium potatoes, peeled and thinly sliced

1½ cups granulated sugar

Juice of 1 lemon

¼ cup water

½ recipe Pastry for 2-Crust Pie (page 418)

½ cup dark brown sugar

1 tablespoon butter

SERVES EIGHT

Boil the potato slices in water over medium heat until they are barely tender. Take care not to cook them too much or they will break. Place the granulated sugar, lemon juice, and ¼ cup water in a saucepan. Simmer the mixture, stirring occasionally, for 5 minutes. Drain the potato slices well (any extra water will dilute the syrup) and carefully add to the sugar-lemon syrup. Bring the syrup to a boil, remove the pan from the heat and allow the filling to cool.

Preheat the oven to 425 degrees.

Roll out the dough and line a deep 10-inch pie plate. Arrange the cooled potato slices evenly over the crust and pour in the remaining syrup. Sprinkle brown sugar over the top of the pie and dot with the butter. Bake for 15 minutes in the preheated oven; lower the heat to 350 degrees and bake for 35 minutes longer. Serve at room temperature or chilled.

Mrs. Knott's Pumpkin Pie

*This orange-flavored pumpkin pie
has a lighter texture than most.
Stiffly beaten egg whites are folded into
the pumpkin custard to produce an airy filling.*

4 eggs

2 cups cooked and strained or
canned pumpkin

1 cup granulated sugar

¾ teaspoon grated orange zest

½ teaspoon ground cinnamon

4 tablespoons butter

⅓ cup orange liqueur

⅔ cup heavy cream, at room
temperature

1 tablespoon cornstarch

½ recipe Pastry for 2-Crust Pie
(page 418)

SERVES EIGHT

Separate the eggs, setting the whites in a mixing bowl. Mix
the yolks with the pumpkin, add the sugar, orange zest, and cinnamon, and beat for 5 minutes at medium speed of an electric
mixer.

Preheat the oven to 350 degrees.

Melt the butter over hot water, then cool to room temperature.
Add the butter and orange liqueur to the pumpkin mixture and
blend thoroughly. Stir in the cream. Beat the reserved egg whites
until they form stiff peaks, sprinkle with cornstarch, and fold into
the pumpkin mixture. Line a deep 10-inch pie plate with dough and
pour in the filling. Bake for 1 hour in the preheated oven. Chill
before serving. Top with whipped cream if desired.

Traditional Pumpkin Pie***

1½ cups cooked and strained or
canned pumpkin

1 cup dark brown sugar

½ cup light brown sugar

5 eggs

3 cups milk

¾ teaspoon salt

¾ teaspoon ground cinnamon

¾ teaspoon ground ginger

½ recipe Pastry for 2-Crust Pie
(page 418)

SERVES EIGHT

Preheat the oven to 400 degrees.

Combine the pumpkin, sugars, eggs, and milk in a large bowl. Stir in the salt and spices and mix all ingredients well. Line a 10-inch pie plate with the dough and pour in the pumpkin mixture. Bake in the preheated oven for 1½ hours, or until a knife blade inserted in the center comes out clean.

Ruth Ellen's Rhubarb Pie

12 stalks rhubarb

1 cup granulated sugar

⅓ cup lemon juice

Pastry for 2-Crust Pie (page 418)

1 teaspoon grated lemon zest

1 tablespoon flour

1 tablespoon butter

SERVES EIGHT

Use a sharp knife to cut or pull the thin outer skins (or ribbons) from the rhubarb stalks. Cut the stalks into ½-inch pieces. Place the sugar in a saucepan, stir in the lemon juice, and cook the mixture at low boil for 3 minutes. Add the rhubarb pieces to the lemon syrup and cook until the rhubarb is tender. Remove from the heat and allow the mixture to cool.

Preheat the oven to 425 degrees.

Roll out the dough and line a 10-inch glass pie plate with one crust. Carefully pour in the cooled rhubarb, sprinkle with lemon zest and flour, and dot with butter. Top with the second crust and crimp the pastry edges together. Slit the top crust in several places to allow steam to escape. Bake in the preheated oven for 20 minutes, then lower the heat to 350 degrees and bake for 30 to 35 minutes longer. Serve warm or at room temperature.

Old Kentucky Shoofly Pie***

*I was born in Kentucky
and molasses-flavored "Shoofly" is one
of my earliest and fondest food memories.
This is a good winter pie
—it can be prepared with ingredients
you have on your pantry shelf.*

1 cup molasses

1 cup simmering water

1¾ cups all-purpose flour

¾ cup light brown sugar or
maple sugar

¾ teaspoon baking soda

12 tablespoons (1½ sticks) butter

½ recipe Pastry for 2-Crust Pie
(page 418)

SERVES EIGHT

Mix the molasses and water until well blended. Sift together the flour, sugar, and baking soda. Use 2 knives to cut 10 tablespoons butter into the dry ingredients to form a coarse meal.

Preheat the oven to 375 degrees.

Roll out the dough, line a 9-inch plate loosely with it, and crimp the edges of the crust. Pour ⅓ cup of the molasses mixture into the pie shell, and sprinkle with ⅓ cup of the flour mixture. Alternate the layers, ending with the flour mixture. Dot the top of the pie with bits of the remaining butter. Bake for 50 minutes in the preheated oven. Serve warm or cool.

Custards and Puddings

Flower Petal Custard

1½ cups rose, marigold, or
    nasturtium petals, or any
    combination of these
  3 cups milk
    1-inch piece vanilla bean
  4 egg yolks, beaten

4½ tablespoons granulated sugar
  ¼ teaspoon grated nutmeg
  ¼ teaspoon salt
  1 teaspoon rosewater

SERVES EIGHT

Preheat the oven to 350 degrees.

If rose petals are used, be sure to cut off the bitter white ends at the bottom of the petals. Crush the flower petals in a mortar with a pestle and place them in a saucepan. Add the milk and vanilla bean and bring the mixture just to the boiling point.

Remove the vanilla bean. Mix the sugar, nutmeg, and salt. Beat the egg yolks and rosewater into the sugar mixture, and continue to beat as you add the scalded milk and flower petals, a little at a time.

Pour the custard into a baking dish. Set the baking dish in a pan with 1 inch of hot water. Bake in the preheated oven for 30 to 40 minutes, or until a knife inserted in the center comes out clean. Chill before serving.

Vanilla Custard

¾ cup granulated sugar
  8 egg yolks
1¾ cups milk

1¼ cups heavy cream
  ½ vanilla bean, split

YIELDS ABOUT FOUR CUPS

Place the sugar in the top of a double boiler. Add the egg yolks, beating until the mixture is thick and pale yellow. Combine the milk, cream, and vanilla bean in another saucepan, and bring to the scalding point.

Gradually add the milk and cream mixture to the sugar and eggs, stirring constantly. Set the custard over hot water, and continue to stir until the custard thickens enough to coat the spoon. Do not allow the mixture to boil or it will curdle.

Remove the pan from the heat and strain the custard. Allow it to cool somewhat, stirring from time to time. Serve warm or chilled.

Miss Philpot's Steamed Apricot Pudding

10 ounces dried apricots	2 cups all-purpose flour
½ cup dark rum	1 teaspoon baking powder
½ cup hot water	¼ teaspoon ground allspice
4 tablespoons butter	¼ teaspoon ground ginger
4 tablespoons shortening	½ teaspoon ground cinnamon
¼ cup light brown sugar	½ teaspoon grated nutmeg
¼ cup granulated sugar	½ teaspoon salt
2 eggs	½ cup chopped walnuts
½ cup unsulfured molasses	½ cup chopped pecans
1 teaspoon baking soda	½ cup currants

SERVES EIGHT TO TEN

Soak the apricots in water to cover for 30 minutes. Drain them well and chop coarsely. Bring the rum and the hot water to a boil over medium heat, boil for 1 minute, pour the mixture over the chopped apricots, and soak for 30 minutes more.

Cream the butter, shortening, and sugars together. Beat the eggs until they are light and fluffy and add to the creamed mixture along with the molasses. Drain the apricots, reserving the liquid. Dissolve the baking soda in this reserved liquid and add it to the molasses and creamed butter.

[437]

Sift the flour, baking powder, and spices together. Beat these dry ingredients into the creamed mixture until well blended, then fold in the apricots, walnuts, pecans, and currants.

Butter a 2-quart, tubular pudding mold and pour in the batter. Secure a sheet of aluminum foil over the top and cover tightly with the mold lid. Set the mold on a wire rack in a large kettle. Ring the sides of the mold with crushed aluminum foil to prevent it from tipping, then add enough boiling water to the kettle to reach ¾ of the way up the sides of the mold. Place another sheet of aluminum foil over the top of the kettle and cover with a tight-fitting lid.

Steam over medium-low heat for 2 hours, adding more boiling water as needed to keep the water level at the original depth. Lift the mold from the boiling water and remove the lid and foil cover. Press the top of the pudding lightly with your fingers. The pudding is done if it springs back when touched. If it feels sticky and looks underdone, recover and steam until the top springs back.

To serve, loosen the sides and center ring of the pudding and set a serving plate on top of the mold. Flip over quickly and shake the pan sharply. Serve the pudding hot with ice cream or Hard Sauce (page 471).

New Orleans Banana Bread Pudding

2 bananas, mashed	4 eggs, lightly beaten
1 cup granulated sugar	3 cups dry bread crumbs
2½ cups milk	½ cup diced citron
¼ cup sweet sherry	2 tablespoons butter
¼ teaspoon grated nutmeg	

SERVES EIGHT

Preheat the oven to 350 degrees.

Mix the bananas, sugar, milk, sherry, and nutmeg together. Beat in the eggs, then add the bread crumbs and citron. Blend the mixture thoroughly, and pour into a buttered casserole. Dot the top of the pudding with butter.

Bake, uncovered, in the preheated oven for 1 hour, or until the pudding is nicely puffed and brown, and the top seems fairly firm when lightly touched in the center. Serve cold or at room temperature.

Long Island Blueberry Pudding

2½ cups blueberries	1 teaspoon salt
4 cups sifted all-purpose flour	4 tablespoons butter
4 tablespoons granulated sugar	¼ cup molasses
8 teaspoons baking powder	1¾ cups milk

SERVES EIGHT

Rinse the blueberries and set them aside to drain. Combine the sifted flour with the sugar, baking powder, and salt and sift again. Cut the butter into the dry ingredients until the mixture resembles coarse meal. Stir the molasses into the milk and add to the flour and butter mixture a little at a time, stirring well after each addition. Dust the blueberries with flour and mix them gently into the batter.

Pour the pudding into a greased pudding mold, cover tightly with aluminum foil, and top with the cover of the mold. Set the mold in a deep kettle. Use crushed balls of aluminum foil around the top and bottom of the mold to keep it upright. Pour enough boiling water into the kettle to reach at least ¾ of the way up the sides of the mold.

Cover the kettle and steam the pudding for 2½ to 3 hours, adding more boiling water to the kettle from time to time if necessary to keep the water level constant. The pudding is done if the top springs back when lightly pressed with the fingers. If the top seems soft and sticky when you test it, seal the mold completely again as you did initially and continue steaming.

To unmold, gently slide a knife around the edges and center of the mold to loosen it. Set a serving plate over the top of the mold, flip over quickly, and shake once.

Serve the pudding hot or cold, topped with Maple Sauce or Hard Sauce (page 471).

Bread-Slice Christmas Pudding

Those of us who dote on bread pudding
bake 2 pans of this superior dessert
to serve 8 persons.

12–14 slices white bread	*1½ cups milk*
5 tablespoons butter	*½ cup light cream*
4 heaping tablespoons currants	*4 eggs*
4 tablespoons chopped citron	*¾ cup granulated sugar*
8 tablespoons orange marmalade	*⅛ teaspoon grated nutmeg*

SERVES FOUR TO SIX

Trim the crusts from the bread and butter each slice generously on one side. Butter a loaf pan and line it with 6 slices of the bread, placing the buttered sides against the pan. Spread the bread with 2 tablespoons of marmalade. Sprinkle 1 heaping tablespoon currants and 1 level tablespoon citron over the bread. Top with 2 more slices of bread and repeat the process until the pan is ⅔ to ¾ full. The final layer should be bread. Beat the milk, cream, eggs, sugar, and nutmeg together and pour just enough over the bread to cover the top slices. Let the pudding stand for 1 hour.

Preheat the oven to 375 degrees.

Place aluminum foil under the pan to catch drippings. Bake the pudding until the top is golden brown and the center is puffed, about 1½ hours.

Bring the pudding to room temperature and then chill it overnight. To unmold the pudding, soak the pan in 1 inch of hot water for 30 minutes, then carefully loosen the sides with a sharp knife and turn the dessert onto a glass plate. Chill and serve cold.

Steamed Carrot and Potato Pudding

*Steamed pudding is an interesting old
country dessert which contemporary gourmets
always find fascinating. This one is particularly
unusual and tasty.*

9 carrots, grated
2 potatoes, peeled and grated
1 cup chopped raisins
1 cup currants
1 cup dark brown sugar
1 cup all-purpose flour
1 teaspoon ground allspice

½ teaspoon salt
1 teaspoon baking soda
1 tablespoon hot water
1 egg
   Sherry, brandy, or whiskey
   Whipped cream or ice cream

SERVES EIGHT

Beat the carrots and potatoes, plus whatever juices result from grating, with the raisins, currants, sugar, flour, allspice, and salt. Mix the baking soda into the hot water and add it, along with the egg, to the pudding mixture. Mix well and pour the pudding into a well-greased, tubular pudding mold. Cover the top tightly with aluminum foil and top with the lid.

Place the mold in a deep kettle and arrange 2 thick circles of crushed aluminum foil around the bottom and top of the mold to prevent it from tipping. Fill the kettle with hot water to reach ¾ of the way up the sides of the mold, seal the kettle tightly with aluminum foil, and top with the kettle lid. Bring the water to a boil, lower the heat slightly, and cook at a slow boil for 3 hours, adding more hot water after 1½ hours if necessary to keep the water level at the original depth. Recover the kettle tightly and continue cooking.

The pudding is done when the top springs back when lightly pressed with the fingers. Loosen the edges of the pudding around the sides of the pan as well as around the tube. Place a plate over the mold, flip it over, and shake it hard to unmold the pudding. While the pudding is still warm, pour sherry, brandy, or other spirits generously over it. Bring it to room temperature, or chill it, and serve with whipped cream or ice cream.

Cake and Bread Pudding***

*This homespun dessert has the warm,
satisfying goodness of bread pudding
plus an unusually light texture.*

3 cups cubed pound cake or other
    cake

1 cup cubed white bread

2 eggs

⅔ cup granulated sugar

2 cups milk

¼ teaspoon grated nutmeg

½ cup raisins

1 tablespoon butter

SERVES EIGHT

Preheat the oven to 350 degrees.

Place the cake and bread in a buttered 8-inch-square glass baking dish. Beat together the eggs, sugar, milk, and nutmeg, and pour over the cake and bread. Mix in the raisins, dot with bits of butter and bake for 55 to 60 minutes.

Mrs. Knittle's Chocolate-Gingersnap Pudding

4 cups milk

2 cups soft, stale bread crumbs

1¼ cups granulated sugar

3 1-ounce squares unsweetened
    chocolate

6 egg yolks

4 tablespoons butter

½ teaspoon salt

1 teaspoon vanilla extract

6 ounces gingersnaps

¾ cup heavy cream, whipped

SERVES EIGHT

Preheat the oven to 350 degrees.

Place 3 cups of the milk in the top of a double boiler, add the bread crumbs, sugar, and chocolate. Cook the mixture over hot water, stirring frequently, until smooth. Lightly beat the egg yolks and combine with the remaining milk, butter, and salt. Combine the egg mixture with the hot liquid. Cook over hot water, stirring constantly, until the pudding thickens. Remove from the heat and stir in the vanilla.

Butter a glass baking dish and pour in about ⅓ of the pudding. Add ½ the gingersnaps, pushing them below the surface of the pudding. Pour more pudding over and add the remaining gingersnaps, pushing them down as before. This method keeps the gingersnaps from floating to the top. Pour in the rest of the pudding, and bake for 1 hour, or until the center of the pudding seems firm to the touch. Cool and chill. Serve very cold, topped with unsweetened whipped cream.

Steamed Chocolate-Whiskey Pudding

5 1-ounce squares unsweetened chocolate

11 eggs

5 egg yolks

13 slices good-quality white bread

1 cup heavy cream

½ pound (2 sticks) butter

4 tablespoons whiskey

1 cup ground blanched almonds

1¼ cups granulated sugar

SERVES TWELVE

Melt the chocolate in the top of a double boiler over boiling water. Beat together the eggs and egg yolks. Place the bread slices in a bowl, cover with the cream, soak for 10 minutes, and beat with a fork until fairly smooth. In a large mixing bowl, cream the butter until light and fluffy. Whip the bread mixture, whiskey, and eggs into the creamed butter. Mix in the chocolate, almonds, and sugar and continue to stir until the ingredients are well blended.

Pour the pudding mixture into a well-buttered, tall 3-quart pudding mold. Cover with a double thickness of aluminum foil and secure the foil with string. Set the mold in a large kettle and pour in enough boiling water to come ¾ of the way up the sides of the mold. Place another sheet of aluminum foil over the kettle and seal with a tight-fitting lid. Steam over medium-low heat, adding more boiling water as necessary to keep the water level at its original depth. After 1½ to 2 hours, lift the mold from the boiling water, remove the foil cover, and check to see if the pudding is firm by pressing the top lightly with your fingers. If it springs back, it is done. If it seems sticky, however, cover the mold again and steam until the top tests done. Then unmold and serve hot with ice cream.

Old-Fashioned Citron Meringue Pudding

4 cups milk

2 cups dry bread crumbs

4 eggs

¼ cup plus 6 tablespoons granulated sugar

¼ cup chopped citron

½ cup chopped golden raisins

¼ teaspoon mace

SERVES EIGHT

Preheat the oven to 350 degrees.

Stir the milk into the bread crumbs. Separate the eggs, reserving the whites in a mixing bowl. Beat the egg yolks until thick and pale yellow; beat in ¼ cup sugar. Add the soaked bread crumbs to the eggs and sugar, along with the citron, raisins, and mace. Stir well to blend. Pour the pudding into a buttered baking dish and bake for 1 hour and 20 minutes. Remove the pudding from the oven and allow it to cool to room temperature. Lower the oven temperature to 325 degrees.

Beat the egg whites until they begin to froth. Continue beating while gradually adding 6 tablespoons sugar. When all the sugar has been added, beat for 5 minutes longer. Heap the meringue in peaks on top of the pudding, making sure it is touching the sides of the dish. Return the pudding to the oven to bake at 325° F. for 20 minutes, or until the meringue is nicely browned. Serve warm or chilled.

Cornbread Pudding

2 cups cornbread crumbs

2 cups bread cubes (sweet bread is best)

2 cups milk

4 eggs

1 cup dark brown sugar

¼ cup molasses

½ teaspoon ground cinnamon

¼ teaspoon ground allspice

¼ cup chopped nutmeats

2 tablespoons butter

SERVES EIGHT

Preheat the oven to 350 degrees.

Place the cornbread crumbs and bread cubes in a buttered, ovenproof bowl. Beat together the milk, eggs, sugar, molasses, cinnamon, allspice, and nutmeats. Pour this mixture over the bread and stir gently until all of the bread cubes are well soaked. Dot with the butter, and bake for 1 hour in the preheated oven. Serve warm or chilled.

Steamed Date and Nut Pudding***

½ cup dark rum

1 cup water

1½ cups pitted dates

4 tablespoons butter

½ cup vegetable shortening

½ cup granulated sugar

¼ cup light brown sugar

2 eggs

½ cup unsulfured molasses

1⅓ teaspoons baking soda

2⅓ cups all-purpose flour

1¼ teaspoons baking powder

½ teaspoon salt

¼ teaspoon ground ginger

¼ teaspoon ground cloves

1 teaspoon ground cinnamon

¾ teaspoon grated nutmeg

1 cup chopped walnuts

SERVES EIGHT TO TEN

Mix the rum with the water in a small saucepan and boil for 1 minute. Pour over the dates and allow to stand for 30 minutes.

Cream together the butter, shortening, and sugars. Beat the eggs until fluffy and add, with the molasses, to the creamed mixture.

Drain the dates, chop them, and reserve the liquid. Stir the baking soda into the reserved liquid and allow it to dissolve before adding to the molasses-shortening mixture. Sift the flour, baking powder, salt, ginger, cloves, cinnamon, and nutmeg together and beat these dry ingredients into the creamed mixture until well blended. Fold the chopped dates and nuts into the batter.

Pour the batter into a well-buttered, 2-quart pudding mold, and secure the top with a tight cover of aluminum foil. Set the mold on a wire rack in a large kettle; crush aluminum foil around the sides of the mold to keep it upright. Add enough boiling water to the kettle to reach ¾ of the way up the sides of the mold. Place another sheet of aluminum foil over the top of the kettle and cover this with a tight-fitting lid. Steam the mold over medium-low heat, adding more boiling water as necessary to keep the water level at the original depth. After 2 hours of steaming, lift the mold from the boiling water, remove the foil cover, and press the top of the pudding with your fingers. If the pudding is firm and springy to the touch, it is done. If, however, the pudding is still very sticky, recover and steam until the top tests done. Serve hot with ice cream or Hard Sauce (page 471).

Turn-of-the-Century French Pudding

4 cups milk

2 cups dry bread crumbs

½ cup plus 6 tablespoons granulated sugar

4 eggs

Juice and grated zest of 1 lemon

4 tablespoons butter, melted

3 tablespoons strawberry preserves

SERVES EIGHT

Preheat the oven to 350 degrees.

Pour the milk over the bread crumbs. Stir in ½ cup sugar. Separate the eggs, reserving the whites in a mixing bowl. Beat the yolks lightly and add to the bread crumb mixture, along with the lemon juice and zest, and melted butter. Blend the mixture well, then pour into a buttered baking dish.

Set the baking dish in a pan filled with 1 inch of hot water. Bake for 2 hours, or until a knife inserted into the pudding comes out clean. Top with strawberry preserves. Cool a bit after removing from the oven. Lower oven temperature to 325 degrees.

Beat the egg whites until they begin to froth. Continue beating while gradually adding 6 tablespoons sugar. When all the sugar has been added beat for 5 minutes longer. Heap this meringue over the pudding and return to the oven to bake for 20 minutes, or until lightly browned. Serve the pudding warm or at room temperature.

Settler's First Indian Pudding***

This is the best Indian Pudding I've ever tasted—
but it really must be served with vanilla ice cream.

7 cups milk	*1½ teaspoons salt*
6 tablespoons butter	*1¼ teaspoons ground cinnamon*
¾ cup yellow cornmeal	*½ teaspoon grated nutmeg*
¼ cup granulated sugar	*Vanilla ice cream*
1 cup molasses	

SERVES EIGHT

Preheat the oven to 300 degrees.

Place 5½ cups milk in a saucepan and set the rest aside. Place over medium heat, and when hot, stir in the butter, cornmeal, sugar, molasses, salt, and spices. Cook, stirring constantly, for about 20 minutes, or until the mixture thickens.

Pour the pudding into a greased baking dish. Carefully pour the reserved 1½ cups milk on top of the pudding, allowing it to float without stirring it in. Bake in the preheated oven for 3 to 4 hours, or until the pudding is set. Serve hot with commercial or Old-Fashioned Vanilla-Custard Ice Cream (page 453).

Pudding in Haste

1 recipe Cornmeal Mush (page
  85)
Molasses
Melted butter

Milk or heavy cream
Ground cinnamon
Grated nutmeg

SERVES EIGHT

Serve individual bowls of steaming hot Cornmeal Mush. Set out pitchers of molasses, melted butter, hot or warm milk or cream, and shakers of cinnamon and nutmeg.

Rice Pudding Deluxe

*Here's a recipe that tastes better
when it is refrigerated overnight.*

4 cups Vanilla Custard (page
  436)
1 cup long grain rice
2½ cups boi'ing water
¾ teaspoon salt

2 cups peach preserves
4 tablespoons rum
1½ cups heavy cream
4 tablespoons granulated sugar

SERVES EIGHT

Prepare the Vanilla Custard as directed, and set it aside to cool. Meanwhile, add the rice and salt to the boiling water, cover, and cook over low heat for 15 minutes. Bite a grain of rice. If it has no hard center, it is ready. If it is a bit hard, recover and cook 5 minutes longer.

Fold the cooked rice into the custard and spoon half the mixture into the bottom of an attractive glass serving bowl. Thin the peach preserves with the rum, and spread half of this syrup over the rice custard. Add the remaining custard to the bowl and top with the remaining peach syrup. Refrigerate the pudding until well chilled, or overnight.

Just before serving, beat the cream until it thickens slightly, then gradually add the sugar and continue to beat until the cream is very thick. Spread the whipped cream over the rice pudding and serve immediately.

Whiskey Pudding

Farmhouse whiskey wasn't always
labeled "for medicinal purposes only"
as this fine old recipe attests.
This dessert must be refrigerated overnight,
so plan ahead.

4 egg yolks	*⅓ cup cold water*
1 cup granulated sugar	*⅔ cup rye whiskey*
¼ cup cold milk	*⅓ cup orange juice*
¾ cup hot milk	*¾ cup crumbled macaroons*
1½ tablespoons unflavored gelatin	*1 cup heavy cream, whipped*
	Candied Violets (page 466)

SERVES EIGHT

Beat the egg yolks and sugar until thick in the top of a double boiler. Beat in the cold milk and then the hot milk. Cook over boiling water, stirring constantly, for 10 minutes, or until the pudding thickens enough to coat the spoon.

Soften the gelatin in the cold water, stir in the whiskey and orange juice, and add to the custard in the top of the double boiler. Stir well. Place the macaroon crumbs in the bottom of a soufflé dish, spoon 7 tablespoons of whiskey custard over them, and refrigerate for 1 hour.

Fold the whipped cream into the remaining custard, spoon into the soufflé dish, and refrigerate overnight. Decorate with whipped cream and Candied Violets.

Sweet Potato Pudding

*Serve this spicy potato pudding
with vanilla ice cream.*

2 pounds sweet potatoes
1 banana
3 tablespoons butter, melted
3 eggs
1 cup granulated sugar
1 cup milk
6 tablespoons molasses

¼ teaspoon grated nutmeg
¼ teaspoon ground allspice
¼ teaspoon ground aniseed
½ teaspoon almond extract
1 cup buttered graham cracker crumbs

SERVES EIGHT

Preheat the oven to 350 degrees.

Scrub the sweet potatoes, place them in a saucepan, cover with water, and boil until soft. Drain, cool, peel, and mash the potatoes and place them in the large bowl of an electric mixer. Mash the banana and add to the sweet potatoes, along with the melted butter and eggs. Beat the mixture at low speed until thoroughly blended.

Stir in the sugar, milk, molasses, nutmeg, allspice, aniseed, and almond extract. Beat until the batter is smooth. Spread the graham cracker crumbs over the bottom and sides of a 10-inch pie plate. Spoon the batter over the crumbs and bake for 1¼ hours. Cut into wedges and serve hot or cold with vanilla ice cream.

Aunt Harriet's Baked Thanksgiving Pudding

3 tablespoons butter
3½ cups hot milk
3 cups dry bread crumbs
3 eggs
¾ cup dark brown sugar
⅔ cup molasses
½ teaspoon salt

¾ teaspoon ground cinnamon
¾ teaspoon ground cloves
½ teaspoon mace
2½ cups raisins
1½ cups currants
½ cup chopped nutmeats (optional)

SERVES EIGHT

[450]

Preheat the oven to 325 degrees.

Mix the butter into the hot milk, stir until melted, then pour the mixture over the bread crumbs. Beat the eggs until light and fluffy, and add to the bread crumbs, along with the brown sugar, molasses, salt, and spices. Stir until well blended, and mix in the raisins, currants, and nuts.

Pour the batter into a well-buttered, decorative pudding mold or other tubular mold. Bake for 3 to 4 hours. Test for doneness by pressing the top of the pudding lightly with the fingers. If it springs back, remove from the oven and cool. Serve with Hard Sauce (page 471) or Old-Fashioned Vanilla-Custard Ice Cream (page 453).

Ice Cream

How to Make Ice Cream

The time and trouble involved in making your own creamy ice cream is well worth the effort. The sweetness of just-picked fruits in thick, pure cream cannot be rivaled.

You will need a churn freezer, either electric or the hand-turned variety, large enough to make at least 2 quarts of ice cream. Both types come with metal freezer cans and directions for use. Also have rock salt or kosher salt and plenty of cracked ice on hand.

Pour your ice cream mixture through a sieve lined with cheesecloth into the metal freezer can provided with the churn. Be sure that the can is only $\frac{2}{3}$ full—the ice cream expands during the freezing process. Cover the can tightly and place it in the freezer tub. Crack ice into fine pieces and pack it, with the salt, in alternating layers around the freezer can—4 to 5 parts ice to 1 part salt is best. Follow the directions for churning provided with your electric freezer.

If your machine is hand-operated, connect the crank to the dasher and begin to turn in steady rhythm until the turning becomes extremely difficult. It can be served at this point as soft ice cream, if you like. If you prefer a firmer cream, take off the can cover carefully so that no salt water gets into the ice cream, remove the dasher, and pack the ice cream down firmly. Cover the can tightly with a sheet of aluminum foil, fill the hole in the can cover with a small cork or crushed aluminum foil, replace the top of the can, and secure as directed. Pour off as much water as possible from the churn and repack with fresh ice and more salt. Place folded newspapers on top to insulate the ice and keep it from melting too rapidly. Allow the ice cream mixture to stand about 2 hours before serving.

If you want to check the progress of the frozen cream, be sure to hold the freezer can down with one hand while you remove the cover. Otherwise, ice will slip beneath the can and you will not be able to secure the top of the freezer.

To achieve really first-rate ice cream, here are a few supplementary hints:

Use exact amount of sugar called for in the recipe—measure carefully. Too much sugar will slow the freezing process.

Supercreamy ice cream is achieved by folding in additional whipped cream after removing the dasher.

Old-Fashioned Vanilla-Custard Ice Cream***

3 cups heavy cream	*8 egg yolks*
1⅔ cups milk	*1 cup granulated sugar*
2-inch piece vanilla bean, split	*¼ teaspoon almond extract*

YIELDS ABOUT ONE AND ONE HALF QUARTS

Scald the cream and milk with the split vanilla bean. Beat the egg yolks and sugar in the large bowl of an electric mixer until the mixture is smooth and creamy. Pour the hot cream and milk into the egg yolks, a little at a time, beating constantly.

Heat this custard over very low flame until it thickens somewhat, stirring constantly. Do not allow it to boil or the egg yolks will curdle. Stir in the almond extract. Place cheesecloth in a large sieve and pour the custard through into the metal freezer can. Chill quickly and follow basic directions for How to Make Ice Cream (page 452).

Banana Split Ice Cream

Stir 3 mashed and sieved bananas into the custard before chilling. After removing the dasher and crank, stir in 6 ounces chocolate bits, 1½ cups coarsely chopped nuts, 1 pint hulled strawberries, 15 chopped maraschino cherries, and 1 cup heavy cream, whipped. Continue as directed.

Eggnog Ice Cream

Prepare the custard as directed, omitting the almond extract. While the custard is churning, soak 6 crushed macaroons in ¼ cup dark rum and whip 1 cup heavy cream with ¼ teaspoon grated nutmeg After removing the dasher and crank, fold in the rum-soaked macaroons and whipped cream. Continue as directed.

Mincemeat Ice Cream

Prepare the custard as directed, omitting the almond extract. While the custard is churning, soak 1½ cups Fruit Mincemeat (page 373) in ½ cup dark rum and whip 1 cup heavy cream. After removing the dasher and crank, stir in the mincemeat and whipped cream. Continue as directed.

Minted Pear Ice Cream

After removing the dasher and crank, stir in 2 cups chopped minted green pears and ¼ teaspoon essence of mint. Continue as directed.

Peach Ice Cream

While the custard is churning, peel and slice 8 peaches. Arrange the slices in a bowl, sprinkle with ½ cup sugar, and set aside for 30 minutes. Mash the peaches with a fork and let stand for 30 minutes longer. After removing the dasher and crank, stir in the peaches. Continue as directed.

Peppermint Ice Cream

After removing the dasher and crank, stir in ¾ pound finely crushed peppermint sticks. Continue as directed.

Strawberry Ice Cream

While the custard is churning, mash 4 cups hulled strawberries with ½ cup granulated sugar and let stand for 30 minutes. After removing the dasher and crank, stir in the strawberries. Continue as directed.

Strawberry-Cherry Ice Cream

While the custard is churning, mash 2 cups hulled strawberries with
¾ pound pitted, chopped Bing cherries. Sprinkle the fruits with ½
cup granulated sugar and let stand for 30 minutes. After removing
the dasher and crank, stir in the fruits. Continue as directed.

Chocolate Chip Ice Cream

4 cups heavy cream	1½ cups granulated sugar
2 cups milk	1 cup grated sweet chocolate
1-inch piece vanilla bean	¾ teaspoon almond extract
9 egg yolks	½ cup finely grated unsweetened chocolate

YIELDS ABOUT TWO QUARTS

Scald the cream, milk, and split vanilla bean. Beat the egg yolks
and sugar in the large bowl of an electric mixer until the mixture is
thick and pale yellow. Stir the sweet chocolate into the scalded milk
and cream and pour the hot liquid into the egg yolks, a little at a
time, beating constantly.

Heat the custard over very low flame, stirring constantly. Do
not allow it to boil or the egg yolks will curdle. When the steam
rises in sheets from the custard it is near the boiling point. Remove
the mixture from the heat and stir in the almond extract. Place
cheesecloth in a large sieve and pour the custard through into the
metal freezer can. Stir in the grated bitter chocolate while the mixture is still hot so the chocolate bits will melt partially. Chill quickly
and follow basic instructions for How to Make Ice Cream (page 452).

Chocolate Chip and Almond Ice Cream

Prepare the custard as directed for Chocolate Chip Ice Cream. After
removing the dasher and crank, quickly stir in ¾ cup blanched
almond slivers and 1 cup semisweet chocolate bits. Continue as
directed.

Raspberry Ice

1 cup water

2 cups granulated sugar

2 cups sieved raspberry puree

2 tablespoons lemon juice

YIELDS ABOUT ONE AND ONE HALF QUARTS

Boil the water and sugar for 5 minutes. Remove from the heat and cool. Add the raspberry puree and lemon juice. Pour this raspberry syrup into a metal freezer can. Chill quickly and follow basic directions for How to Make Ice Cream (page 452).

After removing the dasher, drain off the water, repack the churn with ice, and let stand 2 hours. If a large quantity of ice is not available, wrap the freezer can in a layer or two of newspaper, secure with tightly wrapped aluminum foil, then place in the freezer. Stir the raspberry ice with a fork every 15 minutes until it reaches the proper consistency for serving.

Note: Two cups of other fruit puree such as apricot, blackberry, blueberry, huckleberry, or peach puree, can be substituted for the sieved raspberry puree.

Orange-Lemon Ice

4 cups water

2 cups granulated sugar

1½ cups orange juice

½ cup lemon juice

¼ cup orange liqueur

YIELDS ABOUT TWO QUARTS

Boil the water and sugar in a large saucepan over medium heat for 5 minutes. Remove from the heat and cool. Add the orange and lemon juices and the liqueur. Place cheesecloth in a large sieve and pour the juice mixture through into a metal freezer can. Chill quickly and follow basic instructions for How to Make Ice Cream (page 452).

After removing the dasher, pack the sherbet in ice as directed. If a large quantity of ice is not available, wrap the freezer can in a layer or two of newspaper, secure with tightly wrapped aluminum foil, and place in the freezer. Stir the sherbet with a fork every 15 minutes until it reaches the proper consistency for serving.

Sassafras Ice***

4 good-size pieces sassafras root   *1½ cups granulated sugar*
3 cups water

YIELDS ONE TO ONE AND ONE HALF QUARTS

Boil the sassafras root and water for 3 minutes. Stir in the sugar and boil the mixture for 5 minutes longer. Remove from the heat, discard the roots, and cool the liquid. Place cheesecloth in a large sieve and pour the mixture through into a metal freezer can. Chill quickly and follow basic instructions for How to Make Ice Cream (page 452).

After removing the dasher, pack the sherbet in ice as directed. If a large quantity of ice is not available, wrap the freezer can in a layer or two of newspaper, secure with tightly wrapped aluminum foil, and place it in the freezer. Stir the sassafras ice with a fork every 15 minutes until it reaches the proper consistency for serving.

Snow Cream

Fresh, clean snow
Half and half cream
½ cup granulated sugar

Red vegetable coloring
Vanilla extract

SERVES EIGHT

Set out a clean bowl or basin during a snowfall to collect fresh clean snow. Fill 8 tall glasses or parfait cups with snow. Add as much cream as each glass will hold after it is packed with snow. Sprinkle each with a tablespoon of sugar and a drop of vegetable coloring and vanilla. Beat with a spoon and serve immediately.

Sweetmeats

Pulled Chocolate-Molasses Candy

2 cups light brown sugar
1 cup molasses
⅓ cup light corn syrup
2 tablespoons butter
⅔ cup water

¼ teaspoon salt
4 1-ounce squares unsweetened chocolate, melted
1 tablespoon vanilla extract

YIELDS ABOUT THREE DOZEN PIECES

Place the sugar, molasses, corn syrup, butter, water, and salt in a saucepan. Cook over low heat, stirring constantly, until the sugar dissolves. Continue to cook, stirring frequently, until the hard-crack stage (300 degrees on a candy thermometer). A small amount of syrup will turn brittle when dropped in cold water.

Remove the syrup from the heat and pour it onto a greased platter. Add the melted chocolate and the vanilla. As the candy begins to cool lift the edges with spatula and push them toward the center. Continue until the candy is cool enough to handle.

Lift the candy, fold it into manageable size, then begin to stretch and pull it into long ropes, folding after each pull. As you pull, the candy will begin to stiffen and grow lighter in color. Continue pulling until the taffy is brittle enough to snap. Break it into bite-size pieces.

Chocolate Divinity Fudge

2 cups granulated sugar
⅔ cup water
½ cup light corn syrup
2 egg whites
3 1-ounce squares unsweetened chocolate, melted

Pinch salt
1 teaspoon vanilla extract
1 cup coarsely chopped pecans

YIELDS ABOUT THREE DOZEN PIECES

Prepare a syrup by combining ½ cup sugar with ⅓ cup water. Boil the syrup until a small amount forms a soft but quite well-formed ball when dropped in a cup of cold water (about 238 degrees on a candy thermometer). Combine the rest of the sugar and water with the corn syrup and cook until a hard ball is formed when a bit is dropped in cold water (slightly over the hard-ball stage, about 252 degrees on a candy thermometer).

Remove the syrup from the heat and set it aside to cool slightly. Beat the egg whites until they are stiff but not dry; then beat in the sugar syrup, and continue to beat for 1½ to 2 minutes. Beat the second syrup into the egg white mixture until well blended. Allow the sweetened egg whites to cool. Fold in the melted chocolate, salt, vanilla, and chopped nuts. Turn the fudge into a well-buttered 8-inch square pan. Cool until firm and cut into serving pieces.

Penuche

3 cups granulated sugar	¼ teaspoon salt
½ cup hot milk	1 teaspoon vanilla extract
1¼ cup condensed milk	1 tablespoon grated orange zest
2 tablespoons light corn syrup	¾ cup coarsely chopped pecans
4 tablespoons butter	

YIELDS ABOUT THREE DOZEN PIECES

Place 1 cup sugar in a heavy skillet. Set over medium-high heat; keep the hot milk nearby. Combine the remaining sugar, condensed milk, corn syrup, butter, and salt in a large saucepan. Warm over medium heat, stirring occasionally. Watch the sugar in the skillet carefully and stir it from time to time until it browns, but do not let it burn. Remove the caramelized sugar from the heat and quickly stir in the hot milk. Hold the pan at arm's length because it may spatter. Return the skillet to the heat and cook, stirring constantly, until the mixture mixes, thickens, and forms a syrup.

When the sugar and milk mixture comes to a full boil, stir in the browned sugar syrup. Continue to cook at full boil until a bit of the mixture forms a well-formed or firm soft ball (but not a hard ball) when dropped into a cup of cold water (about 238 degrees on a candy thermometer).

Cool the mixture in the pan until the bottom of the pan feels lukewarm. Using a wooden spoon, stir, or beat thoroughly until the glossy shine disappears and the mixture turns creamy. Quickly stir in the vanilla, orange zest, and pecans, then turn out into a well-buttered pan. Mark into serving pieces before chilling for several hours. Cut into squares when cool and firm.

If your Penuche remains sticky after it has been chilled, it means that the candy had not reached a full soft-ball stage during boiling. This candy "cures" and will firm up if you refrigerate it several days.

Pralines

I use salted, toasted pecans
in this delectable candy because the salt
cuts the sweetness somewhat.

1 Recipe Penuche (page 460)   *3 cups salted toasted pecan halves*

YIELDS ABOUT TWO DOZEN PIECES

Prepare the penuche as directed. Stir in salted pecan halves with the vanilla and orange zest. Drop the mixture by tablespoons onto well-buttered cookie sheets. Allow the pralines to cool, then cover each in plastic wrap and refrigerate until firm.

Peanut Log

1 cup peanut butter
½ pound (2 sticks) butter
1 pound confectioners' sugar
  (4 cups)
6 tablespoons cocoa

2 teaspoons vanilla extract
  Sweet sherry
2 cups coarsely chopped salted
  peanuts

YIELDS ABOUT EIGHTEEN SLICES

Combine the peanut butter and butter in a saucepan and cook over low heat, stirring frequently. When the mixture melts and turns syrupy, remove from the heat and stir in the sugar, cocoa, and vanilla, blending thoroughly. Knead in as much sherry as necessary to make a smooth, but not sticky dough. Shape the dough into a log and roll it in the chopped peanuts until the log is completely covered.

Wrap the bar in plastic or wax paper and refrigerate until firm. Cut into slices before serving.

Old-Time Chocolate Fudge

3 1-ounce squares unsweetened chocolate, shaved fine

3 cups granulated sugar

¼ teaspoon salt

2 tablespoons light corn syrup

1 cup milk

3 tablespoons butter

1 teaspoon vanilla extract

1 cup coarsely chopped walnuts or pecans

YIELDS ABOUT TWO AND ONE HALF TO THREE DOZEN PIECES

Place the chocolate, sugar, salt, and corn syrup in a saucepan; stir in the milk. Cook over medium heat, stirring constantly, until the sugar dissolves. Continue to cook, stirring from time to time, until the mixture reaches 238 degrees on a candy thermometer, or forms a well-formed soft ball when a bit is dropped into cold water.

Remove the pan from the heat and add the butter, allowing it to melt without stirring it in. This is the tricky step in fudge-making. The fudge must stand until the bottom of the pan is warm, not hot, to the touch. When the chocolate mixture is lukewarm, add the vanilla, then beat with a wooden spoon until the glossiness begins to disappear. Quickly mix in the nuts, and turn out the fudge into a buttered 8-inch pan.

Cover with wax paper, mark into serving pieces, and chill until the fudge is cool and firm. Cut into squares before serving.

Chocolate Caramels

1½ cups heavy cream   *¾ cup light corn syrup*
1 cup granulated sugar   *¼ teaspoon salt*
3 1-ounce squares unsweetened chocolate, cut in pieces

YIELDS ABOUT THREE DOZEN

Place ½ cup cream in a saucepan, add the sugar, chocolate pieces, corn syrup, and salt. Cook the mixture, stirring constantly, until the sugar is dissolved. Scrape the sides of the pan to loosen any bits of sugar. Bring to a boil and continue cooking until hot enough to form a well-formed soft ball when a bit is dropped in cold water (about 238 degrees on a candy thermometer). Stir in another ½ cup cream and continue to cook until the mixture reaches the soft-ball stage once more. Stir in the remaining ½ cup cream. Continue to cook, stirring constantly, until the syrup reaches the hard-ball stage (250 degrees), or test by dropping a bit in a cup of cold water. The ball formed should be hard. Remove the caramel mixture from the heat.

Lightly butter a loaf pan, and pour in the candy, scraping the bottom but not the sides of the saucepan. Allow the caramel candy to rest undisturbed until it is cold. Use a knife to mark the loaf into ¾-inch squares. Turn it out of the pan onto a cold surface, set it right side up, and cut it cleanly through along the marked lines. Separate the candy and allow it to stand for 2 to 3 hours before wrapping each piece in plastic wrap.

CHOCOLATE-WALNUT CARAMELS

Add 1 cup coarsely chopped walnuts just after taking the caramel mixture from the heat.

CHOCOLATE-CARAMEL APPLES

Cool the Chocolate Caramel slightly in a lightly buttered bowl. Skewer 8 apples with wooden sticks and dip each into the caramel, turning to coat the entire surface. Place on well-buttered wax paper to dry and harden somewhat.

Candied Apples

8 apples

2 cups granulated sugar

⅔ cup light corn syrup

1 cup water

¼ teaspoon lemon juice

Red food coloring

YIELDS EIGHT

Place the sugar and corn syrup in a saucepan and mix in the water. Cook over low heat, stirring constantly, until the sugar is dissolved. Cook without stirring until the syrup reaches the hard-crack stage (300 degrees on a candy thermometer). Test by dropping threads of syrup into ice water. If the threads are brittle when removed from the water, the hard-crack stage has been reached.

Remove the syrup from the heat and stir in the lemon juice. Set the pan in cold water only long enough to stop it from boiling, then place it over hot water so that the syrup will stay liquid. Stir in as much food coloring as needed to make the syrup an attractive red color. Skewer the blossom ends of the apples on sticks and dip them one at a time into the syrup, twisting them around so that all surfaces are covered. Set the apples upside down on buttered foil or paper until the syrup hardens.

No-Cook Fondant Bonbons

These are fun and easy for children to make.

2½ cups confectioners' sugar

4 tablespoons butter, softened

2–3 tablespoons light corn syrup

½ teaspoon vanilla extract

¼ teaspoon salt

Lemon juice

Food coloring

Pecans, walnuts, or almonds

YIELDS ABOUT TWO DOZEN PIECES

Place the sugar, butter, corn syrup, vanilla, and salt in a large bowl. Use your hands to mix them together until well blended, then add as much lemon juice as necessary to make the dough kneadable, working it with the hands to a firm, smooth paste.

[464]

Divide the mixture into several smaller bowls, adding a few drops of different food coloring to each. Work the food coloring in with the hands until each dough is attractively colored and smoothly blended, then shape into small balls. Finish by squeezing a whole nut into the center of each bonbon.

Kentucky Bourbon Balls***

½ cup semisweet chocolate bits   ⅓ cup bourbon whiskey
1½ cups confectioners' sugar   1½ cups coarsely chopped pecans
3 tablespoons light corn syrup   3¾ cups crushed vanilla wafers

YIELDS SIXTY SMALL BALLS

Melt the chocolate bits over hot water. Sift the confectioners' sugar into a large bowl. Stir the corn syrup into the whiskey and add the mixture, along with the melted chocolate, to the sugar. Mix in the nuts and crushed wafers, stirring thoroughly to blend.

Use your hands to shape the candy into small balls, then dip the balls into additional confectioners' sugar. Store in an airtight box.

Popcorn Balls

*Popcorn balls are fun to make
and may be used to decorate a Christmas tree.
Tie these plastic-wrapped balls, as well as cookies,
nuts, gumdrops, candy canes, and homemade candies
to the branches and nibble the decorations
during the twelve days of Christmas.*

8 quarts lightly salted popcorn   4 cups granulated sugar
1 cup light corn syrup   1 tablespoon vanilla extract
1 cup water

YIELDS ABOUT TWO DOZEN

Prepare the popcorn and set it aside. Place the corn syrup and water in a saucepan and bring the mixture to a boil, taking care to remove any loose sugar crystals that may form along the sides of the pan. Cook the syrup at a full boil until it reaches a well-formed but still pliable ball when a bit is dropped into a cup of cold water (238 degrees on a candy thermometer). Remove the syrup from the heat, stir in the vanilla, and cool.

When the syrup is still warm but cool enough to handle, pour it over the popcorn. Gently stir until all the popcorn is coated. Spread butter generously over your hands and shape the popcorn into 3-inch balls. Cool on a well-greased cookie sheet, then cover each ball in plastic wrap, leaving several inches of wrap on either end to be twisted and secured in candy-kiss fashion. Store in an airtight container.

Frosted Stuffed Dates

24 dates, pitted
12 walnut halves

1 recipe Lemon Icing (page 415)

YIELDS TWO DOZEN

Slit the dates and stuff each with a walnut half. Frost with Lemon Icing. Chill and serve cold.

Candied Violets and Rose Petals

These delicate sugary flowers and petals will add a professional touch to your cakes or desserts.

Use freshly picked violets and float them gently in water to rinse them. Drain on paper towels. Beat an egg white with 1 table-spoon of water. Dip the violets one at a time into the egg white, making sure that the petals are well coated. Set each violet, flower side up, on a plate after dipping, and sprinkle it carefully with granulated sugar. Allow the candy coating to dry thoroughly before storing the violets in an airtight container.

Rose petals may also be candied this way. Be sure to snip off the bitter white ends of each petal before proceeding.

Roasted Salted Nuts

1 pound raw peanuts or other raw nuts

4 tablespoons vegetable oil
Salt

Preheat the oven to 400 degrees.

Arrange the nuts on a cookie sheet, sprinkle with the oil, and stir to coat well with the oil. Roast in the preheated oven, stirring occasionally, until the nuts are golden brown. Remove from the oven and salt to taste while the nuts are still hot.

Glazed Nuts

2⅔ cups granulated sugar
1 cup water
⅓ teaspoon cream of tartar

Pinch salt
1 pound walnut halves, blanched almonds, or other whole nutmeats

Combine the sugar and water in a small saucepan, stir in the cream of tartar and salt. Cook the mixture, stirring constantly, until it reaches the hard-crack stage (300 degrees on a candy thermometer). Test by dropping a bit of the boiling syrup in cold water. If the threads are brittle and snap sharply, remove the syrup from the heat and set the pan in cold water to stop further cooking. Quickly set the pan over hot water to keep the syrup from hardening. Dip the nutmeats one at a time into the syrup to glaze them and place on a greased surface to cool and harden. In damp weather, store the nuts in a dry, airtight container.

Chocolate-Covered Nuts

1 pound shelled almonds
1 cup sweet or semisweet
  chocolate bits

1 tablespoon butter

Roast the almonds according to directions given in Roasted Salted Nuts (page 467) but omit the salt added after roasting. Melt the chocolate bits and butter together over hot water. Dip the nuts, one at a time in the chocolate, drain off the excess chocolate mixture, and arrange on a lightly greased surface until the chocolate coating hardens.

Sugared Nuts

2 egg whites
1 tablespoon water

1 pound whole nutmeats
Granulated sugar

Beat the egg whites lightly with the water. Dip the nutmeats into the mixture, allowing any excess to drip off. Arrange on a platter and sprinkle evenly with sugar. Allow the nuts to dry before storing in an airtight container.

Sautéed Sunflower Seeds

3 cups hulled sunflower seeds
2 tablespoons butter or vegetable
  oil

2 cloves garlic, halved

Shell the sunflower seeds and place them in the skillet with the butter or oil and the garlic. Stir over low heat until the seeds begin to pop. Eat hot or cold.

Sweet Sauces and Syrups

Apple Parings Sauce

*Spoon this thin sauce over warm apple pie
or spread it on buttered toast at breakfast—
either way it's delicious.*

4 cups apple peels and cores from
   thoroughly washed fruit

4 cups water

1 cup granulated sugar

1 cup light brown sugar

YIELDS ONE CUP

Cover the apple parings and cores with the water and bring to
a boil in an enamel saucepan. Boil over medium-high heat until the
liquid is reduced by half. Strain through a cloth, add the sugars, and
cook at a rolling boil until the sauce jells.

Brandy Sauce

1¼ cups dark brown sugar

⅓ cup water

2 egg yolks

⅓ cup heavy cream, whipped

3 tablespoons brandy

Pinch salt

YIELDS TWO CUPS

Bring the sugar and water to a boil in a saucepan, and cook
until the syrup forms a soft ball when a bit is dropped in cold water
(250 degrees on a candy thermometer). Remove the syrup from the
heat. Beat the egg yolks until thick, then add the syrup a little at a
time, beating constantly. Continue to beat until the mixture thickens
and cools. Mix in the whipped cream, brandy, and salt. Serve over
fruit pudding.

Grandmother's Chocolate Sauce

*Here's the sauce to make ice cream and/or
plain cake uncommonly delicious.*

8 1-ounce squares unsweetened
    chocolate
4 tablespoons butter
2 cups heavy cream

2 cups granulated sugar
1 teaspoon vanilla extract
1 teaspoon grated orange zest
2 tablespoons dark rum

YIELDS FOUR AND ONE HALF CUPS

Place the chocolate and butter in a heavy saucepan and stir constantly over low heat until the chocolate is melted.

Pour the cream into a bowl and stir in the sugar. Add to the melted chocolate, raise the heat to medium, and continue to cook, stirring constantly, until the sauce begins to boil. Reduce the heat to low and simmer until the sauce thickens slightly, then add the vanilla, orange zest, and rum. Serve hot.

Grandmother's Chocolate–Peanut Butter Sauce***

8 1-ounce squares unsweetened
    chocolate
4 tablespoons butter
4 tablespoons peanut butter

2 cups heavy cream
2 cups granulated sugar
1 teaspoon vanilla extract

YIELDS FOUR AND ONE HALF TO FIVE CUPS

Place the chocolate and butter in a heavy saucepan and stir constantly over low heat until the chocolate is melted. Add the peanut butter and continue stirring until the chocolate and peanut butter are well blended.

Mix the cream and sugar and add to the chocolate mixture. Raise the heat to medium and stir constantly until the sauce comes to a boil. Reduce the heat and simmer until the sauce thickens slightly, then stir in the vanilla. Serve hot over ice cream.

Hard Sauce

8 tablespoons (1 stick) butter
1½ cups confectioners' sugar

2–3 tablespoons brandy, rum, or whiskey

YIELDS ABOUT ONE CUP

Beat the butter until light and fluffy, then gradually cream in the sugar. Add brandy, rum, or whiskey to taste, and blend in thoroughly.

Lemon Curd

*This sauce is unusually tasty
when it is spread on toast as our
English forefathers did.*

Grated zest and juice of 2 lemons
4 tablespoons butter

1 cup granulated sugar
2 eggs

YIELDS ONE AND ONE HALF CUPS

Place the zest, juice, butter, and sugar in the top of a double boiler. Stir over low heat until the sugar is completely dissolved. Beat the eggs and add them to the pan. Cook over hot water stirring constantly, until the lemon curd thickens. Do not allow it to boil. Spoon into a sterilized jar and refrigerate. Serve on toast.

Maple Sauce

*To create an exceptional dessert,
pour a bit of this delectable sauce
over apple pie or bread pudding.*

1½ cups maple syrup
4 tablespoons butter

1 cup heavy cream

YIELDS TWO AND ONE HALF CUPS

Place the maple syrup, butter, and cream in a saucepan. Bring to a boil, stirring frequently. Cook at a full boil for at least 2 minutes. Serve hot or warm.

Plum Pudding Sauce

1½ cups light brown sugar
1½ tablespoons quick-cooking
   tapioca
⅓ teaspoon salt

2¼ cups boiling water
2 eggs
2 tablespoons butter
3 1-ounce jiggers brandy

YIELDS FOUR CUPS

Mix the sugar, tapioca, and salt together in the top of a double boiler set over boiling water. Slowly add the boiling water to the sugar mixture, stirring constantly as you pour. Cook 5 minutes, stirring constantly.

Beat the eggs to a lemony froth. Stir the hot syrup into the eggs a little at a time. Return the mixture to the top of the double boiler. Continue to cook, stirring constantly for 5 minutes, or until the mixture thickens.

At serving time, reheat the sauce, if necessary, in one pan and the butter and brandy in another. Pour the brandy mixture on top of the sauce, set it aflame and carry to the table. Serve hot over plum pudding or Bread-Slice Christmas Pudding (page 440).

Raspberry Sauce

*Try this sauce spooned over fresh fruit
or pound cake topped with ice cream.*

2 cups raspberries
¾ cup granulated sugar

3 tablespoons raspberry, grape,
   or apple jelly

YIELDS TWO AND ONE HALF CUPS

Carefully rinse the raspberries, drain them thoroughly, and toss lightly with the sugar. Allow to stand for 30 minutes. Use the back of a spoon to press the sugared berries through a fine sieve. Warm the jelly and stir it into the pureed fruit.

Brown Sugar Syrup

2 cups light brown sugar   *4 tablespoons butter*
1½ cups boiling water

YIELDS ABOUT THREE CUPS

Place the brown sugar in a saucepan, stir in the boiling water, and bring to a boil again. Add the butter and cook, stirring frequently, until the syrup thickens and reaches the desired consistency. Serve over pancakes, waffles, scrapple, or plain puddings.

Shaker Cider Sauce

Serve hot over puddings, dessert omelets, and egg-bread.

2 tablespoons butter   *3 cups Grandfather's Boiled-*
2 tablespoons flour   *Down Cider (page 479)*
                                         5 tablespoons sugar

YIELDS ABOUT THREE CUPS

Melt the butter in a skillet and blend in the flour until smooth. Add the boiled-down cider all at once and bring to a boil, stirring constantly. Sprinkle the sugar over the sauce and stir at a low boil until the sugar is dissolved.

Drinks

Old-Fashioned Lemonade

8 cups water
  Juice of 12 lemons
8 tablespoons granulated sugar

Lemon-flavored soda
8 sprigs mint
  Lemon sherbet (optional)

SERVES EIGHT

Bring 1 cup water to a boil. Add the lemon juice and sugar and boil 3 minutes. Stir in the cold water. Chill the mixture. At serving time, strain the lemon mixture into 8 tall glasses, and fill with the cold lemon soda. Top each glass with a scoop of sherbet if desired.

Old-Fashioned Orangeade

8 cups orange juice
1 cup granulated sugar
½ cup lemon or lime juice

Water, club soda, or ginger ale
Mint leaves (optional)

SERVES EIGHT

Bring 1 cup orange juice to a boil, remove from the heat, and stir in the sugar. Pour into a small pitcher and chill. Stir in the remaining orange juice and the lemon or lime juice. Fill 8 tall glasses with ice; strain in the orangeade, filling the glasses ¾ full and add water, club soda, or ginger ale to the brim. Garnish with mint leaves.

Orangeade with Mint

8 cups orange juice
½ cup lime juice
¼ cup lemon juice
⅔ cup granulated sugar or more to taste

Club soda or ginger ale
8 orange slices
8 sprigs mint

SERVES EIGHT

Combine the citrus juices and sugar. Fill 8 tall glasses with ice; pour in the orangeade, filling the glasses ¾ full and add club soda and ginger ale to the brim. Slit the orange slices halfway through and place one on the edge of each glass. Stand 1 mint sprig in each glass as decoration.

Berry Cooler

1½ cups raspberries, blackber-
    ries, or strawberries, alone
    or in combination
¾ cup heavy cream

¾ cup milk
4 ice cubes
2 sprigs mint

SERVES TWO

Rinse and hull the berries. Rub through a fine strainer and discard the seeds. Place the puree, cream, milk and ice cubes in a blender container and blend until smooth. Serve immediately, topped with a mint sprig.

Raspberry-Orange Juice

2 cups fresh raspberries or
    1 package frozen

6 cups orange juice

SERVES EIGHT

Puree the raspberries by forcing them through a fine sieve with the back of a spoon and stir into the orange juice. Serve icy cold.

Note: Strawberries may be substituted for the raspberries.

Deep-South Eggnog

12 egg yolks
 2 cups superfine sugar
 1 fifth bourbon whiskey
 1 cup cognac

1 cup light rum
2 cups milk
6 cups heavy cream
   Grated nutmeg

YIELDS ABOUT TWO QUARTS

[477]

Beat the egg yolks until they are thick and pale yellow. Beat in the sugar until it is well absorbed. Chill the mixture for at least 2 hours.

Place the egg yolk and sugar mixture in a large punch bowl. Gradually add the bourbon, cognac, and rum, stirring constantly to blend well. Mix in the milk and 3 cups cream.

Beat the remaining 3 cups cream until stiff. Pipe through a decorative tube of a pastry bag onto the surface of the eggnog. Sprinkle with grated nutmeg and serve immediately.

Mulled Cider

4 2-inch cinnamon sticks
24 whole cloves
1 gallon apple cider
1 cup light or dark brown sugar

2 teaspoons ground allspice
Grated nutmeg
Butter (optional)

SERVES EIGHT

Tie the cinnamon sticks and cloves in a cheesecloth bag. Heat the cider, stir in the sugar, the cheesecloth bag, and the allspice. Simmer the cider for 20 minutes. Ladle into mugs and sprinkle with nutmeg. A bit of butter can be added to each serving if you like. Serve immediately.

Mint Tea

6 cups boiling water
2 4-inch cinnamon sticks
4 whole cloves

4 whole allspice
2 cups mint leaves
Honey (optional)

SERVES FOUR

Bring the water, cinnamon, cloves, and allspice to a boil. Boil for 1 minute. Stir in the mint leaves. Remove from the heat and steep for 5 minutes. Strain into cups. Sweeten with honey if desired.

Orange Tea

6 tea bags
10 cups boiling water
2 cups orange juice

Sugar to taste
8 mint sprigs
8 orange slices

SERVES TEN

Place the tea bags in an enamel pan. Cover with boiling water and steep for 5 minutes. Remove the tea bags and add the orange juice and sugar. Chill well. Fill 10 glasses with ice cubes and divide the chilled tea between them. Garnish with mint sprigs and orange slices.

Teaberry Tea

Hidden away in the still forests,
these glossy, green leaves with the cheery,
cherry red berries provide a refreshing nibble.

30 teaberry leaves
6 cups boiling water

Honey or granulated sugar

SERVES FOUR

Crush or crumble the leaves and place them in a small glass or enamel pot. Pour boiling water over the leaves and steep for 3 minutes. Strain into teacups. Sweeten with honey or sugar.

Grandfather's Boiled-Down Cider

4 quarts cider

YIELDS THREE CUPS

Pour the cider into a large kettle and place over medium heat. Allow the liquid to cook at low boil until it evaporates to 3 cups Use as indicated in recipes.

[479]

Sassafras Tea

Northeastern Pennsylvania is a land of plenty.
Most of my childhood was spent there,
and I cherish memories of fruit-laden orchards
and field after golden field of heavy rippling grain.
One of the pleasant bounties nature provided
was a sassafras tree which grew
just around the bend from my house,
near the edge of the forest.
The rusty colored sassafras roots provided us
with many a pot of fragrant tea.
Sassafras—warming in the winter,
cooling when iced in the summer,
and marvelous as a spring tonic.

2 3-inch pieces sassafras root or
  bark

4 cups boiling water
  Granulated sugar or honey

SERVES FOUR

Scrub roots and cut into short pieces. Boil the roots and water for 15 minutes or until the tea is red and strong. Serve hot sweetened with honey or sugar, or chill and serve with ice.

PRESERVING FOODS FOR THE WINTER

IF YOUR GARDEN has been properly planned, planted, and cared for (and barring any unpleasant excesses of nature), you are almost certain to have surplus fruits and vegetables as late August rolls around and crops hang heavy waiting for harvest. Your gathering basket should be overflowing with juicy tomatoes, tender squash, and tasty green beans, corn, peppers, cabbage, and eggplant, as well as succulent fruits ripening on trees and vines. Your physical and emotional investment is far too great to allow these treasures to languish on the vine. Now is the time to consider a safari into the wonderful world of food preservation.

Once you experience the satisfaction of nurturing, preserving, and feasting, year-round, on your own home-grown, hand-preserved produce, you'll never again supermarket-shop without a twinge of sadness. The intervention of various middlemen will seem an intrusion—an unfortunate obstruction to the natural order of things.

Contemplation of a root cellar full of fruits and vegetables, all in a state of slumber awaiting your gastronomic pleasure is guaranteed to bring a few secret smiles of satisfaction during the long, cold winter months. You'll no doubt also find yourself sneaking to the cellar to look proudly at bottles of home-dried herbs, shelves full of sparkling jars of cherries, tomatoes, and pickled pears, and your freezer full of corn, asparagus, blackberries, and rhubarb. Feel a bit smug if you wish. It's a pardonable transgression and not at all blameworthy, especially for the novice.

There are five methods of home storage which range from ridiculously easy to quite complicated. None, however, is beyond your capabilities. These methods are: (1) Outdoor storage; (2) Indoor storage; (3) Pickling; (4) Freezing; and (5) Canning. Most vegetables lend themselves to several of these methods. In addition to the foods you grow yourself, you may wish to take advantage of the economically priced surplus of local farmers. Fruits and roots that are a glut on the market at the end of the summer are rarities, and priced accordingly, through the winter and spring. If you have the time and/or money, it may be worthwhile to expend the energy involved. You'll be glad you did.

Outdoor storage

THERE ARE MANY garden vegetables that may be made perfectly comfortable outdoors during the long winter months and harvested with relative ease as you need them. These may be left in the ground where they grew, or stored in pits, mounds, boxes, or barrels insulated with straw, leaves, or sawdust. It is tremendously exciting, especially to the urban dweller new to the world of natural subsistence, to trudge to the garden on Christmas Day, brush aside a light layer of snow, and harvest parsnips, leeks, horseradish, Chinese cabbage, kale, turnips, potatoes, apples, and pears.

A sense of pride and fulfillment are not the only rewards for the outdoor storage enthusiast. This is also one of the most inexpensive methods of preserving foods. If you live in a part of the country where winter temperatures average about 20 to 30 degrees and snowfall does not generally exceed 12 to 15 inches (unless you enjoy digging for your dinner), outdoor storage is certainly one method with which you should experiment. Consult, with the county agent, the local extension service of the state agricultural college, the weather bureau and/or local friends, neighbors, and farmers to determine the desirability of storing foods outdoors during the winter, as well as the outdoor storage methods that have worked best for them.

The Mulching Method

It is possible to winter-harvest parsnips, salsify, horseradish, kale, chard, leeks, collards, and most root vegetables by using this easiest of all methods. Simply leave the vegetables in the ground where they grew and mulch them heavily with a foot to a foot-and-one-half of leaves. Dig through the snow and the warming blanket of leaves to the vegetables whenever you wish to supplement your food supply with the "garden-fresh" variety. The leaves prevent the ground from freezing and harvesting is easy. Be warned, however, that if you live in the far northern states or if the winter happens to be an unusually severe one, your vegetables may freeze and be rendered inedible, with the exception of the parsnips, salsify, and horseradish, which actually improve in flavor when frozen. For this reason it is best to store only a portion of your harvest in this manner and the remainder in one of the more conventional storage methods.

If you have late-maturing Chinese cabbage or celery growing in your garden, a variation of the above method may be used to prolong harvesting for a month or so after the hard frosts begin. Leave the vegetables where they grew but mound an additional 3 to 4 inches of soil around the base of each plant before the first frost. More soil should be banked up and around the tops of the plants as the frosts become more severe. This process will also bleach the vegetables.

Mounds

Select a well-drained site and spread a 4-inch layer of straw over a section of earth about 1 yard square. Cover this layer of bedding with hardware cloth or heavy metallic screening to discourage un-authorized feedings by all types of rodents. Arrange 2 to 3 bushels of winter apples and pears or root vegetables (fruits and vegetables should be stored in completely separate mounds, but two fruits and two vegetables may be stored in a single mound, one on the right and one on the left, separated by straw). Mound the produce on the hardware cloth and pat a thick layer of straw or leaves over the entire mound. Cover this insulating layer with 4 inches of earth tamped over everything but the very top of the mound. Build up the straw in a 4- to 5-inch stack over the center of the mound. Pack more soil around the sides of this stack and cover with a large flat rock or a piece of board held in place by a rock.

Tamp the soil over the entire mound carefully but firmly with the back of a shovel until it is well packed. Scatter 6 inches of straw over all. Small mounds like this one need no additional ventilation and are easier to harvest than larger ones.

Mounds for storing cabbage are somewhat different and not nearly so easy to harvest. Pull heads of cabbage with their roots from your garden and arrange them side by side, heads down, in a row. Cover with a mound of earth. Do not tamp down. Dig a shallow trench around the mound.

Cover the mound with 4 inches of straw and black plastic. To harvest, dig the cabbages out one at a time from one end of the mound.

The Framed Trench

This is actually a method of replanting cabbage in a shallow trench, building a frame around the vegetables and insulating them with straw. Dig a long and narrow trench, 8 inches deep. Pull cabbage plants from your garden with the roots intact. Replant them, close together, patting the soil dug from the trench tightly around their roots. Sink 2- to 3-foot sturdy stakes about 8 inches into the ground around the trench. Nail boards to these stakes and crisscross the top with poles to form a framework with several inches of clearance above the cabbage heads. Pile earth around the boards and heap 2 to 3 feet of straw over the poles.

Barrel Storage

Place a barrel on its side on top of the ground in a well-drained place. Arrange root vegetables in layers of straw and secure the top (which is in this case actually the side) of the barrel. Cover with three layers of straw and two of soil, starting and ending with the straw.

[485]

Root cellars

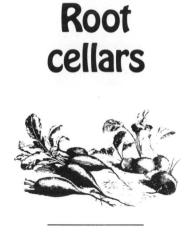

AN ECONOMICAL, CONVENIENT, and practical way to store root vegetables as well as other vegetables and fruits is, not surprisingly,
in a root cellar. Potatoes, onions, carrots, parsnips, turnips, kohlrabi, beets, pumpkins, squash, apples, and pears are all ideal tenants
for long-term residence in a root cellar. Tomatoes, red and green
peppers, and citrus fruits will keep for shorter periods of time.

What Constitutes an Ideal Root Cellar

1. A dirt floor is preferable but a slatted wooden floor set several inches above a concrete floor will do nicely. If installing a complete slatted wooden floor is too expensive or inconvenient, place
boards on concrete blocks or bricks. The idea is to permit ventilation under the boxes of produce. Never place food on a concrete
floor or against a concrete wall or your produce will mildew.

2. Most vegetables and fruits need consistently low temperatures and high humidity to ensure maximum preservation. Indoor
storage space should have one or two windows which may be opened
or closed to regulate temperature, air flow, and moisture. Place one

thermometer in the coldest part of the root cellar and another outside the house. Check daily (when you gather the fruits and vegetables you need for the day's meals) to see if the temperature in the cellar is as low as it was the day before. If not, open the window to permit entry of more cold air. On days when the outside temperature rises above the desired root cellar temperature, be sure to close the window to prevent the storage space from warming up. In general, root cellar temperature should be no higher than 32 degrees. If winter temperatures are likely to rise above 25 to 30 degrees for protracted periods of time, consider other methods of food preservation.

3. The ideal root cellar should have at least one wall of shelves. Since heat always rises this will enable you to arrange the fruits and vegetables that need to be kept coolest on the lower shelves, while the less frigid ones nestle on the higher shelves.

4. In addition to proper ventilation and temperature maintenance root cellar–stored foods need proper humidity to prevent shriveling. Do plan on a few galvanized pans of water set in front of the ventilation and/or a liberal covering of damp sawdust or straw for the floor of the storage place.

Locations for Root Cellars

If your farm and garden plans are in the just-dreaming stage, you are perhaps more fortunate than you realize. If you are planning to purchase a farm or a house in the country, an awareness of the desirability of a root cellar may help you to seek a home with existing storage space. Many Early American homes have no proper or finished basement but merely an excavated space with dirt walls and floors. These can be excavated further and provided with windows and wooden shelves—for a perfect root cellar.

Plans for building a new house can easily be changed to accommodate a root cellar incorporating all of the most desirable features.

Utilizing existing space is more difficult but by no means impossible. Search out an 8-by-8-foot northern corner of your basement in which there is at least one window and through which no heating ducts run (or insulate these well). Build two walls of 2-by-4-foot studding and insulate the walls and ceiling with insulating board. Build an insulated door with felt edging for a tight fit and equip the room with a slotted floor and rough wooden shelves.

An outside stairwell of an existing house can also be easily adapted for fruit and vegetable storage. These usually lead to the cellar and are therefore easily accessible. Cover the stairwell with wood and waterproofing, hang up a thermometer, and you are in business. Arrange the vegetables and fruits according to their fondness for cold, with turnips and parsnips on the top (or coldest) steps and fruits lower down. Place boards or bricks on the stair treads and more boards on the uprights of the stairs to keep the vegetables from leaning against the bare concrete which might cause them to mildew.

If price is no object and you really wish to baby your home-grown fruits and vegetables, buy them an $800 sauna. Saunas make excellent root storage units and the manufacturer will even add wooden shelves for your edible roots at little or no extra cost. A sauna root cellar may be unique and quite a conversation piece, but it might be less expensive and more enjoyable to buy your winter vegetables at a fancy vegetable market and take a plane to Florida for your fruits.

Storing Vegetables and Fruits in a Root Cellar

Make a late planting of vegetables for storage in your root cellar. This should ensure ripe vegetables just before frosts begin to whiten the fields and gardens.

Vegetables and fruits to be stored must be absolutely perfect, with no bruises, cuts, or decay of any kind. It is far better to turn near-perfect tomatoes into tangy tomato sauce and bruised apples into applesauce than to spoil a whole basket of stored fruits or vegetables in order to avoid discarding an imperfect piece.

Handle produce destined for storage with great care. Careless handling may cause hidden bruises which become worse shortly after packing and damage produce stored nearby. It is, in my opinion, a bad practice to wash fruits or vegetables prior to storing. The more handling, the more chance of damage. There are a few authorities who believe it does no harm to clean foods thoroughly before storing but the majority are against it.

Brush the more prominent, larger bits of clinging dirt away with a feather-light touch and trim stems 2-3 inches above the root to prevent "bleeding" and nutrition loss.

ROOT CELLARS

Harvest fruits and vegetables to be root cellar–stored as late as possible in the season. This will give your cellar time to become cool before the foods are stored. A precooled cellar will minimize damage if you are surprised by a warm, Indian summer type day after fruits and vegetables are settled for the winter.

Harvest on a cold, clear, sunny day when rain is not expected.

Never harvest the day after a rainstorm; the vegetables should be left on dry ground anywhere from a few hours to overnight to shed "field heat" and dry out somewhat.

Slightly dampened sawdust is the best packing agent; sand often imparts a strong and rather unpleasant taste to fruits and vegetables. Allow the sawdust to dry out slowly around the produce and to remain dry. Too much dampness keeps the produce from shriveling but causes foods to continue to grow and become woody and tasteless.

Pack produce in cardboard boxes or inexpensive thin wooden baskets. For best results, old containers should be destroyed every year and replaced by new ones. Barrels or strong, expensive wooden boxes may be more esthetic, but these must be well cleaned and aired before reusing.

Fruits and vegetables such as pumpkins and squash must be stored so that they do not directly touch and thereby transmit decay or disease. Onions, potatoes, pears, and apples are exceptions to this and may be stored in baskets if desired.

Thoroughly clean your root cellar during the summer. Sweep it out, discard old produce, boxes, and sawdust and wash down the walls, ceiling, shelves, and floor. Add the sawdust and shredded boxes to your compost heap.

Storage Chart*

Food	Keeps Approximately	Ideal Temperature	Ideal Humidity	Time to Harvest	Special Notes
Acorn squash	6–8 weeks	55°–60°	Dry	Before frost.	Leave stem 2 inches long.
Apples	6–7 months	35°–40°	Moderate	Late as possible before frost, when fruit is mature but firm.	Best varieties —Baldwin, Black Beauty, Cortland, Yellow Newton, Winesap.
Beets	4–5 months	35°–40°	Fairly moist	After light frosts, before hard ones.	Cut tops to 2 inches. Ground dry several hours.
Buttercup and butternut squash	2–4 months	55°–60°		Before frost, when squash is immature.	Leave stem 2 inches long. Cure 1 week at 70° before storing.
Carrots	4–5 months	35°–40°	Fairly moist	After light frosts, before hard ones.	Cut tops to 2 inches. Ground dry several hours.
Grapefruit	3–5 weeks	32°–35°	Fairly moist	Before frost.	Cut stems 2 inches long.
Hubbard squash	2–3 months	55°–60°	Dry	When rinds are hard and tough.	Cure 1 week at 70° before storing.
Kohlrabi	3–4 months	35°–40°	Fairly moist	During light frosts.	

* This chart is based on my own experience and is meant as a guide. You are sure to discover methods that are suitable to your storage space and climate as you go along.

Food	Keeps Approximately	Ideal Temperature	Ideal Humidity	Time to Harvest	Special Notes
Lemons and limes	4–6 weeks	32°–35°	Fairly moist	After reaching true color.	
Onions	3–5 months	35°–40°	Dry	During light frosts.	Hang 1 week outdoors. Braid dried stems together and hang on hooks. Do not handle when frozen.
Oranges	3–5 weeks	32°–35°	Fairly moist	After reaching true color.	
Parsnips	5–7 months	32°	Fairly moist	After freezing occurs.	
Pears	3–5 weeks	32°–35°	Fairly moist	When pale green.	Best varieties —Anjou, Winter Nelis.
Peppers, sweet	4–5 weeks	40°–50°	Very moist	Before frost.	
Peppers, hot	4–5 months	50°	Dry	At any stage; green or fully ripe.	Hang entire plant in a dry place and pick peppers as needed.
Potatoes, late	4–5 months	40°	Fairly moist	After light frosts.	First store in a moist, airy place for 2 weeks, at about 70°. Transfer to a dark corner of the root cellar for storage.

Food	Keeps Approximately	Ideal Temperature	Ideal Humidity	Time to Harvest	Special Notes
Potatoes, sweet	5–7 months	55°–60°	Fairly dry	Before frosts.	Cure 2 weeks at 70° before storing.
Pumpkins	4–6 months	55°–60°	Dry	Before frosts.	Cure 2 weeks at 70° in a moist place before storing.
Rutabagas	4–5 months	35°–40°	Fairly moist	After light frosts, before hard ones.	These have a strong odor during storage.
Tomatoes, green	1–2 months	50°–60°	Fairly moist	Just before first frosts.	Pack in long, shallow boxes. Separate ones that are beginning to ripen from those that are very green. Choose tomatoes as you need them from among the partially ripened ones. Leave 1-inch stems.
Turnips	4–5 months	35°–40°	Fairly moist	After light frosts, before hard ones.	These have a strong odor during storage.
Zucchini	2–3 months	55°–60°	Dry	Before frosts.	Cut stems to 2 inches.

Canning

CANNING IS by far the most complex and difficult of the preserving processes. Care must be taken and rules must be scrupulously followed. There is quite a bit of work involved, but there are few endeavors which give so much pleasure for the time invested. The jewel-like beauty of gleaming jars of ripe red tomatoes, golden peach halves, and green beans set proudly on a cellar shelf would almost be reward enough without the additional pleasure of consuming the food. Although freezing foods is much easier, you may wish to try your hand at canning at least once.

One word of caution—molds, yeasts, and bacteria that cause spoilage in foods are ever-present in the air, water, and soil. These organisms as well as spoilage-producing enzymes in the fruits and vegetables themselves must be destroyed by intense heat or deadly botulism may occur. Use only the approved boiling-water bath or the steam-pressure methods. The first is ideal for fruits, vegetables, and pickled vegetables which have a high acid content. The second is the only safe way to can vegetables. Discount completely any stories you may hear to the contrary. Oven-canning, cold-sealing, or the addition of aspirin, chemical preservatives, or powders are unsafe. For the sake of your health and that of your family and friends, can the slow, sure way or don't can at all.

Equipment

Canners

Boiling-Water-Bath Canner. For fruits, tomatoes, or pickled vegetables, use a water-bath canner. These are available on the market but any large metal container may be used if it is deep enough to permit the water to boil briskly 3 to 4 inches above the tops of the sealed jars. This container must be equipped with a tight-fitting cover and a rack to keep the jars from touching each other or falling against the sides of the container during processing.

You may use your steam-pressure canner for water-bath canning if it's deep enough. Simply arrange the jars in the rack, cover them with water several inches above the tops, cover the canner, but do not fasten the lid. Leave the pet cock wide open so the stream will not build up in the canner.

Steam-Pressure Canner. For all vegetables except tomatoes and pickled vegetables, use a steam-pressure canner. In order to process these low-acid foods safely a temperature higher than that of boiling water is required. The commercial steam-pressure canner comes equipped with a rack and a tight-fitting, easily secured cover with a pet cock or weighted-gage opening.

It is best to follow directions that came with your steam-pressure canner, but if these are lost, here are a few general rules on the use of any steam-pressure canner.

1. Pour several inches of boiling water into the bottom of the canner.

2. Arrange filled and sealed jars in the canner rack so steam can circulate around each container. If two layers of jars are put in, stagger the second layer on a rack set between the two layers.

3. Fasten the cover securely so steam can escape only through the pet cock or weighted-gage opening.

4. Place the canner over medium-high heat until steam pours steadily from the vent for 10 minutes to drive all air from the canner. Then close the pet-cock or put on the weighted gage.

5. Pressure must rise to 10 pounds (240 degrees) to ensure thorough processing of vegetables. The moment the pressure reaches

10 pounds (or the figure given on the Pressure Compensation Chart, page 496), start counting processing time. Keep the pressure from rising and falling by regulating the heat under the canner. NEVER OPEN PET COCK TO LOWER PRESSURE. Be sure that there are no drafts blowing on the canner.

6. Maintain pressure at 10 pounds for as long as specified for the vegetable you are canning.

7. Remove canner from the heat immediately when processing time is up.

8. Allow canner to cool slowly. Never try to help it along by dousing it with cold water or refrigerating it. When pressure registers zero, wait 10 minutes, then slowly open the pet-cock or take off the weighted gage. Unfasten the far side of the cover first and tilt it up so that the steam escapes away from you. Remove jars from the canner and set them, top side up and several inches apart, on a rack or folded towel to cool. Never place the hot jars on a cold surface or in a draft.

Jars

Use only standard canning jars. Jars that formerly contained pickles, mayonnaise, or other purchased foods may not be sturdy enough to withstand the high temperatures of steam-pressure and/or boiling-water-bath canning.

There are two main types of closures for standard jars: (1) the porcelain-lined zinc cap with shoulder rubber ring, and (2) the metal screwband and flat metal lid edged with sealing compound.

Selecting Fruits and Vegetables for Canning

Follow the rules outlined in selecting produce for Root Cellar Storage (page 488). Choose only perfect fruits and vegetables of the highest quality. One bad piece can spoil the barrel or the batch. The time investment in canning is high and it simply doesn't make sense to waste it or the effort and the expense involved to can second-rate vegetables. There is also a greater danger of spoilage and serious illness if the vegetables canned are on the verge of spoiling to begin with.

Pick or buy fruits and vegetables as soon as possible before canning time to preserve their vitamin content. If the fruits or vegetables must be stored, keep them in a cool, well-ventilated place until they are readied for canning.

The Day Before You Can

1. Check over all standard jars and closures and discard any with cracks, chips, dents, or rust.

2. Purchase new jars, closures, and rubber rings as necessary.

3. If your canner has a weighted gage, clean it thoroughly before using. If a dial gage is a feature of your canner, ask your county home-demonstration agent, dealer, or manufacturer about checking it. Your canner pressure gage must be accurate to get processing temperatures needed to keep foods from spoiling. To can vegetables safely 10 pounds of steam pressure must be accurately reached. If your gage is off by more than 5 pounds, replace it. If your gage is inaccurate by less than 5 pounds, use the following Pressure Compensation Chart.

Pressure Compensation Chart

If the gauge reads high:	If the gauge reads low:
1 pound high, process at 11 pounds	1 pound low, process at 9 pounds
2 pounds high, process at 12 pounds	2 pounds low, process at 8 pounds
3 pounds high, process at 13 pounds	3 pounds low, process at 7 pounds
4 pounds high, process at 14 pounds	4 pounds low, process at 6 pounds

4. Clean pet-cock and safety-valve openings by pulling a string through them.

On Canning Day

Preparing Equipment

1. Wash jars, lids, and bands in hot, soapy water, and rinse and dry well.

2. Wash and rinse canner thoroughly without submerging the cover, and dry both pieces well.

Preparing Vegetables and Fruits

1. Wash vegetables and fruits thoroughly in several changes

of water whether or not they are to be pared. Remove the produce and rinse the pan between each washing.

2. Sort produce and group according to size and ripeness so it will be cooked evenly in the jars.

3. Handle produce with care to prevent bruising.

4. Do not allow the vegetables to stand in water after washing or much of the flavor and vitamin content will be poured down the drain with the water.

5. Peel, pit, and cut produce as desired.

The Day After You Can

1. Test the flat metal jar lids by pressing down on the center of the lid. If the lid is down firmly and will not move, the jar is properly sealed. If you find a leaky jar eat the food right away or repack the food and process again as if it were fresh. Check the lid and jar thoroughly before using them again.

2. Remove the screwbands from the jars of canned vegetables if you wish, but do so carefully.

3. Wipe the jars and label them, listing the contents, date, and lot number if you canned more than one lot in one day.

4. Wash the bands and store them in a dry place.

Storing Canned Foods

Store in a cool, dark, dry place. Never store canned foods near hot pipes, stoves, or in sunlight or quality may be impaired.

Checking Canned Foods for Spoilage

Before opening any canned foods, check for signs of spoilage. Puffed or bulging jar lids, leaks, spurting liquid when the lid is lifted, mold, or unpleasant odors are all signs of spoilage. Discard all jars of food that have any of the danger signals listed above.

Home-canned foods that have been improperly processed may contain the poison causing botulism, a serious food poisoning, without displaying any of the telltale signs mentioned above. It is a wise precaution to bring all home-canned foods to a boil, cover, and continue boiling for 10 minutes before using if possible. (Spinach and corn should be boiled 20 minutes.) If the food looks or smells spoiled, or foams during boiling—destroy it!

Methods: Raw Pack or Hot Pack

Choose the canning method you prefer—raw pack or hot pack. Raw pack is easier and the best choice for all vegetables except corn, lima beans, peas, pickled vegetables, or vegetables that are difficult to rid of grit. Nutritional values are sure to be retained by the raw-pack method. Pack clean, cut, raw vegetables in jars, add salt, and cover with boiling water. Adjust closures. Process as directed for the particular vegetable. Raw fruit is covered with boiling water, syrup, or juice.

Hot pack requires slight precooking of clean, cut vegetables in boiling water. Pack the vegetables in jars, add salt, cover with cooking liquid (which contains vitamins and minerals from the produce) or boiling water, and adjust closures. Process as directed for the particular vegetable.

To hot-pack fruits, heat them in syrup, water, steam, or juice before packing. Juicy fruits may be heated without additional liquid and packed in the juices that cook out.

Sugar helps preserve the shape and color of fruits and in most cases enhances their flavor. Sweeten fruits with any mild-flavored, light-colored syrup such as sugar syrup, light corn syrup, or mild honey mixed with sugar and boiled with water to form a syrup. In general dark or strong-flavored sweeteners such as brown sugar or dark honey should be avoided because they discolor the fruit, impose their flavors too strongly, and drown out the delicate natural fruit flavor.

Sugar Syrups

Sugar syrups may be made with either water or fruit juice. Corn syrup or light honey may be substituted for half the sugar in the following. Skim the syrup of froth before using.

Thin Sugar Syrup: 2 cups granulated sugar boiled with 4 cups water or juice will yield 5 cups.

Medium Sugar Syrup: 3 cups granulated sugar boiled with 4 cups water or juice will yield 5½ cups.

Heavy Sugar Syrup: 4¾ cups granulated sugar boiled with 4 cups water or juice will yield 6½ cups.

Processing Times

Follow times carefully. The times given apply only to a specific food prepared according to detailed directions. If you live at an altitude of 1,000 feet or more, consult the chart below to calculate additional processing time.

High-Altitude Processing Times

Altitude	Less than 20 minutes	More than 20 minutes
1,000 feet	1 minute	2 minutes
2,000 feet	2 minutes	4 minutes
3,000 feet	3 minutes	6 minutes
4,000 feet	4 minutes	8 minutes
5,000 feet	5 minutes	10 minutes
6,000 feet	6 minutes	12 minutes
7,000 feet	7 minutes	14 minutes
8,000 feet	8 minutes	16 minutes
9,000 feet	9 minutes	18 minutes
10,000 feet	10 minutes	20 minutes

Yield of Canned Produce from Fresh

The number of quarts of canned food yielded from a given quantity of fresh produce depends upon the quality, condition, variety, maturity, and size of the fruits and vegetables; whether whole, halved, or sliced; and whether it is packed raw or hot. Generally, the following amounts of fresh fruit or vegetables yield 1 quart canned.

Fruits

Fruits	Pounds
Apples	2½ to 3
Berries, except strawberries	1½ to 3 (1 to 2 quart boxes)
Cherries (canned, unpitted)	2 to 2½
Peaches	2 to 3
Pears	2 to 3
Plums	1½ to 2½
Tomatoes	2½ to 3½

In 1 pound there are about 3 medium apples and pears; 4 medium peaches or tomatoes; 8 medium plums.

Vegetables

	Pounds		Pounds
Asparagus	2½ to 4½	Okra	1½
Beans, lima, in pods	3 to 5	Green peas, in pods	3 to 6
Green beans	1½ to 2½	Pumpkin or winter squash	1½ to 3
Beets, without tops	2 to 3½	Spinach and other greens	2 to 6
Carrots, without tops	2 to 3	Summer squash	2 to 4
Corn, in husks	3 to 6	Sweet potatoes	2 to 3

Fruits

Apples

Hot Pack. Pare and core apples; cut in pieces. To keep fruit from darkening, drop each piece into water containing 2 tablespoons each of salt and vinegar per gallon. Drain, then boil 5 minutes in Thin Sugar Syrup or water.

Pack hot fruit in glass jars to within ½ inch of top. Cover with hot syrup or water, leaving ½-inch space at top of jar. Adjust jar lids. Process in boiling-water bath (212 degrees).

Pint jars	15 minutes
Quart jars	20 minutes

As soon as you remove jars from canner, complete seals if necessary.

Applesauce

Hot Pack. Make applesauce, sweetened or unsweetened. Heat to simmering (185–210 degrees); stir to keep from sticking.

Pack hot applesauce in glass jars to within ¼ inch of top. Adjust lids. Process in boiling-water bath (212 degrees).

Pint jars	10 minutes
Quart jars	10 minutes

As soon as you remove jars from canner, complete seals if necessary.

Berries

Raw Pack. Wash and drain berries. Pack into glass jars to within ½ inch of top. For a full pack, shake berries down while filling jars.

Cover with boiling syrup, leaving ½-inch space at top. Adjust lids. jar lids. Process in boiling-water bath (212 degrees).

Pint jars	10 minutes
Quart jars	15 minutes

As soon as you remove jars from canner, complete seals if necessary.

Hot Pack (for firm berries). Wash berries and drain well. Add ½ cup sugar to each quart of fruit. Cover pan and bring to boil; shake pan to keep berries from sticking.

Pack hot berries in glass jars to within ½ inch of top. Adjust jar lids. Process in boiling-water bath (212 degrees).

Pint jars	10 minutes
Quart jars	15 minutes

As soon as you remove jars from canner, complete seals if necessary.

Cherries

Raw Pack. Wash cherries; remove pits, if desired. Pack in glass jars to within ½ inch of top. For a full pack, shake cherries down while filling jars. Cover with boiling syrup, leaving ½-inch space at top. Adjust lids. Process in boiling-water bath (212 degrees).

Pint jars	20 minutes
Quart jars	25 minutes

As soon as you remove jars from canner, complete seals if necessary.

Hot Pack. Wash cherries; remove pits, if desired. Add ½ cup sugar to each quart of fruit. Add a little water to unpitted cherries to keep them from sticking while heating. Cover pan and bring to a boil.

Pack hot fruit in glass jars to within ½ inch of top. Adjust jar lids. Process in boiling-water bath (212 degrees).

Pint jars	10 minutes
Quart jars	15 minutes

As soon as you remove jars from canner, complete seals if necessary.

Peaches

Raw Pack. Wash peaches and remove skins. Dipping the fruit in boiling water, then quickly in cold water makes peeling easier. Cut peaches in half, remove pits, and slice if desired. To prevent fruit from darkening during preparation, drop into water containing 2 tablespoons each salt and vinegar per gallon. Drain just before heating or packing raw.

Pack raw fruit in glass jars to within ½ inch of top. Cover with boiling sugar syrup, leaving ½-inch space at top of jar. Adjust jar lids. Process in boiling-water bath (212 degrees).

Pint jars	25 minutes
Quart jars	30 minutes

As soon as you remove jars from canner, complete seals if necessary.

Hot Pack. Prepare peaches as for raw pack. Heat peaches in hot syrup. If fruit is very juicy you may heat it with sugar, adding no liquid.

Pack hot fruit in glass jars to within ½ inch of top. Cover with boiling liquid, leaving ½-inch space at top of jar. Adjust jar lids. Process in boiling-water bath (212 degrees).

Pint jars	20 minutes
Quart jars	25 minutes

As soon as you remove jars from canner, complete seals if necessary.

Rhubarb

Hot Pack. Wash rhubarb and cut into ½-inch pieces. Add ½ cup sugar to each quart rhubarb and let stand to draw out juice. Bring to the boil.

Pack hot in glass jars to within ½ inch of top. Adjust lids. Process in boiling-water bath (212 degrees).

Pint jars	10 minutes
Quart jars	10 minutes

As soon as you remove jars from canner, complete seals if necessary.

Tomatoes

Use only firm, ripe tomatoes. To loosen skins, dip into boiling water for about 30 seconds, then dip quickly into cold water. Cut out stem-ends and peel tomatoes.

Raw Pack. Leave tomatoes whole or cut into halves or quarters. Pack tomatoes in glass jars to within ½ inch of top, pressing gently to fill spaces. Add no water. Add ½ teaspoon salt to pint jars; 1 teaspoon salt to quart jars. Adjust lids. Process in boiling-water bath (212 degrees).

Pint jars	35 minutes
Quart jars	45 minutes

Hot Pack. Quarter peeled tomatoes. Bring to boil; stir to keep tomatoes from sticking.

Pack hot tomatoes in glass jars to within ½ inch of top. Add ½ teaspoon salt to pints; 1 teaspoon salt to quart jars. Adjust lids. Process in boiling-water bath (212 degrees).

Pint jars	10 minutes
Quart jars	10 minutes

As soon as you remove jars from canner, complete seals if necessary.

Vegetables

Asparagus

Raw Pack. Wash asparagus, trim off scales and tough ends, and wash again. Cut into 1-inch pieces.

Pack asparagus in glass jars as tightly as possible without crushing to within ½ inch of top. Add ½ teaspoon salt to pint jars; 1 teaspoon salt to quart jars. Cover with boiling water, leaving ½-inch space at top of jar. Adjust jar lids. Process in steam-pressure canner at 10 pounds pressure (240 degrees).

Pint jars	25 minutes
Quart jars	30 minutes

As soon as you remove jars from canner, complete seals if necessary.

Hot Pack. Wash asparagus; trim off scales and tough ends and wash again. Cut into 1-inch pieces; cover with boiling water. Boil 2 or 3 minutes.

Pack hot asparagus loosely in glass jars to within ½ inch of top. Add ½ teaspoon salt to pint jars; 1 teaspoon salt to quart jars. Cover with boiling-hot cooking liquid, or if liquid contains grit use boiling water. Leave ½-inch space at top of jar. Adjust jar lids. Process in steam-pressure canner at 10 pounds pressure (240 degrees).

Pint jars	25 minutes
Quart jars	30 minutes

As soon as you remove jars from canner, complete seals if necessary.

Green Beans

Raw Pack. Wash beans. Trim ends and cut into 1-inch pieces.

Pack raw beans tightly in glass jars to within ½ inch of top.

Add ½ teaspoon salt to pint jars; 1 teaspoon salt to quart jars. Cover with boiling water, leaving ½-inch space at top of jar. Adjust jar lids. Process in steam-pressure canner at 10 pounds pressure (240 degrees).

Pint jars	20 minutes
Quart jars	25 minutes

As soon as you remove jars from canner, complete seals if necessary.

Hot Pack. Wash beans. Trim ends and cut into 1-inch pieces. Cover with boiling water; boil 5 minutes.

Pack hot beans loosely in glass jars to within ½ inch of top. Add ½ teaspoon salt to pint jars; 1 teaspoon salt to quart jars. Cover with boiling-hot cooking liquid leaving ½-inch space at top of jar. Adjust jar lids. Process in steam-pressure canner at 10 pounds pressure (240 degrees).

Pint jars	20 minutes
Quart jars	25 minutes

As soon as you remove jars from canner, complete seals if necessary.

Beets

Hot Pack. Sort beets for size. Cut off tops, leaving an inch of stem and root. Wash beets, cover with boiling water, and boil until skins slip off easily, 15 to 25 minutes, depending on size. Skin and trim. Leave baby beets whole. Cut medium or large beets into ½-inch cubes or slices; halve or quarter very large slices.

Pack hot beets in glass jars to within ½ inch of top. Add ½ teaspoon salt to pint jars; 1 teaspoon salt to quart jars. Cover with boiling water, leaving ½-inch space at top of jar. Adjust jar lids. Process in steam-pressure canner at 10 pounds pressure (240 degrees).

Pint jars	30 minutes
Quart jars	35 minutes

As soon as you remove jars from canner, complete seals if necessary.

Pickled Beets

Hot Pack. Cut off beet tops, leaving 1 inch of stem and root. Wash beets, cover with boiling water, and cook until tender. Skin and slice beets. For pickling syrup, use 2 cups vinegar (or 1½ cups vinegar and ½ cup water) to 2 cups sugar. Heat to boiling.

Pack beets in glass jars to within ½ inch of top. Add ½ teaspoon salt to pint jars; 1 teaspoon to quart jars. Cover with boiling pickling syrup, leaving ½-inch space at top of jar. Adjust jar lids. Process in boiling-water bath (212 degrees).

Pint jars	30 minutes
Quart jars	30 minutes

As soon as you remove jars from canner, complete seals if necessary.

Carrots

Raw Pack. Wash and scrape carrots. Slice or dice.

Pack raw carrots tightly in glass jars to within 1 inch of top. Add ½ teaspoon salt to pint jars; 1 teaspoon salt to quart jars. Cover to within ½ inch of top of jar with boiling water. Adjust jar lids. Process in steam-pressure canner at 10 pounds pressure (240 degrees).

Pint jars	25 minutes
Quart jars	30 minutes

As soon as you remove jars from canner, complete seals if necessary.

Hot Pack. Wash and scrape carrots. Slice or dice. Cover with boiling water and bring to boil.

Pack hot carrots in glass jars to within ½ inch of top. Add ½ teaspoon salt to pint jars; 1 teaspoon salt to quart jars. Cover with boiling cooking liquid, leaving ½-inch space at top of jar. Adjust jar lids. Process in pressure canner at 10 pounds pressure (240 degrees).

Pint jars	25 minutes
Quart jars	30 minutes

As soon as you remove jars from canner, complete seals if necessary.

Corn

Raw Pack. Husk corn and remove silk. Wash. Cut from cob at about ⅔ the depth of kernel.

Pack corn in glass jars to within 1 inch of top; do not shake or press down. Add ½ teaspoon salt to pint jars; 1 teaspoon salt to quart jars. Cover with boiling water, leaving ½-inch space at top of jar. Adjust jar lids. Process in steam-pressure canner at 10 pounds pressure (240 degrees).

Pint jars	55 minutes
Quart jars	85 minutes

As soon as you remove jars from canner, complete seals if necessary.

Hot Pack. Husk corn and remove silk. Wash. Cut from cob at about ⅔ the depth of kernel. To each quart of corn add 1 pint boiling water. Heat to boiling.

Pack hot corn in glass jars to within 1 inch of top. Cover with boiling cooking liquid, leaving 1-inch space at top of jar. Or fill to within 1 inch of top with mixture of corn and liquid. Add ½ teaspoon salt to pint jars; 1 teaspoon salt to quart jars. Adjust jar lids. Process in pressure canner at 10 pounds pressure (240 degrees).

Pint jars	55 minutes
Quart jars	85 minutes

As soon as you remove jars from canner, complete seals if necessary.

Hominy

Hot Pack. Place 8 cups of dry field corn in an enameled pan; add 8 quarts water and 2 ounces lye. Boil vigorously for 30 minutes, then let stand for 20 minutes. Rinse off the lye with several hot water rinses. Follow with cold water rinses to cool for handling.

Work hominy with the hands until dark tips of kernels are removed, about 5 minutes. Separate the tips from the corn by floating them off in water or by placing the corn in a coarse sieve and washing thoroughly. Add sufficient water to cover hominy by about 1 inch, and boil 5 minutes; change water. Repeat 4 times. Then cook until kernels are soft, 30 to 45 minutes, and drain. This will make about 6 quarts of hominy.

Pack hot hominy in glass jars to within ½ inch of top. Add ½ teaspoon salt to pint jars; 1 teaspoon salt to quart jars. Cover with boiling water, leaving ½-inch space at top of jar. Adjust jar lids. Process in steam-pressure canner at 10 pounds pressure (240 degrees).

Pint jars	60 minutes
Quart jars	70 minutes

As soon as you remove jars from canner, complete seals if necessary.

Green Peas

Raw Pack. Shell and wash peas. Pack in glass jars to within 1 inch of top; do not shake or press down. Add ½ teaspoon salt to pint jars; 1 teaspoon salt to quart jars. Cover with boiling water, leaving 1½-inch space at top of jar. Adjust jar lids. Process in steam-pressure canner at 10 pounds pressure (240 degrees).

Pint jars	40 minutes
Quart jars	40 minutes

As soon as you remove jars from canner, complete seals if necessary.

Hot Pack. Shell and wash peas. Cover with boiling water. Bring to boil.

Pack hot peas loosely in glass jars to within 1 inch of top. Add ½ teaspoon salt to pint jars; 1 teaspoon salt to quart jars. Cover with boiling water, leaving 1-inch space at top of jar. Adjust jar lids. Process in steam-pressure canner at 10 pounds pressure (240 degrees).

Pint jars	40 minutes
Quart jars	40 minutes

As soon as you remove jars from canner, complete seals if necessary.

Summer Squash

Raw Pack. Wash but do not peel squash. Trim ends. Cut squash into ½-inch slices; halve or quarter to make pieces of uniform size.

Pack raw squash tightly in glass jars to within 1 inch of top. Add ½ teaspoon salt to pint jars; 1 teaspoon salt to quart jars. Cover with boiling water, leaving ½-inch space at top of jar. Adjust jar lids. Process in steam-pressure canner at 10 pounds pressure (240 degrees).

Pint jars	25 minutes
Quart jars	30 minutes

As soon as you remove jars from canner, complete seals if necessary.

Hot Pack. Wash squash and trim ends; do not peel. Cut squash into ½-inch slices; halve or quarter to make pieces of uniform size. Add just enough water to cover. Bring to boil.

Pack hot squash loosely in glass jars to within ½ inch of top. Add ½ teaspoon salt to pint jars; 1 teaspoon salt to quart jars. Cover with boiling cooking liquid, leaving ½-inch space at top of jar. Adjust jar lids. Process in steam-pressure canner at 10 pounds pressure (240 degrees).

Pint jars	30 minutes
Quart jars	40 minutes

As soon as you remove jars from canner, complete seals if necessary.

Freezing

THE REWARDS of the freezing process are obvious. Not only is this the easiest technique for preserving produce but it is the one that best retains the garden-fresh, just-picked taste of fruits and vegetables.

Basically, freezing is a three level process: (1) Assemble your produce—either from your garden or someone else's; (2) Blanch the produce (although this is not vital to successful freezing); and (3) Wrap and freeze. Freezing is a relatively simple process with virtually no pitfalls. It doesn't require great skill or know-how to achieve superb results. Ultimate success depends on the quality of the produce and the speed and efficiency with which that produce goes from stalk to freezer.

Vegetables

Blanching

Like almost everything else in life, there are two sides to this question. One school maintains that blanching is an unnecessary and somewhat laborious process that has outlived its usefulness. The other insists that blanching is not at all difficult and that the bit of extra effort involved preserves vitamins, minerals, and flavor and is worthwhile. I heartily concur with the latter.

All living, growing plant life contains enzymes, one of whose functions it is to aid in the ripening process. Unless enzyme action is arrested, it continues until the fruit or vegetable passes from ripe, to riper, to overripe, to rotten, accompanied by changes in color, taste, and texture. Blanching stops the enzyme action which would otherwise continue through the stages preparatory to freezing and through the early stages of the actual freezing process as well.

Blanching also helps preserve the natural color of the produce; it removes chemical sprays to which the fruits and vegetables may have been subjected, washes away ingrained dirt, and kills virtually all bacteria which may be lurking in the food. Perhaps most important, blanching helps maintain the nutritive value of fruits and vegetables because it destroys the enzymes which in turn destroy the vitamins.

Basically, blanching is a quick, partial, high-temperature cooking process. Produce is steamed or boiled for a brief period and then rapidly cooled. Precise times required are specified in the section for freezing individual vegetables.

Some authorities prefer steaming to boiling, particularly for sliced vegetables as this seems to be less destructive to vitamins and minerals. Leafy vegetables, however, don't take too kindly to the steaming process and boiling is the much preferred technique.

Boiling

Use a large enameled pot of at least 2 gallon capacity, equipped with tight-fitting lid and a wire-mesh basket with handles. Do not use copper or iron pots.

For cooling, you will need at least 1 pound of ice for each pound of blanched vegetables.

While the water is heating to a boil, wash your produce thoroughly, discarding overripe, immature, badly bruised, or damaged specimens. Place 1 pound of perfect produce (2 pounds is not too much for small, compact vegetables such as beans or peas) into your mesh basket, immerse into vigorously boiling water, cover tightly, and begin to count from the time you put on the lid.

After the recommended time has elapsed, remove produce and plunge into ice water for the same amount of time produce has boiled, or until vegetables are thoroughly cool. Drain well, wrap, label, and place in freezer.

Steaming

Use a large pot of at least 2 gallon capacity equipped with a rack which will keep the vegetables well above the 2 inches of water at the bottom of the pot. A wire-mesh basket with handles as well as a tight-fitting lid are also necessary. You may use a large pressure cooker, but *don't clamp down the lid,* as pressure is not required.

For cooling, you will need at least 1 pound of ice for each pound of produce.

Put 2 inches of water into the pot, bring to a vigorous boil, put approximately 1 pound of produce into a wire basket, lower onto the rack, and immediately close lid tightly.

After steaming for the specified amount of time, plunge the produce into ice water for the same amount of time produce has steamed, or until vegetables are thoroughly cooled.

Drain well, wrap, label, and place in freezer.

Wrapping

Wrapping is of prime importance. Most failures occur because inadequate attention was paid to this all-important aspect of the gentle art of freezing. There are two reasons for this. First, dehydration can and does occur in the freezer. Moisture can be quite literally sucked out of frozen produce and the consequences are dry, tasteless vegetables barely fit for consumption.

Problem two is oxidation. Unless prevented from doing so, the oxygen in the air will attack produce and in the process destroy the vitamin and mineral content.

Overcoming these problems is relatively simple. You must use packaging materials and techniques that are both moisture-proof and airtight, thus insulating your produce from the deleterious effects of dehydration and oxidation.

There are a great many freezer wrapping materials and devices available, from plastic containers (square are more practical than round, and tight lids are a must) to plastic bags, glassine-lined paper boxes, plastic-lined paper bags, and many, many more. I prefer plastic boxes with snap-tight lids. They are moisture-proof and airtight, they pack and stack well, and they can be used over and over again, which compensates for their high initial cost. When using rigid containers always leave at least a ½-inch space at the top to allow for expansion. There are a few instances where bags are more practical, but these must be handled with extreme care as they puncture easily.

Select the container size on the basis of family size. The more of you there are to feed at each sitting, the larger your individual containers must be.

Beware of glass jars. They can be used successfully, but they are extremely fragile when frozen and must be handled very gently. It is particularly difficult and even hazardous to extricate frozen foods from them.

Labeling

It is a good idea to label every package of food you freeze. Each package should be labeled with content, quantity, and date frozen. Maintain a running inventory of quantities and varieties originally frozen and amounts still left in your freezer.

Freezing

Be sure to leave an inch or two of space between packages to allow for air circulation and don't jam your freezer with more than it can adequately handle.

It takes approximately 24 hours for the average package of produce to achieve a completely frozen state. And remember, organization will enable you to get your hands on precisely what you want when you want it.

How to Freeze

Asparagus. Harvest, cut into 6-inch lengths, tie into bunches, thin spears with thin spears, medium with medium, and large with large. Boil large spears 4 minutes, medium 3, and thin 2 minutes. Cool, drain, package, and freeze.

Green or Wax Beans. Harvest before full maturity. Wash, cut ends, and remove strings. Cut or leave whole, as you prefer. Boil whole beans 3 minutes, cut beans 2 minutes. If steam-blanching, add 1 minute. Cool thoroughly, drain well, pack, and freeze.

Lima Beans. Shell, sort beans into large (boil 4 minutes), medium (boil 3 minutes), and small (boil 2 minutes). Cool, drain, package, and freeze.

Soybeans. Harvest when bright green, wash thoroughly, and boil for 5 minutes. Cool, remove beans from pods, package, and freeze.

Beets. Select small beets, wash well, and boil until tender. Cool, peel, slice or dice, package, and freeze.

Broccoli. Pick young shoots (less than 1 inch thick), trim, and wash. To remove lurking insects, soak in salt water for 30 minutes. Rewash, cut lengthwise into uniform pieces leaving heads approximately 2 inches or less. Boil for approximately 3 minutes (4 minutes for steam-blanching), cool, drain on paper towels, package gently, and freeze.

Brussels Sprouts. Harvest dark green specimens, trim, wash thoroughly, and sort into small, medium, and large (more than 2 inches). If insects appear to be present, soak in salt water for 30 minutes. Rewash and boil large heads 5 minutes, medium 4 minutes, small 3 minutes. Add 1 minute for steam-blanching. Cool quickly, drain, package, and freeze.

Carrots. Harvest small, tender, young specimens, wash well, and boil small whole carrots 4 minutes, "sticks" 3 minutes, slices 2 minutes.

For steam-blanching add 2 minutes. Cool quickly, drain well, package, and freeze.

Cauliflower. Break into small florets about 1 inch across, wash well, and blanch for 3 minutes in boiling water to which lemon juice has been added. The juice of 1 lemon per gallon of water keeps cauliflower from turning dark. Cool, drain, package, and freeze.

Corn. There are a number of techniques for freezing corn. Harvest ears that are just ripe. Test by piercing a kernel with your fingernail. If a white, milky juice spurts out, the corn is ready. Bear in mind that freezing whole cobs takes up a great deal of room.

Husk corn, wash, and boil large ears for 7 minutes, medium ears for 5, and small ears for 4 minutes. If steaming, add 1 minute. Cool quickly, wipe dry, wrap each ear separately in freezer paper, and freeze.

Whole kernels: Cook as above, cool, cut off kernels, place in container, and freeze.

Creamed corn: Use imperfect ears for creamed corn. Husk, wash, and blanch in boiling water for 4 to 5 minutes. Cool quickly and cut the top portion of kernels from the cob and place in a bowl. Scrape the cobs with blunt edge of a knife squeezing the creamy hearts of kernels into the bowl. Stir well, store in refrigerator until cold, and then place in a rigid container, and freeze.

Herbs. Most herbs can be frozen successfully. Simply wash whole leaves, dry on paper towels, package, and freeze. No blanching is necessary.

Peas. Harvest peas before they are mature, shell, and blanch in boiling water for 1 minute. Cool quickly, package, and freeze.

Sweet Potatoes. These must be cooked before freezing. Scrub the potatoes well then boil or bake them and cool at room temperature. Peel, cut into uniform slices, and, to prevent darkening, dip into lemon juice and water solution (juice of ½ lemon to 1 quart water) for about 10 seconds. Dry, package, and freeze.

Spinach. Select dark green leaves, remove large stems, and thoroughly wash unblemished leaves. Blanch in boiling water for 2 minutes. Drain, dry, package loosely, and freeze.

Squash. Use small, tender squash. Wash, slice (don't peel), and blanch in boiling water for 3 minutes or steam for 4 minutes. Cool quickly, drain, package, and freeze.

Tomatoes. Tomatoes can be frozen but I like the flavor and texture of the canned ones better. If you have surplus tomatoes but no surplus time for the more difficult and lengthy canning process, try this method. Harvest small, just-ripe tomatoes, wash them, and place in 3 inches of boiling water until their skins break. Remove, peel, and core. Allow to cool at room temperature, refrigerate until cold, pack in rigid containers, and freeze.

Berries and Fruits

Berries and fruits are far easier to freeze than vegetables because they require little preparation and no blanching. There are, however, a few points to remember. . . .

1. Work quickly. The less time that elapses between harvesting and freezing the better.

2. Again, as with vegetables, the higher the quality of the berries and fruits, the better the results! Freezing doesn't improve flavor. It only preserves what is already there.

3. Never pick more than you can process at one time.

4. Use only aluminum, stainless, or enamel pots. No copper, iron, or galvanized.

5. Have plenty of ice on hand.

6. Fruit juices are acid. Use good, leakproof containers.

Three Basic Ways to Package Berries and Fruits

Wet Pack—No Sugar

Wash your fruits or berries in ice water, drain, and pack in a waterproof container. If you are dealing with a fruit that darkens easily cover with water containing a citrus acid solution, cover, and freeze.

Sweetened Dry Pack

When freezing fruits which discolor, prepare your sugar by mixing 2 teaspoons of ascorbic-citric powder into each 2 cups of sugar you plan to use. Now prepare your fruit as you would to serve it. Sprinkle some sugar in the bottom of the container, cover with a layer of fruit, and continue to alternate sugar and fruit to within ½ inch of the top of the container.

For berries or fruits which do not discolor, proceed as above with untreated sugar.

Dry Pack

This is the quickest, easiest way to freeze. Simply wash your fruits or berries in a colander with ice water to firm them up. Then drain, place in a rigid container, and freeze.

How to Keep Fruit from Discoloring

A great many fruits—apples, bananas, peaches, among them—turn dark after peeling. Happily, however, there is an antidote. Ascorbic and citric acids prevent, or at least slow up, the oxidation process which causes fruits to darken. The heavy concentration of these acids in citrus fruits explains why those fruits retain their natural color long after they have been peeled. You can prevent fruits from darkening by using those same acids yourself.

Pickling

Pickles fall into four broad classifications.

Brine pickles, also called fermented pickles, take approximately 3 weeks to cure and include dilled cucumbers, green tomatoes, and sauerkraut.

Fresh-pack or quick-process pickles include crosscut cucumber slices, whole cucumber dills, and sweet gherkins. They are brined for several hours and then subjected to boiling vinegar and various seasonings and spices. They are quick to prepare and can be seasoned to taste.

Fruit pickles, which include watermelon rind, pears, and peaches, are generally prepared from whole fruits simmered in a spicy, sweet-sour syrup.

Relishes are prepared from chopped fruits and vegetables, seasoned to taste, and cooked to the desired consistency. Chutney, piccalilli, and pepper-onions are included in this category.

Ingredients

Good results depend upon the quality of the ingredients selected and the proportions in which they are used.

Fruits and Vegetables

Select firm fruits, slightly underripe, tender vegetables, and un-waxed cucumbers. Use them as soon after harvest or purchase as possible. Do not use any fruit or vegetable with even the slightest hint of mold.

Salt

If available use pure granulated salt; uniodized table salt may be used but shun iodized salt as it has a tendency to darken pickles.

Use high-grade cider or distilled white vinegar of 4 to 6 percent acidity (40 to 60 grain). Never use vinegars of unknown acidity. Cider vinegar blends flavors well but may darken light-colored fruits and vegetables. Never dilute vinegar unless the recipe specifically recommends that you do so. If you prefer a less sour taste, add sugar.

Sugar

Granulated white or brown sugar may be used. Light-colored pickles are achieved with white sugar.

Spices

Whenever possible, use fresh herbs and spices. Spices deteriorate rapidly when the weather is damp and warm. If they cannot be used immediately, store in airtight containers in a cool, dry place.

Equipment

Heat pickling liquids in stainless steel, aluminum, glass, or un-chipped enamelware. Never use copper, brass, iron, or galvanized utensils. For fermenting or brining use a crock or stone jar, un-chipped enamel-lined pan, or large glass jar, bowl, or casserole. Use a heavy plate or large glass lid which fits inside the container to keep the vegetables submerged in the brine.

Other convenient tools of the pickler's art include measuring spoons, large wooden stirring spoons, ladles, colanders, tongs, funnel, wooden chopping board, and sundry other kitchen gadgets.

Water-Bath Canner
See Canning Fruits and Vegetables (page 494).

Glass Jars and Lids
See Canning Fruits and Vegetables (page 495).

Checking Canned Foods for Spoilage
See Canning Fruits and Vegetables (page 497).

Canned Pickles and Relishes

Brined Dill Pickles

20 pounds (about ½ bushel)
  cucumbers, 3–6 inches long
¾ cup whole mixed pickling spice
2–3 bunches fresh or dried dill

10 cloves garlic (optional)
2½ cups white vinegar
1¾ cups pure granulated salt
2½ gallons water

YIELDS NINE TO TEN QUARTS

Cover cucumbers with cold water. Wash thoroughly, using a vegetable brush; handle gently to avoid bruising. Take care to remove any blossoms. Drain on rack or wipe dry.

Place half the pickling spices and a layer of dill in a 5-gallon crock or jar. Fill the crock with cucumbers to within 3 or 4 inches of the top. Place a layer of dill, remaining spices, and optional garlic over the top of cucumbers. Thoroughly mix the vinegar, salt, and water and pour over the cucumbers.

Cover with a heavy china or glass plate or lid that fits inside the crock. Weight the plate to keep the cucumbers under the brine. A glass jar filled with water makes a good weight. Cover loosely with clean cloth. Keep pickles at room temperature. Scum may start forming in 3 to 5 days; it should be removed as formed. Do not stir pickles, but be sure they are completely covered with brine. If necessary, make additional brine, using original proportions.

In about 3 weeks the cucumbers will have become an olive green and should have a good flavor. Any white spots inside the fermented cucumbers will disappear in processing.

The original brine is usually cloudy as a result of yeast development during the fermentation period. If this cloudiness is objectionable, fresh brine may be used to cover the pickles when packing them into jars. In making fresh brine use ½ cup salt and 4 cups white vinegar to 1 gallon water. The fermentation brine is generally preferred for its added flavor and should be strained before boiling.

Pack the pickles, along with some of the dill, into clean, hot 1-quart jars, add garlic, if desired. Avoid too tight a pack. Cover with boiling brine to within ½ inch of the top. Adjust jar lids.

Process in boiling water for 15 minutes (start to count the processing time as soon as hot jars are placed into the actively boiling water).

Remove jars and complete seals if necessary. Set jars upright, several inches apart, on a wire rack to cool.

Fresh-Pack Dill Pickles

17–18 pounds cucumbers (slightly less than ½ bushel), 3–5 inches long

2 gallons 5 percent brine (¾ cup pure granulated salt per 1 gallon water)

1½ quarts white vinegar

¾ cup pure granulated salt

¼ cup granulated sugar

2¼ quarts water

2 tablespoons whole mixed pickling spice

2 teaspoons whole mustard seed per quart jar

3 heads fresh or dried dill per quart jar, or 1 tablespoon dill seed per quart jar

1–2 cloves garlic per quart jar (optional)

YIELDS SEVEN QUARTS

Wash cucumbers thoroughly; scrub with vegetable brush; drain. Cover with 5 percent brine; set aside overnight; drain.

Combine vinegar, salt, sugar, water, and pickling spice tied in a clean, thin, white cloth; heat to boiling. Pack 7 to 10 cucumbers into each clean, hot 1-quart jar. Add mustard seed, dill, and garlic to each jar; cover with boiling liquid to within ½ inch of the top of jar. Secure jar lids.

Process in boiling water for 20 minutes (start to count the processing time as soon as hot jars are placed into the actively boiling water).

Remove jars and complete seals if necessary. Set jars upright, several inches apart, on a wire rack to cool.

Miss Robin's Brined Pickles in a Crock

*Miss Robin Smith of Williamsport, Pennsylvania,
contributed this recipe for spicy sweet and
sour pickles. The quantities will depend upon
the size of the crock you use.*

Whole cucumber pickles	*Granulated sugar*
Salt	*Allspice*
Water	*Whole cloves*
White vinegar	*Cinnamon sticks*

Pack the cucumbers in a crock. Make a brine of salt and water that will hold up an egg. Pour this over the cucumbers and leave uncovered for 3 weeks. Pour off and discard the brine. Wash the pickles and the crock well. Repack the pickles in the crock and cover with vinegar. Let stand for 2 weeks.

Pour off the vinegar and discard it. Cut the pickles into cubes. Weigh the pickles and measure out 1 pound less of sugar than pickles. Prepare several cheesecloth bags with spices.

Arrange a layer of sugar, a bag of spices, and a layer of pickles, and continue this layering until all the pickles are used. Let stand for a few days, stirring frequently. The pickles are now ready to use.

Mildred Peace's Dill Pickles

1 quart cider vinegar	*4 quarts cucumber pickles (½ peck)*
3 quarts water	*Fresh dill*
¾ cup pure granulated salt	
Garlic cloves	

YIELDS FIVE OR SIX QUARTS

Bring the vinegar, water, salt, and 1 garlic clove to a rapid boil. Place a sprig of dill in the bottom of each jar, pack in the cucumber pickles lengthwise, and top with another sprig of dill and half a garlic clove. Fill clean jars to ½ inch of top with the boiling vinegar mixture and seal immediately.

Process in boiling water for 20 minutes (start to count the processing time as soon as hot jars are placed into the actively boiling water).

Remove jars and complete seals if necessary. Set jars upright, several inches apart, on a wire rack to cool.

Sweet Gherkins

7 pounds (5 quarts) cucumbers, 1½–3 inches long

½ cup pure granulated salt

8 cups granulated sugar

6 cups white vinegar

¾ teaspoon turmeric

2 teaspoons celery seed

2 teaspoons whole mixed pickling spice

8 1-inch pieces cinnamon stick

½ teaspoon fennel seed (optional)

2 teaspoons vanilla extract (optional)

YIELDS SEVEN TO EIGHT PINTS

First day. Wash cucumbers thoroughly; scrub with vegetable brush; stem ends may be left on if desired. Drain cucumbers, place in large container, and cover with boiling water. Six to 8 hours later drain, cover with fresh, boiling water.

Second day. Drain, cover with fresh, boiling water. Six to 8 hours later drain, add salt, cover with fresh, boiling water.

Third day. Drain, prick cucumbers in several places with table fork. Make syrup of 3 cups sugar and 3 cups vinegar; add turmeric, celery seed, pickling spice, and cinnamon. Heat to boiling and pour over cucumbers. (Cucumbers will be partially covered.) Six to 8 hours later drain syrup into pan, add 2 cups sugar and 2 cups vinegar to syrup. Heat to boiling and pour over cucumbers.

Fourth day. Drain syrup into pan, add 2 cups sugar and 1 cup vinegar to syrup. Heat to boiling and pour over pickles. Six to 8 hours later drain syrup into pan, add remaining 1 cup sugar and the vanilla to syrup; heat to boiling. Pack pickles into 8 clean, hot 1-pint jars and cover with boiling syrup to within ½ inch of the top. Secure jar lids.

Process for 5 minutes in boiling water (start to count processing time as soon as water returns to the boil). Remove jars and complete seals if necessary. Set jars upright, several inches apart, on a wire rack to cool.

Dilled Green Beans

4 pounds (about 4 quarts) green beans

¼ teaspoon crushed hot red pepper per pint jar

½ teaspoon whole mustard seed per pint jar

½ teaspoon dill seed per pint jar

1 clove garlic per pint jar

5 cups white vinegar

5 cups water

½ cup uniodized salt

YIELDS SEVEN PINTS

Wash beans thoroughly; drain and cut into lengths to fit pint jars. Pack beans into clean, hot jars; add pepper, mustard seed, dill seed, and garlic.

Combine vinegar, water, and salt; heat to boiling. Pour boiling liquid over beans, filling jar to within ½ inch of the top. Adjust jar lids.

Process in boiling water for 5 minutes (start to count processing time as soon as water returns to the boil). Remove jars and complete seals if necessary. Set jars upright, several inches apart, on a wire rack to cool.

Sauerkraut

50 pounds cabbage   *1 pound uniodized salt*

YIELDS SIXTEEN TO EIGHTEEN QUARTS

Remove the outer leaves and any undesirable portions from firm, mature, heads of cabbage; wash and drain. Cut into halves or quarters; remove the core. Use a shredder or sharp knife to cut the cabbage into thin shreds about the thickness of a dime.

In a large container, thoroughly mix 3 tablespoons salt with 5 pounds shredded cabbage. Let the salted cabbage stand for several minutes to wilt slightly; this allows packing without excessive breaking or bruising.

Pack the salted cabbage firmly and evenly into a large clean crock or jar. Using a wooden spoon, tamper, or your hands, press down firmly until the juice comes to the surface. Repeat the shredding, salting, and packing of cabbage until the crock is filled to within 3 or 4 inches of the top.

Cover cabbage with a clean, thin, white cloth (such as muslin) and tuck the edges down against the inside of the container so that the cabbage is not exposed to the air. Put a weight on top of the cover so the brine comes to the cover but not over it. A glass jar filled with water makes a good weight.

At ideal room temperature of 70° fermentation is usually completed in 5 to 6 weeks.

To store. Heat sauerkraut to simmering. Do not boil. Pack hot kraut into clean, hot jars and cover with hot juice to ½ inch of top of jar. Adjust jar lids. Process in boiling-water bath 20 minutes per quart. Count processing time from moment hot jars are placed into actively boiling water. Remove jars, complete seals if necessary, and set jars upright to cool.

Pickled Peaches

12 cups granulated sugar

2 quarts white vinegar

7 2-inch pieces cinnamon stick

2 tablespoons whole cloves

16 pounds (about 11 quarts) peaches

YIELDS SEVEN QUARTS

Combine sugar, vinegar, cinnamon, and cloves. (Cloves may be put in a clean cloth, tied with a string, and removed after cooking, if not desired in packed product.) Bring to a boil and let simmer, covered, about 30 minutes.

Wash peaches and remove skins; dipping the fruit in boiling water for 1 minute, then quickly in cold water makes peeling easier. To prevent pared peaches from darkening during preparation, immediately put them into cold water containing 2 tablespoons each salt and vinegar per gallon. Drain just before using.

Add 1½ to 2 pounds peaches at a time to the boiling syrup and heat for about 5 minutes. Pack hot peaches into clean, hot 1-quart jars. Continue heating and packing until all the peaches are done. Add 1 piece cinnamon and 2 to 3 whole cloves (if desired) to each jar. Cover peaches with boiling syrup to within ½ inch of the top of jar. Adjust jar lids.

Process in boiling water for 20 minutes (start to count processing time after water returns to the boil). Remove jars and complete seals if necessary. Set jars upright, several inches apart, on a wire rack to cool.

Watermelon Pickles

6 pounds (½ large melon) watermelon rind

¾ cup uniodized salt

3 quarts plus 3 cups water

2 trays (2 quarts) ice cubes

3 cups white vinegar

8–9 cups granulated sugar, depending upon sweetness desired

1 tablespoon whole cloves

6 1-inch pieces cinnamon stick

1 lemon, thinly sliced and seeded

YIELDS FOUR TO FIVE PINTS

Pare rind and all pink edges from the watermelon. Cut into 1-inch squares or fancy shapes as desired. You should have about 3 quarts of rind. Cover with brine made by mixing the salt with 3 quarts cold water. Add ice cubes. Let stand 5 or 6 hours.

Drain; rinse in cold water. Cover with cold water, bring to a simmer, and cook until fork-tender, about 10 minutes. Drain.

Combine vinegar, sugar, remaining water, and spices (tied in a clean, thin white cloth). Boil 5 minutes and pour over the watermelon. Add spice bag and lemon slices. Let stand overnight.

Heat watermelon in syrup to boiling and cook until watermelon is translucent, about 10 minutes. Pack hot pickles loosely into clean, hot 1-pint jars. To each jar add 1 piece cinnamon stick from spice bag; cover with boiling syrup to within ½ inch of the top. Adjust jar lids. Process in boiling water for 5 minutes (start to count processing time when water returns to the boil). Remove jars and complete seals if necessary. Set upright on wire rack to cool.

Corn Relish

2 quarts whole kernel corn (16–20 ears fresh corn or 6 10-ounce packages frozen)

2 cups diced sweet red pepper

2 cups diced green pepper

4 cups chopped celery

1 cup chopped onion

1½ cups granulated sugar

4 cups white vinegar

2 tablespoons uniodized salt

2 teaspoons celery seed

2 tablespoons dry mustard

1 teaspoon turmeric

¼ cup flour (optional)

YIELDS SEVEN PINTS

Fresh corn: Remove husks and silks. Cook ears of corn in boiling water for 5 minutes; plunge into cold water. Drain; cut corn from cob but do not scrape cob.

Frozen corn: Defrost overnight in refrigerator or for 2 to 3 hours at room temperature. Place containers in front of a fan to hasten defrosting.

Combine peppers, celery, onion, sugar, vinegar, salt, and celery seed. Cover pan and bring to the boil, then boil uncovered for 5 minutes, stirring occasionally. Mix dry mustard and turmeric and blend with a little boiling liquid; add to boiling mixture along with the corn. Return to boiling and cook for 5 minutes, stirring occasionally. This relish may be thickened by adding ¼ cup flour blended with ½ cup water at the time the corn is added. Frequent stirring will be necessary to prevent sticking and scorching.

Pack loosely while hot into hot, sterilized 1-pint jars, filling to within ½ inch of top. Adjust jar lids.

Process in boiling water for 15 minutes (start to count processing time as soon as water returns to the boil). Remove jars and complete seals if necessary. Set jars upright, several inches apart, on a wire rack to cool.

Sylvie Mutchler's Tomato Relish

12 red or green sweet peppers, seeded	6¾ cups granulated sugar
10 large onions	2 tablespoons celery seed
4 quarts green tomatoes	2 tablespoons mustard seed
½ cup salt	4 cups cider vinegar

YIELDS TEN PINTS

Put the peppers, onions, green tomatoes, and salt through a grinder. Stir well. Let stand overnight. Drain and discard liquid.

Mix all ingredients, bring to a boil and cook over medium heat for 20 minutes. Pack into hot, sterilized jars and seal tightly. Store in refrigerator.

If extended storage without refrigeration is desired, this should be processed in boiling water. Pack the boiling hot relish into clean, hot jars to within ½ inch of the top. Adjust jar lids. Process in boiling water for 5 minutes (start to count processing time when water in the canner returns to boiling point). Remove jars and complete seals if necessary. Set jars upright, several inches apart, on a wire rack to cool.

Sylvie Mutchler's Spanish Relish

6 green peppers, seeded
6 sweet red peppers, seeded
12 large onions
3 quarts green tomatoes
½ cup salt
1 stalk celery, minced

4 quarts tomatoes, peeled, seeded, and finely chopped
2 gallons cider vinegar
3 pounds granulated sugar
1 tablespoon whole cloves
1 tablespoon ground cinnamon

YIELDS FIVE QUARTS

Put the peppers, onions, green tomatoes, and salt through a grinder. Stir well. Let stand overnight. Drain and discard liquid.

Mix the celery, tomatoes, vinegar, sugar, cloves, and cinnamon. Stir in the marinated vegetables and boil until tender.

Piccalilli

4 cups chopped green tomatoes (about 16 medium)
1 cup chopped sweet red pepper
1 cup chopped green pepper
1½ cups chopped onion
5 cups chopped cabbage (about 2 pounds)

⅓ cup uniodized salt
3 cups white vinegar
2 cups (firmly packed) light brown sugar
2 tablespoons whole mixed pickling spice

YIELDS FOUR PINTS

Combine vegetables and salt; let stand overnight. Drain and press in a clean, thin, white cloth to remove all liquid.

Combine vinegar and sugar. Place spices loosely in a clean cloth and tie with a string. Add to vinegar mixture. Bring to a boil.

Add vegetables, bring to a boil, and simmer about 30 minutes, or until there is just enough liquid to moisten vegetables. Remove spice bag. Pack hot relish into clean, hot 1-pint jars. Fill jars to within ½ inch of top. Adjust lids.

Process in boiling water for 5 minutes (start to count processing time as soon as water returns to the boil).

Remove jars and complete seals if necessary. Set jars upright, several inches apart, on a wire rack to cool.

Tomato-Pear Chutney

2½ cups quartered fresh or canned tomatoes

2½ cups fresh or canned diced pears

½ cup seedless white raisins

½ cup chopped green pepper

½ cup chopped onions

1 cup granulated sugar

½ cup white vinegar

1 teaspoon salt

½ teaspoon ground ginger

½ teaspoon dry mustard

⅛ teaspoon cayenne

¼ cup chopped pimiento

YIELDS TWO PINTS

When fresh tomatoes and pears are used, remove skins; include syrup when using canned pears.

Combine all ingredients except pimiento. Bring to a boil; cook slowly until thickened, about 45 minutes, stirring occasionally. Add pimiento and boil 3 minutes longer.

Pack the hot chutney into clean, hot jars, filling to the top. Seal tightly. Store in refrigerator.

If extended storage without refrigeration is desired, this product should be processed in boiling water. Pack the boiling hot chutney into clean, hot jars to within ½ inch of the top. Adjust jar lids. Process in boiling water for 5 minutes (start to count processing time when water in canner returns to the boil). Remove jars and complete seals if necessary. Set jars upright, several inches apart, on a wire rack to cool.

Sylvie Mutchler's Mincemeat

5 cups ground beef

10 cups peeled, cored, and chopped apples

5 cups granulated sugar

2½ cups cider vinegar

3½ cups apple cider

3 pounds raisins

1 pound currants

1 quart pitted sour cherries

1 teaspoon salt

1 teaspoon ground allspice

1 teaspoon whole cloves

1 teaspoon grated nutmeg

YIELDS SIX QUARTS

Simmer all ingredients together for 20 minutes. Pack the boiling hot mincemeat into clean, hot jars to within ½ inch of the top. Adjust jar lids. Process in boiling water for 5 minutes (start to count processing time when water in the canner returns to boiling point). Remove jars, and complete seals if necessary. Set jars upright, several inches apart, on a wire rack to cool.

Refrigerator Pickles and Relishes

Cucumber Ketchup

2 medium cucumbers

1 medium onion

3 tablespoons plus 2 teaspoons white vinegar

⅓ teaspoon salt

⅔ cup ketchup

⅛ teaspoon black pepper

YIELDS ABOUT ONE AND ONE HALF CUPS

Grate the cucumbers into a large shallow bowl. Grate the onion into the same bowl. Add 3 tablespoons vinegar and the salt. Stir briefly to mix. Fit a plate into the bowl to rest directly on the cucumber mixture. Place a heavy jar on the plate to weight it and set the mixture aside for 1 hour.

Press down on the plate and pour off the liquid in the bowl, continuing to drain every 20 minutes or so until no liquid remains. Remove the plate and jar. Stir the ketchup, pepper, and remaining vinegar into the cucumbers, pour the mixture into a jar, seal, and refrigerate for 2 days before using. Cucumber ketchup can be used wherever pickle relish is called for, and is especially good on hamburgers.

Pickled Carrots

2 *small cloves garlic, crushed*
1 *large bay leaf*
½ *cup vegetable oil*
½ *cup dry white wine*
1 *cup white vinegar*
½ *cup water*
2½ *tablespoons granulated sugar*

¾ *teaspoon salt*
  Pinch dried thyme
2 *sprigs fresh tarragon*
15–18 *young carrots, peeled and quartered*
2 *tablespoons minced parsley*

YIELDS TWO PINTS

Place the garlic, bay leaf, oil, wine, vinegar, water, sugar, salt, thyme, and tarragon in a large saucepan. Bring this marinade to a boil and simmer for 5 minutes, stirring once or twice. Add the carrots and parsley. Reduce the heat, cover, and simmer until the carrots are barely tender.

Remove the saucepan from the heat and chill the carrots in the liquid. Discard the bay leaf and place the carrots in jars. Strain the marinade over the vegetables and cover the jars. Store the carrots in the refrigerator where they will keep for 2 to 3 weeks.

Eggplant Pickles

1 *eggplant*
  Salt
2 *teaspoons dry mustard*

3 *tablespoons soy sauce*
3½ *tablespoons granulated sugar*
3½ *tablespoons tarragon vinegar*

YIELDS ONE QUART

Quarter the eggplant lengthwise and cut into ¼-inch slices. Arrange these pieces on a plate, sprinkle with salt, and allow to stand for 15 minutes. Make a paste of the mustard, soy sauce, sugar, and vinegar. Squeeze the eggplant pieces between paper towels to remove the liquid, and place in a quart jar with a lid. Pour in the vinegar mixture, tighten the lid, and gently rotate the jar until all pieces are soaked with the paste. Refrigerate for at least 3 hours, gently rotating the jar from time to time. Serve cold.

Baltimore Relish

2 tablespoons granulated sugar

1½ teaspoons celery salt

½ teaspoon salt

¼ teaspoon prepared mustard

¼ cup white vinegar

2 cups finely shredded cabbage

1 sweet red pepper, finely shredded

YIELDS ABOUT THREE CUPS

Combine the sugar, celery salt, salt, mustard, and vinegar. Blend well. Mix the cabbage with the chopped pepper and pour the dressing over. Refrigerate overnight. Serve cold.

Cauliflower Relish

2 small heads cauliflower, quartered and cored

2 cups small white onions, peeled

2 sweet red peppers, seeded

2 green peppers, seeded

2 carrots

2 cups lima beans

½ cup salt

2 cups cider vinegar

2 cups granulated sugar

½ cup flour

1 teaspoon turmeric

1 teaspoon poppy seeds

YIELDS TWO PINTS

Coarsely chop all vegetables (small lima beans may be left whole) and place them in a large bowl. Cover the vegetables with water and the salt and let soak overnight.

Pour the vegetables and the liquid into a saucepan. Place over medium-high heat and bring to a boil. Drain off the liquid and reserve the vegetables. Place the vinegar, sugar, flour, and turmeric in a large saucepan and cook, stirring constantly until thickened. Add the poppy seeds to the reserved vegetables and cook until the vegetables are barely tender, stirring from time to time to avoid sticking. Pour the relish into hot, sterilized jars and seal tightly. Refrigerate.

Cranberry-Orange Relish

6 cups cranberries
3 large oranges

3 cups granulated sugar

YIELDS SIX CUPS

Wash and pick over the cranberries, discarding any soft ones.

Grate the zest from the oranges, taking care not to include any of the bitter white pith. Cut away and discard the exposed white underskin. Section the oranges and discard the seeds. Put the raw cranberries and oranges through a food mill, add the sugar and orange zest, and mix thoroughly. Chill for several hours before serving cold.

Pickled Blackberries

2 quarts blackberries
1 cup white vinegar
2 cups granulated sugar
½ teaspoon grated nutmeg

½ teaspoon ground allspice
½ teaspoon ground cloves
1 teaspoon ground cinnamon

YIELDS THREE PINTS

Rinse the blackberries, discarding any imperfect ones, and pat them dry. Place the vinegar in a large saucepan, stir in the sugar and spices, and bring the mixture to a boil. Simmer over low heat for 15 minutes, add the berries, and simmer for 10 minutes more. Pour hot into hot, sterilized jars and seal. Refrigerate until needed.

8-Day Cherry Pickle

2 quarts firm ripe cherries	1 teaspoon ground allspice
2 cups white vinegar	1 tablespoon ground cinnamon
2 cups granulated sugar	1 teaspoon ground cloves

YIELDS TWO QUARTS

Wash and dry the cherries, retaining the stems, and place them in a crock. Bring the vinegar, sugar, and spices to a boil in a large saucepan. Pour the mixture over the cherries. Cover the crock and refrigerate for 24 hours.

Drain the vinegar mixture into a saucepan, and bring to a boil. Immediately pour over the cherries. Repeat this procedure every day for 8 days. The pickled cherries may then be served or stored in the refrigerator for later use.

Jellies, jams, conserves, and preserves

IF YOUR GARDEN produces an overflow of berries or fruits, or if neighboring farmers have berries and fruits for sale at temptingly low prices, you may wish to try your hand at putting up sweet spreads for your home-baked breads. The spreads you can make are:

JELLY. A clear, firm spread made only from the juice of the fruit; the pulp is discarded.

JAM. Made from crushed or pureed fruits in a soft jelly.

CONSERVES. Made from a mixture of fruits including citrus fruit, raisins, and occasionally, nuts.

MARMALADE. A soft jelly with pieces of fruit or citrus fruit rind.

PRESERVES. Made with whole or large pieces of fruit in a slightly jellied syrup.

The Four Primary Ingredients

Fruit

Fruit provides jellies, jams, etc., with their characteristic flavor. It also furnishes a portion of the pectin and the acid required to make the spread jell.

Pectin

Pectin, a natural substance present in all fruit (the riper the fruit the less pectin present), is vital to the jell process. To assure jelling, commercial fruit pectins—liquid or powder—are generally recommended. Their presence assures a satisfactory jell, allows for the use of riper, tastier fruit, shortens cooling time, increases yield and produces a predictable result in a specific length of time.

Powdered and liquid pectin are not interchangeable. Powdered pectin is mixed with the unheated fruit juice; liquid pectin is added to the boiling juice and sugar mixture. Boiling time is the same— generally 1 minute—whether liquid or powered pectin is used. Time accurately beginning when mixture has reached a full rolling boil that cannot be stirred down.

Acid

Acid, present in varying degrees in all fruit, is also a requirement for jell formation and flavoring. Products utilizing fruits which are low in acid require the addition of lemon juice or citric acid.

Sugar

Sugar is a preserving agent, contributes to the flavor, and helps jell formation.

Equipment

A large (8 to 10 quart) kettle with a broad, flat base is essential. To extract juice use a fruit press or jellybag. The latter may be made of several thicknesses of closely woven cheesecloth or unbleached muslin supported by a special stand or colander.

Other helpful equipment includes measuring cups, scale, candy thermometer, ladles, a clock or timer, and appropriate knives, bowls, choppers, mashers, and pitting spoons.

Containers

Airtight seals are essential. Use only perfect canning jars capable of being tightly sealed. Jellies or other fruit preserves firm enough to be sealed with paraffin may be put up in jelly glasses.

Thoroughly wash and rinse all containers immediately before use, and keep them warm in a low oven or in hot water to avoid breakage when being filled with hot jelly or jam.

All lids, bands, and rings should be thoroughly washed and rinsed. Some may require boiling. (Refer to manufacturer's directions.)

Filling and Sealing Containers

To Seal with Lids: Use only standard home-canning jars and lids. *For jars with two-piece lids:* Fill hot jars to ⅛ inch of top with hot jelly or fruit mixture. Wipe jar rim clean, place hot metal lid on jar with sealing compound next to glass, screw metal band down firmly, and stand jar upright to cool. *For jars with porcelain-lined zinc caps:* Place wet rubber ring on shoulder of empty jar. Fill jar to ⅛ inch of top, screw cap down tight to complete seal, and stand jar upright to cool. Work quickly when packing and sealing jars. To keep fruit from floating to the top, gently shake jars of jam occasionally as they cool.

To Seal with Paraffin: Use this method only with mixtures that make fairly firm products. Use only enough paraffin to make a layer ⅛-inch thick. A single thin layer—which can expand or contract readily—gives a better seal than one thick layer or two thin layers. Prick air bubbles in paraffin. Bubbles cause holes as paraffin hardens; they may prevent a good seal. A double boiler is best for melting paraffin and keeping it hot without reaching smoking temperature.

For Jelly: Pour hot mixture immediately into hot glass containers to within ½ inch of top and cover with hot paraffin.

For Jam, Conserves, and Marmalades: Remove from heat and stir gently at frequent intervals for 5 minutes. This will help prevent floating fruit in the finished product. Before each stirring, skim off all foam that appears on the surface. Pour into hot glass containers to within ½ inch of top. Cover immediately with hot paraffin.

Preliminary Preparation

Wash fruit in cold, running water and prepare to extract juice as directed in the recipe. Juicy berries require no heating for juice extraction but most firm fruits require heat to start the flow of juice.

Juicing

Place prepared fruit in a damp jellybag or fruit press. Twist, squeeze, or press bag tightly for greatest yield. Restrain juice through several thicknesses of damp cheesecloth or a damp jellybag, but do not squeeze.

Jellies

Blackberry or Strawberry Jelly

3 quarts blackberries or straw-
berries (to yield 4 cups fruit
juice)

7½ cups granulated
sugar
1 bottle liquid pectin

YIELDS TWELVE SIX-OUNCE JELLY GLASSES

To prepare juice. Select fully ripe berries. Sort and wash; remove any stems or caps. Crush the berries and extract juice.

To make jelly. Measure juice into a kettle. Stir in the sugar. Place on high heat, and, stirring constantly, bring quickly to a full rolling boil that cannot be stirred down.
Add the pectin and heat again to a full rolling boil. Boil hard for 1 minute.
Remove from heat and skim off foam quickly. Pour jelly immediately into hot jars and seal.

Cherry Jelly

3 pounds or 2 quarts sour
cherries (to yield 3 cups
cherry juice)
½ cup water

7 cups granulated sugar
1 bottle liquid pectin

YIELDS ELEVEN SIX-OUNCE JELLY GLASSES

To prepare juice. Select fully ripe cherries. Sort, wash, and remove stems but do not pit. Crush the cherries, add water, cover, bring to a boil quickly. Reduce heat and simmer 10 minutes. Extract juice.

To make jelly. Measure juice into a kettle. Stir in the sugar. Place on high heat, and, stirring constantly, bring quickly to a full rolling boil that cannot be stirred down.

Add the pectin and heat again to a full rolling boil. Boil hard for 1 minute.

Remove from heat and skim off foam quickly. Pour jelly immediately into hot jars and seal.

Currant Jelly

3 quarts currants (to yield 5½ cups currant juice)
1 cup water

1 package powdered pectin
7 cups granulated sugar

YIELDS TEN OR TWELVE SIX-OUNCE JELLY GLASSES

To prepare juice. Select fully ripe currants. Sort, wash, and crush, but do not remove them from the stems. Add water, cover, and bring to a boil quickly. Reduce heat and simmer for 10 minutes. Extract juice.

To make jelly. Measure juice into a kettle. Add the pectin and stir well. Place on high heat and, stirring constantly, bring quickly to a full rolling boil that cannot be stirred down. Add the sugar, continue stirring, and heat again to a full rolling boil. Boil hard for 1 minute.

Remove from heat and skim off foam quickly. Pour jelly immediately into hot jars and seal.

Grape Jelly

3½ pounds Concord grapes (to yield 5 cups grape juice)
1 cup water

1 package powdered pectin
7 cups granulated sugar

YIELDS ELEVEN OR TWELVE SIX-OUNCE JELLY GLASSES

To prepare juice. Select fully ripe grapes. Sort, wash, and remove stems. Crush grapes, add water, cover, and bring to a boil quickly. Reduce heat and simmer for 10 minutes. Extract juice. To prevent formation of tartrate crystals in the jelly, let juice stand in a cool place overnight, then strain through 2 thicknesses of damp cheesecloth to remove crystals that have formed.

To make jelly. Measure juice into a kettle. Add the pectin and stir well. Place on high heat and, stirring constantly, bring quickly to a full rolling boil that cannot be stirred down.

Add the sugar, continue stirring, and bring again to a full rolling boil. Boil hard for 1 minute.

Remove from heat and skim off foam quickly. Pour jelly immediately into hot jars and seal.

Plum Jelly

4½ pounds plums (to yield 4 cups plum juice)
½ cup water

7½ cups granulated sugar
½ bottle liquid pectin

YIELDS ELEVEN SIX-OUNCE JELLY GLASSES

To prepare juice. Select fully ripe plums. Sort, wash and cut into pieces; do not peel or pit. Crush the fruit, add water, cover, and bring to a boil quickly. Reduce heat and simmer for 10 minutes. Extract juice.

To make jelly. Measure juice into a kettle. Stir in the sugar. Place on high heat and, stirring constantly, bring quickly to a full rolling boil that cannot be stirred down.

Add the pectin and bring again to full rolling boil. Boil hard for 1 minute.

Remove from heat and skim off foam quickly. Pour jelly immediately into hot jars and seal.

Jams, Conserves, and Fruit Butters

Because these products contain fruit pulp or pieces of fruit, they tend to stick to the kettle during cooking and require constant stirring to prevent scorching.

Blackberry Jam

3 quarts blackberries (to yield 6 cups crushed blackberries)

1 package powdered pectin
8½ cups granulated sugar

YIELDS ABOUT FIVE PINTS

To prepare fruit. Select fully ripe berries. Sort and wash; remove any stems or caps. Crush the berries. If they are very seedy, put part or all of them through a sieve or food mill.

To make jam. Measure crushed berries into a kettle. Add the pectin and stir well. Place on high heat and, stirring constantly, bring quickly to a full boil with bubbles over the entire surface.

Add the sugar, continue stirring, and heat again to a full rolling boil. Boil hard for 1 minute, stirring constantly. Remove from heat; skim.

Fill and seal containers.

Cherry Jam

3 pounds or 2 quarts sour cherries (to yield 4½ cups ground or finely chopped pitted cherries)

7 cups granulated sugar
1 bottle liquid pectin

YIELDS ABOUT FOUR AND ONE HALF PINTS

To prepare fruit. Select fully ripe cherries. Sort and wash; remove stems and pits. Grind the cherries or chop fine.

To make jam. Measure prepared cherries into a kettle. Add sugar and stir well. Place on high heat and, stirring constantly, bring quickly to a full boil with bubbles over the entire surface. Boil hard for 1 minute, stirring constantly.

Remove from heat and stir in the pectin. Skim.

Fill and seal containers as directed.

Grape-Cranberry Jam

3 pounds Concord grapes (to yield 3 cups grape juice), or 2 6-ounce cans frozen concentrated grape juice

1½ cups water

2 cups (½ pound) cranberries

1 teaspoon finely grated orange zest

1 package powdered pectin

7 cups granulated sugar

YIELDS ABOUT FOUR PINTS

To prepare grape juice. Sort and wash grapes; remove stems. Crush grapes, add water, cover, and bring to boil over high heat. Reduce heat and simmer for 10 minutes. Extract juice as for jelly. To prevent formation of tartrate crystals in the jam, let juice stand in a cool place overnight. Strain through 2 thicknesses of damp cheesecloth to remove crystals that have formed.

If frozen grape juice is used, dilute it with water.

To make jam. Combine grape juice, cranberries, and orange zest in a kettle. Add the pectin and stir well. Place over high heat, and, stirring constantly, bring quickly to a full boil with bubbles over the entire surface.

Add the sugar, continue stirring, and heat again to a full rolling boil. Boil hard for 1 minute, stirring constantly. Remove from heat and skim.

Fill and seal containers.

Peach Jam

3 pounds peaches (to yield 3¾
cups crushed peaches)
¼ cup lemon juice

1 package powdered pectin
5 cups granulated sugar

YIELDS ABOUT THREE PINTS

To prepare fruit. Select fully ripe peaches. Sort and wash; remove stems, skins, and pits. Crush the peaches.

To make jam. Measure crushed peaches into a kettle. Add the lemon juice and pectin and stir well. Place over high heat, and, stirring constantly, bring quickly to a full boil with bubbles over the entire surface.

Add the sugar, continue stirring, and heat again to a full rolling boil. Boil hard for 1 minute, stirring constantly. Remove from heat and skim.

Fill and seal containers.

Pickled Blueberry Jam

This unusual jam is spectacular with game, duck, or pork.

8 cups blueberries
2 cups water
⅔ cup wine vinegar
4 cups granulated sugar

2 teaspoons whole allspice
2 teaspoons crushed cinnamon
stick
2 teaspoons whole cloves

YIELDS ABOUT THREE PINTS

Rinse the blueberries, pick them over, and place them in a kettle. Add the water, vinegar, sugar, and spices which have been tied together in a cheesecloth bag. Bring the mixture to a boil, lower the heat, and simmer until the jelling point is reached. Remove and discard the cheesecloth bag and spoon the hot pickled blueberry jam into jars. Seal.

Apple Butter

I usually cook apple butter on a bread-baking day,
when I plan to spend most of the day at home.
The combination of mouth-watering aromas—
spices and yeast—are particularly satisfying.

20 *medium apples*	1 *teaspoon ground allspice*
2 *quarts water*	1 *teaspoon ground cinnamon*
1½ *quarts apple cider*	1 *teaspoon ground cloves*
4½ *cups granulated sugar*	

YIELDS FOUR EIGHT-OUNCE GLASSES

Wash and mince the apples without removing the cores, seeds, or peel. Place in a saucepan with the water, and cook over medium heat until the pulp is soft. Use the back of a spoon to force the apple pulp through a sieve, discarding the peels and seeds.

Heat the cider to a very low boil and stir in the apple pulp with its juice, and the sugar. Stir frequently during the next 40 minutes to keep the thickening apple butter from scorching. Mix in the allspice, cinnamon, and cloves. Stir constantly as the mixture thickens to spreading consistency. Pour into hot jars and seal.

Greengage Plum and Apple Butter

1 *pound greengage plums*	¾ *teaspoon ground cinnamon*
1 *pound apples, quartered*	½ *teaspoon grated nutmeg*
1 *cup apple juice*	⅓ *teaspoon ground cloves*
2 *cups light brown sugar*	

YIELDS TWO SIX-OUNCE GLASSES

Place the unpitted plums and the apples in a large kettle; add the apple juice and bring to a boil. Simmer until the plums are soft.

Puree the mixture by forcing it through a fine sieve with the back of a spoon, discarding the pits. There should be about 4 cups of puree. Add the sugar and spices and cook over medium heat, stirring constantly, until the mixture reaches the consistency of apple butter. Pour at once into hot, sterilized jars and seal immediately.

Pear-Rum Butter

2 pounds pears	2 cups light brown sugar
¾ cup pineapple juice or other fruit juice	¾ teaspoon grated nutmeg
	¼ teaspoon ground cloves
¼ teaspoon grated orange zest	¼ cup light rum

YIELDS TWO EIGHT-OUNCE JARS

Peel the pears, halve, and cut away the cores and threads. Chop coarsely and place in a kettle with the fruit juice and orange zest. Bring to a boil, reduce heat, and simmer, covered, until the pears are tender. Puree the mixture by pressing it through a fine sieve.

Mix in the sugar, nutmeg, and cloves, and return to medium heat. Cook, stirring occasionally, until the mixture is thick. Pour 1 to 2 tablespoons of light rum into each hot, sterilized jar, fill the jars with the pear mixture, and seal.

Tipsy Peach and Plum Butter

4 pounds peaches	2½ teaspoons ground cinnamon
2 pounds plums	2 teaspoons ground nutmeg
3½ cups orange juice	¼ teaspoon ground cloves
⅓ cup lemon juice	⅔ cup bourbon whiskey
4 cups light brown sugar	

YIELDS ABOUT SIX SIX-OUNCE JARS

Scald the peaches in hot water for a few seconds, then dip in cold water, and slip off the skins. Chop the peaches and discard the pits. Place the chopped peaches and the whole plums in a kettle and add the fruit juices. Bring to a boil, cover, and simmer over low heat until the plums are tender. Puree the mixture by forcing it through a fine sieve with the back of a spoon. Mix in the sugar, cinnamon, nutmeg, and cloves. Return to low heat and simmer, stirring constantly, until the mixture reaches the consistency of apple butter.

Pour 2 tablespoons of bourbon into 6 6-ounce hot jars. Fill the jars with the hot fruit butter and seal immediately.

Cantaloupe Butter

4 medium cantaloupes

3 cups light brown sugar

½ teaspoon ground ginger

½ teaspoon ground cloves

¼ cup lime or lemon juice

YIELDS FOUR EIGHT-OUNCE JARS

Discard the seeds and skins from the cantaloupes and coarsely chop the pulp. Place in a kettle, cover, and simmer over very low heat for about 10 minutes, or until the fruit is soft. Puree the cooked melon by forcing it through a fine sieve. Mix in the sugar, ginger cloves, and lime juice and return the pulp to medium heat. Cook, stirring occasionally, until the mixture thickens to spreading consistency. Pour at once into hot jars and seal.

Damson Plum–Orange Conserve

1½ pounds damson plums (to yield 3½ cups finely chopped damson plums)

1 cup finely chopped orange (1 or 2 oranges)

Zest of ½ orange, finely shredded

2 cups water

½ cup seedless raisins

1 package powdered pectin

7 cups granulated sugar

½ cup chopped nutmeats

YIELDS EIGHT EIGHT-OUNCE JARS

To prepare fruit. Sort and wash plums and remove pits. Chop plums fine. Combine orange and zest, add the water, cover, and simmer for 20 minutes.

To make conserve. Measure chopped plums into a kettle. Add orange, raisins, and pectin and stir well. Place on high heat and, stirring constantly, bring quickly to a full boil with bubbles over the entire surface.

Add the sugar, continue stirring, and heat again to a full rolling boil. Boil hard for 1 minute, stirring constantly. Stir in the nuts. Remove from heat and skim.

Fill and seal containers.

Preserves

Select fruit at the firm-ripe stage for preserves. If the fruit is to be left whole, it should be of uniform size and good shape.

The method used in making preserves differs somewhat with different fruits. Directions for making two popular kinds of preserves are given here.

Strawberry Preserves

2 quarts strawberries (to yield   4½ cups granulated
  6 cups prepared berries)   sugar

YIELDS TWO PINTS

To prepare fruit. Select large, firm, tart strawberries. Wash and drain berries; remove hulls.

To make preserves. Combine prepared fruit and sugar in alternate layers and let stand for 8 to 10 hours or overnight in the refrigerator or other cool place.

Heat the fruit mixture to boiling, stirring gently. Boil rapidly, stirring as needed to prevent sticking.

Cook to 221 degrees, or until the syrup is somewhat thick, about 15 or 20 minutes. Remove from heat and skim.

Fill and seal containers.

Damson Plum Preserves

3 pounds damson plums (to yield   5½ cups granulated sugar
  6 cups prepared fruit)   1 cup water

YIELDS ABOUT SIX EIGHT-OUNCE JARS

To prepare fruit. Sort and wash plums. Remove pits with a pitting spoon, leaving plums whole.

To make preserves. Dissolve the sugar in the water, and bring to a boil. Add the plums and boil at 221 degrees, stirring gently, until the fruit is translucent and the syrup is thick. Remove from heat and skim.

Fill and seal containers.

Index

INDEX

Ham(s) (*Continued*)
  gravy, red-eye, 242
  hock with beans and potatoes, farmhouse, 145–146
  and kale soup, 125
  with mushrooms and cream sauce, 149
  ponhaws, 84–85
  schnitz un knepp, 147–148
  slices with red currant glaze, Philadelphia, 148
  stuffing for eggs with curry sauce, 93
  and tomato sauce stuffing for artichokes, 246
Hard sauce, 471
Harden-off, 13
Hasenpfeffer, 205
Hash
  browns, country-style, 296
  chicken, 97
    in parchment pancakes, 97
  down East corned beef, 167
  red flannel, 167–168
Hazelnut stuffing, Irene's, 224
Herb(s), 33–34
  consommé, 114
  drying, 34
  freezing, 34, 518
  fresh vs. frozen vs. dried, 34
  sauce, 236–237
  soup, 126
Herbed
  carrots, 265
  mayonnaise, 335
High-altitude processing times, 499
Hollandaise sauce, 240
Hominy
  canning, 509
  salt pork, beans, and, 153
Honey(ied)
  -buttermilk soup, Elsie Dunlop's, 136
  corn on the cob, 274
  mint-honey-yoghurt sauce, 338–339
  nut loaf, 394–395
"Hootsla," eggbread, 360

Horseradish
  cream, 340
  sauce, fresh-cooked, 340
Hot caps, 13
Hot pack, 498–499
Hotbed, 13
Hunter's marinade, 217

Ice
  orange-lemon, 456–457
  raspberry, 456
  sassafras, 457
Ice cream
  banana split, 453
  chocolate chip, 455
    and almond, 455–456
  eggnog, 453–454
  how to make, 452–453
  meringue pie, topped, 430
  mincemeat, 454
  minted pear, 454
  old-fashioned vanilla custard, 453–454
  peach, 454
  peppermint, 454
  strawberry, 454
    -cherry, 455
Icebox cookies, oatmeal, 410
Icing
  lemon, 415
  orange butter-cream, 415
    See also Frosting, Glaze
Indian pudding, settler's first, 447

Jam
  blackberry, 547
  cheddar cheese and, filling for baked sandwich omelet, 91
  cherry, 547–548
  definition of, 539
  grape-cranberry, 547
  peach, 548
  pickled blueberry, 548
Jars, for canning, 495
Jelly, 543–546
  -baked apples, 365
  blackberry, 543
  cherry, 543
  currant, 544